Advance Praise for
Unis vers Cythère

"Josef Chytry's *Unis vers Cythère* is a highly creative and imaginative contribution to the emerging fields of political aesthetics and socio-aesthetics. In the first part of the volume, the author provides a rich and lively exploration of the way in which theatre, art, and the image of the polis interact with political thinking to create a kind of erotic of politics. In doing so, Chytry significantly expands our understanding of the idea of justice and gives us a fascinating account of the way that the threads of civic art and dramaturgy are subtlety woven into our notions of truth, fairness, and love. The volume ranges happily through antiquity, early modernity, the travails of the twentieth century, and the collapse of Communism. From there, Chytry turns his attention to the contemporary development of aesthetic economies. He offers an engaging and astute account of large-scale artistic enterprises, from Wagner's Bayreuth to the Italian film studio Cinecittà, and explores the growing role of the poetic and the artistic in management and organization theory. *Unis vers Cythère* is a serious meditation on the role of theatre, performance, and the arts in modern management, and art as a managerial practice—and a shrewd rumination on aesthetics as the inspirer of our grandest as well as our most intimate conceptions of politics. This is a first-class work."

Peter Murphy, Associate Professor of Communications,
Monash University, Australia

"The field to which Josef Chytry has been a pioneer with his great study *The Aesthetic State* (1989) has undergone a dramatic expansion in international academia over the past decade. Today it is a fact that in the areas of socio-economics and management, aesthetics is regarded as one of the most important perspectives for the study of social innovation and economic enterprises. Many of us who have relatively recently joined the field of aesthetic social science are most indebted to the earlier work of Dr. Chytry. He is one of the few researchers in the field who is globally regarded as thoroughly competent in both philosophy and cultural studies. With this work he will with certainty contribute to an increased understanding of interactions where artistic creativity affects social innovation."

Pierre Guillet de Monthoux, Professor of General Management,
Stockholm University, Sweden; Professor of Philosophy
of Management, Copenhagen Business School, Denmark

Unis vers Cythère

PETER LANG
New York • Washington, D.C./Baltimore • Bern
Frankfurt am Main • Berlin • Brussels • Vienna • Oxford

Josef Chytry

Unis vers Cythère

Aesthetic-Political Investigations in Polis Thought and the Artful Firm

PETER LANG
New York • Washington, D.C./Baltimore • Bern
Frankfurt am Main • Berlin • Brussels • Vienna • Oxford

Library of Congress Cataloging-in-Publication Data

Chytry, Josef.
Unis vers Cythère: aesthetic-political investigations
in polis thought and the artful firm / Josef Chytry.
p. cm.
Includes bibliographical references.
1. Aesthetics—Political aspects. 2. Political science—Philosophy.
3. Industrial management. I. Title.
BH301.P64C493 190—dc22 2009017950
ISBN 978-1-4331-0732-0

Bibliographic information published by **Die Deutsche Nationalbibliothek**.
Die Deutsche Nationalbibliothek lists this publication in the "Deutsche Nationalbibliografie"; detailed bibliographic data is available on the Internet at http://dnb.d-nb.de/.

Cover illustration: Sandro Botticelli, *Abundance or Autumn*, a drawing

Author photo: Sophia Chytry

The paper in this book meets the guidelines for permanence and durability of the Committee on Production Guidelines for Book Longevity of the Council of Library Resources.

Peter Lang Publishing, Inc., New York
29 Broadway, 18th floor, New York, NY 10006
www.peterlang.com

Printed in Germany

To the memory of
Stan Antosik

The magic that fights for us, the Eye of Venus that charms and blinds even our opponents, is *the magic of the extreme*, the seduction that all that is uttermost exercises: we immoralists—we are *the uttermost ...*

Friedrich Nietzsche, *The Will to Power* [749]

Faune, l'illusion s'échappe des yeux bleus
Et froids, comme une source en pleurs, de la plus chaste:

Stéphane Mallarmé, *L'après-midi d'un faune*

TABLE OF CONTENTS

PREFACE

Unis vers Cythère forms a continuation of my ongoing project to formulate and disseminate a new faculty of thought called "cytherics."

In a previous volume *Cytherica: Aesthetic-Political Essays in an Aphrodisian Key* (Peter Lang, 2005), I defined cytherics as "the sighting and siting of aphrodisian—aesthetic-erotic—environments" and based my definition largely on the results of the extensive historical account of German thought provided in *The Aesthetic State: A Quest in Modern German Thought* (University of California Press, 1989). While *Cytherica* furnished a background of intellectual-historical themes leading to the formulation of cytherics as well as a series of studies designed to demonstrate the efficacy of this new faculty, *Unis vers Cythère*—the title taken from the last words of *Cytherica*—introduces two new areas for the further implementation of cytherics.

The first area marks what I call **polis thought** and propose as a subdivision of academic political theory. The four chapters comprising this first part are intended to encourage attention to the "polis" element in political thinking and history. Thus the first chapter argues the case for its inclusion in academic political theory before elaborating the distinctive "cytherean" components of polis thought. The second chapter challenges a commonplace critique of the application of aesthetic categories to politics resorting to the metaphor of the political "artist" as sculptor of the inert masses, before widening its counter to cover more general aestheticization of politics claims. The third chapter then advances and further develops Peter Murphy's recent theory of civic justice as a literal, and not just metaphorical, openness that the polis/city historically provided for disputation and rhetoric, but also for performance, ceremony and the carnivalesque. Finally, the fourth chapter reads the Czech philosopher Jan Patočka as an important contributor to polis thought in terms of Patočka's influence on the Czech Velvet Revolution of 1989 first set off in the Magic Lantern theatre of Prague/Praha, while it also locates him within the larger context of the Central European polis thought of Martin Heidegger, Hannah Arendt, Herbert Marcuse, and Karl Löwith.

The second area covers what I label the **artful firm**, drawing on two separate concepts, "the art firm" and "artful making," already in use among business, firm and management theorists. Four chapters investigate discrete elements in such contemporary efforts to connect aesthetics and management. The first chapter studies the body of recent literature on the theme and concludes with its own concept of the "artful firm" as the most promising synthesis of the results of this early research. The second chapter, influenced by Pierre Guillet de Monthoux's "art-firm" reading of the composer Richard Wagner's project of the Bayreuth music drama festival, re-evaluates Wagner's cultural intentions for establishing Bayreuth and suggests the entrepreneurial reading as an effective summation of Bayreuth as both a management and a cultural-spiritual enterprise committed to the "total artwork." The third chapter associates the creation and success of the major Italian film studio, Cinecittà, with ecumenical or "cosmo-political" goals which the postwar Italian neorealist (and "second neorealist") filmmakers cultivated, and it briefly evaluates Cinecittà's present significance for the social and political context in which such neorealist and second neorealist goals no longer have currency. Finally, the fourth chapter highlights a major contributor to formal management theory, James G. March, by reading his resort to poetry as integral to his broader interpretations of the role of organizations and managers in economic and social life and the governance of political democracy.

Polis Thought and The Artful Firm form suggestive areas for the further cultivation of cytherics. They encourage a more widespread appreciation of an openness for the kind of civic life that promulgates not only pluralistic political contestations but also enhances ongoing tendencies toward theatricality, the performative and the carnivalesque. For reasons stated in the text, these are conditions that reinforce the overriding cause of "the sighting and siting of aphrodisian—aesthetic-erotic—environments," the working definition of cytherics.

These two major areas of Polis Thought and The Artful Firm are themselves bounded by two briefer essays. The first, introductory essay assesses ancient Mediterranean modes of international hegemony known as "thalassocracy" associated originally with Cretan Minoan neopalatial civilization and carried forth into classical Hellenic, specifically Athenian, political life. The second, concluding essay "arrives" at the "landfall" of "theatrocracy," a term coined by Plato against Athenian democracy, but which here by contrast is favorably employed to signal the furthest development of the Athenian polis during the Periclean era toward a union of the theatrical and the political that transcended, while encompassing, classical participatory democracy.

In accordance with the terms and definitions that it has developed and drawing on the concepts of polis thought and the artful firm, *Unis vers Cythère* thus concludes with the cultural and political vision—"beyond democracy"—of a *thalassic theatrocracy*. It is hoped that this result will stimulate new discussion on the character of these interrelated areas of humanities, politics, history, management, and aesthetics.

ACKNOWLEDGMENTS

I gratefully acknowledge their interest in aspects of this project shown by Ivan Chvatík, John Dobson, Frederick M. Dolan, Pierre Guillet de Monthoux, James G. March, Peter Murphy, Robert Pirro, Ignacio Valero, and Thierry Weil.

The California College of the Arts kindly provided faculty travel grants enabling my participation in a number of relevant conferences, as well as a Faculty Development Grant which helped defray the subvention costs for this book. In addition, the Institute of Management, Innovation and Organization at the University of California, Berkeley, generously supported my participation in two conferences honoring James G. March.

Some of these chapters were published earlier in somewhat different versions in scholarly journals and books. I am thankful to the following publishers for their permission to publish the versions in this book: *Aesthesis*, *History and Theory*, Lexington Books, and Oxford University Press.

As always, my daughter Sophia and son Gabriel constituted the mast that ultimately made possible this particular *embarquement* toward Cythera.

EMBARQUEMENT: THALASSOCRACY

And then went down to the ship,
Set keel to breakers, forth on the godly sea, and
... winds from sternward
Bore us on outward with bellying canvas,
Circe's this craft, the trim-coifed goddess.

....

A lost kind of experience?
scarcely,
O Queen Cytherea,
che'l terzo ciel movete.
Ezra Pound, *The Cantos*[1]

θαλασσο-κρατία: Thalassocracy, a word marked out, if not invented, by the historian Herodotus to embrace the policies of the tyrant Polykrates on the isle of Samos as well as to recall the ancient statesmanship of Minos, mythical ruler of the isle of Crete. Full of "power" (κρατία) in the direct, lexical sense, but different from the "power" of the "people" (*Demos*) or the power of the "best" (*Aristos*). Rather, power devolving upon those same "wine-dark" Seas (*Thalassa*).

Simultaneously a convenient term of entry into the more material dimensions of history and politics that valorize commerce, trade, international politics.[2] Herodotus himself apparently intended the term (θαλασσοκρατέειν) to cover some form of rule by Polykrates over "Ionia and the islands."[3] A subsequent account by Thucydides elaborated this thought into a realpolitik reading of mastery over the seas started by Minos with the establishment of a navy, control of the Cyclades islands, and appointment of governors, putting

[1] Pound [1996], 3, 637 (Cantos I, XCI).

[2] For Miller [1971], 1-3, 96, thalassocracy as found in Hellenic writings is suggestive not only of a concept of local historiography, but perhaps also "a concept unifying a treatment of Universal History," suggesting new notions of "political geography" that underscore the importance of an international market, economics, and of process and movement (versus the typical Greek bias toward institutions).

[3] Herodotus [1960], *Histories*, iii.122. In reference to the key passage on "*ruling* Ionia and the islands," the verb ἄρξειν could mean mastery, rule, governing, or perhaps just leadership.

down piracy while maintaining revenue collections.[4] For the classical historians, in short, thalassocracy at the least implied a deliberate policy by a ruler, some sort of control over islands which enforced the collection of revenues, and some degree of centralization.[5]

Complications ensue with the subsequent Hellenistic elaboration of these ideas into what was apparently a full-scale register of "thalassocracies" supposedly dating from the fall of Troy (1184/3 BCE) to the onset of the Persian wars (481/480 BCE). Through more recent evidence going back to Eusebius' possible use of a list from Diodorus Siculus, something like seventeen thalassocracies have been marked down, the last five (519-481 BCE) forming the historically verifiable examples for Herodotus and Thucydides.[6] It is the first twelve then which belong to the transition from something like a mythical reservoir of information coming out of the Trojan wars to the more recent historical material. That transition reiterates the importance of "Minos" as "creator" of an "original" thalassocracy—whatever that might imply for a culture prior to the Trojan wars—and the elements that the earlier Minoan cultures had set into play for the later articulation of the more firmly political and hegemonical ("historical") concerns of Herodotus and Thucydides. It is therefore incumbent to turn to Minoan civilization for a first stab at the originary implications of "thalassocracy."[7]

I

"Minoan" civilization refers to a process of cultural development dated roughly between 2300 and 1375BCE on the fertile island of Crete comprising the southern boundaries of the Aegean Sea. Generally 2300-2000BCE appears to be a period of growth when sets of Cretan villages accompanied by the

[4] Thucydides [1992], *Histories*, i.4. Although Thucydides brings up "thalassa" in reference to the "Hellenic seas," he does not actually use the word thalassocracy. The contributors to the 1984 symposium on "Minoan thalassocracy" are therefore generally mistaken in referring to Thucydides rather than Herodotus as initiator of the concept of thalassocracy. Hägg & Marinatos [1984], 221.

[5] Following Miller [1971], 24-25. According to Thucydides it might also perhaps suggest, with regard to Phokaian dominance at a certain stage, a leadership of free Ionians (27 [note 34]).

[6] A recent German translation of an Armenian translation of the *Chronographica*, which forms the first volume of Eusebius' *Chronika*, reveals what is supposed to contain the direct quote from Diodorus' original register of thalassocracies. See Miller [1971], 5.

[7] Hägg & Marinatos [1984] provide the technical results of an important 1984 conference on the theme of a "Minoan thalassocracy."

foundations of the classical Mediterranean economy of grains, grapevines, and olives gave rise to the surplus agriculture that promoted subsequent advances in civilization. As a result, the next period, 2000-1700BCE, called the Minoan protopalatial, witnessed the emergence of complexes—erroneously labeled "palaces" by Arthur Evans—which reveal a far more expansive phase, probably connected with increasing participation in, and perhaps relative mastery over, the neighboring seas and sustained contacts with the wealthier civilizations of the eastern Mediterranean.

Then comes something catastrophic: an epochal volcanic explosion that the most recent scientific dating locates around 1628-1613BCE on the neighboring island of Thera.[8] It is, however, followed by an even more bounteous cultural period—associated with the great independent centers of Knossos, Phaistos, Malia, and Zakros[9]—and the confirmed extension of Minoan presence throughout the Aegean Sea: from Cythera to Rhodes and from Crete to Kea just off the shores of Attica—a period labelled the neopalatial.[10] Again, a further cataclysm, this time marked by burning remains indicating invasions, warfare, and perhaps further earth convulsions, brings an end to this neopalatial period around 1450BCE, with the exception of Knossos which apparently functions effectively until 1375-1350BCE. After that, Crete is flooded by Mycenaean outsiders from the Peloponnesus and elsewhere who have expanded their own hegemony over the seas, and this Minoan-Mycenaean mixture forms the period for the historical dating of the ruler later known as Minos, with a *floruit* of 1250/1249 BCE and Minos' own death around 1204/1203 BCE.[11] By this stage we are very close to the classic datings for the fall of Troy at 1184-1183 BCE, and the line of rulers extending from Minos on can be traced directly into the world of Homeric genealogy.[12]

The most striking period of Minoan civilization is therefore clear. It is during the neopalatial period, 1628-1613BCE to 1375BCE, that the great age of Minoan cultural and military-naval hegemony should be marked. When

---

[8] This dating stems from the recent work by the team led by Walter L. Friedrich utilizing an advanced carbon-14 reading for the large branch of an olive tree alive at the time. Reported in *Science*, 312: 5773 (28 April 2006), 508-509.

[9] Marija Gimbutas explicitly refers to these as "Minoan city-states." Gimbutas [1999], 133. Marinatos [1972], 11.

[10] One clear case for actual Minoan colonization is Cythera; there is also some evidence for Rhodes. These two islands incidentally mark the Aegean limits of Minoan presence. J. N. Coldstream & G. L. Huxley, "The Minoans of Kythera," in Hägg & Marinatos [1984], 107-113; also 222.

[11] Miller [1971], 82.

[12] Using the dating by Eratosthenes. According to Homer [1970], *Iliad*, xiii.450-452, Minos is the father of Deucalion, father of Idomeneus, who fights the Trojan Deiphobos.

Herodotus pinpoints thalassocracy as at the roots of Minos' rule, his reference probably encompasses the far more brilliant period of thalassocratic governance of which the Minoan-Mycenaean ruler known as Minos was no doubt a late beneficiary. If there is a single clear image and document attesting to what a Minoan-style thalassocracy might have entailed during this period, it may well be the magnificent wall-paintings discovered after 1967 on neighboring Thera, a "Minoanized" society.[13] Particularly the magnificent frescos of the West House reveal the undulations of a society and culture—vessels, harbors, households, spectators, processions—fully saturated in a life of the sea.[14]

Approaching its characteristic features as suggested by contemporary archaeological evidence, neopalatial Crete seems a difficult phenomenon to grasp. Even while contemporary scholars gently chide their predecessor Arthur Evans for unreflectively applying categories drawn from contemporaneous Near Eastern and Egyptian cultures such as "palaces" for the extensive habitations on Crete, for their part these same scholars seem to bend over backward in slipping in more fashionable categories of theology and class economics. Ever on the lookout for the primacy of gods, goddesses, priests, priestesses, and social stratifications, they confess themselves puzzled, at least at the outset, by certain recurring features of neopalatial Crete that are not to be found elsewhere.

First, the architecture itself fails to provide definable focal points such as chapels that might serve as obvious cult centers; nor are there cult images or statues to provide further orientation. This means that it is impossible to specifically identify anything like prominent gods or goddesses, priests or priestesses, or even prominent persons as rulers or kings.[15] If there are shrine settings, each seems autonomous, thus meriting the description "cluster of shrines."[16] In general, "rulership" is taken to have been "multifarious" and

[13] The general view remains that Thera was politically independent from Minoan Crete, although deeply influenced by its association with Crete, with Akrotiri looking directly in the direction of Crete. Thus Spirodon Marinatos' paeans to Minoan civilization as the first "United Kingdom in the history of the world" appear excessive. Marinatos [1972], 12. Wolf-Dietrich Niemeier wonders whether the relation of Crete to such Minoanized islands compares with that between Athens and the rest of the Delian League. "The End of Minoan Thalassocracy," in Hägg & Marinatos [1984], 205.

[14] As J. Lesley Fitton describes it: "a pictorial programme" on "the theme of the sea, ships, journeys, and other lands" with Akrotiri representing "a thriving town, with all the vitality of a sea-port and a place where different people met." Fitton [2002], 171. Excellent reproductions of this extensive tableau may be found, e.g., both in Morgan [1988], after 234, and Doumos [1992], 64-85.

[15] Peter Warren even suggests "a relative absence of class (intra-unit) division or group (inter-unit) division," adding that Minoan architecture "denies social division." "The Place of Crete in the Thalassocracy of Minos," in Hägg & Marinatos [1984], 39.

[16] Marinatos [1993], 50, 75, 110, 119, 177, 143; Fitton [2002], 152, 175.

"flexible" at best, rather than anything resembling excessive centralization.[17] Such lack of concern for obvious displays of power and monumentality fits with the overall aesthetics of surviving works, which avoid the moumental, even the impressive wall-paintings tending toward human representations that are less than life-size.[18]

Without the obvious testimony of aggressive Egyptian or Middle Eastern affirmations of divine and human power, without anything like representations of rulers as warriors decimating their hapless opponents, Minoan Crete leaves interpreters stymied in their desperate need for the familiar landmarks of hierarchy, domination, and stratification.[19] What then can be said of the positive evidence? While the vast apparent maze—"labyrinth" is of course a Minoan invention—of the concentrated civic complexes (alternatively labeled palace, temple, cult center, or even the composite "temple-palace") does suggest some sort of consolidation process initiating the protopalatial period circa 2000 BCE, the key feature to such complexes may well be the recurring presence of its large and imposing central courts.[20] Here it would appear that "rulers" and "people" came in contact for purposes generally summarized loosely as "public," "ceremonial," "ritual." That these great courts are the predecessors to the later agoras of the Hellenic polis cannot be doubted, whatever the specific differences in their respective functions: at the least they epitomize gathering points, assembly venues, and no doubt spectating vistas. Since the neopalatial period no less yields highly attractive and in some cases wealthy and luxurious town-houses outside such complexes confirming that there would have been other substantial options for ordinary, "secular" human contact and sociability, the central courts would have had to fulfil a more "ritualistic" and "governance" set of functions.[21] Thus these central courts are probably the most revelatory elements toward explaining the organizational principles of Minoan Crete constituted by the great complexes of Knossos, Phaistos, Malia, and Zakros.

Second, the principle of the female is given striking prominence. Whether or not such prominence confirms a strong matriarchal rule, at the very least it underscores the high status of women in Minoan iconography compared with their later roles in Mycenaean and Hellenic societies.[22] Again, it remains a

---

[17] Marinatos [1993], 111, 243.

[18] Fitton [2002], 152-153; Hawkes [1972], 53 ff.

[19] Marinatos [1993], 243.

[20] This important claim is effectively made by Marinatos [1993], 43, 110.

[21] Fitton [2002], 135-145.

[22] Marinatos [1993], 192; Fitton [2002], 178. For all her advocacy of Cretan religion as an extension of "Old European" religion, Gimbutas grants that the latter's stress on life and death cycles cannot be confirmed in the case of Crete: "Life, rather than death, primarily characterized Minoan culture." Gimbutas [1999], 144.

controversial matter to claim either a single goddess principle or a multitude of goddesses, or for that matter the interrelationship of goddess to priestess—let alone the overall pertinence of these categories to the evidence.[23] The safest account then would be to mark out a female principle consistently represented as belonging to an exemplary naturalistic landscape, perhaps even a fertility-religious-sacred landscape, from which she draws her power and is the object of adorants.[24] Wearing a flounced skirt and displaying bare and ample breasts, she is characteristically surrounded by flowers, trees, animals, dolphins, and birds, often flanked by griffins, and apparently exclusively protective of her own sex.[25] As her counterpart, a male figure—more frequent and masterly than the conventional matriarchal perspective on Minoan Crete has conceded—is represented as young, athletic, a master of towns and animals (which are voluntarily drawn to him), never bearded, old, "wise." Where male and female appear together, the possibility of something akin to a sacred marriage is not unlikely, since the male is never a votary of the female.[26]

Third, it is difficult to make sense of characteristic modes of rule and domination that depend on the martial or even the prominently economic. That only leaves, for the interpreter, the vague areas of "religion" and "ritual" to pigeonhole Minoan Crete to conventional accounts of hierarchical and stratificatory social systems.[27] If therefore a theistic nomenclature for the isle continues to be insisted upon, perhaps the least problematic would be: an adorant theacentric henotheism tilting toward feminine polytheism.[28] But given the unsettled status of whether the Minoans even made use of anthropomorphic allusions to deities, a less controversial point of departure seems warranted. "Nature"—in fact the more relevant term would be the Hellenic *phusis* rather than the Latin *natura*—seems ubiquitous in all the available representations. The fecund female celebrant surrounded by her human and non-human adorants emerges from a flourishing *phusis*, and in particular—granted the ubiquitous

---

[23] Nikolaos Platon refers to "the Great Goddess in her special role of a Sea-goddess" as well as the "marine goddess." "The Minoan Thalassocracy and the Golden Ring of Minos," in Hägg & Marinatos [1984], 67.

[24] Marinatos [1993], 162, 198.

[25] Marinatos [1993], 162, 192.

[26] Marinatos [1993], 166-174, 188, 190. This tableau of a larger female body juxtaposed to the slimmer male body finds its equivalents in contemporary beach cultures throughout the world. Consider the case of Rio de Janeiro and its fabled Copacabana Beach which during its better days in the 1950s was (pejoratively) described as "a Cythera where one basks in the sun, swims in the cool waters, and enjoys the pleasures of life with nonchalance." J. O. de Meira Penna (1956), cited in Evenson [1973], 115, and the relevant photographs in Botting [1977], 7, 120-129.

[27] Marinatos [1993], 75, 244; Fitton [2002], 153, 154.

[28] Marinatos [1993], 165; Fitton [2002], 178.

role of the thalassic environment for Crete—from a Horizonal boundary between sea and sky, between the thalassically experiential and its "beyond."[29] From that perspectival line, unique again to Cretan iconography when compared with Egypt and the Near East, the Minoan female induces "visionary epiphanies" through her arrival by sea and is received by single solitary—rather than collective—individuals. These epiphanies reveal distance perspective, exploiting the liminality of a "beyond" from which the figure manifests in definite—not random—places such as columns and trees.[30]

Fourth, therefore, considering what might serve as the content of the "ritual" itself, the iconography regularly displays bull sports, athletic games for young men, ceremonial processions, the harvesting of saffron and crocuses. Looking in this context toward what might be inferred about a Minoan "aesthetic" in general, its characteristic features are invariably described as fluid, shapely, "springy."[31] Such characteristics spill out into such mundane facts as the extraordinary number of pots and liquid containers in Minoan households and the relation of their female principle to liquidity.[32] "Naturalness" is the term constantly—albeit too loosely—deployed to account for those arresting vistas of supple bodies at home in an extraordinarily "natural" setting of land, sea, and skies.[33]

II

From these features that stand out as exceptional—lack of clear cultic or theistic references, marked prominence of the female principle, a set of unique representational features linked to nature-*phusis* and the seas, and the fluid, flowing character of the Minoan aesthetic—a different reading may provide a more helpful entry into this "thalassocratic" world. The period 1600-1200 BCE forms more or less the most frequent datings for that exceptional flock of Aegean heroes and heroines carrying such names as Daedalus, Orpheus, Heracles, Perseus, Theseus, Jason, Pentheselia, Oedipus and Dionysus. What

---

29 Marinatos [1993], 163, 169.

30 Marinatos [1993], 175-181, 243. The epiphany may be sometimes associated with arrival by boat.

31 Fitton [2002], 147. Hawkes argues the case for the Cretan initiation of the theme of *Homo ludens*. Hawkes [1972], 72-73.

32 Regarding possible identifications of female deities through extrapolating from Linear B evidence, there is some support for a deity with the name Pipituna as well as a "priestess of the winds," both without counterparts in later Mycenaean and Hellenic pantheons. Fitton [2002], 177.

33 Marinatos [1993], 177; Fitton [2002], 159.

marks these heroes is their framework of adventures, quests, and wanderings, which served as the more mobile, liminal elements to Aegean thalassocratic societies. Its pragmatic-economic ramifications make up that search for precious metals, gemstones, amber, and metallurgy that epitomizes the designation of *Sonnenkinder*, or "children of the sun," for these heroes.[34]

It is some such "questing" economics that helps qualify, and clarify, any attempt to interpret such thalassic societies as somehow "matriarchal." If J. J. Bachofen is rightly considered the originator of the terminology of mother- and father-right in anthropological and sociological literature, his work also contains some important qualificatory categories for our purposes. Bachofen argued for a somewhat unwieldy set of five stages of human development of which two were matriarchal and a succeeding three patriarchal, culminating in the presumably ultimate reign of the solar male principle of Apollo. But notwithstanding the eccentric prejudices of this nineteenth-century Basel patrician, he may have also been the "most inspired interpreter ... of the moral orders—*Aphroditean as well as* Demetrian—of the goddess."[35] Even if for Bachofen the exemplary matriarchal stage was the "Demetrian" one of conjugal motherhood, settled agriculture and communities, it was necessarily both preceded and succeeded by what Bachofen termed "the hetaerism of Aphrodite," or "the hetaerist-Aphroditic stage of sexuality."[36]

For Bachofen his preferred "historicity of matriarchy" had to support this "historicity of hetaerism," because the latter in his view stood originally for a state of unregulated sexual relations corresponding to the "natural" conditions of an originary "swamp" existence of wild plant life (*iniussa utronea creatio*).[37] Even more suggestively, these Aphroditean elements then recurred at the later "male" stage when the Dionysian cult came into prominence and brought with it the recurrence—indeed the highest development—"of a thoroughly Aphroditean civilization." For his part Bachofen regarded with distaste this Aphroditean revitalization as coterminous with the political call for "democracy." Despite this, he had to grant that "all special privilege is odious to this goddess": the *ius naturale* is "the Aphroditean law," upholding the crucial juridical position that this justice is common not just to the human race but to all living creatures.[38]

---

[34] Perry [1968], and the stimulating, if gossipy, reflections of Green [1976].

[35] Joseph Campbell, introduction to Bachofen [1967], xliii (emphasis added).

[36] Bachofen [1967], 99; Campbell in Bachofen [1967], xlvii.

[37] Bachofen [1967], 94, 97.

[38] Bachofen [1967], 102, 189. According to Bachofen, the ancients invariably recognized this inseparability of "carnal" and "political emancipation;" indeed, it was largely responsible for the doom of the ancient world (103). Bachofen attributes this reading of the *ius naturale* to the

Putting aside the prohibitively difficult task of matching Bachofen's claims to specific historical periods between the Minoan and later Hellenistic-Roman ages, what stands out is the available candidacy of Bachofen's "Aphroditean" account for making more sense of the kinds of priorities that might have ruled Minoan neopalatial thalassocracy than the conventional matriarchal account (ironically also deriving from him). Relating to the manifold opportunities—economic, exploratory, metallurgical—for the adventuring talents of young males capable of scouring the seas for appropriate treasures, the principle of a fertile sea-goddess centralizing such flows at such exemplary centers as Crete could well have given rise to a panoply of activities, habitations and habitudes appropriately summed up under the heading of thalassocracy.[39]

III

In Homeric storytelling one site bears a remarkable resemblance to this scenario. The Phaiakaians, islanders dwelling somewhere out upon that thalassic terra incognita beyond the isle of Cythera (παρέπλαγξεν δὲ Κυθήρων) according to the directives of the *Odyssey*, have been occasionally identified with Crete itself.[40] While the strong presence of a Phaiakaian king (Alkinous) and queen (Arete) may be more suggestive of subsequent Mycenaean features, certain characteristics of the Phaiakaian style of life seem apropos for what has been surmised so far about neopalatial Crete and its "thalassocratic" strains.

First and foremost is the Phaiakaians' thalassic liminality in location and vocation. Originally inhabitants of Hyperia, the very rim of the known world, the Phaiakaians still take pride both in living far away from the rest of humankind in their thalassic expanses—"off at the world's end" (ἔσχατοι)—and in being able to reach at any time "the edge of the world" (τηλοτάτοι) thanks to their matchless sailing capacities.[41] Children of the sea-god Poseidon, the Phaiakaians are the exemplary sailor folk famed for their craftly commitment to

writings of the jurist Ulpian. Through Ulpian Bachofen specifically attributes to "Aphrodite": (1) the desire of the two sexes to generate, (2) solicitude for one's offspring, (3) the bond of mother and child, and (4) the securing of freedom and equality for one's progeny.

[39] Hawkes explicitly makes the case for identifying the Minoan exemplary female figure with Aphrodite through the Minoan cults of the dove, the seashell, and the garden. Hawkes [1972], 81-83.

[40] Homer, [1970], *Odyssey,* ix.81; Willetts [1962], 127-129. When adjusting to his arrival in Ithaka, Odysseus lies to his patroness Athene with a story that uses verifiable historical markers for the eastern Mediterranean: he has presumably heard about Ithaka on "the spacious land of Crete" and was brought to Ithaka's shores by a "Phoenician" fleet which then returned to its city of "Sidon." Homer [1970], *Odysssey*, xiii.256-257, 272, 285.

[41] Homer [1970], *Odyssey*, vi.4, vi.205, vii.322.

masts and oars and vessels that they love to sail across the "foam-flecked seas" (πολιὴν παρόωσι θάλασσαν).[42] Indeed, their sailing capacities exceed the plausible: their ships are as swift as birds or "as thought itself" (νοήμα);[43] they use no steersman, nor even steering oars, but know "by instinct" what their crews are thinking or propose to do; they can sweep fearlessly across the immensities of the sea; and they are acquainted with every polis and every fertile land.[44] Small wonder then that they believe themselves so close to the gods that they actually rub shoulders with them and can experience them directly without disguise.[45]

Second, the Phaiakaians are not only the ultimate sailor people, they also excel in "nimble footwork, dance, and song"—suggesting an intrinsic affinity between a thalassic mastery and love for the choral activities of song and dance: indeed their original home Hyperia was described as a "land of spacious-dancing circles" (ἐν εὐροχόρῳ).[46] To prove their supremacy, King Alkinous enthusiastically calls upon his best dancers to perform (παίσατε) for the benefit of their guest Odysseus, and the latter unhesitatingly concurs after the performance.[47]

And third, the Phaiakaians display the full panoply of a polis in all its Homeric glory. Beautifully laid out by its founder Nausithous, father of Alkinous, to optimize its natural and civic capacities, Phaiakaia's capital city Scheria is a model of civilized life. Above all, their assembly site (ἀγορή) is specially marked out and admired by the visitor Odysseus—who recalls by contrast the complete lack of any such amenity for assembling, consultation, or law-making among the Cyclops as the prototype of an uncivilized, atomized society. Not surprisingly, the agora is cleverly located right next to the harbored ships so that the Phaiakaians can assemble and consult with minimal disturbance to their daily thalassic responsibilities and joys.[48]

[42] Homer [1970], *Odyssey*, vi. 272; vii.36. Despite his irritation toward the Phaiakaians for their hospitable reception of strangers, Poseidon nonetheless admits that they are "born of my own stock" (xiii.130).

[43] Homer [1970], *Odyssey*, vii.36. In taking Odysseus to Ithaka, the Phaiakaian vessel is described as quicker than "a wheeling falcon, the quickest thing on wings" (xiii.87).

[44] Homer [1970], *Odyssey*, viii.447-563. If the men are thus skilled in sailing, that skill is matched by the Phaiakaian women's dexterity at the loom (vii.107-110). The interelationship of shiply crafts and weaving crafts is a familiar one to sea-oriented societies.

[45] Homer [1970], *Odyssey*, vii.205. Such proximity also marks the Trojan-Phyrgian relation to the gods in the *Iliad* and the Homeric hymns.

[46] Homer [1970], *Odyssey*, viii.253; vi.4.

[47] Homer [1970], Odyssey, viii.250-251, viii.382-384. Compare Hawkes on the Minoan sites for dance and dramatics. Hawkes [1972], 60, 74-75.

[48] Homer [1970], *Odyssey*, vi.266, vii.44, viii.5, ix.112. It has been suggested that this account can be taken as an ideal vision of the Ionian polis. Roebuck [1959], 40, and comparable citations

Granted that this Homeric account belongs to "poetry" rather than to "fact," its very persuasiveness as narrative helps to indicate alternative readings of thalassocracy that might be less crudely oriented toward the obviously power-political and hegemonic meanings later ascribed to the term by the classical chroniclers. For what stands out is the possibility of interpreting a society in terms of its being entirely given over to the ramifications of sea-life, enjoying a kind of "hegemony" over it in terms of unprecedented capacities to cover its expanses but no less to benefit from the sea's effects on island culture, society and economy. This is a *thalasso*-cracy, but, as in the cases of *demo*-cracy or *aristo*-cracy, the power it signifies is that of the substantive itself, in this case the sea (*thalassa*) as it is manifested in the reality-sense of that people. True, such might be the case for any island people, but it is no less possible that there are special cases, as in the story of the Phaiakaians, where this thalassic principle corresponds to the development of exceptional human faculties in relation to the seas—something perhaps in which neopalatial Crete excelled without being necessarily the formal center of an empire or hegemonic island power.[49]

Such readings may have become more narrowly directed by the martiality of the Mycenaean age and more sharply after the fall of Troy with the onset of the Hellenic dark ages—periods regarded by native chroniclers as the onset of an "iron age" when the communication, complicity and coition between gods and men were broken once and for all.[50] It would therefore not be implausible that by the age of Herodotus and Thucydides all that remains of the originary implications of a thalassocracy is the notion of political and hegemonical rule over suppliant islands and mainlands by a centralizing, taxing, and hegemonic force. On the other hand, those originary implications—as suggested by cultural remains on neopalatial Crete and the Homeric story of Phaiakaia—could still resurface even within the realpolitik language of a Thucydides whose sympathy for the thalassocracy theme was part and parcel of his advocacy on behalf of Athenian fifth-century policy by Themistocles and Pericles to create a great Aegean sea power centered on Athenian *demokratia*. But those originary implications would need a separate concept to be extracted from this unfolding theme of thalassocracy.

---

in Chytry [1989], xxxix-xl.

49 There is also the helpful suggestion by Mario Benzi of a *koine* or "a collaboration between smaller groups which had minor cultural differences but also much in common." Hägg & Marinatos [1984], 113.

50 The final such "heroic" coition being the union of Aphrodite with the Trojan prince Anchises giving birth to Aeneas: "And beautifully-crowned Cytherea [Κυθέρεια] gave birth to Aeneas." Hesiod & Homer [1914], *Theogony*, 1008.

In our concluding “landfall,” we provide such a concept as “theatrocracy” and wed it to the conditions of what thalassocracy had so far—through collective memory, myth, history and chronicle—brought into operation for the fifth-century Athenians, at the very moment when they too, like the Homeric Phaiakaians, sailed out to the edge of their knowable universe.

IV

Assuming then that neopalatial Crete around 1650 BCE merits the term thalassocracy in our revised sense, it is perhaps additionally suggestive that the ensuing castastrophe of 1628-1613 BCE seems not have destroyed the amenities of this civilization but may even have helped ornament important features of the neopalatial period. For a “cytherean” interpretation of the phenomenon, it is tempting to link the myth of Aphrodite Anaduomene—the presencing or surfacing of Aphrodite as the Sea-goddess of Love— to a naturalistic event, one which resembles the mythical account of the splash of Ouranos’ “testicles”—the, as it were, generative power of the Heavenly proper—upon the surface of the Aegean Sea, from which foam the future Queen of Cythera presumably burst forth in all her swelling brilliance. If formal academic history reveals this Event as an unprecedented volcanic explosion that tore out the isle of Thera proper—its traces all too clear from the disgorged crescent shape of the present isle of Santorini—and flung it out to catalyze massive repercussions by water, land and air, submerging and shaking to their roots a host of neighboring lands and civilizations, the receiving denizens of Crete must have been among the first to absorb by sight, sound, and odor, something that would become fundamental to their culture and its history from that stage on. Something Hesiod would later confirm as the “awesome” (αἰδοίη) shine of the Sea-goddess’s epochal Adventus.

PART ONE

POLIS THOUGHT

CHAPTER ONE

Cytherics as a Mode of Polis Thought

Political Theory and the Relevance of the Sighting-Siting of Aphrodisian Environments

The theory of the polis ... is, in a certain sense, political theory in its purest form.
J. G. A. Pocock[1]

The subject-matter of modern political philosophy ... is not the polis or its politics, but the relation between philosophy and politics.
Robert D. Cumming[2]

Notwithstanding some forty years of pluralistic, postmodern, and anti-essentialist priorities in discussions of political methodology, political thought habitually returns to certain guidelines. Unlike more recent subject-matter (among others, critical theory, cultural studies, visual studies), these can be traced all the way back to ancient Greek writers from Herodotus and Thucydides to Plato and Aristotle and to the earliest formulations of a theme called "politeia" (πολιτεία).[3]

Yet although it is plausible to regard contemporary political theory and philosophy as direct successors to such a theme, it is no less true that there remain important differences between the modern priorities of political theory and the theorizing of the ancient Greeks. Unlike the moderns, the latter remained largely bound to the phenomenon of the "polis," the characteristic Hellenic "political" community.[4] The decisive factor for the change from the ancients to the moderns is the emergence of the modern security-territorial

[1] Pocock [2003], 74.

[2] Cited in Arendt [1982], 22.

[3] As Manville & Ober [2003], 10, point out, "politeia" encompasses not only "constitution," but also "community of citizens," "form of government," and even "way of life."

[4] Even canonical histories of (western) political theory which extend their reflections to pre-Hellenic contexts grant: "It is in the polis that political theory began and it is to the polis that we now turn." Thomas Landon Thorson in the fourth edition of Sabine [1973], 17.

("sovereign") state in the fifteenth and sixteenth centuries. The complicity between this "political body" and the concurrent rise of, on the one hand, mercantilist, capitalist and industrial economies and, on the other, a "natural philosophy" (later called "science") increasingly inseparable from technology and the latter's institutionally pedagogical needs (the research center, the large-scale university) helped overturn the apparent relevance of the "ancients." Thanks, however, in part to a body of thought in the European tradition starting in the late eighteenth century that was indebted to German Hellenism of the classical period of Johann Joachim Winckelmann and Johann Wolfgang von Goethe, interest in the concept of the polis has succeeded in re-entering modern thought and raising anew the challenge of the polis.

I

For the ancient world discussion about the political nature of humankind invariably assumed the existence of life in the polis—even if the polis had lost its ultimate claims of autonomy under imperial Roman rule.[5] To look at such originary texts of formal "political thought" as Plato's *Republic* (or *Politeia*) and Aristotle's *Politics* is to be firmly reminded of such polis priorities.[6] Yet even these maiden efforts in "political theory" owe their problematizations to a prior foundational text. If the polis was for the Greeks the very "matrix of civilization," then the standard polis, indeed the very first one elaborated in Greek literature, was Homer's Troy, labeled by Homer himself as the "sacred polis" (ἱερὴν Πόλιν).[7] Whatever later formal theorists in the Greek tradition might make of the polis in descriptive or normative terms, they were bound to work through the prior "vision" that this canonical poetic narrative and metric had already laid out for them and Hellenic paideia in general.

This vision carries five central implications. *First*, it *is* a vision: an "idiogrammatic" image of the polis "that suggests a vision of the city as a schematic whole" whose space is poetically conceived in an "idealized"

[5] Extending from the Ionian creation of the polis around 900-750 BCE to the Hellenizing civilization of the second sophistic of the late second and early third centuries CE. Lane Fox [1986], Swain [1996].

[6] Martin Heidegger strictly describes Plato's work as bearing the proper title: "The 'Dialogue' about the Essence of the πόλις." Karl Löwith points out the extent to which Aristotle gave emphasis to actually functioning poleis in the Hellenic world through an encyclopedic effort to furnish a series of political studies of their constitutions. "Platons Lehre von der Wahrheit" [1942], in Heidegger [1967], 119; Karl Löwith, cited in "Regaining the Cosmos: Karl Löwith contra Martin Heidegger," in Chytry [2005], 53-55.

[7] Bernard Knox, in Homer [1990], 30-31.

fashion.[8] *Second*, what is enclosed is *sacred* (ἱερός). Unlike the Roman city (*urbs*) which is never sacred, or the Near Eastern city where sacredness is reserved to the temple precincts, the Homeric polis *as a whole* is sacred[9] *Third*, it promotes an openness, not merely metaphorically but also literally as the gathering point for the spatiality of the free inhabitants, including—remarkably enough, given the patriarchalist proclivities of the later classical polis—its women, all of whom occupy a tremulous position of humanity between the heavenly and the earthly.[10] *Fourth*, even though the polis is sacred, it is permitted to "fall," thus raising issues of political and metaphysical conflict that give birth to a genre and poetic mode of awareness called "tragedy," which later poleis, particularly the Athenian, henceforth attached to their self-conceptions of the polis as such.[11] And *fifth*, this tragic outlook, far from implying a permanent setback, encourages the redemptive prospect of creating new Troys in a future that, historically at least, will include the Rome of Aeneas, the Britain of Geoffrey of Monmouth, the France of François Ronsard, and even the California of Garcí Rodriguez de Montalvo.[12] Above all, what remains paradigmatic is the absolute standard of this "sacred polis" for future thought concerning a distinctly human life: "Whereas the twentieth-century image of the megalopolis ... is soberly aware of a postindustrial urban blight, the polis in Homer, *as in later Greek philosophical writing*, was exalted as the crowning achievement of humankind."[13]

Modern thought valorizing the polis then starts with Martin Heidegger and his students, as well as other thinkers indebted to his thought. If the original paradigm of Troy was "the point where the threads of events crisscross and the

---

[8] Scully [1990], 8, 9, 23, 46-47, 89.

[9] And no polis is more frequently mentioned as sacred than "sacred Ilion/Ilios" (΄Τροίης ἱερον, Ἴλιος ἱρή). Homer [1970], *Odyssey* i.2, *Iliad* iv.46. Scully also points out that the most sacred places in Homer are the poleis. Scully [1990], 17, 23.

[10] Much of this idiogrammatic essence to the original Homeric vision of polis is captured by Aristotle's later insistence that the polis is something to be grasped in one glance or overview (εὐσύνοπτος). Scully [1990], 56, 96, 113. Aristotle [1967], 1326b. Similarly, as Scully notes, there is a parallel between this original Homeric vision of polis and Aristotle's later formal definition of the polis in terms of a partnership committed to a "good" or "beautiful" life.

[11] Quite apart from a number of transgressions registered against Troy throughout its history, there remains the outstanding fact that Zeus permits its destruction, in spite of his declaration that it remains his favorite polis and Hektor —the name etymologically descended from "holder of the polis"—his favorite polis defender. Homer [1970], *Iliad* iv.44-47, xv.610-612, xxiv.66-68.

[12] For the details behind this Trojan foundation of Montalvo's "California" along with an explanatory genealogical diagram, see Chytry [2006b], 23-29.

[13] Scully [1990], 127 (emphasis added), cf. also 125-127.

metaphysical place on which the sacred fiction of the poem turns,"[14] Heidegger furnishes a comparable definition of the polis: "πόλις is translated as state or city-state; this does not capture the full sense. πόλις means rather the site, the Da, in which and as which Da-sein as the historical is. The πόλις is the history site, the Da, *in* which, *out of* which, and *for* which history happens [*Geschichte geschieht*]."[15]

Quite independently of Homeric philological research, Heidegger provides an ontological justification for the primacy of the "sacred polis" through his own philosophy of human being (*Da-sein*) as an "openness" (*Da*) for "Being"(*Sein*) proper, attributing important priorities to point, place, site, and scene. Yet Heidegger never built in an effectively political manner upon his insight. It is his student Hannah Arendt.[16] who surpasses Heidegger by arguing for not only the fundamental distinction between society (*societas*)—the social—and the polis—the political—but also the superiority of the latter over the former.[17] Only the polis—the political—can be the "sphere of freedom" because only there can genuine action and speech occur, effecting "the shining brightness we once called glory." Real action means first and foremost "a definite space"and a "structure built" for action to take place: this space is "the public realm of the *polis* and its structure the law."[18] Arendt further brings to bear the centrality of persuasion—the goddess Peitho (Πείθω)—over violence (βία) as the essential mode of polis communicability. As a result she valorizes theatre as "the political art par excellence; only there is the political sphere transposed into art."[19]

In turn, two other Heidegger students, Herbert Marcuse and Karl Löwith, further develop Heidegger's original insight. Marcuse is best known for his

---

[14] Scully [1990], 116-117.

[15] Heidegger [1966], 117 (emphasis in original). This definition is first dated 1935.

[16] Asking at the conclusion of *On Revolution* what it was for the Greeks "that enabled ordinary men, young and old, to bear life's burden," Arendt answers in her very last sentence: "it was the polis, the space of men's free deeds and living words, which could endow life with splendor—τὸν βίον λαμπρὸν ποιεῖσθαι." Arendt [1963], 285.

[17] The confusion between the two goes back, claims Arendt, to the "profound misunderstanding expressed in the Latin translation of 'political' as 'social'." Arendt [1958], 27.

[18] Arendt [1958], 29, 160, 174; Arendt [1963], 2. As Arendt stresses, "legislator and architect belonged in the same category." Nonetheless it must be admitted that Arendt prefers to regard the polis as ultimately a matter of communication that does not require a given physical space (177).

[19] Arendt [1958], 26, 167. Indeed I would further distinguish between *per-suasion* and *suasion*, preferring the latter as a softer—and more correct—translation of πείθω. Suasion is also preferable for translating the Latin *Suada* (goddess and concept). Not only does "suasive" take the sting out of the *per*-suasive, it also allows for distinguishing between its usage and contemporary exploitations of the word persuasion to denote a scheming mode of control.

activist attempts to fuse Freud and Marx in a post-industrial political thought that made rare direct use of Schiller's theory of the aesthetic state to imagine what he called "a nonrepressive culture" concretized "at the level of mature civilization." In his most radical writings of the 1960s and 1970s Marcuse goes on to invoke an "aesthetic ethos of socialism" compatible with his Schillerian vision: "Art transcending itself would become a factor in the reconstruction of nature and society, in the reconstruction of the polis, a political factor."[20] Meanwhile Löwith, better known for his exposure of the theological presuppositions underlying the modern historical consciousness, devotes a substantial part of his intellectual-historical inquiries to saving the centrality of the polis in Greek thought from modern attempts to subordinate it to a universal philosophy of history. For Löwith the great classical thinkers and historians from Aristotle to Machiavelli remained riveted not on a single historical vector but on the polis itself, a position that he even detects, albeit partly obscured, in Karl Marx's "Polis of the future" no less than in the more traditionalist Jacob Burckhardt's advocacy of important polis characteristics of intimacy against the modern power-state (*Machtstaat*).[21]

Finally, the Czech philosopher Jan Patočka brings polis thought directly into the arena of political activity through his influence on the Czech dissident movement that culminated in his student Václav Havel's Velvet Revolution of 1989.[22] As a polis thinker Patočka attaches his justification of the Czech dissident movement to his Heideggerian vision of the original Hellenic polis as the site for the first clear Word of the eventing of being as a Heraclitean *polemos* manifesting the ungroundedness of freedom as a "shaking" and the polis as the arena for "shakenness" (*otřes*, *otřesenost*). His "solidarity of the shaken," which is meant to allude to all modern potential dissident movements, remains firmly committed to a politics of "the realm of the discovery of freedom and the ground of truth" that the historical polis had first embodied and that survives in the distant recollections of a philosophy true to its polis origins.[23]

These opening moves on behalf of a modern polis thinking continue to find fresh extensions and interpretations in contemporary scholarship. Peter Murphy

---

[20] "Marcuse: Aesthetic Ethos," in Chytry [1989], 430, 434. See also the recent collection of Marcuse's writings in Marcuse [2005] and Marcuse [2007].

[21] "Regaining the Cosmos: Karl Löwith contra Martin Heidegger," in Chytry [2005], esp. 53-56. In Burckhardt's case the actual experience of life in the city-state of Basel gave an added impetus. However Burckhardt, graduating from his earlier philhellenism to a more balanced portrayal of the Hellenic polis, critiqued the analogy commonly drawn in his time between the Hellenic polis and Swiss cantons. Cf. Gossman [2000], 297-346, esp. 301.

[22] Patočka attended Heidegger's lectures in 1933 as a student of Heidegger's own teacher Edmund Husserl. See also Chapter 4 below.

[23] For details and relevant citations, see Chytry [2006a].

has developed a powerful theory of justice seen as part and parcel of the openness where humans literally gather and assemble, fostering the character of mutual exchange, contest, competition, recognition, balancing and harmony which constitute the political realm. This literal spacing fits with the polis emphasis on performative, ceremonial and carnivalesque traits to being human and in effect gives birth to justice, fairness and equity. For Murphy such lived experiences of justice were crucial to the "Mediterranean city" and he proposes to follow its implications to the global level of "portal cities" which have spawned art, artisanship, commerce and trade societies.[24]

For Robert Pirro who is influenced by the polis thought of Hannah Arendt, Arendt points the way to the very idea of a "politics of tragedy." Pirro shows not only that, following Arendt, tragedy promoted a polis mode of life which meant a way without "authority" through its pedagogical effects on the polis citizenry, but also that it is possible to formulate equivalents to ancient tragedy through modern storytelling which will promote political freedom "as a mode of being that is accessible, continuous and durable."[25] In subsequent work Pirro has marked out the cases in which a tragic outlook serves such political purposes and those in which it does not, looking both to Germany and to its apparent tragic "opposite," the United States, for his empirical components.[26]

A former student of, and collaborator with, the Marxist philosopher Louis Althusser, Jacques Rancière in his more recent works has fully embraced an approach to politics as "a matter of building a stage and sustaining a spectacle or 'show'."[27] For Rancière politics "is always about creating a stage" and invariably takes the form "of the establishment of a theatrical and artificial sphere."[28] His arguments are meant to uphold the "disruptive equality" that historically has served the people, workers and public against claims for an orderly and hierarchical inequality; hence Rancière's turn against Plato by

---

[24] Murphy [2001] and personal communication. See also Chapter 3 below. The important collection of essays on the modern relevance of the Hellenic legacy edited by Arnason & Murphy [2001] should also be mentioned. Murphy himself is influenced by the Central European thought of Agnes Heller and writes favorably of Hannah Arendt but remains highly critical of Heidegger. Heller herself has promoted the Central European tradition of "the Great Republic" which she traces back to Kant. Heller [1985]. Heller went on to occupy the Hannah Arendt Chair of Philosophy at the New School University of New York City. However, Peter Murphy questions any significant polis proclivities to be found in Heller's thought. Personal communication (27 December 2006).

[25] Pirro [2001], 76.

[26] Personal communication. Pirro has also written effectively on the Czech case of Václav Havel and his "political uses of tragedy." Pirro [2002].

[27] Hallward [2006], 111.

[28] Rancière, cited in Hallward [2006], 111. See also "Landfall: Theatrocracy" below.

arguing the advantages for the *demos* of the openness and unconfinement offered by the Athenian "theatrocracy" which Plato himself so vehemently upbraided.

Finally, Alan Singer's advocacy of aesthetic reason and aesthetic community shows how postmodern anti-aestheticism can be placated in terms fully conversant with critical thinking. Following on Arendt's faith that the aesthetic judgment can be pivotal for making political order through the standard of the aesthetic state, Singer has retrieved the "ethical artifice of the polis" by his theorizing of "a context of human choice-making constrained by social recognition."[29] Calling upon the concepts of translatability, deliberation, choice, and training "in reciprocal recognition as the argumentative touchstones for a cognitivist aesthetic," Singer succeeds in recuperating the ancient resort to tragedy for its "deliberative boundary-negotiating contextualism" and hence on behalf of a "strictly cognitive" sense of community.[30]

Absorbing these points of departure by the original list of modern polis thinkers (Heidegger, Arendt, Marcuse, Löwith, and Patočka) and more recent contributors (Murphy, Pirro, Rancière, and Singer) and linking them with the five principal features of polis thought earlier stated, the following list of major areas for further development and research suggests itself.[31]

First, the "aesthetic-political." Particularly since the 1980s a deluge of works, and nomenclatures, favoring the reference point of the aesthetic-political has produced a series of political and ideological prescriptions ranging from "paraesthetics," "aesthetic politics," "aesthetic statism," "aesthetic community," all the way to "kallipolis."[32] No doubt some of this interest reflects an earlier discussion around Walter Benjamin's famous theme of an "aestheticization of politics" *(Ästhetisierung der Politik)* and his call for a "politicization of art" (*Politisierung der Kunst*).[33] Nonetheless, the "aesthetic-political" has not remained bound by such Benjaminian concerns. Thus, one prominent example of the "aesthetic-political" that has emerged is the ideal of the "aesthetic state"

---

[29] Singer [2003], 41.

[30] This perfunctory summary barely touches on the wealth of Singer's arguments. Singer [2003], 226.

[31] It will be noted that the first three areas of the following eight headings are in fact derived from the fate of the polis theme between the fall of the polis in late antiquity and its contemporary articulations and clarifications.

[32] Carroll [1987], Ankersmit [1996], Kaiser [1999], Murphy [2001], Singer [2003].

[33] An important counter in left intellectual circles to Benjamin proved to be Michel Foucault's increasing valorization of the "aesthetic-political" in his positive readings of a contemporary "aesthetics of existence" for the "politico-aesthetic choice" in ethical life. Foucault [2003], 112-114. More details on Foucault's aesthetics of existence are in Chytry [2008a]. For a criticism of Foucault's "mistaken" "Journey to Greece," see, e.g., Daraki [1986].

(der ästhetische Staat des schönen Scheins) derived from the German poet-philosopher Friedrich Schiller's famous 1794-5 essay *Letters on the Aesthetic Education of Man*. Investigation of central contributors to this theme—from the Hellenism of Winckelmann and the *Goethezeit* of Friedrich Schiller's and Goethe's "classical" Duchy of Weimar to the modern thought of Heidegger and Marcuse—has been followed by an extension of the theme to other regions and cultures.[34] Latin American figures espousing the aesthetic state have been traced in the careers of such influential writers and movements as the Mexican scholar Alfonso Reyes and the Mexican youth movement Ateneo de la Juventud.[35] Similarly, Schiller's ideal has been shown at the core of the modern Chinese thought of Zhang Jingsheng in his calls for a "republic of beauty".[36] Even in its own terms, "aesthetic state" has been reconfigured as "aesthetic statism" to cover relevant areas of English literary thought that include Samuel Taylor Coleridge, Matthew Arnold and John Ruskin.[37] And contemporary efforts to marry management-firm analyses to aesthetic priorities have led to the important discovery of the relevance of Schiller's theory of play and oscillation for the development of the concept of an "art firm."[38]

Second, the architectural and theatrical-dramatic. Leonardo Bruni helped revive ancient polis thought in the Florentine Renaissance by "showing" the literal architectonic beauty of Florence prior to the particulars of its administration and governance.[39] By the same token, a work of the architectonic stature of Leon Battista Alberti's *De Re Aedificatoria* (1472) turned out to be equally a contribution to polis thought for the care with which it imagined not simply relevant architectural themes (the revival, to take the most prominent example, of the classical orders of architecture) but the very vision of the whole polis as a civic domain in which aesthetic and political considerations were

---

[34] Schiller [1967], Chytry [1989]. Against merely "cultural" readings of Schiller's theory, it is worth noting that Schiller intended to provide a political "constitution" for his aesthetic state. See the relevant passage published in *Die Horen* and discussion in the editors' foreword in Schiller [1967], 300, in which Schiller states: "Since no good state should be without its *constitution*, it is legitimate to require one for the aesthetic state also" (emphasis in original), and he promises "a first attempt at one, which I have destined for this journal."

[35] Legras [2003], Conn [2002].

[36] Lee [2006].

[37] Kaiser [1999]. Kaiser claims that "aesthetic statism" is meant to emphasize those thinkers who explicitly —rather than just implicitly—granted the guiding importance of the aesthetic for the political sphere.

[38] Guillet de Monthoux [2004]. As Guillet de Monthoux puts it, "Schiller awakened my desire for a learned kind of management" (20). See also Chapter 5 below.

[39] Bruni went on in his mature treatise on the Florentine constitution—composed entirely in classical Greek—to confirm explicitly that his Florence was indeed a "politeia" (περὶ τῆς πολτείας τῶν Φλωρεντίνων). "On the Florentine Constitution," in Bruni [1987], 171-174.

mutually supportive.[40] These priorities then brought in the equal salience of drama and theatre. Once ancient tragedy as music drama was revived by the Florentine Camerata experiments in *dramma per musica*, this motif could be traced through the perambulations of the musical-theatrical tradition to the grand aesthetic-political ventures by that fan of the Athenian polis, Richard Wagner, and his creation of the Bayreuth temple to art.[41] Indeed, spoken theatre and such ancillary rivulets as the burgeoning commedia dell'arte tradition are of equal relevance, particularly where such streams extend into the distinctively modern-technological media of Italian cinema, both neorealist and Napolitano-comedic.[42] Finally, more recent work on the subversive "Cytherean" features of seventeenth- and eighteenth-century French opera-ballets against the absolutism of Louis XIV open up even more expansively "libertine" and political features of the theatrical contribution to the polis theme.[43]

Third,"artistism" (German *Künstlertum*, French *artistisme*), understood as a social-communal contextuality for the artist temper. The subject-matter of "Bohemia," "avant-garde," and even "counterculture" has formed the object of a variety of more recent scholarly investigations. These works often have in mind the locating of Bohemia within the needs of early industrial society in Paris around 1820-1840, the avant-garde within "advanced" radical positions largely coming out of Bohemia after 1870, and counterculture linking up with dissident movements prominent in the 1960s.[44] Nonetheless, it is also worth calling upon a broader historical canvas to point out that the first of these movements, Bohemia, clearly succeeds the varied stages of the presence of "libertinism" and "libertines" in early modern France, and that such movements owe their origins to artistically-oriented life styles emerging from the more prosperous workings of Italian, specifically Florentine, Renaissance society.[45] This line of influence confirms the affinity between the Florentine variant of an "art" movement[46] and larger issues of a *rinascita* of classical urban and civic

---

[40] Alberti's concern was not a mere architectural revival, but a return "to the essential, universal human values embodied in the classical city," i.e. the polis. Borsi [1977], 230.

[41] See Chapter 6 below.

[42] More generally, see Chapter 7. Also, such contemporary cinematic ventures as Federico Fellini's Studio 5 at *Cinecittà* ("cine-city") suggest polis priorities of ceremonial, carnival, and commedia. Fellini [1989].

[43] Cowart [2001] and below.

[44] Seigel [1986], Poggioli [1968], Goffman & Joy [2005]. The latter work, while somewhat excessive in parts, is at least a promising effort to widen use of the term counterculture to other epochs.

[45] Wackernagel [1981].

[46] Marked, for example, by the sense of community among the culture-makers of the early Florentine Renaissance (Alberti, Brunelleschi, Ghiberti, Donatello, Masaccio).

society and politics driving what would be subsequently called Florentine civic humanism.[47]

Fourth, the "artful firm," a term—drawing on two already current notions, "the art firm," and "artful making"—utilized for addressing contemporary management and firm theories aiming toward the potential marriage of the aesthetic domain and organizations ranging from enterprises to business firms.[48] While some of this management theorizing is presently premature for going so far as to posit "the aesthetic firm as a *polis*," such arguments are an encouraging sign that management minds are for the first time also becoming attuned to the proximity of *polis* thought.[49]

Fifth, studies of the cultural phenomenon of the "city" insofar as the latter supports polis thought. This area covers the body of work associated with Lewis Mumford (particularly his *City in History*) and might be contrasted to the large-scale yet a-polis accounts of the city by Peter Hall.[50] It also covers comparative studies of the city in a variety of cultures besides the western, such as the Chinese and the Mesoamerican as well as the civic functions of the campus or university city and the urban focalizations of the presently globalizing internet galaxy.[51] Finally, recent work on the contemporary economic and military viability of the "small" state should form part of speculation on the pragmatic relevance of the polis.[52]

Sixth, empirical studies of presently existing "city-states" from the perspective of the tips they accord the serious searcher of polis characteristics. A valuable introduction to the role of the city-state throughout history has been recently furnished by Geoffrey Parker.[53] In addition, two relevant cases are the Principality of Monaco[54] and the economically flourishing city-state of Singapore (and to a lesser extent the quasi-autonomous Chinese entity of Hong Kong) as well as the city-states of the Persian Gulf. Since such examples as

---

[47] Baron [1955], Holmes [1969].

[48] "Art firm" is from Guillet de Monthoux [2004] while "artful making" is from Austin & Devin [2003].

[49] Dobson [1999], 159. Also: "The firm becomes a nurturing community, a *polis*" (132). These views reflect the author's adoption of certain positions from the ethical philosophy of Alasdair MacIntyre. See also Chapter 5 below.

[50] Mumford [1938], Mumford [1961], Hall [1998].

[51] See also Chapters 3 and 8 below.

[52] For the present viability of small states, see Lind [1994], 92-94; for future possibilities, see the comment that "future technologies ... may create pockets of military capability that will allow very small states to hold off larger ones" in Cohen [1996], 53.

[53] Parker [2004].

[54] For ancient Massalia (Μασσαλία) and its *comptoirs* (*Gallia graeca*), see Benoit [1965]; for modern Monaco, cf. "The Setting: Monaco and its Princes," in Englund [1984], 173-203, and Veszelits [2006].

Singapore, Hong Kong and Dubai are not historically connected with polis tradition, they can also serve as useful control devices.[55]

Seventh, the theme of interstellar "city-states" of the future. Although small-scale space stations seem the most likely immediate option for the transition to human colonization in space, the long-run prognosis valorizes the city-state model—small or large—as the most appropriate civic form. Thus the physicist and futurist Freeman Dyson envisages space city-states along the lines of Renaissance Italian city-states. This makes good cultural sense since the only historical precedents for such voyages and settlements on earth have been long-term voyages to the "ocean sea." While the Polynesians are the unquestioned champions in this regard, a strong candidate for second place would be ancient Hellenic colonization of the Mediterranean basin: "The image of the future in which more humans will live on space colonies than will live on Earth is something that has precedent in the Greek experience."[56]

Finally, *eighth*, reconsiderations of classical studies of the historical polis, insofar as such studies aid in the further clarifications of the phenomenon of polis. This would include contemporary political theory that makes use of ancient history—or parallel periods such as the Italian Renaissance—for its inferences and conclusions. Such works carry important lessons for revitalizing polis thinking even if their authors are generally more concerned to apply them to a-polis themes related to globalizing republics like the United States and political-economic agglomerates like the European Union.

A program of this range, driven by the five principal features of polis thought, helps distinguish polis thought from a variety of alternatives in political theorizing. Although polis thought shares a great deal with the civic republicanism associated with J. G. A. Pocock, its emphases on the openness that encourages associations between the aesthetic and the political clearly marks it off from civic republicanism's prime concerns.[57] And while the critical

---

[55] For Singapore, see Regnier [1991]; for Hong Kong and the Persian Gulf city-states, see "The Globalization of the City-State" in Parker [2004], 213-214. Parker notes that the city-state has been far more characteristic of the Mediterranean region, less so in China and India, but adds that its more recent disappearance in Europe has been accompanied by its emergence "for the first time in other parts of the world" such as Southeast Asia and the Middle East (16).

[56] Richard B. Lee, "Models of Human Colonization: !Kung Sun, Greeks, and Vikings," in Finney & Jones [1985], 185-186.

[57] Besides Pocock [2003], cf. Honohan [2002] and Olsen [2006]. Significantly, themes related to the aesthetic-political are entirely absent in Honohan's helpful summation of civic republicanism. Olsen, for his part, brings in the concept of "placeness" in drawing on Hannah Arendt's relevance for the theme of property, but he avoids touching on the more comprehensive understanding of place, site, theatre and stage which the polis approach in principle offers. "Hannah Arendt and the Disintegration of Property," in Olsen [2006], 247; 229-262.

theory school of Theodor Adorno and Max Horkheimer has contributed a good deal to a broader reading of both the critical and emancipatory dimensions of art and the aesthetic dimension for politics, among its members it is really only Herbert Marcuse, who as earlier noted, remained unfailingly affirmative in his critical reading of the prospects for a revival of the polis.[58] Finally, notwithstanding important shared directions with Rawlsian liberalism, John Rawls' own strictures point out that his justice as fairness approach may resemble civic republicanism but should not be identified with the kind of "civic humanism" he explicitly associates with the city-states (poleis) of Athens and Florence.[59]

II

The first part of this chapter presented an argument on behalf of making room for polis thought within political theory proper. This second part goes on to claim that within such polis thought cytherics as a faculty of thought should be given particular consideration.

Cytherics names a faculty of thought defined as "the sighting and siting of aesthetic-erotic or aphrodisian environments."[60] The purpose behind this definition is to broaden the larger modern post-Kantian concern with the "aesthetic" to encompass as well the "erotic." It thus supports nineteenth- and twentieth-century attempts to broaden the concept of the aesthetic in a manner that more explicitly recognizes the permutations of the original icon for an aesthetic way of thinking: Aphrodite or Venus, whose iconological function was meant to subsume not only the subject-matter of "beauty" but also of "love." By fusing this new (in fact more ancient) "aesthetic-erotic" subject-matter within the comprehensive term "aphrodisian," cytherics signals a region, environment, "isle" for the appropriate discursive arena of the aesthetic-erotic or aphrodisian, since "Cythera" (Cythère, Κύθηρα) has characteristically epitomized an isle upon which "the aphrodisian presence—*luxe, calme et volupté*—is paramount."[61]

Through this unifying concept of the "aphrodisian" to encompass both the aesthetic and the erotic, it becomes possible to utilize ancient texts that clarify the character of the "aphrodisian" proper as a "sun-duo" (σύνδυο), defined as the dynamics of the togetherness of the two in contrast to the unity of a one.

[58] Marcuse [2005} and [2007].
[59] Rawls [2001], 142, 144.
[60] For a full presentation, see Chytry [2005].
[61] "The Foundations of Cytherics,' in Chytry [2005], 127, and more generally 121-146.

Evoking "Cythera" through the term "cytherics" then takes on a more political direction by encouraging the conceptualization of pilgrimages toward the desired goal of an "isle," with its "landfall" beginning the implementation of a realm in harmony with the aphrodisian priorities—already recorded in the relevant literature and iconology—that such an isle might legitimately embody.[62]

Although at first such concerns suggest little more than charming conceits culled from ancient and modern belles lettres, in fact there are solid historical facts to confirm the founding of "Cytheras" throughout the Mediterranean world. Classical antiquity included such sacred precincts and pilgrimage sites as the original isle of Cythera of Uranian Aphrodite off the coast of Greece, Aphroditian Paphos on Cyprus, and Venereal Eryx/Erycina on Sicily. Moreover, in such cases as the Carian polis of Aphrodisias specifically and exclusively devoted to the goddess, there is the clear evidence of the functional workings and fame of a literal "political" or polis entity devoted to Aphrodite.

Once the Roman statesman Sulla supplicated this "aphrodisian" polis of Aphrodisias in the first century BCE, the cult of the Aphrodisias goddess was specifically introduced into the political priorities of Roman rule and legitimation.[63] Particularly the Julio-Claudian line of rulers already claimed its origins (via "Ascanius" or "Iulus" from, according to Virgil, "Ilus"-"Ilos") in the legendary Aeneas' wanderings from fallen Troy to Latium. This appropriation reflects the larger patterns of the acceptance of "Venus" in the early Roman pantheon of deities. What seems to have begun as a generalized mixture of magical incantation and religious propitiation was personalized in the sixth-fifth centuries BCE at the sanctuary of Lavinium to incorporate the respective Etruscan and Hellenic deities Turan and Aphrodite into the distinctively Latin "Venus."[64] Such personalization absorbed both the seductive-amorous elements of the latter and the religio-magical respectability of the former within the master epithet of *Concilium* or "conciliation"/"conciliator" under the new cult of *Venus Frutis.*[65]

This "Venus" appellation allowed the Romans to enjoy the security of Latin autochthony while comfortably absorbing newer external strands of aphrodisian

---

[62] Boedeker [1974], Grigson [1976], Friedrich [1978].

[63] Confirmed by the uniquely "free" status which Caesar Augustus later granted this exactly cytherean polis of Aphrodisias and which Roman emperors consistently reconfirmed until as late as the mid-third century CE. Schilling [1954], 282; Erim [1986], 32. More generally see Moon [2000], 24-29.

[64] The Indo-European root "uen" for "to "desire" or "to become prosperous" turned into the divine Latin "uenia," whence "uenerari"/"venerate."

[65] Schilling suggests that the Etruscan word "Frutis" may well stem from the Hellenic word "Aphrodite." Schilling [1954], 79.

genealogy and history. Hence, Roman acquisition of Sicily in the first and second Punic wars brought in the spectacular cult of Aphrodite Erycina on Mount Eryx, further historicizing the myth of the Aeneadae already celebrated in Magna Graecia and now identified with the epithet of *Victrix* for helping the Romans resist and eventually defeat the great challenge of Hannibal in 217-215 BCE. Then, having reached the Eastern Mediterranean lands originally giving birth to the cult of Aphrodite and the myth of Troy, the major Roman conquerors Sulla, Caesar and Augustus went on to bind personal, family, and Roman success and prosperity to the Asian sanctuaries, thus rounding out a Mediterranean chain of sacred aphroditian centers extending from Aphrodisias to Mount Eryx and Laurentian Rome proper. Uniting the divine *uenia* with the human *ueneratio*, this "'venusian' religion" confirmed the genealogical superiority of the Julio-Claudian line while dominating the civic, poetic and philosophical standards of Augustan Rome which incorporated as well the "cytherean" and "paphian" ("cyprian") Aphrodite into the venusian universe.[66] Under this broader reading of Venus, the polis of Aphrodisias lent the star-and-crescent cosmic symbolism of its goddess to Caesar's *Venus Genetrix*, thus reintroducing the "nature" ("physical") or "garden" aspect of the goddess that had been first absorbed centuries earlier through the Sicilian cult of Aphrodite ἐν κήποις. This aspect was now poetically and philosophically augmented, via Lucretius and Virgil, to encompass the entire cosmic universe,[67] all the while that triumphant Roman leaders continued to exploit the "victory" theme (*felicitas/victoria*) through their incorporation of the martial Aphrodite ('Αφροδιτη στρατεία).[68]

If the high point proper of this venusian religion took place under Caesar and his celebration of *Venus Genetrix* with her massive temple by the Forum of Caesar, its ramifications extended over the entire Antonine period of flourishing poleis under imperial hegemony (96-180CE). Sanctified by the newer cosmic reading, the Patron Goddess of Gardens was allied with her amorous attributes to stimulate the second sophistic civilization of the Hellenistic East which forged the Greek novel with its cultivation of amorous couples seeking and

---

[66] Schilling [1954], 265. In his classic Roman epic *Aeneid*, Virgil made sure that his hero's divine mother Venus was addressed by the gods more often than not as "Cytherea." Virgil [1966], *Aeneid*, v.800, viii.615, x.86.

[67] The cosmic precedence of Aphrodite had already been philosophically argued by the Presocratic Magna Graecia philosophers Parmenides and Empedocles.

[68] Schilling [1954], 22-23, 30, 379, 290. The link between these two themes is the prosperity that fecundates the land and its trees and also brings about military victories. In this regard the Aphrodisias *labrus*, a double-headed axe, also seems to have played a contributory role in tandem with the Latin *fasces*. This symbol may have stemmed originally from the "labyrinth" of ancient Cretan Knossos, denoting royal and sacerdotal power.

realizing happiness in mythical renditions of either pre- or non-Roman Hellenic poleis.[69] Roman Hellenism meanwhile, particularly under Hadrian, embarked on consciously Hellenizing projects which, after the destruction of Jewish Jerusalem in 135 CE and its replacement by the Roman city Aelia Capitolina, even included the construction of a temple of Aphrodite over the reputed Tomb of Christ and a sculpture of Aphrodite over Golgotha, the reputed setting for his Crucifixion.[70]

Not surprisingly, the fourth-century Roman swing toward Christianity under Constantine, prodded by his Christian mother Helena, led immediately to the destruction of this same temple and the building over its base of the Church of the Holy Sepulchre,[71] the symbolically pregnant start to a thorough campaign of obliteration of the cytherean universe in favor of Christian icons, including the Madonna, to replace the Lady of the Dove throughout all her Mediterranean sanctuaries.[72] The end of classical antiquity is thus the start of a highly ambivalent, if not hostile, Christian-Roman attitude toward the entire range of venusian-aphroditian phenomena: if that attitude remained obdurately against the fleshly challenges contained in "Aphrodite," it could not entirely divest itself of the "uenerari" at the core of the venus theme.[73] The implications of such ambiguity however only surfaced centuries later in the Italian Renaissance.

As spokesman for the Florentine Platonism of the late fifteenth century, Marsilio Ficino was the first to mark out the centrality of Cytherean or Uranian Venus. Ostensibly following Plato's *Symposion*, he argued for an *amor divinus*

---

[69] Swain [1995], 101-131, who emphasizes an important Hellenizing ideological component to this explicit denial of a Roman reality for the polis-devotions of the Greek novel's favored couples. As he notes regarding the premises of the Greek novel, "the Greek world for the novel of the past—a world without Rome—is the only possible setting;" "the city is the centre of Hellenic civilization" for heroes; and "the heroes should be two young people from the urban elite," all of which leads to a new ethic of the harmonious couple (109-110).

[70] For the temple of Aphrodite over the tomb of Christ, see Tsafrir [1999], 158-160. For the statue of Venus over Golgotha, see Heckscher [1956], 29. "In crucis rupe, statua ex marmore veneris": Heckscher refers to rumors of "a marble statue of Venus crowning the hill of Golgotha," pointing out that for such Church Fathers as Eusebius and Ambrosius, this site was also known as *Venerarium*. Between Hadrian and Constantine, although "we have information about a small Jewish congregation in Jerusalem, the city became pagan." Tsafrir [1999], 159.

[71] According to the new language of Christianity, one must erase the "dreadful grave of souls, and the gloomy shrine of lifeless idols to the impure spirit they call Venus." Eusebius, *Vita Constantini*, cited by Tsafrir [1999], 160, also cf. 163 (notes 40, 41).

[72] The destruction of the temple of Aphrodite and the building of this church marked the major initial stages of the triumph of Christianity over "paganism," according to Tsafrir [1999], 160. Tsafrir also notes that building a church immediately on top of a ruined temple was "very uncommon" in the fourth and fifth centuries (163 [note 50]).

[73] Schilling [1954], 380; cf. also Grigson [1976], 228-229.

corresponding to the faculty of *nous* or *intellectus* in contrast to the more *amor humanus* of Paphian or Cyprian Venus.[74] Such teachings he saw as highlighted in the classically Renaissance works (*Primavera, Nascita di Venere*) of Sandro Botticelli, confirming the gravity with which the Renaissance largely approached such icons. In the critical work *Hypnerotomachia Poliphili* (1467/1499), the isle of Cythera became the ultimate goal of a quest that was not merely amorous but meant to reintroduce the entire classical world, its mystery cults, and the aphroditian religiosity that had been shattered by an intervening Christianity.[75] Combining the characteristic Renaissance genres of painting, sculpture, architecture, and ecological landscaping, this work reveals the extent to which as of 1500 certain sophisticated Renaissance minds had already reached a unified vision of the cytherean vocation.[76]

From this stage on, the cytherean theme increasingly stands for radical traditions of thought and behavior that sat uneasily with the orthodoxies of the sixteenth and seventeenth centuries. Sensuous, alchemical, utopian, it fed into currents of "libertine" resistance to seventeenth-century royal absolutism which eventually surfaced within oppositional cultural formations in Louix XIV's France and the succeeding Regency period.[77] Recent work on the cultural politics of the "Cythera" theme in French letters and performance arts during this period has underscored its "subversive" components favoring a "cytherean" or "aphroditian" domain of peace, love and fruitfulness against the martial elements of French absolutism.[78] Such exploitation of the Cythera theme has been traced back to Giambattista Marino's poem *Adone* (1623) through its French translation by Jean Chapelain which identified "Cythera" as a symbol of "transcendental beauty" and as "a renewal of civilized epicureanism associated with Venus and her island home."[79] By the end of the seventeenth century this sacred island accordingly came to stand for "a political" or "subversive utopia"

---

[74] For a more detailed account with references, see "The Foundation of Cytherics," in Chytry [2005], 128-131.

[75] At the very center of this "isle of Cytherea" the "divine Venus stood naked in the middle of the transparent and limpid waters of the basin ..., reflecting the Cytherean body." Colonna [1999], 362 (a diagram of the isle is located on 475).

[76] For a Jungian reading of the work's major mission in terms of classical antiquity and the ancient mystery cults, see Fierz-David [1987], 26-27. Also Blunt [1937-1938], 118.

[77] On alchemical readings of the *Hypnerotomachia Poliphili* in 17th century France through Béroalde de Vervillle (1600), see Blunt [1937-1938], 123-126. As Blunt notes, during this period alchemy "was associated with free thought," understood as "the simple libertine Epicurean doctrine of self-indulgence," with the group around Bérolde classified by Blunt as "Bohemian" (125).

[78] See in particular Crow [1985], Plax [2000], and Cowart [2001].

[79] Cowart [2001], 464.

that was explicitly "anti-absolutist," feeding into a wide range of currents—including its use as a "bogus publication site"—that helps explain the subversive undertow to the impact of Antoine Watteau's famous painting *Pelerinage à l'isle de Cythère* of 1717 and its *fête galante* motifs: "a voyage of transformation, at once personal, political, and societal, that both leads to and is Cythera."[80] Indeed, by this stage the physical realm of the theatre proper was taken to be "Cythera," a siting of celebrations of peace, equality and freedom opposed and superior to the political alternatives of the era of Louis XIV and its aftermath.[81] Linked with characteristic Enlightenment motifs of happiness (*bonheur*) and civic virtue, this theme pervades eighteenth-century European culture—even leaping across the Pacific Ocean to baptize the newly discovered isle of Polynesian Tahiti in 1768 as "La nouvelle-Cythère."[82]

More currently, aphrodisian motifs play a provocative role in European thought. Through his treatment of beauty as an incitement to "aphrodisian bliss," the philosopher Friedrich Nietzsche has strongly influenced modern thought to incorporate ecstatic components within the aesthetic and the erotic.[83] Moreover, since Sigmund Freud's speculations on the alternative of "Cythera" as "the model of human society" (which Freud rejected), thinkers influenced by him and Nietzsche have articulated new valorizations and nomenclatures for what the Marxist philosopher Herbert Marcuse has termed "the aesthetic-erotic environment" or "aesthetic Eros," while that erstwhile critic of the "carceral archipelago," Michel Foucault, has chosen the "aphrodisia" to epitomize the ancient ethical substance that Foucault has called upon to support his own vison of a new "aesthetics of existence."[84]

A striking advocacy on behalf of "Aphrodite" has even been fashioned within the discursivities of current media theory and history. Although known primarily for his inquiries into the primacy of "hardware" influences helping to shape and reinforce the proclivities of a digital epoch, Friedrich Kittler has turned resolutely toward the goddess in his idiosyncratic revival of German Hellenism. Having earlier drawn a fundamental distinction between

---

80 Plax [2000], 108-153; Cowart [2001], 461-464, 475, 473. Cowart notes that "the term actually became synonymous with a French underground press" (476).

81 One strong ancient support for this modern reading of Cythera is the opposition of the Aphrodite cult of Sicilian Eryx (as well as Cyprus) to blood sacrifices in cultic preference for flowers, herbs, and incense. Schilling [1954], 237. The Sicilian philosopher Empodocles stresses this aversion to blood sacrifices in his praise of the Golden Age of Kupris (fragment 128).

82 Bougainville [1958], 137. For an articulate historical account of the concept of happiness (*bonheur)* for modern liberal theory, see G. Chytry [2005].

83 See Chytry [2007].

84 References in "The Foundation of Cytherics," in Chytry [2005], 131-132, and Chytry [2008a].

"Aphrodite" as the "aphrodisia" of the female goddess beyond desire and "Eros" as the "erotica" of the male god constituting desire—and lack—Kittler has launched a magisterial work on music and mathematics, the first part of which he significantly names "Aphrodite."[85]

Assembling a rich variety of philological, historical, illustrative and rhetorical weapons, *Aphrodite* argues the case for the uniqueness of the Greek alphabet in presiding over the origins of mathematics and the latter's subsequent progeny of computer-digital language.[86] Kittler posits "song" at the origins of that same alphabet and its uniqueness in providing a perfect phonetic match between sound and writing through its precise rendition of both consonantal and vowel ("AEIOU") sounds. Such "song"—rather than the conventionally argued primacy of calculation and reckoning by monarchical scribes—inspired the creation of this alphabet from the very different characteristics of the Phoenician syllabary—including the use of Greek letters for numbers. In turn, this startling fact, namely, that "the alphabet of the Greeks sings," may be attributed to the intimate relations between earlier, pre-literate "hearings" of the Sirens, of Circe, and of Calypso, all of whom Kittler correctly locates under the master presencing of "Aphrodite," the goddess who brings love, happiness, even the stillness of the seas for the safe haborings of her questing heroes, and those who receive her through the ears, the heart—and presumably the genitals: "Music and Script are united in Love."[87] Accordingly, "it is alone love which music teaches," and from the writing system of the Greek alphabet a mode of reproduction is invented which cannily encourages the invention of mathematics through the master concept of Harmonia—daughter of Aphrodite and Ares— in an eventually geometrical direction. As Kittler shrewdly puts it, "the papyrus rolls are spooled like sound tracks," and mathematics was not invented for its own sake but "for music."[88]

Kittler clearly means to draw important conclusions from his aphrodisian approach for a reading of the present ubiquity of computer-driven media. Between the Greek alphabet and the contemporary computer universal sign

[85] Kittler [1995], 37; Kittler [2006]; Kittler & Vismann [2001].

[86] A much milder case for the connection between the ancient Greeks and computers was made earlier by Bolter. Comparing "computer man" and "ancient man," Bolter, a classicist as well as computer-science graduate, wrote: "In fact, the attitude toward history fostered by electronic technology is like that of the ancient Greeks, who lived in the present both in their politics and in their literature." Bolter [1984], 224.

[87] Kittler [2006], 115, 108, 128. Thus Circe is a "Doppelgängerin Aphrodites" (27); from Thrace through Illyria to Magna Graecia, "Zeirene" meant "Aphrodite schlichtweg" (44), and Calypso, already known as "Kythera," "ist eine der Gestalten Aphrodites" (68).

[88] Kittler [2006], 213, 133; also: "Vom Vokalalphabet bis zum Assembler-Code" (133). Armitage [2006], 35.

system, he detects a close working relationship: to this extent there is an underlying affinity between "Homer" and "Hardware." Still, Kittler is far from inferring an aphroditian future for the unfolding digital world. Rather, his gambit appears to be to angle toward a critique of the primarily war-oriented underpinnings of at least fast-paced technological innovations by suggesting an earlier affinity between love ("Aphrodite") and the original pre-mechanical universal language of the Greek alphabet as fashioned by Homer and his Sapphic and Sophoclean heirs but subsequently lost. Accordingly, as the last literal words of his *Aphrodite* affirm, Kittler's rhetoric has become increasingly direct in its supplications to the goddess: "Aphrodite, remain close to us."[89]

III

According to the above narrative, cytherics captures important dimensions of relating the aesthetic-erotic, or the "aphrodisian," to social, cultural and political priorities between classical antiquity and modernity. This section concludes by summarizing and highlighting these affinities between cytherics and polis thought.

Accepting that the original "vision" grounding polis thought was "sacred Troy," it is notable that "Aphrodite" was in fact the "most loyal female protectress" of Troy as well as "the primary goddess of the Troad"—the region in which Troy was located with its favored Mount Ida—who brought her benevolence to all its human and natural landscape, and even, in divine union with Anchises, helped restart civilization (through such "New Troys" as Rome and London) after the tragic fall of Troy.[90] Moreover, this same Troy and Venus-Aphrodite was subsequently appropriated by the Romans for their genealogical and political legitimations. Indeed, as Hannah Arendt has argued in the case of the United States of America, even the Founding Fathers of its Constitution, although claiming to be forming a new order (*novus ordo saeclorum),* admitted to being a "second Rome," their own model Rome having

[89] Kittler had earlier commented: "Computers may be copying machines, but, thanks to Aphrodite, we are not. The way from her to now and back must always be given over again." Armitage [2006], 27-28; Kittler [2004]; Kittler [2006], 337. Cf. also the website interview, "Rock Me, Aphrodite," dated 27 May 2006, http://www.heise.de/tp/r4/artikel/22/22695/1.html (page 6). For a valuable introduction to war and media theory, see Winthrop-Young [2002]. Kittler stresses in a recent interview that in order to regain the lost theme of "love in Europe," we must bring "a female Goddess" to our side: "it is very important to argue that Aphrodite, the Goddess of love and beauty, is a Goddess for *all* animals, inclusive of men and women." Armitage [2006], 30 (emphasis in original).

[90] Scully [1990], 35, 36.

in fact read *its* own origins as that of being "a second Troy," a resurrection of the *gens Hectorea*, and a deliberate attempt to "reverse the order of events" of the tragedy of Troy's fall.[91] The Rome of the Founding Fathers, at least according to Arendt, had thought of itself as "the resurgence of Troy and the re-establishment of some city-state that had existed before and of which the thread of continuity and tradition never had broken."[92]

It follows then that to advocate polis thought, as this chapter does, effectively renews the ancient Romans' celebration of a universal empire rounding out ancient polis practices in terms congenial to the Roman cult of Aphrodite-Venus. If meanwhile the post-Renaissance vocation of Cythera has been largely to favor "subversive" anti-absolutist utopias immersed in happiness and coupledom, this result in fact confirms the subsequent adversarial status of the polis in modern political and technological life through the image of perhaps the most dramatic "polis" alternative ("Cythera") to such a life.

The cytherean option in other words nourishes the richest tradition for evaluating and reinforcing the project of the original vision of sacred Troy. And since this vision serves as both our starting-point and paradigm for the legitimacy of polis thought for political theory proper, endorsing a faculty of thought called cytherics offers one of the more promising approaches toward the further growth and cultivation of that polis thought:

> nusquam abero et tutum patrio te limine sistam.[93]

---

[91] For Virgil the "tragedy" of Troy's fall was reinforced by the Trojans' "blamelessness," as Venus insists to her son Aeneas: "no blame to Helen of Sparta's hated face/no, nor to Paris": rather, it was the gods who were to blame. Virgil [1966], *Aeneid*, ii.5, ii.601-603, iii.2.

[92] Arendt [1963], 210, 211. Arendt [1963] distinguishes between the "new Rome" sought by the Americans and the abandoned alternative of "Rome anew," which in her view broke the American tie to "the prehistorical memories of Greece and Troy" (211).

[93] "I am always with you, to guide you safely home." Venus/Cytherea to her son Aeneas. Virgil [1966], *Aeneid*, ii.620.

CHAPTER TWO

Sculpting States

Revisiting a Theme in the Aestheticization of Politics Polemic

My dearest wish would be to be able to wander about in Italy as an unknown painter.
Adolf Hitler[1]

Alas, at the very outset of our adventure a cyclops threatens.[2]

Standing in the way of acknowledging the perseverance of polis thought within contemporary aesthetic-political discursivities is an unbending aversion to what has come to be labeled "aestheticization of politics" (*Ästhetisierung der Politik*). In a frequently cited article Martin Jay lays out a helpful taxonomy of examples of such aestheticization of politics that have served as objects of concern and censure: the callous application of the category of beauty to the deaths of human beings, the victory of the spectacle over the public sphere, the sensuous expression of a rationality claiming to realize "the literary absolute," the emphasis on the sensual dimension in the aesthetic to conceal values of truth and falsehood—and, finally, the state-artist expressing his or her "will through the shaping of unformed matter."[3]

With his characteristic Solomonian acumen, Jay attempts to right some serious imbalances in the anti-aestheticization of politics arguments against such examples. Nonetheless, his efforts are more by way of bringing up other more positive factors in the relation of aesthetics (or art) to politics than systematically questioning all these specific examples—and therefore the legitimacy of the arguments against them—in their own terms. This chapter takes up probably the most sensational of these examples—the last on Jay's list—and sees what merit, if any, the claims on behalf of such an example contain.

---

[1] Hitler [2000], 11. As the dating of 21-22 July 1941 indicates, this comment took place at the start of Hitler's epochal attack on the Soviet Union.

[2] An earlier version of this chapter was presented as an invited paper at the Southern Political Science Association annual meetings in New Orleans, Louisiana, on 10 January 2008.

[3] Jay [1992], 44. The article was also subsequently published in Jay [1993]. Jay's own reading of aesthetic experience is further developed in "Returning the Body through Aesthetic Experience: From Kant to Dewey," in Jay [2005], 131-169.

Simply put, the argument is that a prime case of aestheticization of politics is the proposition—gladly espoused by despots, tyrants and brutalists—that the state and its denizens should be treated as "matter" for the ruler or "state-artist" to mold and sculpt in the manner of the practising sculptor.[4] Strongly imbedded in this claim is the implication that such denizens are to be regarded as "inert matter" (in Jay's words, "pliable material") or some such insalubrious, and disempowering, metaphor—presumably emulating the stance of conventional sculptors toward their objects. The ruler who "sculpts states" in this manner is therefore trying to extend art and aesthetic standards into the political and state-forming realms. The anti-aestheticization counter is, obviously, that this prime example of claiming to bring aesthetics into politics encourages and legitimates a practical politics that exploits such "aesthetic" justifications in order to engage in despotic actions and policies. Aestheticization of politics is, in short, the handmaiden of illiberalism, often indeed of political fascism.

Of course some such move was the purport of Walter Benjamin, the Marxist thinker who first coined the phrase—and charge—of *Ästhetisierung der Politik* in his 1936 classic *The Work of Art in the Era of Technical Reproducibility.*[5] Actually Benjamin's thesis, itself distilled from his earlier probing analyses of the presumed fascist attraction to the aesthetic domain for ideological purposes, reflects a nuanced understanding of the new forcefulness of modes of organized violence in World War I in which individuals and soldiers in trench conditions were both stupefied and traumatized by the literal "spectacle" of total warfare around them on a daily basis.[6] Himself admirer and translator of Marcel Proust, Benjamin was no doubt aware of the perceptive passage in Proust's massive work which described the aesthetic appeal of the spectacle of aerial warfare above Paris in the latter days of the first world war.[7]

For both Proust and Benjamin the answer was not, however, to exclude the aesthetic from the political but to rethink relations that had been dramatically overturned by contemporary systems of hegemony and warfare. If Proust came up with a highly sophisticated revitalization of the aesthetic sensibility, Benjamin actively called for a "politicization of art" (*Politisierung der Kunst*). Whatever the latter might mean, it hardly entailed surrendering to fascism a

---

[4] See the 1933 cartoons depicting Adolf Hitler as "Germany's Sculptor" *[Der Bildhauer Deutschlands*] by O. Garvens, in Spotts [2002], 97.

[5] Benjamin [1973].

[6] Benjamin [1979].

[7] This "spectacle d'une grande beauté esthétique" is expanded by the narrator's friend Robert Saint-Loup (an aristocratic socialist) into a comparison of the sirens accompanying it with Wagner's Ride of the Valkyries. Proust [1954], 758-759 (*Le temps retrouvé*).

realm of human sensitivity and experience to which Benjamin himself made signal contributions.

Still, Benjamin's terminology and stance came to be bequeathed to the understandable commitment by later liberal and progressive thought to expose the multitudinous tools employed by European fascism against the integral individual and community. This commitment is worth taking seriously. But it will only be properly served once the threads presumably making up the aestheticization of politics phenomena are appropriately disentangled. It is in this spirit that our own choice of exploring the statesman-as-sculptor metaphor is designed, and we begin by looking more directly at traditions of thought which could be said to have encouraged and eventually culminated in the fascist appropriation of this metaphor.[8]

I

For Hannah Arendt it all begins—as does so much else in the problematics of the political—with Plato and a critical passage from his *Republic* (420). Arendt gives the gist of the passage as follows: "In the *Republic*, the philosopher-king applies the ideas as the craftsman applies his rules and standards; he 'makes' his City *as the sculptor makes the statue*" (203).[9] Unfortunately, Arendt's reading appears somewhat flawed, for all that this particular passage states is the contention that the ideal polis should be arranged to serve the whole and not just the parts, and in support of this contention Plato evokes the hypothetical case of "painting a statue" (ἀνδριάντα γράφοντας) by giving each part the color that works for the whole rather than the part as such (*Republic* 420c).

Arendt might have been better served by citing a different passage in which Plato imagines statescraft to be akin to the work of "artists" (ζωγράφοι) (500e). Key to Plato's injection of his hypothetical artist into the political is that he "wipe out" all human habits and patterns in order to give himself a "clean canvas." Indeed, Plato's artist is unique for refusing to start work on an

[8] It should be noted that "the impetus to sculpt society" has been also associated with Stalinism and Soviet attempts to shape a new man. Hedin [2004], 179. This larger reading stems from use of Zygmunt Bauman's metaphor "the Gardening state" to cover modern European efforts at more conscious state planning which then took extreme forms in the cases of modern totalitarian regimes. According to Amir Weiner, the key to this "sea change" was the discovery of the modern masses as not only a source of political legitimacy but also "as a raw material by which to mold a purer, healthier and more aesthetic society." Amir Weiner, "Introduction: Landscaping the Human Garden," in Weiner [2003], 2. I leave it to scholars of Stalinist civilization to ferret out possible exploitations of the statesman-as-sculptor metaphor.

[9] Arendt [1958], 203, 360 (note 68) (emphasis added).

individual or a polis without first being assured of this clean canvas (καθαρὰν). From this starting-point the Platonic artist then sketches out an outline of his polity (ὑπογράψανθαι ἂν τὸ σχῆμα τῆς πολιτείας), going back and forth between his model and his vision of such ideals as justice (δίκαιον) and beauty (καλὸν) until he comes up with a "most beautiful picture" (καλλίστη ... ἡ γραφὴ) (501a-c).

All this seems innocent enough other than perhaps the unsettling suggestiveness behind the demand for a tabula rasa; yet creating a polis, a polity, a utopia has been often premised on just such craftly working principles and should not cause undue stir.[10] In any event, notwithstanding the parallels between such a political painter and the political sculptor, it remains the case that, formally anyway, we do not have here an explicit assertion of the statesman-as-sculptor metaphor.[11]

Instead of ferreting out every such "artist" move in the history of western thought, it makes more sense to jump directly to the nineteenth century and seek out a more characteristic pre-fascist environmentality of thought. Obviously candidates would have to evince at least viscous attraction to brutality and a violence that is unforgiving, hurtful, even sadistically homicidal. The first language that effectively stirs up this witches' brew in the European imaginal belongs to Friedrich Nietzsche, and undoubtedly he must figure, whatever his own ultimate intentions, as the provocateur for all future brutalists once he lets loose his rhetorical cannonades of the late 1880s—before falling (presumably) to the "knifelike pains of the 'little sea maid'."[12] Yet Nietzsche himself turns out to be fronting a far more dapper personality. It is in the slippery yet curiously aggressive readings of his Basel patrician colleague and academic idol Jacob Burckhardt that we detect hints of the earliest tonalities and stances of what will become the pre-fascist histrionics of such future aesthetic brutalists as Maurice Barrès, F. T. Marinetti, and Gabriele d'Annunzio.[13]

These readings come to a head in Burckhardt's most prominent work *The Civilization of the Renaissance in Italy* (1860), particularly, for our purposes, its

---

[10] At least outside the projections of Karl Popper.

[11] But cf. Wolin [2004], 42-44, who argues that Plato's "quest for suitable materials was essentially a search for a political *tabula rasa*" (44).

[12] Thomas Mann's rendering of the entry of syphilis into the life of his "Nietzschean" composer Adrian Leverkühn in *Doktor Faustus*. Mann [1948], 539.

[13] In his study of Burckhardt, Lionel Gossman refers to "the legendary wicked tongue of the Baseler" in which he also includes Burckhardt's colleague J. J. Bachofen. Gossman [2000], 206. In this regard it is worth recalling Burckhardt's own description of his favored Florentines as bearing "sharp eyes and wicked tongues" as well as engaging in "evil-speaking." Burckhardt [1869], 129.

key chapter: "The State as Artwork."[14] Although it is tempting to read this phrase in terms sympathetic to Burckhardt's overall commitment to the beautiful in classical and Renaissance cultures, in fact it has nothing to do with "beauty" or any of the higher objectives of art.[15] Strictly speaking "state as artwork" simply means: "the state as outcome of reflection and calculation" (*als berechnete, bewusste Schöpfung*).[16] In turn, the potential and need for calculability is attributed to the lack of a prior legitimacy accessible to those new Italian states which were concocted by a wide variety of medieval and renaissance political adventurers, particularly soldiers of fortune (*condottiere*). Burckhardt's prose therefore veers excitedly between an almost voluptuous rendering of the unspeakable brutalities exercised by such amoral state-creators and his somewhat more moderate acknowledgment that those states did best which brought under control such maniacal tendencies toward bloodlust and vengefulness.[17]

Of course Burckhardt, inveterate champion of a challenged nineteenth-century patrician (e.g. anti-democratic) humanism, is the first to assert that all power is inherently evil.[18] Nonetheless, it is difficult to miss the underlying self-congratulatory pulsation to his uncensored accounts of Italian bloodlust. In the final analysis it fits with his larger assertions regarding the origin of the state itself as emerging either from a "violent process" or from violence proper (*die Gewalt*): for Burckhardt it is "an apriori self-understanding" that the birth of the state is inseparable from "terrible convulsions."[19]

Absent Burckhardtian "humanism" and one is left more or less with what became the typical Nietzschean stance on the state, its origins and its slave-

---

[14] I follow the conventional English title, although strictly speaking the correct translation for the German title would use "culture" rather than "civilization." The distinction between these two terms proved an area of major contention for German writers of the nineteenth and twentieth centuries.

[15] Gossman correctly chastises such misreadings of Burckhardt's notion, particularly critiquing the views of Edward Rosen. Gossman [2000], 533 (note 126).

[16] Burckhardt [1869], 2. Also: "der Staat war ein wohl berechnetes und organisirtes Kunstwerk" (36), and: "Kunstwerke, d.h. bewusste, von der Reflexion abhängige, auf genau berechnete sichtbaren Grundlagen ruhende Schöpfungen" (71). This defining feature presumably also shaped international relations as "ein Werk der Kunst" (71).

[17] In fact Burckhardt's rather purple prose tends to disguise his simultaneous argument that on the whole the best of the Italian Renaissance culminated in republics like Venice and particularly Florence, states whose legitimacy was founded on something more virtuous and ethical than lust for power (e.g. Burckhardt [1869], 59). This latter position seems at variance with Burckhardt's claim that the state as artwork was to be found in a "more complete and more clearly defined type" among the "tyrant states" (*Tyrannenstaaten*). Burckhardt [1869], 3.

[18] "Power [*Macht*] is in itself evil [*böse*]." Burckhardt [1941], 83; also 166.

[19] Burckhardt [1941], 78.

sustaining essence—along with an unambiguous assertion of the state-as-sculpture metaphor. Indeed Nietzsche's often scandalous reading of Renaissance men and Renaissance politics is generally a simply more manic variant on his colleague Burckhardt's historiography.[20] Thus Nietzsche came to read the first state as emerging from the violent acts of a master morality of conquerors seizing pacific agricultural communities in order to "hammer" them into shape, thereby externalizing their own proneness toward violence and brutality onto an outside body of enslaved individuals. Regarding this action as a kind of "artwork" perpetrated by these noble-aristocrat types, Nietzsche went on to prominently exploit the state-sculptor metaphor: "In them rules that frightful artist's egoism which gazes forth like bronze and, like a mother in her child, knows itself to be eternally justified in the 'work'."[21]

It might be legitimately countered that there is something highly problematic about comparing such brutalism with a mother's love for her child. What is nonetheless significant about this account is how Nietzsche remains oblivious to the inconsistency in such statements as he presses on with his favored project of philosophizing "with a hammer."[22] Such "sculpting" in fact reflects Nietzsche's idiosyncratic account of the very process of creation itself. In one of his most quoted passages, Nietzsche proclaims: "For all creators are hard. And it must seem bliss to you to press your hand upon millennia as upon wax, bliss to write upon the will of millennia as upon metal—harder than metal, nobler than metal. Only the noblest is perfectly hard."[23] Just in case the point is missed, Nietzsche further amplifies this account by declaring that for his favored ideal being (*Übermensch*), "man" is "something non-form, raw material, an ugly stone in need of the sculptor."[24]

---

[20] A prominent example: Nietzsche's famous joke in his concluding *The Antichrist* that Cesare Borgia almost became pope—which would have presumably realized the triumph of Renaissance morality over the (later) Reformation—was very probably derived from Burckhardt's 1860 speculation on the near-selection of Borgia through the machinations of his father Pope Alexander VI, a step that for Burckhardt would have "secularized the States of the Church" (*Kirchenstaat*). Burckhardt concludes dramatically: "If one pursues this hypothesis, the fantasy loses itself in an abyss." Burckhardt [1869], 92, 95.

[21] Nietzsche [1966], ii, 827 (*Zur Genealogie der Moral* ii [17]).

[22] I have attempted a more favorable reading of Nietzsche's other comments on a mother's "labor of love" in Chytry [2005], 147-166.

[23] Nietzsche [1966], ii, 460. This passage in *Also sprach Zarathutra* is cited as the ending of *Götzendämmerung* (1033).

[24] Nietzsche [1966], ii, 1139 (*Ecce Homo*). "Der Imperativ: 'werdet hart!', die unterste Gewissheit darüber, *dass alle Schaffenden hart sind*, ist das eigentliche Abzeichen einer dionysischen Natur." (1140 [emphasis in original]). Cf. Nietzsche's gloss on the need to be hard in a letter to his friend Franz Overbeck: "*hier* ist Abhärtung nötig und, der Erziehung halber, eine gelegentliche Grausamkeit" (2 May 1884). Nietzsche [1966], iii, 1219 (emphasis in original).

Such Burckhardtian-Nietzschean rhetoric only then needs the very real traumas of the first world war to conflagrate into the slash-and-burn language of early fascism. Already in the postures and slogans of such prominent Italian literary figures as Gabriele D'Annunzio and F. T. Marinetti the configurations of the fascist stance are metamorphosing from pseudo-noble detachments of a pre-war excitability into the vengeful militarism of the early post-war out of which European fascism hatched. If a relatively straightforward trajectory for fascism is to be envisaged from D'Annunzio and Marinetti to Benito Mussolini and Adolf Hitler, two common features stand out: all four acquired prominence because of their talents as unusual and compelling declaimers/orators[25] and all four exploited that prominence to advocate— and, more importantly, factically engage in—localized acts of violence: "the fisticuff, the sprint and the kick," in Futurism's pungent lucubrations. Indeed it is tempting, if not strictly accurate, to sum up the basic vector of fascism as precisely this combustible mix of declamation/oratory and violence. In any event, behind this vector all four figures acknowledged the encouragement of that supreme prophet of the *superuomo/ Übermensch*: Friedrich Nietzsche.[26]

Of these four, Gabriele D'Annunzio (1863-1938) was the first to take up such Nietzchean cudgels as part of his literary contributions to *fin de siècle* aesthetic decadence. D'Annunzio's literary popularity was only to grow as he turned more aggressively toward favoring martial and war themes, and emerged in World War I as the most famous and daring flying pilot for the Italians. From 1914 on all his writings were committed to the achievement of a Greater Italy, and during 1919-1920 D'Annunzio accomplished the unique creation of a temporary "operatic state" in Fiume for which he wrote a stirring constitution exalting music and medieval corporations as the backbone of a new Italian city-

---

Compare Adolf Hitler's frequent approbation of being "hard." Spotts [2002], 125.

[25] For D'Annunzio, see Rhodes [1959], 144-149. Marinetti learned his art of declamation in the Paris of Alfred Jarry and French Symbolism. Berghaus [1996], 36-38.

[26] For D"Annunzio, Rhodes [1959], 50-51; for Marinetti: Berghaus [1995], 12-13, 65; for Mussolini: Mack Smith [1981], 12. The case for Hitler is far more sparse notwithstanding the Führer's undoubted attraction to a Nietzschean "will to power" vocabulary—or "triumph of the will," a phrase which, according to Kershaw, Hitler provided Leni Riefenstahl for the title of her noted film on the Third Reich. Kershaw [1998], 526. Despite vague allusions to reading Nietzsche in Linz, Vienna, and the Landsberg prison, Hitler seems to have been more acquainted with Schopenhauer. In 1944 Hitler claimed he had carried with him Schopenhauer's work throughout the first world war. Hitler [2000], 720. Kershaw mentions Hitler's gift of Nietzsche's collected works to Mussolini on the latter's sixtieth birthday. Kershaw [2000], 597. In one extended comment on Kant, Schopenhauer and Nietzsche as the greatest German thinkers, Hitler does conclude that "Schopenhauer's pessimism ... has been far surpassed by Nietzsche." Hitler [2000], 720.

state.[27] In fact the younger Mussolini was very much indebted to the inspiration of this "Mediterranean superman"[28] whose Fiume gambit was intended perhaps to precede his own original "March on Rome" which this politically shrewder fascist emulator appropriated in October 1922. Right to his death D'Annunzio was placated by gifts, land, lavish publication of his oeuvre, and titles by a Duce who regarded him as his only potential rival on the political landscape.[29]

For F. T. Marinetti (1876-1944) D'Annunzio was a key inspiration through the mix of literature and gesture that he contributed to the pre-history of Marinetti's most famous provocation, the Futurist Manifesto of 1909.[30] While by then D'Annunzio's aestheticist prose had become outdated for Marinetti's Futurist obsession with novelty, speed, and wholesale destruction of past cultural landmarks,[31] Marinetti was launched on a similar trajectory into the arms of militarism and violence, like D'Annunzio stirred by Italian successes in Libya and—much later—in Abyssinia.[32] Although the Manifesto and its successor expressions fit under the radical bohemianism of the prewar period, by 1918 Marinetti's founding of the *Partito politico futurista*, later absorbed into Mussolini's *Fasci di combattimento*, qualifies as the first significant politically institutional move toward the birth of Italian Fascism and its battalions. Even if Marinetti continued to retain, as did D'Annunzio, a certain aloofness from political fascism, he still dedicated his *Futurism and Fascism* (*Futurismo e fascismo*) of 1924 to his "dear and great friend Benito Mussolini,"[33] and lauded the latter's most bellicose actions right up to the collapse of 1943-1944 and his own death. For his part Mussolini was all too willing to relegate both authors to the "artistic" wing of political fascism.

That Benito Mussolini (1883-1945) was himself more effective than D'Annunzio or Marinetti in actually seizing and retaining political power in postwar Italy is due largely to the Duce's comparative political conservatism in allying with more traditional forces, as well as a shrewdness that eschewed some of the wilder, if more "poetically" declamatory, gestures of D'Annunzio and Marinetti.[34] Still, Mussolini's own self-identity had emerged from the same

---

[27] Rhodes [1959], 163, 141, 181-189.

[28] The title of a chapter in Rhodes [1959], 48-52. See also the reference to Marinetti's *superomismo*. Blum [1996], 75.

[29] Mack Smith notes that D'Annunzio alone—along with the king of Italy—was treated by Mussolini "as almost an equal." Mack Smith [1981], 112; also 208.

[30] On Marinetti's innovation in creating an "art of making manifestos" as itself a mode of rupture and revolution, see Blum [1996], 29.

[31] Berghaus [1995], 45-47, 72.

[32] Blum [1996], 145.

[33] Marinettti [1983], 489.

[34] In D'Annunzio's case, there remained a lingering loyalty to left-wing causes and worker

arenas of aesthetic politics of D'Annunzianism and Futurism that his predecessors had so dramatically cultivated. Besides, Mussolini's only genuine skill turned out to be that of orator and declaimer, precisely the "gifts" that had ensured fame and notoriety to D'Annunzio and Marinetti, leavened with a willingness to bash heads in street and meeting encounters.[35] It is in this agitator-oratorical relation to the "people" that the more solidly grounded Duce of 1932 then seems to have first enunciated the statesman-as-sculptor metaphor for an explicitly fascist regime.

The Mussolini interviewed in 1932 may be regarded in retrospect as at the height of his dictatorship. Rounding out a highly theatrical-artistic impression of himself and his deeds, this Mussolini confesses to a marked disgust for the mass—"for me nothing but a herd of sheep in so far as it is not organized"—which is incapable of ruling itself.[36] The *orator* Mussolini then gets to work on this presumably recalcitrant material with his declamations, theatrics and festivals—including the putative Roman salute[37]—but interestingly the art metaphor that takes over in his account becomes that of *sculpture*:

> When I then feel the masses in my hands ... I feel myself a piece with this mass. And yet there remains a piece of aversion, as the poet feels toward the material on which he works. Does not the sculptor many times strike [*zerschlägt*] the marble out of fury [*aus Wut*] because he has not shaped it with his hands in accordance with his first vision? Here the matter sometimes even stands up against the sculptor.

Pausing dramatically for effect, Il Duce forcefully concludes: "Everything depends on *mastering the masses like an artist*."[38] In this same interview

---

concerns that is perhaps best expressed by his continued friendship with the Socialist Federation of the Mariners in Genoa, the one organization which had come to his aid in the Fiume venture. Rhodes [1959], 221. As for Marinetti, a splendid example of his political sagacity was his apparent proposal in 1919 to personally fly over the Vatican in an airplane, kidnap the Pope, and then drop him into the Adriatic sea. Rhodes [1959], 203 (note 1)—an interesting contrast to Mussolini's more crafty compromise of a Concordat with the Papacy in 1929.

[35] Mack Smith points out the Young Mussolini's admitted lack of talent in writing and music, thus leading to his ambition to become "a great orator, a modern Demosthenes." In fact, Mussolini turned out to be more of a "Cagliostro" than a "Garibaldi," although Mack Smith admits that Mussolini, while not producing very good speeches, did develop an effective declamatory style. Mack Smith [1981], 21, 112, 126.

[36] Mussolini [1932], 123.

[37] Mussolini describes the Roman salute as "hygienischer, ästhetischer und kürzer" than the handshake. Mussolini [1932], 112.

[38] Mussolini [1932], 129 (emphasis added). This is the passage to which Jay gives prominence, drawing on Mack Smith. Jay [1992] 44-45. The original text stems from a conversation in Italian between Ludwig and Mussolini, which Ludwig then wrote down in German. That version was subsequently submitted to Mussolini and retranslated into Italian (with some changes and omissions). I have therefore used as most reliable the original German

Mussolini does somewhat qualify the machismo of this statement by admitting that unlike the sculptor the politician-statesman deals with "living material" *(eine lebendige Materie)* which is "changeable" (*veränderlich*) and "flexible" (*flexibel*), but all that this qualification concedes is the lack of final certainty in the kind of product that he can expect to "sculpt" in comparison with the genuine sculptor.[39]

Something of a neophyte in relation to what by 1932-1933 had become a fixed set of gestures and poses in an already established Italian fascism, Adolf Hitler (1889-1945) gladly recalled the stirring influence upon him of Mussolini's dramatic March on Rome of 1922 for his own 1923 Munich putsch.[40] This would be hardly surprising since Hitler's own rise to power resembles Mussolini's in terms of his exploitation of declamation and localized violence in Bavarian environments not too dissimilar from the post-war Milanese atmospherics nurturing D'Annunzio, Marinetti, and Mussolini. Once appropriately incarcerated in Landsberg prison for his treason, Hitler undertook to set down his ideas in the two-volume *Mein Kampf*, the most intriguing part of which concerns Hitler's coming of age as a speaker before the masses. "I could speak" (*Ich konnte reden*)—the young agitator's exultation at discovering his calling in Munich beerhalls after the frustrations of abortive architectural and painterly ambitions pursued in pre-war Vienna and Munich was laced from the start with the young war veteran's equal exultation over the formation of a "fighting organization," the "brutal worship of the blackjack" (*die rohe Anbetung des Gummiknüttels*).[41] It is this double achievement—speaking to the masses side by side with the organizational capacity to bash in potentially interfering heads—that constitutes the core of Hitler's apprenticeship in fascist political thought and behavior.[42]

---

text in Mussolini [1932].

[39] Mussolini [1932], 189. Jay does not comment on this qualification by Mussolini.

[40] Hitler [2000], 10, also 266-269.

[41] Hitler [1925] 377, 363. In fairness to Hitler this phrase is actually a charge that Hitler mentions as coming from the pusillanimous bourgeoisie and intellectuals before the "Red" violence. Nonetheless Hitler is happy to provide his own praise of the "rücksichtslose Energie unserer Versammlungsleitung und das brutale Draufgängertum unseres Saalschutzes." Hitler [1927], 126. The text of both volumes is replete with self-congratulatory references to the "fighting organization" of the NSDAP that he shaped with fellow veterans. Approaching Moscow in late 1941, Hitler fondly recalled those early days of "thrashing" with great relish: "I preferred men who didn't mind getting their hands dirty." Hitler [2000], 126, 128.

[42] Hitler's childhood friend August Kubizek claims to have been already stunned by Hitler's oratorical effectiveness in their early friendship: "Such rapture I had only witnessed so far in the theatre, when an actor had to express some violent emotions.... There is no doubt that my friend Adolf had shown a gift for oratory from his earliest youth." Kubizek [1955], 13, 18.

As might be expected from the Mussolini example, Hitler therefore also brought in potentially sculptural metaphors as part of his eulogy of the "magic of the spoken word" *(Zauberkraft des gesprochenen Wortes)*.[43] Like Mussolini Hitler saw the masses as intrinsically "slow-moving" (*Schwerfälligkeit*) and "lazy" (*faul*), potentially hostile and not to be indulged. Hitler's remedy as "a mass-meeting speaker" *(Massenversammlungsredner)* and "popular orator" (*Volksredner*) was to exploit this character by letting himself be borne in such a way that his words came to him in the symbiotic conditions of a mass meeting and thus were enabled to reach the "hearts" of his audience.[44] When such a connection took place, it produced states of "intoxication" (*Rausch*) and "enthusiasm" (*Begeisterung*) which Hitler did not hesitate to identify with "mass suggestion" (*Massensuggestion*). Thus the orator was automatically an "agitational orator" (*agitiriender Redner*) and all great historical events were due, as in the cases of the French and Russian revolutions, to agitators: "Thus it has always been and so will it always be."[45]

It is in this sense that Hitler spoke originally of the "Führer" as a type. The Führer, or Leader, was both a great psychologist and demagogue, for "to lead means to be able to move the masses" *(denn Führen heiss: Massen bewegen können)*. If such a Führer-type then included great "theoretical" and "organizational" abilities, one could with justification speak of "the great man" (*den grossen Mann*).[46] In other words, "to lead" was identical with the actions of the "agitational speaker" creating the appropriate conditions to "move" the "slow-moving," "inert," potentially "hostile" masses. To do so, such a speaker needed to use words "which like hammer blows *[die Hammerschlagen ähnlich*] can open the gates to the heart of a people." He must form "granite principles" (*granitene Grundsätze*) to rule the "wavering" (*schwankenden*) views of the "broad masses." After all, Marxist agitators and orators (*Volksredner*) had already succeeded by "hammering at the masses" (*auf die Massen einhämmerten*) and thus acquiring "a marvelous knowledge of this human material" (*eine fabelhafte Kenntnis dieses Menschenmaterials*).[47]

---

[43] A possible direct—and indirect—source on crowd psychology for both Mussolini and Hitler is Gustave Le Bon's *The Crowd* (1895). Mack Smith [1981], 127; Kershaw [1998], 652 (note 126).

[44] Hitler [1925], 110, 195; Hitler [1927], 111, 108, 110, 112.

[45] Hitler [1927], 121, 118: "Und das war noch immer so und wird ewig zu bleiben." Hitler emphasized the importance of "Pathos" and "Geste" for the *Volksredner* (110). Kubizek recalls that already the young Hitler "was in the habit of emphasizing his words by measured and studied gestures." Kubizek [1955], 19.

[46] Hitler [1927], 230, 231.

[47] Hitler [1925], 111; Hitler [1927], 10, 114-115. Hitler's Press Chief Otto Dietrich, noting a change in Hitler during 1935-1936 toward massive self-adulation, gives as evidence Hitler's

If Hitler toyed with such sculptic metaphors as part of his technique to "move" the masses, his propaganda minister Joseph Goebbels (1897-1945) was already obsessed with the statesman-as-sculptor metaphor prior to acquiring the reins of power. The only genuine "intellectual" among Hitler's henchmen,[48] Goebbels had already written a novel *Michael* in the early 1920s which exhausts the metaphor as a central visceral feature of his protagonist's character and aspirations. From the outset Goebbels' protagonist declares the identity of statesman and sculptor:

> Art is an expression of feeling. The artist differs from the non-artist in his ability to express what he feels. In some form or other. One artist does it in a painting, another in clay, a third in words, and a fourth in marble—or even in historical forms. The statesman is also an artist. *For him, the nation is exactly what the stone is for the sculptor [Für ihn ist das Volk nichts anderes, als was für den Bildhauer der Stein ist]*.[49]

But what is of even greater relevance is the manner in which this same protagonist, committing himself to the people and the workers against the bourgeois classes, embarks on a direct confrontation with matter by becoming a coal miner.[50] There in the depths of the darkness and among sweating, swearing, laboring peers, Goebbels' young visionary apparently learns the very meaning of Goebbel's triumvirate of highest values: Geist or spirit, Work, and Struggle.[51] If the "spirit" element is somewhat difficult to extract from the novel's posturings, the collaboration of work and struggle, even war, is made transparent through Goebbel's ejaculatory prose:

increasing prohibition of "unrequested political discussion"; Hitler "wanted to speak, not to listen. *He wanted to be the hammer*, not the anvil." Cited in Kershaw [1998], 531 (emphasis added). Also compare Mussolini: "Wenn man den Leuten das nicht einhämmerten, ... so schläfen sie ein." Mussolini [1932], 116.

48 Goebbels had received a doctorate in romantic literature from the university of Heidelberg under the supervision of Stefan George scholar Friedrich Gundolf. Albert Speer notes that in party circles Goebbels was always called "the Doctor" since the "party simply did not have many doctors of philosophy among its members in those days." Speer [1970], 54 and 54 (note *).

49 Goebbels [1987], 14 (emphasis added). Michael's beloved declares to him: "you think artistically even in politics" (30). Goebbels [1937], 21.

50 Although evidently Goebbels himself never worked in a mine, his friend Richard Flisges was a miner as well as (leftist) intellectual. After Flisges' death in a mining accident, Goebbels resolved to leave a "literary monument" to his friend in the form of the novel. Goebbels' later commitment to Horst Wessel and the song Wessel had written as a National Socialist symbol resembles this earlier stylization of the death of Flisges. Reuth [1993], 46-48, 113.

51 Thus: "Soldiers, students and workers shall build the new Reich," and after a fatal mining accident Michael "was buried as a worker, student and soldier." Goebbels [1987], 97, 130. Goebbels' anticapitalism is reflected in the admonition: "Bury all the capitalists in the world" (108), although his admiration for the worker does not extend to equality: "Everyone not equal, but all of us brothers" (121).

> I hear the banging of a thousand hammers. Dins and screams around me. I feel as
> if I were about to black out ....
> *I hammer and hammer* [*Ich schlage und schlage*]. I hit my hands. Unbearable pain!
> The blood runs down my thumb and forefinger ....
> I shall not stop until I collapse.
> I feel as if I were screaming, bellowing like a hungry beast.
> Fire splashes from the stones. I strike flames! I strike light.
> I am no longer a human being. I am a titan. A god![52]

Like Hitler and Mussolini, Goebbels' Michael has only contempt for the masses: "Ah, they never foment .... The masses are carried along." And like his fascist peers, he is an intrepid foe of "aestheticism," that characteristic bourgeois failing and proof of degeneration.[53] Thus the only sensibly manly option is to hammer away at recalcitrant matter, both in concrete manual "work" and in the "work" of shaping a folk and therefore a state: "I feel free only when the pit is full of crashing and booming .... Work! Create! Put your shoulders to the wheel!"[54]

II

Goebbels' strident rhetoric is in important respects the culmination of the fascist appropriation of the statesman-as-sculptor metaphor. More transparently than all other such invocations, it clarifies the underlying intent and visceral needs of that appropriation. Directly opposed to any variant of bourgeois "aestheticism," this approach comes down to the anticipated joy in striking and smashing objects: "I want to give shape," as Goebbels' frustrated protagonist wails.[55]

Still, it remains to ask whether calling upon variants of mining labor or other forms of strictly manual labor expresses more than just a laboring equivalent of bashing in heads.[56] Even if it is conceded that the "aestheticization

[52] Goebbels [1987], 104 (emphasis added). Goebbels [1937], 127. This passage no doubt reflects Goebbels' attraction to the Nietzschean adage: "Flamme bin ich sicherlich" which Goebbels cites elsewhere in the novel (42). The entire novel is studded with references to Nietzsche and his works.

[53] Goebbels [1987], 27, 47. Compare Hitler [1925], 194, and Mussolini, cited in Mack Smith [1981], 135.

[54] Goebbels [1987], 113. A "state" is a "folkhood that has taken form" (17).

[55] Goebbels [1987], 99.

[56] The most charitable explanation for this fascist misunderstanding of the sculptural vocation might be that it confused sculpture with the prior and more physically arduous task of cutting stone, or "stonemason." At least this was why Michelangelo Buonarroti's father did not want him to become a sculptor. According to Ascanio Condivi, Michelangelo's contemporary biographer, the father "would never suffer his son to be a stonemason. Nor was it any use" that

of politics" label might accurately reflect the *intentions* behind these fascist approaches, it does not automatically follow that its users have legitimately *captured* any fundamentals to discernibly aesthetic or artistic activity. To concede this point prematurely betrays a serious tactical error, since it simultaneously concedes the position that art can be so easily commandeered. It is therefore incumbent on defenders of art and the aesthetic dimension to look carefully at this putative appropriation of the statesman-as-sculptor metaphor. Obviously what is necessary to ask is: what actually does a practicing sculptor think and do? How does the sculptor relate to his/her material? And: what aims does the sculptor have in mind? To answer such questions, two sources would seem indispensable: the actual views of practicing sculptors and those of formal theorists of the art of sculpture.

Fortunately a key discussion involving perhaps the paradigmatic Sculptor in western civilization, Michelangelo Buonarroti, and his erstwhile philosophical admirer, Benedetto Varchi, in 1540s Florentine Renaissance debates on the *paragone* ("comparison") of the arts furnishes a valuable starting point.[57] Michelangelo's most notable poems had exploited the affinities between the art of the sculptor and the art of the lover as he addressed his poetic Beloved by stressing the "hidden form" that needed to be excavated or carved out (*per levar*). According to this reading, the ideal lover-artist (*l'ottimo artista*) held a conception (*concetto*) of what was potentially present in the "material," and by substraction—rather than addition—drew out "a figure that's alive/and that grows larger whenever the stone decreases."[58]

Accepting this general approach, Varchi drew more methodically on the Florentine Neoplatonism that had inspired Michelangelo and also on the recently revived Florentine concern for Aristotle to valorize the "difficulty" in the sculptor's artistry on matter. Somewhat akin to the alchemist and lover, the sculptor's magic was in "mirroring his soul with that of his subject and then drawing forth from the material what he sees reflected in his own soul."[59] Such a process presupposed that the form was already in the material itself, thus confirming in an Aristotelian manner that all true composites were always a unity of form and matter. The artist who wished to draw the concept from his

---

he was instructed "how much difference there was between a sculptor and a stonemason." Ultimately the father only gave way because of Lorenzo the Magnificent's intervention. Cited in Buonarroti [1987], 13.

[57] See the informative study by Mendelsohn-Martone [1978].

[58] Nos. 151 and 152 in Buonarroti [1991], 302-305, following the translation by James M. Saslow. Other relevant poems include No. 62 (157), No. 236 (400-401), No. 240 (406-408), 242 (409-410), 247 (419), 275 (464)

[59] Mendelsohn-Martone [1978], 169.

material had to acknowledge "the similarly unrealized potential present in both" himself and what was hidden in matter.[60] Although ostensibly Varchi's purpose was to equalize the arts of sculpture and painting, in fact this reading gave preference to the sculptor, and indeed to the resemblance of the latter to the true lover. The sculptor's relation to his marble block could be compared to the lover's relation to his Beloved. The difficulties both encountered in extracting a hidden "concept" were not due to the inherent recalcitrance of the "matter" of the Beloved's heart or of the marble block, but to the task of finding a proper correspondence between the "concept" residing within the artist-lover and that residing within the marble-heart. Although somewhat diffident to formal theorizing on the subject of the sculptor's practice, Michelangelo largely approved this reading by Varchi, the basis for a series of influential lectures given by Varchi in Florence in 1546 and publication in 1550.[61]

At the other end of the historical spectrum, Henry Moore's distinctively modernist body of work, looking partly to the prior formal aesthetics of Roger Fry and influencing the subsequent aesthetic thought of Herbert Read, is a useful reference-point for its apparent dropping of the Renaissance-classicist concerns of Michelangelo and Varchi. To be sure, Moore always acknowledged the inspiration of Michelangelo himself for his own calling as a sculptor, and his comments on his craft and intentions reaffirmed what he called "the humanist organic element" as "of fundamental importance in sculpture, giving sculpture its vitality," as well as the importance of a "long and intense study of the human figure" for the starting sculptor.[62] Nonetheless, the familiar classicist criteria for great art take a back seat to a newly heightened preference for organic standards and elements of vitality reaching even into that characteristically modernist terra incognita of the "unconscious" and the "archetypal."[63]

Moore would have been the first to acknowledge the formal guidance of Fry's bold readings of African and Mexican art and sculpture which, further encouraged by exhibitions of actual works in the British Museum, confirmed his own commitment to the credo known as "truth to material" and the priority of

---

[60] Mendelsohn-Martone [1978], 214, 232-233, 271-272, provides references to the use of Aristotelian terms concerning essence or *sostanza* (214). Mendelsohn-Martone notes that Varchi's resort to Aristotle (versus Plato's theory of the Ideas) allows for recognition of the form of the product being "distinct from but inherent in matter" (214).

[61] In his letter to Varchi dated March 1547, Michelangelo acknowledges receipt of Varchi's treatise and furnishes his own definition of sculpture (largely reflecting the gist of the particular poems on which Varchi had discoursed): "I mean by sculpture work which is fashioned by dint of taking away [*per forza di levare*]; what is done by way of adding is similar to painting." Buonarroti [1987], 120 (No. 33); the Italian is in Varchi [1550], 82.

[62] Moore [1967], 29, 68, 115; also 175-186.

[63] Read [1965], 257-259; Rawson [1997], 4.

three-dimensionality for sculpture.[64] What this meant for Moore is argued in his explicit call for liberation from what Moore labeled classicist "Greek spectacles," a liberation freeing the sculptor:

> to recognise again the importance of the material in which he works, to think and create in his material by carving direct, *understanding and being in sympathy with his material* so that he does not force it beyond its natural constructive build, producing weakness; to know that sculpture in stone should look honestly like stone.[65]

From this comment it is easier to appreciate the impact of Mexican art on Moore, "unsurpassed," in his view, in the history of stone sculpture for the degree of its "'stoniness', by which I mean its truth to material, its tremendous power without loss of sensitiveness, its astonishing variety and fertility of form-invention and its approach to a full three-dimensional conception of form."[66]

As himself an unabashed vitalist, Moore certainly did not intend to concede the sculptor's authority; as he put it, the sculptor should remain master of his material: "Only, not a cruel master." And, "though he still respects his material and doesn't ask it to do what it can't, he has to master it and not be at its mercy."[67] Still, granted this much, Moore's account of his sculptor's art is generally consistent in its focus on the sculptor's obsession with the shape and form of things and with a direct active relation to the individual qualities inherent in his material. There is even something of the rhetoric of Michelangelo and Varchi in Moore's claim: "It's as though you have something trying to make itself come to a shape from inside itself."[68]

Finally, as a provocative contrast to both the classicist-Renaissance and modernist practices of sculpture, it is worth taking a look at what the foremost sculptor in the German fascist pantheon, Arno Breker, himself had to say about his vocation.[69] Celebrated as the "German

---

[64] Moore calls Fry's *Vision and Design* "the most lucky discovery for me." Moore [1967]. 49; Fry [1924]. For Moore's stress on three-dimensionality and the surprises it offers over two-dimensionality, see Moore [1967], 62, 148, 266.

[65] Moore [1967], 57 (emphasis added).

[66] Moore [1967], 159. The importance of this passage is stressed in Read's analysis of Moore's work. Read [1965], 65.

[67] Moore [1967], 113.

[68] Moore [1967], 60; cf. also 58-60, 69.

[69] Notwithstanding the neutral political tonality maintained in the selection of Breker's writings in Breker [1990], Breker's letter to architect Hermann Giesler dated 29 November 1977 testifies to the sculptor's expressed view of Hitler twenty years after the fall of the Third Reich: "Hitlers primitive, verblendete Gegner ahnen nicht, dass hier ein Mensch stand, der ein neues—auch architektonisches—Zeitalter gestalten wollte." Apparently for Breker Hitler was the answer to the Versailles Diktat: "Das gesamte Drama hat sich auf einen anonymen Menschen gestürzt, und die Vorsehung hat ihn bestimmt, den verhängnisvollen Zustand zu brechen." Giesler [1978],

Michelangelo,"[70] Breker committed his work to a classicist aesthetics which fit the Nazi regime's neo-classicist leanings and he eventually became the Führer's favorite artist in an artform, sculpture, that also became the latter's favorite. Yet, for all his strivings, it seems generally clear that Breker's oeuvre failed to achieve genuine classical standards: "Breker's creations do not feature the Hellenic sense of proportion and harmony: they intimidate and dominate the viewer."[71] All the more relevant therefore are his accounts of what he at least thought he was trying to produce with his putative classicist effects as an "expression of the absolute harmony in the universe."[72]

Stressing the importance of the material proper for the sculptor's task, Breker emphasized sensitivity to the "uniqueness" of that material and consistently advocated resort to the hands and repetitive processes of tangible contact with the material. The "spiritual shaping process" then began with a "consideration of nature." Nature itself already carried a kind of "writing" which the sculptor "translated" into a language distinctly human. All important artworks began with "the spiritualization of matter," which Breker regarded as a "divinely inspired process" (God was the first Sculptor), one which resembled the Creation's Song of Songs. Even if Breker's own priorities upgraded man as the crowning achievement of this creation, particularly the athletic man, and this slant led to his denigration of most art since 1900-1910 as deforming the human image, genuine sculpture remained committed to "the convincing translation of the natural form into the art form." The sculptor worked with an awareness that his work captured things in a material that would outlast time. "The flowing into each other of forms: that is sculpture."[73] Thus, far from suggesting an abusive relation by the sculptor to natural materials, Breker repeatedly warned against anything less than deepest respect toward material to yield in principle the human equivalent of the divine creative process.

---

523. See also the informative article on the unrepentant postwar Breker by Petropoulos [2002].

[70] The judgment actually of French sculptor Aristide Maillol happily adopted by the German press. Petropoulos [2002], 208, 218. Breker learned from Maillol and admired his reintroduction of the importance of the primal power of nature and of volume to sculpture. Breker [1990], 181, 219.

[71] Petropoulos [2002], 212; also: "His works lacked the harmony and sense of proportion present in classical or Renaissance works. The monumental figures were anything but lithe and graceful" (210).

[72] Breker [1990], 244. Also: the classical as a "balance of all forces" (243).

[73] Breker [1990], 155, 156, 159, 235, 240, 243. For Breker's critique of modern art, see 172-175; for his praise of the Greek commitment to the sports and athletic image of man, see 173, 210. Breker emphasized that his own greatest experience in art had been Michelangelo's David (218).

III

From this cursory survey of some critically positioned sculptors' comments on their craft along with some formal aesthetic philosophies germane to their self-understandings, let us turn to somewhat more formalized attempts to develop an aesthetics of sculpture. It is perhaps worth noting that all such efforts characteristically begin with the lament that of all the major "fine arts" sculpture has secured the least formal attention until recently, serving more as a subordinate of, on the one hand, painting, and, on the other, architecture. Whether this is strictly historically true or not, such criticism has carried with it the tendency to firm up once and for all the autonomy of sculpture and what genuine sculptors presumably do from all the other arts.

Thus Herbert Read's influential 1954 lectures—subsequently published as *The Art of Sculpture*—pinion sculpture's autonomy to what he calls the "haptic sense" for the all-aroundness or three-dimensionality that sculpture is uniquely positioned to exploit and cultivate.[74] Sculpture is precisely "an art of palpation —an art that gives satisfaction in the touching and handling of objects." For all that, Read is clear that the sculptor already assumes "a power imminent in all things," including inanimate objects, and thus works consciously not on "a lifeless object, but a living form."[75] Only from this perspective can it be confirmed that the sculptor realizes his unique vocation of calling upon "the palpable and ponderable qualities of the object." Thus all materials are—here Read quotes John Ruskin—"most precious materials for true masters."[76]

Although granting that Read is one of the few theorists concerned with sculpture's autonomy, F. David Martin remains dissatisfied with what he regards as the excessive narrowness of Read's prioritization of touch.[77] In Martin's view, the haptic function is minimal when compared with the space or force field surrounding a sculpture. Drawing on Martin Heidegger's language of being-in-the-world, Martin prefers to give emphasis to the "enlivening space" which he thinks sculpture furnishes, thus bringing into play "a sacred space, a dwelling nearness."[78] Whatever the effectiveness of Martin's own claims, it is at least evident that Martin's purpose is to underscore sculpture's function of encouraging "our spatial withness with things," "our withness with things as

---

[74] Read [1961], 30, from the Greek *haptikos*: "able to lay hold of."

[75] Read [1961], 49, 43. Read is thoroughly conversant with the positions taken by Michelangelo and Varchi (62).

[76] Read [1961], 66, 77. Read quotes Auguste Rodin to the effect that Rodin's figures seem "to blossom from within to the outside, like life itself" (73).

[77] Martin's work incidentally provides a valuable appendix surveying the statements of practicing sculptors on their art. Martin [1981], 223-230.

[78] Martin [1981], 62, 221, 12-13.

thingly," helping us to develop a more sensitive belongingness in the world.[79] Martin himself has been criticized for his undervaluation of the qualities of palpability underscored by Read and questioned for his Heideggerian language. Nonetheless, these same critics also applaud his efforts to claim for sculpture the vocation of helping to reconnect us with the "visible, tangible three-dimensionality of the things of the world."[80]

Philip Rawson, who is known for his expertise in non-western (Tibetan, Indian, Chinese and Southeast Asian) arts, notes the historical association of sculpture with traditions in which it "kept alive intensely felt meanings for whole societies" compared with sculpture's contemporary isolation in museum displays. Rawson's ecumenical approach to what sculpture has globally meant recognizes the variety of languages unique to the contact between the viewer and the three-dimensional object. If sculpture begins with "an inert lump of matter," it becomes sculpture proper "only when we learn how to question a lump for its shapes and their meaning." The sculptor must call on "inner matrixes of formal relationship" to convert multiple meanings "into formal coherence." Thus sculpture for Rawson is foremost a language of human communications in which the life given to this "inert piece of material" comes from the person who gives it meaning. Once the work on material and physical making brings in metaphorical implications and "formal imaginative technique" is added to the mix, sculpture reaches a richness of expression that is comparable to general spoken and musical linguistic structures.[81]

IV

Whatever the differences articulated in these selections from formal theory on the art of sculpture (or from practicing sculptors' reflections on their art), there is nothing here that might be remotely aligned with the statesman-as-sculptor metaphor. Indeed, our survey might be rightly accused of overkill given the evident gap between the sophistication of such accounts and the crudity of the users of the statesman-as-sculptor metaphor. But that is precisely the point. Simply to acknowledge the existence and priority of these accounts for an understanding of sculpture is to question from the outset any genuinely

[79] Martin [1981], 124; also "our physical withness with things," "the spatial withness basic to being-in-the-world" (135). Cf. as well the citations in Rogers [1983], 164. Martin argues that "truth to materials is always subordinated to truth to things" and lists as examples such traits as the sullen, intractable, porous and opalescent which such truth to things makes accessible (184).

[80] Martin [1981], 184.

[81] Rawson [1997], 1, 5, 6, 24, 155.

"aesthetic" element behind the exploitation of the statesman-as-sculptor metaphor by its users.

Nonetheless, it is worth making the effort if only to break down the validity of the larger "aestheticization of politics" motif where it seeks to accuse the aesthetic of an intrinsic vulnerability or attraction to fascist cooptation. Of course, our particular case—the statesman-as-sculptor metaphor—is but one of several characteristics listed by Jay, and it would be necessary in principle to submit the others to comparable critique. Still, such is the weakness of this particular claim that it justifies a second look at the aesthetics of politics issue in general.

To do so, we distinguish between the sensationalist effects of the kinds of argument found in Susan Sontag, Philippe Lacoue-Labarthe, or a cinematic work like Peter Cohen's *The Architecture of Doom*, and more serious recent literature delving into the functions of art and the aesthetic in the Third Reich.[82] We draw this distinction because these earlier works helped set the atmospherics for the notoriety of the aesthetics of politics gambit for modern—and postmodern—social critiques and should not be bunched with the more welcome tendency by recent literature to consider the topic with the requisite scholarly and theoretical seriousness.

What is so potentially problematic about the effects wrought by Sontag, Lacoue-Labarthe, and Cohen is their implicit encouragement of the identity between aesthetics and fascism, whereas this recent scholarship aims to empirically clarify the variegated functions of art and the aesthetic within the overall framework of fascism. At the core of the formers' error is not so much the understandable and important task of working out elements of a distinctly fascist aesthetics—in this respect, all societies or cultural formations, including Stalinism or Maoism, may be said to carry their own aesthetics[83]—as the tendency to equate fascist aesthetics with the intrinsic vocation or function of aesthetics in general. This tendency stems no doubt from a reading of the fascist relation to the aesthetic as a far more extensive and inclusive one than that found among other societies or ideologies, particularly those with a more pragmatic, "materialist," or practical bent (such as, putatively, the Anglo-American). But even if that were true, it would not then follow that such significantly inclusive concern with the aesthetic confirms in its turn the importance of the fascist reading *for* the aesthetic. After all, it could very well be the case that one reason for fascism's obsessiveness with the ubiquity of the

[82] Compare Cohen [1989], Lacoue-Labarthe [1987], and Sontag [1981] with, e.g., Eltin [2002], Huener & Nicosia [2006], Kershaw [1998], Kershaw [2000], Petropoulos [1996], Reichel [1991], Scobie [1990], and Steinweis [1993]

[83] For Stalinism, see Kotkin [1997] but also Hedin [2004].

aesthetic for its own larger aims is the depleted and impoverished reading and experience of the aesthetic that it carries. In contrast, the aesthetic may play a more modest role within non-fascist liberal politics, but only because the latter's sense for the aesthetic is richer in its comparative pluralism and therefore more in line with the original liberal project of the aesthetic as set out by the Enlightenment thought of Kant and Schiller.

Consider for a start the somewhat blatant case of *The Architecture of Doom* with its closing admonition in cadence with cinematic displays of the smoking hulk of 1945 Berlin and paintings depicting leading Third Reich henchmen: "Defining Nazism in traditional political terms is difficult, mainly because its dynamic was fueled by something different from what we usually call politics. This driving force was to *a great degree aesthetic*. Its ambition was *to beautify the world through violence*."[84] Beyond its sensationalist intent, what is the purport of these charges? Is it that Nazism utilized violence in order to destroy forces that it held stood in its way of creating a permanently "beautiful" society? Or was the violence integral to the cultivation of a distinctive Nazi sense of "beauty" (assuming that "beauty," however understood, remained the compass for a Nazi aesthetics)?

The two aims are not necessarily similar. In the former option, the "violence"—by which one presumably means the governmental apparatus utilizing such institutions as the S.S. to obliterate "parasites" through political exploitation (from euthanasia programs to eventually extermination camps) of a pseudo-biological vocabulary invoking bacteria and similarly charged metaphors—would presumably "cleanse" the society of its parasitical elements and thus bring into play a sanitarily "healthy" ethnicity. There is much footage in *The Architecture of Doom* which would seem to confirm this reading. But in that case the "cleansing" process would involve the very elite of the Nazi regime—the S.S. and its henchmen—to a direct involvement in the continuously "unbeautiful" task of brutality and execution that apparently even S.S. leader Heinrich Himmler was himself unable to endure directly. As for the beneficiaries—presumably the newly physically purified nordic people of Greater Germany—of such salutary sacrifices, their "beauty" was regarded more as a facet or consequence of "health" than that "beauty" as such

---

[84] Cohen [1989] (emphasis added). Also, the final destruction of Berlin is equated with Hitler's "final and decisive theatrical mission." With such a jaundiced sense of the political elements in Nazism, it is no surprise that the film concludes there was "no real political motive" behind Nazism's genocidal liquidations, overlooking the obvious point that the political motive, derivable from the available evidence of documents and political acts, was clear: the extermination of Jews and related "parasitical" peoples within the overall mission of creating a new Eurasian empire to be ruled by Germans and Nordics in an unfolding planetary hegemonical struggle with such rivals as the "Anglo-Americans."

functioned as the standard or paradigm. Such, at least, was the Führer's own "aesthetic" position, for whom "a healthy and forceful body" always came first.[85] If, as he emphasized in 1938, "every true art must in its expression bear the stamp of beauty," then the "ideal for all of us lies in the cultivation of what is healthy. *Only* what is healthy is right and natural, and what is right and natural is *therefore* beautiful."[86] In any case, whatever the qualifications to be imputed to the presumed adulation of the beautiful in Nazism, the formal position derivable from the official ideology is that the violence was taken to constitute lamentable but necessary acts for making possible the ensuing permanent rule of the "beautiful" (as the "healthy").[87]

More seductive is the other option: the equation of violence itself with fascist aesthetics. Given, as has already been shown, the proclivity of fascism for direct violent confrontation, this reading makes a modicum of sense. Sontag, herself clearly fascinated by the renewed 1970s interest in Nazi art, invokes the label of "fascinating fascism" which links an original Nazi "theatre" of führer masters exercising sexual mastery over "feminine" masses to a contemporary "theatricalization of sexuality" most thoroughly embedded in contemporary flirtations with sadomasochism.[88] This fascination goes back to the fact—she thinks—that such Nazi organizations as the SS were "the ideal incarnation of fascism's overt assertion of the righteousness of violence" and that the SS dramatized this point "by linking themselves to certain aesthetic

[85] Hitler [1943]. 407. Hitler even chooses boxing as the paradigm; after all, the "folkish state" is not meant "to breed a colony of peaceful aesthetes and physical degenerates" (410).

[86] Cited in Spotts [2002], 279 (emphasis added), from the Nuremberg party rally of 1938. This primacy of "health" also meant that for the Nazis the body should become "like steel" [*gestählt*]" and was metaphorically regarded as "metal." H. Bromsky, cited in Reichel [1991], Bildteil. To make the distinction as clear as possible, Hitler strenously affirmed to Fritz Wiedemann that he would have nothing to do with a Jewish woman however attractive she might be, nor with modern music however beautiful it might possibly sound: the "Partei könne in Sachen moderner Musik ebenso wenig eine Konzession machen wie er, Hitler—obwohl nicht unempfänglich für weibliche Reize—sich jemals mit einer Jüdin und *sei sie noch so schön*, einlassen könnte." Wiedemann [1964], 207 (emphasis added). I owe this revealing reference to Spotts [2002], 293.

[87] A similar approach is seen in Stalinism by Generation K scholars who argue that Stalinism's goal was aesthetic: "to weed out members of the 'parasitic classes' in order to achieve what a 1952 Soviet article on the concept of the beautiful describes as 'The idea of communism, as the highest, most harmonious, most complete form of human existence on earth'." Accordingly, violence "was but a technique employed towards the higher aim of remaking society." Hedin [2004], 175.

[88] Sontag [1981], 102, 104-105. "Never before" Nazism "was the relation of masters and slaves so consciously aestheticized" (105).

standards" as "an elite military community that would be not only expressly violent but also supremely beautiful."[89]

Ostensibly these passing thoughts are intended by Sontag to clarify some themes in the adumbration of a distinctly "fascist aesthetics." Whether or not her particular proofs are historically compelling, her reading very quickly turns Nazism into an "utopian aesthetics" implying an "ideal eroticism" which Sontag then states "stands for an ideal or rather ideals that are persistent today under other banners," including "the ideal of life as art, the cult of beauty," and a variety of other traits. Before readers can catch their breath, Sontag's listing spills over into "youth/rock culture" and all sorts of adversarial movements of the 1970s, including prostrations before spiritual gurus.[90] Such analytical clumsiness thus tars the aesthetic, the beautiful, the very "ideal of life as art" with fascist or crypto-fascist leanings. Yet Sontag herself suggests that fascist aesthetics was, even in its own terms, subordinate to a higher standard: the fascist style "*at its best* is Art Deco," implying that even fascist aesthetics needs a more nuanced reading than she provides.[91]

Lacoue-Labarthe's analysis raises even more questions. After a few intellectual-historical moves concerning the German tradition, he feels justified in "risking" his own label: Nazism as a "national-aestheticism" (*national-esthétisme*).[92] Having made his obligatory bow to Benjamin's "aestheticization of politics" gambit, quoted Goebbels on politics as art (in a 1933 letter to the conductor Wilhelm Furtwängler), and invoked director Hans Jürgen Syberberg's reading of the Third Reich as a kind of *Gesamtkunstwerk*, Lacoue-Labarthe is ready to furnish his own contribution to what he sees as a fixation in German intellectual history: "the City [*Cité*] as a work of art," based on the presumably insidious impact upon Germans of (1) the view of politics as a "plastic factor" in the strict sense, (2) adulation of the Greeks as "the people of art" and "the political people par excellence," and (3) an organic reading of politics.[93] Tracing this larger tradition all the way back to Thucydides' account of Pericles' funeral oration, Lacoue-Labarthe quickly backpedals that he is not trying to suggest an incipient fascism among the proponents of the tradition, only that German Nazism succeeded in twisting such themes to its own purposes. However, as he makes no effort to distinguish between an "authentic" understanding of such a tradition and the fascist misuse of that

---

89 Sontag [1981], 99.

90 Sontag [1981], 90-91, 93, 96, 96-97.

91 Sontag [1981], 94 (emphasis added).

92 Lacoue-Labarthe [1987], 91.

93 Lacoue-Labarthe [1987], 92, 93, 102-108.

tradition, Lacoue-Labarthe leaves the indelible impression that perhaps such distinctions are not after all that significant.

That one can collect citations from Hitler or for that matter from Goebbels that the Third Reich might fancy itself as a kind of "aesthetic state" and that politics was being propagandized as somehow "art" in the new dispensation[94] is hardly evidence of an actually practising political structure any effective account of which must necessarily commingle the categories of the aesthetic and the political (the minimum one might expect of an analysis yielding an "aestheticization of politics" germane to a political regime). It can be conceded that the Nazi regime developed and deployed a highly complicated set of relations to notions derivable from the aesthetic and to the production and standards of art; but what sustainable inferences can be drawn?

V

Here is where the more recent literature, less prone to such earlier grand accounts of National Socialism that took its propagandistic claims at face value, comes in. The first notable result is that from studies of the relevant Nazi organizations concerned with the arts, anything like a consistent Nazi aesthetic policy is impossible to single out since there was an overall lack of consensus regarding aesthetic standards.[95] Even in the case of Hitler himself, there is actually little evidence, if any, of "direct links between Hitler's own artistic visions and their implementation in cultural policy." Moreover, part of the problem with isolating such a phenomenon as "Nazi art" is that empirical studies are increasingly revealing more continuities with the arts and aims of the previous Weimar period as well as the succeeding post-1945 Bundesrepublik period, and also raising important questions about the similarities between much of Nazi art and architecture and the rest of the cultural world of the 1930s and 1940s. As a result, the general conclusion of one recent survey of this growing literature is that it is no longer a question of "Nazi art" but rather "whether Nazi art ever was."[96]

At the same time, such research has given a somewhat more respectful picture of Hitler himself as an idiosyncratic *Kulturträger*, or "culture-bearer." Self-taught painter, architect, even furniture designer, performance artist and

---

[94] E.g. the citation from the Nazi Ministry of Propaganda's celebration of the 180th anniversary of Friedrich Schiller's birth (1939): "Lehre vom ästhetische Staat—Schillers Lebengrösstes Vorbild." Cited in the introduction by Wilkinson and Willoughby to Schiller [1967], cxlii.

[95] Steinweis [1993]; Pirro [1994], 147; Potter [2006], 587. Also Huener & Nicosia [2006], 1-13, for a judicious introduction to the state of the discussion circa 2006.

[96] Potter [2006], 594, 598; Reichel [1991], 376.

orator, choreographer and scenographer of the great spectacles of the 1930s, civic and highway transportation planner—Hitler has to be recognized, whatever the merits of his works and projects, as an artist and designer of sorts, even, in his daily habits, a bit of a bohemian life-styler; moreover, his knowledge of architectural history and operatic, especially Wagnerian, music and performance was, in the view of experts, remarkable for a layperson. Accordingly, it turns out not to be surprising that Hitler did indeed have grand visions, whatever the genocidal tools employed for their realization, of an ultimate *Kulturstaat* in which he and his regime would conscientiously promote and make readily available to the German populace the fruits of artworks and cultural products.[97] Such visions included practical plans for the expansion and ready availability of opera houses and theatres throughout the German world; rebuilt city centers with recognizably cultural orientations in accordance with presumably neoclassical designs; creation of city forums in ostensible emulation of classical antiquity; magnificent autoroutes through landscapes made aesthetically attractive and available for the ecological citizen; unparalleled culture collections, including huge museum holdings; finally, even planetariums in every significant civic area.[98] Whatever the ultimate practicability of all these projects, there is more than sufficient evidence that a substantial number were underway when they were derailed by the expenses of the war;[99] indeed in many cases Hitler continued to insist on their implementation notwithstanding the financial and material costs to the war effort.[100]

---

[97] Spotts [2002], 9, 401. With his extensive research (and prior work on Bayreuth), Spotts has made a major contribution toward an understanding of the role of art and the aesthetic for Hitler's vision of his culture state. See however Potter [2006], 593-594, for some relevant concerns about Spotts' residual commitments to older approaches toward Nazi culture and politics.

[98] Hitler [2000], (20-21 February 1942) 322-323, (5 June 1942) 514.

[99] Besides the excellent reproductions in Spotts [2002] (and to a lesser extent Reichel [1991]), the reader is encouraged to peruse the extensive number of illustrations and photographs in the autobiography by Hitler's "other" architect Hermann Giesler. Besides the familiar Speer-inspired plans for Berlin (or "Germania"), key examples are Munich—the spiritual city of National Socialism—as well as Weimar as the one case of a city forum actually built, and finally Hitler's favored hometown enterprise in Linz. Giesler [1978]. Perhaps given Giesler's continued commitment to his Führer after the war, this work has been generally ignored in favor of excessive deference to the ostensibly repentant Albert Speer's importance for Hitler's overall architectural vision.

[100] Hitler actually found a silver lining in the terrible bombing of German cities during the war for helping to facilitate the massive reconstruction he envisaged. Spotts [2002], 385. Even during the war Hitler held firm to the necessity of rebuilding shattered theatres and opera houses, insisting that theatre was essential to citizens and that its absence would break down the continuity on which performance culture depended. Spotts [2002], 282-287; Speer [1970], 388-

How far do such disclosures rehabilitate the "aestheticization" reading? Any reconsideration must include Hitler's *own* stated reservations about the final claims of politics over art and the artist. Characteristically the artist was for him but a naif in political matters,[101] and Hitler himself occasionally lamented that he had not pursued his artist's vocation instead of entering politics.[102] Nor was Hitler's own National Socialist party sympathetic to his more flamboyant artistic tastes. Especially with regard to the most notorious case of Bayreuth and Wagner, it is notable that Hitler's love for the Idea of Bayreuth, the Wagner family, and musical experiences of Wagner's works were generally regarded as "batty" by Party functionaries, and Hitler consistently failed to draw them into Wagnerian ecstasies even when attendance at Wagner music dramas was mandatory. Ironically, Bayreuth turned out to be the one cultural enterprise entirely free of National Socialist party control.[103]

As to the phenomena that are usually invoked to confirm "aestheticization" —the speeches, the rallies, the spectacles—there remains the question of the degree to which these are purely (or primarily) propaganda efforts on behalf of an explicitly political cause or are themselves constitutive of a politics as such. Actually there is evidence that in some cases the effects of these events on Hitler himself cannot be primarily attributed to an external political purpose, in which case one must wonder what aesthetic results the "politics" of these effects was meant to induce in himself and his audiences. At the very least the claim that Hitler "theatrically" planned his own Wagnerian-suicidal *Götter-dämmerung* seems forced, a rhetorical temptation to which even such conscientious scholars as Ian Kershaw have succumbed. Not only can Hitler's physical and mental deterioration be regarded as a steady proof of his obsessive efforts at gaining victory right to the last moment, but it also seems evident that he had a more rational understanding of his situation than these later chroniclers. First, as Kershaw has shown at length, Hitler's strategy was always that of the all-or-nothing gambler, an approach that worked for some twenty-

389.

[101] E.g. the case of Adolf Ziegler who was not punished for a treasonable political act because he was like all artists, according to Hitler, "ein schlechter Politiker." Goebbels [1993], (21 August 1943) 336.

[102] Speer [1970], 123, 386; Spotts [2002], 327; and Hitler's own comments preferring the arts or philosophy to "the path of politics," in Hitler [2000] (25-26 January 1942), 251. Also: "Wars pass by. The only things that exist are the works of human genius. This is the explanation of my love of art." Hitler [2000] (25-26 January 1942), 251.

[103] Spotts [2002], 256; Chytry [2007]. Of course Hitler may have simply hoped to wear down the Nazi oldtimers with his Bayreuth religiosity. At the very least however, this case exposes the elementary error of automatically equating Hitler's aesthetic preferences with National Socialist doctrine.

odd years right to the late fall of 1941; Hitler himself reminded his followers in the latter stages of the war that he had faced more daunting odds in the earlier phases of his political career.[104] And second, Hitler was all too aware that, as he himself put it, "we have chalked up so much that we have to win; otherwise our entire people—and in first place we ourselves, with all that is dear to us—will be wiped out."[105] He correctly recognized that there was no chance whatsoever that he and his followers would be allowed any role or presence in a post-Nazi Germany.

More often, however, such aestheticization phenomena are attributed to the overriding purpose of a "schöner Schein" or "lovely illusion" intended to cover up contradictory or harsh political goals that the regime did not intend the populace to grasp directly.[106] But if that is so, then clearly Nazi aestheticization is an incomplete "aesthetic" politics at best, and there remains the further suspicion that not all Nazi racial and hegemonical politics can be ultimately traced back to Hitler's "aesthetic ideals."[107] Indeed, Kershaw's exhaustive study of Hitler and Nazi social and political history reveals the degree to which aestheticization formed but a modest component to the Third Reich's overall political aims and practices. If Kershaw's thesis is on the right track that Nazi governance can be most effectively described as a "working toward the Führer," then its politics and resultant political goals must be read in terms of the variety of political actors and organizations producing the personalized rule of the Führer state as a panoply of overlapping and competing agencies which over time eroded administrative overview, promoted radical ideological goals, and sustained Führer absolutism.[108]

---

[104] Kershaw [2000], 613, 745. With regard to the Polish crisis of 1939, Goering, aiming for a compromise, is cited as stating, "it is time to stop this *va banque*." To which Hitler supposedly replied, "it is the only call I ever make." Taylor [1964], 305.

[105] Cited in Kershaw [2000], 386.

[106] The term "schöner Schein," as used for example by Reichel, is clearly intended to invoke Friedrich Schiller and his *Letters on the Aesthetic Education of Man*. Curiously however, Reichel never raises the relevant Schiller references to draw up differences—or similarities. Reichel [1991].

[107] Spotts [2002], 11.

[108] Kershaw [1998], 526-539. Kershaw is drawing on a statement by Werner Willikens, State Secretary in the Prussian Agricultural Ministry in 1934, that "It is the duty of every single person to attempt, in the spirit of the Führer, to work toward him" (527). Kershaw's reading may be the best explanation so far for the actual operations of the Nazi state and its governance, since it accounts for its radical degree of personalization as well as the constant competitiveness of the difference agencies—governmental, military, party—that helped shape the history of that state. In general Albert Speer seems correct for predicting that notwithstanding its *Volksgemeinschaft* ideology, in time the Führer state "would have arrived at a kind of caste society." Speer [1970], 65.

Add to this mix the increasing relevance of war to the Nazi ideology and it is necessary to extend that ideology to comprise political-military commitments toward rearmament at the expense of solvent government financing which in time led to the genocidal racism and military expansionism of the 1940s.[109] Once embarked on such expansionism, the Führer state found itself enmeshed in extermination policies concentrated on the new conquests in Poland and eastern Europe and on behalf of a Greater German empire that would permanently include vast numbers of non-Germans. Even if it might be argued that extermination of undesirable elements, such as east European Jews, was a time-limited venture to be followed by the exclusive presence of "beautiful" (because racially "healthy") nordic Germans in Hitler's state, the expectation of the permanent existence of primarily Slavic subordinates in the forthcoming Greater Germany clearly was not. Given further Hitler's own clear pronouncements on how such a populace would be treated in unsanitary and barbaric segregation, it must be conceded that any "beautiful" new Order would contain a huge body of necessarily "unbeautiful," presumably racially inferior creatures operating into the indeterminate future.[110]

But supposing for the sake of argument that war conditions did somehow deform some pristine Nazi vision, what can be still said about that vision? It may be conceded that Nazi aesthetics claimed a privileged relation to classical antiquity: for Hitler, Myron's Diskobolos (of which the regime owned the best copy) and the Roman Pantheon were absolute standards. But what were the general results of this presumed commitment? Instead of emulating the harmony and humanity of classical sculpture with its ideal of *sophrosyne*, Nazi sculpture is accurately regarded as brutalist and martial in its exaggerations of the human male form.[111] While presumably aiming for neoclassical balance, Nazi architecture ended up with an overbearing massiveness that underscored raw power and domination in its neo-Baroque leanings.[112] Finally, with regard to

---

[109] Kershaw [1998]. 302. Kershaw quotes a perceptive 1928 editorial in the *Frankfurter Zeitung* which already captures this essential feature of Hitler's ideology: Hitler "has taken war ideology perfectly literally" (302).

[110] Hitler's merciless vision for this future slave populace marks his more extravagant declarations during the Russian campaign of 1941-1942 and thankfully comes to a permanent halt after the defeat at Stalingrad. Hitler [2000] (27 July 1941), 15-16, (8-11 August 1941), 24, (3 March 1942), 354-355, (11 April 1942), 423-426.

[111] Spotts [2002], 185.

[112] Speer [1970], 76-77. Or: "bloated rectilinear structures with endless colonnades." Spotts [2002], 335. Giesler however insists that Hitler's concept of "Klassizität" was "die klare, disziplinierte Ordnung," confirming "die zeitlose Endgültigkeit," and blames Speer for his "Gigantomanie" in contrast to Hitler's "massvoll, ja bescheiden" standards. Giesler [1978], 206, 32

the great spectacles, the people were "reduced to unthinking automatons" since the underlying structures for such spectacles obsessively latched on to formal arrangements of blocks of masses and exclusive isolation of the leader.[113]

At most, certain resemblances with the intended power of Roman architecture, certainly as seen through Mussolini's Italy, may be claimed, but such resemblances merely help to underscore the chasm between Hitler's visions and classical Hellenism. Notwithstanding his professed adulation of the Greeks,[114] Hitler lacked a clear access to Athenian standards and achievements, the fount after all of classical German Hellenism. His martial proclivities drew him at best to the Spartans but all more unambiguously to imperial Rome.[115] Even where he praised such Athenian accomplishments as the Parthenon, he resolutely refused to accept that they could have anything to do with Athenian democracy, but rather must be attributed to the "great Doric leader" theory, in this case Pericles.[116] Perhaps the best example of this absence of any intrinsic affinity with the Athenian enterprise may be gleaned from the grand project of creating Greek-style theatres throughout the Nazi realm during the 1930s. Such a *Thingspiel* project ultimately floundered because Nazi administrators had no satisfactory way of accommodating themselves to a flourishing rhetorical and dialogical tradition that is germane to the properly theatrical.[117] This standing contradiction between mere spectacle and genuine theatre is as good as any for underscoring the National Socialist failure to become sufficiently "aestheticized"—certainly in an identifiably Hellenizing direction.

VI

To misuse the heritage of classical antiquity in such a manner is not simply an antiquarian indelicacy; it is no less than a form of cultural misuse. For all his alleged erudition and saturation in history, Hitler never took a first step toward

---

[113] Granted these readings, it is difficult to see why Spotts then interprets the spectacles as a viable "political" substitute of participation for the loss of debate and elections: "his pageanty and rites provided the populace, now deprived of debate and elections, with a stronger sense of political participation than ever before." Spotts [2002], 57; also 60, 69.

[114] "When we are asked about our ancestors, we should always point to the Greeks." Hitler [2000] (18-19 January 1942), 225.

[115] Following Scobie [1990] in general, and especially 14-15. For Hitler the "Roman Empire never had its like. To have succeeded in completely ruling the world!" Hitler [2000] (2 November 1941), 111. One additional problem was that whereas Mussolini's Italy might ethnically claim the Roman Mediterranean heritage, this, as the fascist architectural theorist Plinio Marconi noted, was not available to Hitler's Germany. Scobie [1990], 4-5.

[116] See the account in Giesler [1978], 203; also 99.

[117] See the account in Scobie [1990], 75-77.

perhaps the most invaluable gift of that heritage: the polis. And as the ancient texts incessantly warn about hubris, for his oversight Adolf Hitler was fated to pay.

For in his last years Hitler did find one apparently glimmering consolation in the wreck of his expansionist and genocidal ambitions: the reconstruction and glorification of his hometown of Linz. As Hermann Giesler, the architect entrusted to what became Hitler's dearest project, relates, Hitler after 1939—that is, from the onset of the war—clung to every detail of plans for the renovation of Linz that he intimately shared with Giesler. Here, at long last, would be fulfilled his youthful operatic, architectural, and city planning dreams—the new Order on a civic and personally relevant scale at the site where he first experienced Wagner's *Rienzi*—directed toward the city that was meant to serve as his retirement home and mausoleum.[118] Historians attracted to the last months of Hitler's life are fond of reflecting on the February 1945 photograph of the Führer in his bunker gazing dreamily at the elaborate model of Linz that Giesler had recently prepared for him. But whatever hopes for a National Socialist future still lingered, they were to be entirely blasted away in a few months, along with all functional vestiges of the Third Reich.

Discussing their project, Hitler had proposed—at least according to Giesler—that the Linz city hall (*Stadthaus*) be designed to represent its citizens (*Bürger*) since city representation comprised the citizens and mayor rather than Reich or party Gauleiter officials.[119] This curiously rare affirmation of civic rights, if such it was, goes entirely against the grain of Hitler's lifelong hostility to the public realm, discursivity, parliament and parties, even the agonistic voices of living theatre, let alone the implacable purifications of tragedy.[120] Oblivious even to the wealth of the tradition of German Hellenism, Hitler's affair with classical antiquity proved as impoverished as his general sense for anything outside his cultural borders of fin-de-siècle Munich painting, Viennese neo-Baroque architecture, and the pseudo-aesthetics of total mobilization. As with the notorious case of the statesman-as-sculptor metaphor that we have tried to unravel, Nazi "aestheticization of politics" was not simply misguided; it cannot even be classified as sufficiently "aesthetic."

---

[118] Giesler [1978], 213-217, 89-104, 478-486 on the city that Hitler called his "Heimatstadt" (213). In 1938 Linz numbered 100,000 inhabitants (with a projected growth of up to 350,000 according to the new plans).

[119] Giesler [1978], 95.

[120] Hitler claimed to have been impressed by only two historical "constitutions": the Papacy and the constitution of the city-state of Venice. Hitler [2000] (31 March 1942), 386. Speer notes that among Hitler's film choices for his considerable library, there were, "interestingly enough, never those with tragic plots." Speer [1970], 69.

Still, any such attempt to usurp the aesthetics and politics of prior classical traditions is a reminder of the countervoice to Nazi aestheticization (along with its gambit of the statesman-as-sculptor metaphor). It is through classical German Hellenism that "aesthetics" not only became a recognizably distinctive area of discourse, but also provoked thought of its corresponding "politics," a politics that assumed as its goal the realization of the promise of freedom launched by the French Revolution. In the closing words of Friedrich Schiller's *Letters on the Aesthetic Education of Man*, this politics of the realm of *schöner Schein* is dramatically announced. It blinds the cyclops[121] once and for all:

> No privilege, no autocracy of any kind, is tolerated where taste rules, and the realm of aesthetic semblance [*das reich des schönen Scheins*] extends its sway ... In the aesthetic state [*In dem ästhetischen Staate*] everything—even the tool which serves—is a free citizen, having equal rights with the noblest; and the mind, which would force the patient mass beneath the yoke of its purposes, must first obtain its assent.[122]

[121] Consider Hitler's declaration of "undertaking this *Cyclopean task* which the building of an Empire means for a single man." Hitler [2000] (25-26 September 1941), 44 (emphasis added).

[122] Schiller [1967], 226-229 (letter 27.11). Also Jay [1992], 51-52, and Pirro [1994], 147.

CHAPTER THREE

Fair Play

The Openness of Polis Justice

Having critiqued the statesman-as-sculptor approach within aestheticization of politics thematics, polis thought can now turn directly to its own legitimations. In his justification of civic—or polis—justice, Peter Murphy extends our project a firm helping hand.[1]

Driving *Civic Justice*,[2] Murphy's provocative venture in theory and history, is a single and irresistible idea: whatever else it may entail, Justice is primarily about sculpting real, concrete civic spaces wherein human beings can enact a performative reality best captured by the categories of dance, drama, music, athletics, and thought. This genial idea takes on a plethora of articulations throughout a work equally containing a set of bold, occasionally mistaken but almost always stimulating, readings in the thousand and one controversies constituting "western culture." Yet the idea sustains sufficient cogency in itself to mark out *Civic Justice* as a central contribution to that growing field of interest in contemporary critical and political theory called the "aesthetic-political."[3] Peter Murphy may not be the last word on the subject, but he has issued a powerful challenge to regnant theories of justice with his civic- or, more properly, *polis*-oriented approach to the general play of human and institutional fairness.

As expected, any such approach is deeply indebted to the spirit of Hellenism. Hellenism has regained some of its classical vigor through the work of such contemporaries as Martin Heidegger and his erstwhile students Hannah Arendt, Karl Löwith, and Herbert Marcuse.[4] If Murphy shows little awareness of, or interest in, this tradition of German Hellenism initiated by Winckelmann

---

[1] A slightly earlier version of this chapter was published in *History and Theory*, 43:1 (2004), 83-106.

[2] Murphy [2001].

[3] Relevant literature in the field includes: Ankersmit [1966]; Benjamin [1973]; Carroll [1987], Chytry [1989], Chytry [2005], Jameson, Bloch et al [1977], Jay, "'The Aesthetic Ideology' as Ideology: Or What Does It Mean to Aestheticize Politics?" in Jay [1993], 71-83, Kaiser [1999], Man [1996], Megill [1985], North [1001], Redfield [1996].

[4] Notwithstanding his generally critical reading of his protagonists, Wolin [2001] can serve as a recent introduction to Heidegger and his students. See also Chapter 4 below.

and Goethe[5]—probably the most potent recovery of the Hellenic paradigm since the Italian *Quattrocento*—it is because his own Hellenism claims to eschew primarily theoretical approaches in favor of concrete constructions of civic spaces by artisans, artists and architects. Of course such concreteness is itself the stuff of theory, and Murphy's own starting-point of the ancient Ionian creations of both the polis and philosophy grants, reasonably enough, the interweaving of theory and praxis for his exemplary narrative. Still, wherever he can, Murphy is quick to dismiss the theoretical drift of the mere thinker or utopianist in favor of the practical arts of founding, hollowing out, and celebrating such civic spaces. In turn, these spaces sustain for Murphy a kind of expansive necklace of "republic of strangers" that in his view has facilitated movement, openness, and exchange in geographies that are, as in the case of Murphy's favored Mediterranean basin, boundedly (*peras*) oceanic.[6] Ultimately—so Murphy's historical moral —this "proliferation of cities in the Mediterranean from the eighth century B.C.E. on marks the beginning of Western civilization."[7]

Not surprisingly therefore, the punctuations in Murphy's narrative, for all the latter's original readings, remain indebted to the familiar and favored sites of classical historiography: (i) "Classical Antiquity" or "Graeco-Roman civilization," starting with the Greeks and emulated (however inadequately) by the Romans (Chapters 1-4); (ii) "the Renaissance", succeeding the dark ages of antiquity's breakdown with the revival of the classical spirit in high medieval and Renaissance Florence as well as in other Renaissance city-states like Venice (Chapters 5-7); and (iii) "Modernity," concluding with a globalizing world-system increasingly dominated by cunningly adept Anglo-American "blue-water" trade empires and continental or imperial republics (Chapters 8-11). While the brevity of a "concluding" chapter (Chapter 12)[8] betrays the degree to which Murphy's own thinking is probably still in fertile process, the near-identity between his titles for the first and the last full chapters—"Kallipolis" ("the beautiful polis")[9] and "The City Beautiful"— accentuates clearly enough the "aesthetic-political" pathos underscoring his overall trajectory.

---

[5] In separate articles, Murphy does touch in passing on this German tradition. Murphy [1993] and Murphy [1998]. Also Arnason & Murphy [2001].

[6] Murphy [2001], 9, 315. Hence: "Greek civilization was a *civilization of the sea*, of the coastal periphery, *not of the land*" (29 [emphasis in original]).

[7] Murphy [2001], 45.

[8] This two-page summary is more an announcement of Murphy's probable future project: the "philosophical history of the American republic of strangers" (316) which will presumably carry forward Murphy's reflections on the ambiguous contributions of the United States to the civic republican tradition in which he largely locates civic justice. See Pocock [2003].

[9] Suggestive—and attractive—as this term is for Murphy's purposes, I do not believe that it

I

What, then, is the Justice appropriate to this "beautiful Polis"? This is the question that Murphy purports to answer, first in a series of readings historically located in the archaic and classical Hellenic periods, then through a sequence of combative exchanges with alternative legitimations of justice from the Judaeo-Christian challenge to, eventually, the specifications of mercantilist, capitalist and industrial modes of secularization. While some may regret that Murphy's theory of justice is articulated less through a direct theoretical formulation than through the vagaries of a "philosophical history"[10]—Murphy's way of conceding the broadly traditionalist historiography of *Geistesgeschichte* and history of ideas on which he terminologically and taxonomically relies—the patient reader invigorated by Murphy's almost disconcerting honesty of intellectual partisanship will appreciate the advantages of his nimble moves between theory and history for his justification of the standard of civic justice.

Justice, according to Peter Murphy, is the quite literal—and not simply metaphoric—openness which enables humans to gather and assemble together as the free beings they immanently are. In turn, such openness protects and nurtures the character of mutual exchange, contest, competition, recognition, balancing and (potentially at least) *harmonia* that girds the sociability, conviviality and agonistics of the ζῷον πολιτικόν, that "species-being" uniquely suited to the polis. In its turn, polis (the *Cité* in Rousseau's explicit sense[11]) is the very *siting* of that openness, justified in its ultimate claims on human allegiance (along with the entire civic and urban tradition of western civilization) by the persistent dynamics of such openness in continually balancing forces that constitute no less, at least for Murphy, the classical meaning of reason and rationality as such.

What is vital to stress in this reading is the concreteness of this agora, this "city center" or "civic space" which "no one" rules or is permitted to rule. First comes the literal space, the center, the openness;[12] then follows inevitably the

---

was ever used by the ancient Greeks themselves. There is no direct citation to that effect in Murphy's text, and my own researches have only come up with Aristotle's "τὸ ζῆν εὐδαιμόνως καὶ καλῶς" ("a happy and beautiful life") as an appropriately Aristotelian standard for the paradigmatic polis. Aristotle [1967], 1281a. On the other hand, the resemblance between Murphy's Kallipolis and Friedrich Schiller's coinage of "aesthetic state" (*der ästhetische Staat*) for his cultural ideal in the *Aesthetic Letters on the Education of Man* (1794-95) merits further inquiry. See "Schiller: The Theory of the Aesthetic State," in Chytry [1989], 70-105.

10 Murphy [2001], 316.

11 Rousseau [1968], 61 (note *) (I.6).

12 "The foundational act of ancient politics was to create the city center (*agora, forum*)." Murphy [2001], 298. As to how that open space originally began, Murphy speculates, without

flowering of those peculiar graces—reasoning, art, philosophy, music, athletics, all those grand gestures of the performative, ceremonial and carnivalesque core to being human—in relation to which standards of justice, fairness and equity not only flourish but may even be said to receive their very origins and character.[13] This is praxis with a vengeance, for it validates the polis-founder, the polis-architect, the polis-performer—that is, the architectural[14] and artisan makers, as well as the political actors, directly ("statesmen") and indirectly ("performing artists") engaged pragmatically in such tasks—to the detriment of the thinkers and theorists who are less about factically creating spaces than speculating on their detritus. It no less validates historical periods in which such praxis is at its premium: from Ionian colonizations and consolidation to the architects and architectural theorists of the Florentine and Italian Renaissance. Finally, it validates economies, and the key actors in those economies, of open-ended market and trade societies plying the bounded seas, along with the metics who are less citizens than artisanly and commercial laborers ("foreigners"—at least to citizenly status and legality) of the continuous flow of goods—and ideas—that link together these separate, discrete civic centers; while at the same time it disparages all that smacks of patrimonial and imperialistic priorities, the two consistent scourges to Murphy's civic standard.

Whenever this formula works, it produces something that looks to be quite "beautiful": *Kalli-polis*. This is Murphy's ultimate, and most controversial, claim, distinguishing his ideal at the same time from primarily commercial or capitalistically-dominated societies and helping to explain his skepticism toward much of world history since the Iberians first headed out into those "blue waters" of global imperialism. Its justification rests on the manner in which Murphy's account couples the material developments that made for the original Ionian polis with the intellectual advances of early Ionian philosophizing. Obviously the first thinkers did not create the polis, but their thought both mirrored and in significant ways refined underlying juridical implications of the practical fashioning of the polis—in Murphy's phrasing, "thinking the *polis*"[15]—by coming up with three reinforcing modes of thought.

---

elaborating, that "the great spaces of antiquity" emerged "from something very simple, viz. the *choros* or dancing place" (303). See also "Landfall: Theatrocracy" below.

[13] "The city formed the citizen through the ethos of, and participation in, the public festivals, drama, music and dance, philosophizing, rhetoric, and athletics of the city." Murphy [2001], 281. Murphy criticizes American public spaces for lacking "the spirit of carnival" (302).

[14] Murphy alludes to the republic as "an architectonic public, not a religious culture." Murphy [2001], 282.

[15] Murphy [2001], 44.

First, Anaximander introduced the principle of balance to philosophy, and by implication, the primacy of a mode of social and political form "in which parts were arranged in opposition rather than in hierarchy." This thought was directed against the formlessness of the principle of the "infinite" in favor of defining the "state of justice" as "limited" (*peras*) or the bringing about of equilibrium—an *isonomia*—celebrating a "center" for that equilibrium in which "public space" could emerge as an agora "metaphorically equidistant from all households in the city." Second, Heraclitus argued for an attunement (*harmonia*) holding together discordance and conflict as the constitutive elements of an overall *kosmos*: "Conflict is justice because discordance attunes; it harmonizes." Such balancing validated the concept of ratio and public power as that power which maintains open spaces for "contestory engagements," along with the patronage less of rulers than of judges, juries, assemblies and spectators whose task it became to exercise judgment in the unfolding of the dynamics of such spacings. And finally, Pythagoras and the Pythagoreans introduced the doctrine of the mean and the image of scales as the attunement of opposites through the standard of ideal ratios—the intervals of the musical scale—with its model of proportionality and the ideals of limit, moderation and order.[16]

The end result of these primarily philosophical innovations turned out to be a distinctive approach compatible with the creation of civic spacings—the legislation of what is conventionally called "classical architecture" with its commitment to balance, proportionality and symmetry—as well as the birth of a mode of thinking the mean ("reason") and of public power as the embodiment and protection of such thinking. Put together, civic creation, architecture, reason and public power confirmed the birth in turn of something called "beauty": "The ordering was beautiful ... because it was well—which is to say justly—proportioned." Its political ramifications are evident from Murphy's insistence that such beauty inevitably bore the imprint of freedom in so far as creating "a beautiful world, the *kallipolis*," entailed hostility to tyranny or despotism.[17]

Framing Murphy's "civic justice" argument perhaps more compactly than Murphy himself intends, one might therefore put it this way: the open space I come across in (and as) the core to the polis is akin to the cerebral force field where thinking enjoys the purity of its pulsations and impulses.[18] These latter,

---

[16] Murphy [2001], 46, 50, 51, 54.

[17] Murphy [2001], 49, 31, 32.

[18] That is, I take it, the thrust behind Murphy's claim that the classical Greeks, in contradistinction to Neoplatonic (Plotinus) and Dantean readings, "sought to produce a rounded world capable of being taken in at a glance. But for the Greeks this occurred at the point of intersection of counterposed intellectual and corporeal shapes as they tested each other's limits in

far from being irrational, are constantly resolved into dynamically alive patterns, proportionalities, symmetries. Precisely such resolutions embody the content and character of justice, and since it was (civic) openness—agonal/agoric and cerebral—that brought about such justice, justice is both "civic" in this sense and also manifests as "beauty" in producing or reinforcing qualities of proportionality and symmetry for settlement of the underlying discordances and contestatory elements in civic and intellectual life: "Like all core systems of social meaning, the meaning of the *Kallipolis* was internal to itself and circular."[19]

II

A lived standard of this order would be no mean accomplishment for any historical period. Nor is Murphy reluctant to hold it forth as the one genuine standard of justice for all societies, notwithstanding the difficulty of replicating the unique Ionian conditions of the original miraculous plant. The challenge for Murphy's subsequent narrative is to show how historically this "civic justice" was almost immediately challenged, subordinated, misused, indeed regularly overcome, only to repeatedly slip back into public discursivity in a wide variety of guises.

Indeed, corruption sets in almost at the outset. No sooner is this Ionian model transferred to the political soil of Cleisthenes' Athens than it experiences not only its finest moment through the latter's constitutional reforms of 508 BCE but also the stirrings of a fatal slide toward imperialism. The Athenians of Cleisthenes, it is true, "were the first to realize" what the Ionian philosophers "thought," in that their new constitution mixed together elements of participation to produce a share in citizenship in the literal public spaces, including the "theater," of the city, but, alas, the "soul of Attica" was "not equipped for the bearing of this legacy."[20] Rather than Cleisthenes' standard of *isonomia*, or balance, Athenians went on to create the *demokratia* of "a none-too-glorious imperial hegemony."[21] The critical, and fatal, difference between these two standards, according to Murphy, is that *demokratia* entailed an atavistic loyalty to the soil—Athenian soil—and celebrated the civic religion of worshipping Athens proper rather than allowing for the continued elaborations

the central space of the city" (148).

[19] Murphy [2001], 49.

[20] Murphy [2001], 55, 60, 65.

[21] Murphy [2001], 66. Cleisthenes' polis as such was *not* a "democracy" (60), according to Murphy.

of the principles of fluidity, mobility and openness characterizing the ideal of "isonomic politics."[22] Inevitably such autochthonous patriotism turned into imperialism, that is, the expansion of Athenian soil to encompass other soils, since love for Athens blinded Athenians to the legitimate existence of other poleis that were absorbed into their Delian confederacy. Murphy is quite unforgiving about this turn: "The eyesight of *dêmokratia* is myopic, and not only because of the desire for mastery." Murphy's entire account of the classical fifth century is punctuated by denunciations of this "Eastern-style behavior," the "irrational acts" and the "enormous self-destructiveness" with regard to the "disasters that the Athenians brought on themselves," against which their Doric rival Sparta "understandably" did whatever was necessary to bring down the empire.[23]

The consequences of such hubris have become, of course, a commonplace to cultural history: in disgust, philosophy in the persons of Socrates and Plato withdrew from the living polis to pursue "the little publics of philosophers and their auditors," a step that was tantamount to philosophy's increasing forgetfulness of "the public space" of the Ionian enlightenment. Concrete political power migrated to the patrimonial and imperialistic principles embodied by the Macedonian monarchy over polis life and eventually by that mother of all imperiums, the Roman republic weaving a Mediterranean supremacy through careful exploitation of alliances and subsequent "fraternal" takeovers.[24]

Even so, particles of civic justice maintain their occasional afterlife in classical antiquity. Philosophers in the Hellenistic genre of Stoicism pushed avidly for civic virtue even if they excluded the element of agon that had pervaded the earlier model. Roman traditions of justice (from *ius*, etymologically referring to a joining or fitting together), Roman admiration for trustworthiness and faithfulness (*fides*), and Roman celebration of the Forum as

---

[22] Murphy [2001], 80. In a separate work, drawing on Lévêque & Vidal-Naquet [1996], Murphy cites the authors' linkage of Pythagorean numerology with the meta-tribal system set up by Cleisthenes' Athenian constitution. At the same time, Murphy notes that by retaining the concept of tribal hero-figures for each deme or neighborhood, Cleisthenes' plan still depended upon tribal emotion and identity. Murphy [1998], 110-1.

[23] Murphy [2001], 69, 66, 67. Presumably because as "an imperial democracy" (70) Athens was singularly concerned with land expansion, Murphy insists that its thalassic hegemony must not be read as "thalassocentric" (65), that is, Athens should not be regarded as contributing in this regard to the sea-oriented openness that Murphy himself eulogizes. Murphy goes to the extent of charging: "Athenian politics had descended into the under-belly of the city, into the sewer of factionalism and chaos" (75). See "Landfall: Theatrocracy" below for a different reading of Periclean Athens.

[24] Murphy [2001], 75, 80-83.

a place of assembly, contest, and exchange encouraged a nonpatrimonial reading of the *res publica*; indeed the Romans were partially so successful in legitimating their expansion by championing an ethics of treaty partnerships that was not overly onerous for the societies they swallowed up. Roman pursuit of *res publicae*—that is, the gathering together of people in public spaces—even produced "the liveliness, drama, and theater of public life in public spaces."[25]

Nonetheless, the persistent pull of the patrimonial dimension in Roman social and private life undermined these contributions to the public sphere. The Imperium Romanum became in time an urban civilization of city-states, but it was never constructed on the basis of a functional urban economy. Rather, the Roman economy depended on the despotic slave household ultimately associated with vast estates of senatorial latifundia.[26] Moreover, the "classical" culture of which this conglomerate operated as the official Mediterranean protector was in general an importation from Hellenistic priorities that had already lost contact with Ionian isonomic politics. Notwithstanding the Roman creation of "humanism" as its special contribution to civic thematics, the later course of antiquity reinforced hierarchy, imperium and professional bureaucratism, strangling the ethics of the poleis to which the earlier empire had at least paid lip service and culminating in the Roman collapse of the fourth and fifth centuries in the forms of an increasingly localized patrimonialism that privatized social life through estate management and the strict religious hierarchy of a Romanized Christianity.

Fortunately, so long as commerce and trade prospered on the bounded seas, cities and the civic life from which "civic justice" and the cult of public "beauty" originated held their own.[27] True, the coming of the Germanic kingdoms in the west further favored agrarian patrimonial patterns—a case of *domus* over *emporion*—but Murphy thinks that it was the triumph of Islam which dramatically shrank Mediterranean trade, leaving little beyond Byzantium and its oceanic heir Venice to carry forth "the classical love of public appearances and its stress on the pleasure of the eye." By the same token, once Islamic Mediterranean hegemony was loosened around the eleventh and twelfth centuries, the revival of international commerce reawakened in the Italian city-states the "public-aesthetic" character of isonomic politics, as these

---

[25] Murphy [2001], 85-87, 111.

[26] Murphy [2001], 104, 116.

[27] Charmingly Murphy goes so far as to argue that association with the (bounded) sea intrinsically reinforces a tendency toward celebrating beauty through the continued experience of the naturalistic beauty of the sea itself and its "azure" qualities. Murphy [2001], 123.

cities, particularly Florence, "developed a *theatrical* quality, and a much closer relationship to the *mores* of the public world of the actor."[28]

While it is not perfectly clear what in fact caused the Florentine commitment to the kind of productivity that, as Murphy puts it, was geared to the "art-industry" of "aesthetic refinement"—other than some pre-existent "Florentine feel for beauty and excellence"[29]—what *is* clear is that the Italian Renaissance stage of civic justice is far more dichotomous than the original Hellenic model. This split reflects the obvious problem of reconciling priorities belonging to a "pure" civic domain with those reflecting medieval Christian patrimonial and familial practices. According to Murphy, a revived commercial life is sufficient to explain the partial return of the older Greek values of cosmopolitan association, along with the "Greek-Roman" "love of beauty"; on the other hand, church, family, and even urban workshop standards of thrift reflected no less the intervening influences of medieval society and economy. Hence, the Renaissance fell short of a pure sense for civic justice; its celebrated cosmopolitanism tended to be restricted to a mere "mercantile cosmopolitanism" rather than ascending to a true "cosmopoiesis," or self-creation of the civic sphere as such.[30] Not the regained polis, but a territorial monarchy along the lines of medieval France, on the one hand, and the "Muslim-Roman" imperialism of Emperor Frederick II, on the other, appeared as the only viable alternatives to this confined urbanity.

It is this basic dichotomy between civic and patrimonial-imperialist patterns that then forms the basis for Murphy's readings of a host of late medieval and Renaissance conundra. Thus, Murphy congratulates Dante for emulating the original Odyssean visionary journeys of Greek sailors through his epic rhetoric of wandering and arrival; yet he also points out that Dante was equally driven by a disenchantment with, rather than desire to found, the city. His worldly city being riven by factionality, Dante's response was the public space of the heavenly garden which symbolized less the force field of dynamic competitivenes than the promise of perfection through diversity.

Nor, for Murphy, is there apparently much that is "civic" in the civic humanism of the celebrated Florentine *Quattrocento*. True, humanism was

[28] Murphy [2001], 126, 128 (emphasis in original). Murphy goes to some lengths to invoke the language of theatricality in describing these city-states, e.g. "Florence epitomizes this southern theatricality" (129). Frank E. Manuel and Fritzie E. Manuel have similarly described the Italian commune of the thirteenth century as beginning "to conceive of itself as a thing of beauty in which religious and aesthetic elements were fused." Manuel & Manuel [1979], 177.

[29] Murphy [2001], 129. To drive home his claim, Murphy italicizes the following statement regarding Florence: "Production was the production of beautiful things, things for aesthetic display" (129).

[30] Murphy [2001], 130, 134.

driven by the fertilizing influences of civic, rather than local or national, life, to posit an ideal of beauty that "is not an aesthetic ideal in the modern sense, but a public-political one."[31] But the humanists were basically commentators, not creators of civic spaces, and in due course what remained of their civic orientations was transformed into the "mystical humanism" of the later court of Lorenzo the Magnificent presided over by Marsilio Ficino. Neither ruler nor philosopher was concerned so much with "city building" as with the "interpretation of texts;" yet civic justice can only operate where builders, not mere commentators, rule. Even if Plato, Aristotle and Cicero had been pragmatically writers, they were "architects of the city in words," these words giving "shape to the living city." In contrast, Ficino ignored "the aspiration of the citizen of the *polis* to objectivate and to build the city" in favor of "the aspiration to fathom the mystery of the word of God through interpretation, commentary, exegesis, and so on." Wherever monotheism with its greater concern with the hermeneutics of interpreting canonical texts predominates, even the ecumenical goal inspiring Ficino and such followers as Pico della Mirandola to incapsulate the entire cultural heritage of the Mediterranean world in a cosmopolitan philosophy and theology is at grounds incompatible with "the building of civic places and spaces in which public action could unfold and be immortalized." In short, Judaeo-Christian-Islamic standards and Graeco-Roman conceptions cannot really mix—even "today."[32]

Put broadly, this incompatibility marks the failure of Murphy's post-Ionian "city tradition" to engage in active creation, or *cosmopoiesis*, "in advance of founding the city-republic." To commit to imitation, as the Florentine civic humanists and their heirs attempted to do with regard to the model of classical antiquity, falls short, by definition, of an originative acting and making. Hence, rather than the familiar authors of the Renaissance, Murphy argues that one must look rather to the architects and their "civic humanism" for the kind of creative work that he is espousing. "Somehow" Florence resisted the humanist extravagances of Florentine culture and allowed its architects to engage in the pragmatic "wise ruling of space" along with their "desire for a city of art, and an art of perfect balance." These workings on the literal civic realm did in fact "achieve the *komospoiêsis* of Florence" by the lengthy contributions made from Brunelleschi through Alberti to Pacioli, and eventually inspired that grand summation of classical Renaissance architecture and civic planning, Andrea Palladio. Common to this imposing list of innovators was their vital

[31] Murphy [2001], 163. Thus, "in the classic humanist sense, a constitutional order is an order of beauty."

[32] Murphy [2001], 168, 171, 172. In Murphy's precise words: it is not clear whether they "can be fully reconciled" (172).

commitment to draw on patterns that might fashion the "social form of the city," i.e. the *kallipolis*, "the beautiful city."[33]

Indeed, it is a good thing that they did, for early modernity turns out to be even less predisposed to Murphy's civic ideal. Summed up under the ruling principle of "Baroque," all the apparently secularizing tendencies of the early modern age that might be likened to the genuine civic concerns informing Murphy's "city tradition" prove sharply incompatible with the latter. The baroque "mind," which for Murphy is "the paradigm of the modern mind," is basically "phantasmagorical." Notwithstanding a hefty list of attributes that includes longing for infinity, becoming, speed and movement, as well as an underlying dissatisfaction with the given that encourages caprice, monumentality and outlandishness, Murphy's Baroque may be summed up as an overall obsession with *dynamis*, with ceaseless and meaningless impetus toward change of any order or magnitude. Even the state-formations of the baroque age, however much the Dutch Republic and Puritan Commonwealth may differ from French absolutist monarchy, shared a predilection for "dynamic law" and "dynamic justice," offering clear contrasts to classical standards of balance and equipoise.[34] Common to the gamut of such state-formations was the new concept of sovereignty with its supportive rationalizing agents of bureaucracy and standing armies, seeking not to create civic spaces as such but ever more offices and organizations. To be sure, the classical ideal survived "precariously" in such forms as Dutch republicanism and French classicism, but much of the former was wedded to antinomian "Protestant-Hebraic" models in search of a New Jerusalem by way of oceanic crossings to the New World.[35] As to theories of the social contract first adumbrated by English liberal circles, their a-teleological, rights-based emphasis on the making of laws and institutions rather than cities was far removed from the classical "making of a city (with its beautiful things and deeds)."[36]

Murphy's modern hopes are therefore confined to two candidates: post-1688 Commonwealthman Britain and the unique venture in republicanism embodied by the United States of America. As one might predict by this stage in Murphy's narrative, both experiments prove seriously flawed. Deeply influenced by the antinomian concerns of Puritan politics, the Britain of the

---

33 Murphy [2001], 154, 173, 184, 175, 192.

34 Murphy [2001], 214, 222. Murphy specifies such contrasts as the dynamic open urban space of the baroque that can only be walked through in comparison with the centeredness of classical civic spacings that encourages congregating. He also points out that the radial diagonals of baroque space challenge classical grid patterns.

35 Murphy [2001], 195, 212. For Murphy the 1620 separatists sought an "ocean, not sea, crossing," something "unimaginable to Hellenic odysseans" (212).

36 Murphy [2001], 214.

Glorious Revolution does touch on elements of the civic model through the Commonwealthman legacy that goes back to James Harrington and Henry Neville, and Murphy acknowledges that at least the Third Earl of Shaftesbury was consistent in his commitment to Hellenic standards of balance, taste and the creative artist.[37] Yet the Commonwealthmen, in his view, were generally partisans on behalf of a "gothic limited monarchy" rather than a republic, in so far as they represented country and landed-property interests that reflected feudal, or "gothic," considerations of patrimonies counterweighting princely power.

At all events, Britain during the eighteenth century was more in search of a "transoceanic trading empire" than of a "thalassocentric" republic, in the course of which its reputed "neo-classicism"—again, excepting Shaftesbury—was driven and shaped by Augustan Roman imperial standards. These neoclassicists, lacking even the depth and strength of the Italian Renaissance recovery of Hellenism, confined their innovations to the observer of creation rather than the creative process itself; as a result, they largely invented the field of "aesthetics" concerned with receptive rather than productive faculties, with criticism rather than creation. In an important sense, this aesthetics was the intellectual counterpart to British constitution-making. If the constitution represented "an eclectic accommodation" not so much creating a balancing of forces as the consolidation of "a partially rationalized state" obsessed with laws and budgets rather than the concrete building of cities and public spaces, neoclassicism epitomized an "aestheticization of citizenship" in which the citizen was demoted to a mere observer and passive participant in the process of creation, political or otherwise.[38]

Under these circumstances, the growing importance of the category of the "sublime" is a reminder of the underlying baroque approach of modern "rationality" as opposed to classical "reason."[39] The modern-baroque tendency to master infinite space is forced to recognize pure contingency, but then attempts to master it through overcoming the terror of sublime nature with its calculative resources. Not Shaftesbury but Robinson Crusoe is the hero of this Augustan neoclassical legacy, and for all its attraction to exoticism and sublimity, the market society that Britain put permanently in place, eventually formalized by that canonical interpreter of market dynamics and ceaseless growth, Adam Smith, came to celebrate both the image of wilderness and the

---

[37] Shaftesbury took "seriously the legacy of Hellenism and its understanding of the importance of *kosmopoiêsis*." Murphy [2001], 238.

[38] Murphy [2001], 238, 239, 244, 246.

[39] Murphy [2001], 232.

power of industry and invention to master that wilderness, both external and internal, in its scenarios of infinite development.

Hence the final twists to Murphy's tale in treating of that strange mixture of Puritan antinomianism and classical balance of powers that helped form the Republic capable of both overthrowing British rule and embarking on a more far-reaching exemplification of baroque spatial and territorial mastery. Indeed, for Murphy, this American Republic is a striking case of "a republic without the *res publica*"—or for that matter, "without the *res publicae* (public things)." What Murphy means by such formulae is that on the one hand the United States drew richly on classical political and constitutional construction, while on the other it reflected Puritan preferences for an "ascetical republicanism" grounded in the free farmer unsympathetic to the very idea of the City or of the kind of leisure devoted to public spaces supportive of music, dance and drama.[40] In principle the U.S. constitution did not regard the state as "a public thing" in the classical sense: "It was not a city or polity [a *civitas* or *polis*], but a set of institutions," and its purpose was "not the augmentation of the city and its brilliant shining forth" but, in time, "the building of a continental empire" consumed not with the image of the "city center, the signifying core of a polity, where the assembling and relating of diversity takes place," but with that of the Frontier.[41]

Murphy, it is true, does detect two interesting, if minor, exceptions to this general American pattern. In his cultivation of the idea of the country villa and particularly in his plans for the University of Virginia where he betrayed "the great spirit of the polity," Thomas Jefferson seems to have been aiming for a standard halfway between urban and rustic concerns. His "southern republican imagination" perceived villa life as a "little republic," and in his Monticello project which drew on Roman models and Palladian standards, Jefferson showed evident classicist leanings. Yet the Jeffersonian villa ideal was paid for by the slavery of the plantation economic system, and to that extent excluded large numbers from the active life. No doubt the American welfare state eventually solved Jefferson's particular dilemma, but at the same time it showed little concern for "creating public artifices of great beauty." Generally American public spaces have failed to function as arenas in which individuals can "consociate" and "freely walk in public."[42]

---

[40] Murphy [2001], 258, 269, 281, 298. Also: "a politicized Calvinism," a "Christian Sparta" (256).

[41] Murphy [2001], 265, 266, 276. In general the Founding Fathers did not believe in "the enduring places—agoras, forums, piazzas—where classical antinomies were displayed and played out" (277).

[42] Murphy [2001], 277, 288, 2191, 297. Even the village commons pattern in New England

Nor does Murphy's second exception fill in this lacuna. The City Beautiful movement of the late nineteenth century at least showed that Americans too could feel a faith and love for their cities; perhaps such port city cases as New York and San Francisco even suggest a minor breakthrough of sorts for the city ideal. Yet the philosophy behind the movement celebrated open planar spaces rather than filled cubic space and, in any case, most American public space remains empty, remote: "foreboding."[43]

III

For Murphy the conclusion to his sweeping narrative is damning. To this politics and system of laws and justice based on the entire modern "failure of *kosmopoiêsis*" must be blamed a host of characteristic vices of the modern age from urban deterioration, sprawling suburbia, formless growth to electoral cynicism, spread of unskilled jobs in the service-consumer sectors, modern welfarism, shoddiness of public spaces, lack of civic greatness, even the "worldlessness" of contemporary psychological inner explorations.[44]

And yet the United States, while it sees itself as a "republic of sturdy farmers and enlightened actors," might well ascend to the "plastic dimension of the *res publica*" if it could only exploit its own underground history as a "republic of strangers."[45] This "other" history, which presumably remains to be written as Murphy's sequel to this book, might well succeed in elevating the liminal elements of the story of all Americans as "strangers" or immigrants and newcomers, and therefore as heirs to the isonomic politics of those Mediterranean strangers—Greek metics, Roman perigrini, medieval vagantes, and Italian merchants—who first founded "civic justice." This promising conclusion could also conveniently match important motifs in contemporary critical, feminist, transculturist, and post-colonial theorizing that celebrates open-endedness, fluidity, hybridity, and nomadism.

Instead of pursuing this promising path, the rest of this chapter will seek instead to augment and perhaps even improve Murphy's argument as it presently stands. Not only are there specific areas in the content of his history that might benefit from adjustments, revisions and changes, but the overall framework also invites substantial reconstruction with regard to formal theory.

---

with its central square lacks the volumetric form and depth of classical public space (299).

43 Such is his skepticism about American public spaces that Murphy must resort to the *choros* of the Congo Square in New Orleans to find one of the most important "vernacular public spaces" in North America. Murphy [2001], 311.

44 Murphy [2001], 12.

45 Murphy [2001], 316.

Confining this section to the former task, the *first* question to raise is whether Murphy has got his historical parameters just right for the origins of the tradition he unfolds and upholds. Since Murphy's originative heroes are not those of classical Hellenism and Periclean Athens, there seems no necessary taxonomic reason to begin, as he does, with the Ionian enlightenment, when a much clearer origin for some of Murphy's priorities—thalassocentrism, ritualistic and performative spaces, city-states living in apparent peace with one another, and relatively open-ended life styles—is already discernible in the "adorant theacentric" character of Minoan Cretan civilization, important elements of which were to be transmitted into the Ionian component of the later Hellenic age.[46]

It is true that Murphy's juxtaposition of Ionian political and philosophical factors cannot be replicated in the Minoan case (inaccessibility to Minoan script automatically shutting out that option). On the other hand Minoa offers what Murphy needs as a clear connection between economy and society, particularly in the concept of "thalassocracy" that Herodotus employed to trace important classical political-economic patterns back to the mythical Minos' rule over island and adjoining sea.[47] Indeed thalassocracy as applied by the ancient chroniclers and historians provides a unique glimpse into Hellenic political thinking that emphasized the economic dimension of politics and the project of a history of the international market. Moreover, the notion helps chronologize history from the fall of Troy (c. 1184 BCE) to the onset of the Persian wars through the policies of Polykrates of Samos in the sixth century.[48] It therefore also allows for a direct connection with the "nautical" policies of Themistocles and Pericles for fifth-century democratic Athens.[49]

This connection conveniently leads into the *second* area in which Murphy's content could stand some revision. While Murphy's animus toward the imperial phase of classical Athenian politics is understandable, he errs as a result of that animus in leaving out what must remain the exemplary polis in a story of this magnitude. One may sympathize with Russell Meigg's canonical conclusion that the Athenians of the empire phase "could have made more concessions to

[46] "The Minoan Religion in Crete," in Gimbutas [1999], 131-50; Marinatos [1993]. "The Minoan city was concentrated round a centre formed by the palace and a kind of agora, an open place for festal and possibly political gatherings." Wycherley [1976], 2.

[47] For more details see "Embarquement: Thalassocracy" above.

[48] Miller [1971], 176-7. More broadly, the term is applied by Clifford Geertz in his analysis of the "thalassocratic" bazaar states of Java. Geertz [1980], 87.

[49] For the argument that Thucydides used Minoa as "a prototype of Aegean imperialism" in the favorable sense that both imperialists and subjects benefitted from sea power, see Connor [1984], 24-25.

the general Greek passion for autonomy without undermining their position,"[50] but one should not ignore the obvious counterpoints that Meiggs—and others—have repeatedly and persuasively made: that Sparta (and Corinth), not Athens, precipitated the Peloponnesian War by its resort to preventive war; that in general Athens supported democratic regimes throughout the Mediterranean world and was fiercely opposed by oligarchic regimes backed by Sparta; that notwithstanding their experience of the Athenian empire, former members of that empire quickly signed up with Athens after thirty years of experiencing Spartan imperialism following the end of the Peloponnesian war; and that with one exception—411 BCE—classical Athenian democracy was only overthrown by outside forces and that all Athenians—not just the "poor"—continually showed by their actions that they clearly preferred that democracy over all known alternatives even when deprived of the benefits of imperial rule.[51]

Murphy fails to sufficiently recognize the degree to which the entire Athenian venture serves the cause of civic justice by unveiling a history that carries to unprecedented levels the goal of what Plato later derided as not just "democracy" but: "theatrocracy"[52] By this interesting neologism, Plato intended to chastise the Athenian proclivity for theatricality in all aspects of its public life, from sessions of the political assembly to ritualistic and explicitly dramaturgical expressions—as opposed to Plato's favored elite judges of the tasteful and the correct. Taken more positively, however, the term reminds us that what is retrospectively regarded as a final arrival—the explicit completion of the constitutional reforms for "radical democracy"[53] in 362BCE under

---

[50] Meiggs [1975], 412.

[51] Indeed, it was Macedonian imperialism that finally brought this fascinating experiment to an end. Meiggs [1975], Ste. Croix [1972], Forrest [1966], esp. 38, and Jones [1969], esp. 42. Jones has amassed the necessary evidence to argue that the benefits of imperialism and slave labor could be nullified without undermining Athenian democracy. In expressing admiration for the Spartan alternative, Murphy does not sufficiently consider the long and brutal nature of Spartan control over its "helots," the Messenians, without which Sparta's fabled egalitarian and tightly minority society would have been impossible. Indeed, once the Messenians broke free of Spartan control in 371BCE, Spartan power almost instantly dissolved. Forrest [1968].

[52] See "Landfall: Theatrocracy" below for more details. This term is also used by Friedrich Nietzsche, no doubt intending to invoke Plato, in his attacks on Wagnerian "Theatrokratie." Nietzsche [1967-], 3:4, 389, 403-8, and 6:3, 36. Political theorist Eric Voegelin, in supporting Plato, states the position the following way: "theatrocracy" supplants the "old musical order of the polis" by replacing the educated ruling class with the "people at large" which "arrogated to itself the right to applaud what pleased and to criticize what displeased without regard to quality" and thus made primary "judgment according to pleasure without insight." Voegelin [1957], iii, 245.

[53] Following Aristotle's phrase "extreme democracy" (δῆμον ... τὸν ἔσχατον). Aristotle [1967], 1277b.

Ephialtes and Pericles—might well have been, for the intrepid Athenians themselves, simply a stage toward a fully operational *thalassic theatrocracy*, possibly the most adequate formal political terminology for the kind of ideal that Murphy's own text envisages: an experiment boldly unfolded by the generation of the 440s before being brutally undercut by the oligarchic aggressions of the Dorian league. Indeed, some hint of this stage is suggested by that remarkable text assigned to the "Old Oligarch"—probably composed around 425-415BCE—in which most of Murphy's heroes, from slaves to metics, are reluctantly accorded the courage to embody a society in which all members live roughly equal lives, share mutual respect for each other's private and public personae, and achieve remarkable heights of everyday democratic decisionmaking—employing such distinctively democratic institutions as the lot—on behalf of the twin pillars of an expanding seapower linking them with all parts of the thalassic universe and a matchless devotion to festival and ceremony, to temple-construction and ritualistic spacings.[54]

Nor, *third*, having ignored Minoan Crete and downplayed theatrocratic Athens, does Murphy evince adequate concern for the contributions of Islamic civic society to his story.[55] Notwithstanding the account of the Mediterranean economy slanted toward Eurocentric readings on which Murphy depends to argue the case for an absolute decline until the Italian "recovery" of the eleventh and twelfth centuries, Islamic Andalusia (*al-Andalus*) serves as an essential transmitter between late antiquity and the early Italian Renaissance civic societies at both the material and cultural levels.[56] Far from undercutting the Mediterranean economy, this Islam, grounded but vastly improving upon earlier classical achievements in Roman Hispania, helped create the rich syncretism of Islam, Judaism and Christianity under conditions that after the evaporation of the centralized Umayyad Caliphate of Córdoba in 1031 became the "turbaned Italian Renaissance"[57] of "city states" of the *taifa* ("party") period in the

[54] See "Landfall: Theatrocracy" below for more details.

[55] In referring to a European later middle ages disinterest in Plato, Murphy mistakenly comments that it was "a reflection of an equal disinterest on the part of Arab scholars in Plato." Murphy [2001], 168. That Plato was central to Arabic and Islamic philosophizing during this same period may be confirmed by consulting Rosenthal [1992]. For Andalusian admiration for Plato, see Averroes [1956]. For his devotion to Plato, the great Andalusian Sufi Ibn 'Arabī was surnamed the Platonist, the "son of Plato" *(Ibn Aflatūn)*. Corbin [1969], 21.

[56] In contrast to Murphy's dependence on the work of Henri Pirenne, other studies argue that "the Islamic conquest had more nearly the opposite effect than that posited by Pirenne: it opened the Mediterranean, previously a Roman lake, by connecting it with the Indian Ocean, converted it into a route of world trade." Glick [1979], 190; also 318-9 (note 1) for further evidence.

[57] Emilio García Gómez, cited in Gerber [1992], 56.

eleventh century.[58] Resembling the later Italian Renaissance in the intensity of cultural and political competition among such leading city-states as Sevilla, Granada and Córdoba, the "peace of the taifa kings" not only produced a remarkable burst of agricultural, economic and trade prosperity as a result of which these "statelets of eleventh-century Spain" became enviably rich (certainly to their Christian European neighbors), but it also incited a profound "flowering of the arts" that benefitted all three religious cultures.[59] To be sure, these city-states largely gave way to Castillian expansion by 1248, but Nasrid Granada, aptly titled 'the last Islamic city-state in Europe,"[60] managed to survive until 1492 and reached new levels of economic prosperity through its agricultural and manufacturing innovativeness, financed largely by its continued commercial operations within a vast Mediterranian emporium.[61] Even Granada's most memorable product, the palace-city of the Alhambra, shows undeniable roots in "classical" no less than "Islamic" architectural aesthetics with its beguiling play of nature and cosmos, theatricality and illusion, secular grandiosity and esoteric pedagogy.[62]

If Murphy unfairly ignores Islamic al-Andalus, he, *fourth*, overlooks the originality behind the Florentine civic humanism which does form part of his narrative. By simply singling out Leonardo Bruni's *Panegyric to the City of Florence* (*Laudatio Florentinae Urbis)* as the one exception to his general dismissal of the civic humanists for being imitators rather than innovators, Murphy not only misses the many salutary contributions that Bruni himself did make to Florentine civic republicanism and the Florentine valorization of wealth-creation in augmenting that tradition,[63] but he also ignores the avant-gardist thrust behind the humanists' work of the early *Quattrocento,* along with

---

[58] For the outside reader, essential texts into Andalusian history and culture are Jayyusi [1992], 2 vols., and Menocal, Scheindlin & Sells [2000]. Specific accounts of the taifa city-state period are Wasserstein [1985] and, an "insider's" view, the autobiography of a taifa ruler, Tibi [1986].

[59] Fletcher [1992], 87, 87-88, 97.

[60] Menocal [2002], 10.

[61] Grabar [1978], 37; Pedro Chalmeta, "An Approximate Picture of the Economy of Al-Andalus," 741-758, and Olnia Remie Constable, "Muslim Merchants in Andalusī International Trade," 759-773, both in Jayyusi [1992], ii.

[62] Grabar [1978], 157, and Ruggles [2000], 209-222. While cities like Sevilla and Córdoba were originally Roman centers, Granada represents a relocation by Berber Zīrid rulers of the previously Roman city of Elvira (Illiberis) slightly eastward to the natural fortress location of the Alhambra mass. Fletcher [1992], 82.

[63] Other important works by Bruni include his *Oratio Funebris on Nanni degli Strozzi*, the lengthy *History of the Florentine People*, and *On the Politeia of the Florentines* (composed in Greek). Baron [1966]. For an instructive introduction to Bruni's contributions to a positive reading of wealth-creation for the city-republic tradition, see Bruni [1987].

their larger impact on the later *Quattrocento* and the architecturalist bias driving Murphy's overall reading of the Italian Renaissance.[64]

In this respect, the key figure must certainly be Leon Battista Alberti. If Murphy mentions him in passing, it is only as a charter member of Murphy's own stable of Renaissance architects. In fact, Alberti, the one unquestioned *uomo universale* of the period, confirms by his humanist enterprise the intimate affiliation between theory and practice among the civic humanists. Not only is he the author of foundational works on the arts of painting, sculpture, and architecture—even the latter classic, *On the Art of Building* (*De re aedificatoria)*, is more a grand treatise (and original work of literature) on civic spacing and the aesthetic-political ideal of *Civitas* inspiring the humanists than a mere summary of architectural and building principles: "the work of a lifetime" as "the culmination of an attempt to relate art to politics and morality."[65] Equally important, Alberti was a practising painter, sculptor, musician and architect to a degree noted and admired by his contemporaries and by posterity. Finally, Alberti wrote originally on a wide range of more explicitly humanist topics such as ethics and family, the relation of formal to vernacular languages, and the life of contemplation and meditation, all of which significantly helped to shape not just the theory but also the pragmatic reality of civic humanism and the city-republic ethos.[66]

Alberti's deserved status as *uomo universale* brought into play a type that Murphy moreover underplays, namely the artist as universal being, which would grow into a fundamental feature in the story of civic justice from this date on (including its further augmentations in the Romantic and neo-Romantic cults of the genius).[67] For such contemporaries as the humanist Cristoforo

---

[64] On the Florentine "humanist avant-garde" of the early *Quattrocento*, see Holmes [1969]. The strong sense of a common project driving the major art-innovators Brunelleschi, Ghiberti, Donatello and Masaccio is captured by Leon Battista Alberti in the prologue to *On Painting* (*Della pittura*) (1434), when he states his solidarity with these friends and their collaborative work in terms extolling Florence, "our city, adorned above all others." Alberti [1966], 39.

[65] Borsi [1989], 221. The work was also immediately recognized as "a model of learned Latin writing." Alberti [1988], xviii.

[66] George Holmes calls Alberti's *On the Family* (*Della Famiglia*) "something like an introduction to social attitudes" which brought out "both the appropriation of humanist concepts to urban society and the gap between them." Holmes [1969], 145. Compare this conclusion to a more recent study of the whole Alberti: "Nothing that he built of stone expressed Alberti's ideals more fully than his lifelong effort to create a rich and responsive social world to make, out of the rhetoric he prized so deeply, not only an art of composition, but a model for all forms of intellectual and artistic community." Grafton [2000], 339.

[67] For an excellent contemporary justification of this title, see Gadol [1969]. Gadol appropriately starts her study with Cristoforo Landino's famous eulogy of the outstanding capacities of Alberti. The term *uomo universale* itself receives its formal justification in Baldesar

Landino and the Laurentian poet Poliziano,[68] Alberti was capable of plumbing the very secrets of nature through his knowledge and practice of proportionalities, the play of language and even his acuity of social analysis. Landino's praise is worth noting in particular because he is mainly responsible for passing on to the later *Quattrocento* this model of Alberti the creator.[69] As himself a leader in Florentine culture in the generation of Marsilio Ficino (whom Landino taught) that succeeded Alberti, Landino thus represents "the link between the Neoplatonism of the latter part of the century and the humanism and artistic-scientific developments of early quattrocento Florence," confirming that Alberti (who had also been one of Ficino's auditors) "contributed to the outlook and interests of late fifteenth-century Florence" through his "own literary achievements, ethical ideas, and aesthetics."[70]

Once this continuity is acknowledged, it becomes more clear why much of what the earlier civic humanists had inaugurated in their social, ethical and historical works would pass through this Neoplatonic culture to culminate in the politico-historical works and careers of the later Florentine thinkers Francesco Guicciardini and Niccolò Machiavelli. Unfortunately, even in the case of these more prominent names for future European historiography and political theory, Murphy nowhere mentions the former and merely treats the latter as a product of the failing political fortunes of the early Florentine *Cinquecento*.[71]

Castiglione's *The Courtier* (*Il Cortegiano*) of 1528, whence it passes through translations and imitations into the thought and practice of the sixteenth-century European Renaissance.

[68] Landino's and Poliziano's encomnia are translated in Borsi [1989], 263.

[69] Interestingly, at least for the continuing debate on the putative opposition of the earlier to the later Florentine *Quattrocento*, Landino's Alberti embodied not the *vita activa* but a *vita contemplativa* which, fused with civic concerns, raised a new standard of the *vita composita.* For the key dialogue on such notions, see the *Disputationes Camaldulenses* of Landino [1980], originally completed in 1472 and made available in 1480, presumably based on a gathering in 1468 (one year before the more famous gathering of 1469 that inspired Ficino's dialogue on Plato's *Symposium*, one of the critical texts for interpretations of the thought of the late Florentine *Quattrocento*). For a complete study of the *Disputationes* in these terms, see Rombach [1991].

[70] Gadol [1969], 231. As Gadol herself warns, this is not to argue the case for identity of views between the earlier and the later Florentine *Quattrocento.* It is rather to emphasize the need for more nuanced readings between the three phases of the Florentine contributions to civic humanism: the civic humanism of 1400-1450, the more ecumenical ambitions of the later "Neoplatonic" culture of Ficino and Landino around 1450-1500, and the radical republican phase of Guicciardni and Machiavelli, 1500-1530, preceding and encompassing the fall of republican Florence.

[71] Holmes points out the continuity between the "immaturity and awkwardness" of the works of the Bruni generation which still revealed "the vision of an independent secular republic" and "the masterpieces of humanist and political writing" of Machiavelli and Guicciardini. Holmes [1969], 157, 167. See also Gilbert [1965].

If Murphy does not follow through sufficiently on his own hint of the positive implications contained in Bruni's civic humanism, he, *fifth*, similarly falls short of pursuing the larger positive impact of his hint with regard to Shaftesbury's eighteenth-century Commonwealthman aesthetics. Whatever the merits to Murphy's restricted reading of Shaftesbury's influence on British neoclassical thought and society in the eighteenth century, it is certainly the case that Shaftesbury enjoyed his greatest vogue elsewhere among European intellectuals and societies resisting the general fashion on the Continent for the new Britain of Locke and Newton. Above all, Shaftesbury became the model for a generation of writers confined to the petty court life in the German-speaking world of the mid-eighteenth century.[72] Johann Joachim Winckelmann, the inaugurator of German classicism, drew heavily on the "philosophical rhapsodies" of Shaftesbury for his evangelical Hellenism and celebration of the Athenian city-state.[73] Moreover, Wieland, Goethe and Schiller, the founders of that unique German experiment in a modern Athens, "classical Weimar," were deeply indebted to Shaftesbury; indeed, two of them, Wieland and Goethe, were born and brought up in German "free cities."[74]

For these representatives of "classical Weimar," it was no large imaginative step to adjudicate between the city-state priorities and culture of Winckelmann's Athens and the conditions in which they not only lived but hoped to establish as an exemplar of the ideal of *Kultur*. The history of this experiment and its cultural-political influence on subsequent German thought is substantial, extending from Schiller's advocacy of an aesthetic political state to Marx's vision of a creative *Gemeinwesen*, Wagner's praxis of his Bayreuth theatrocracy, and Nietzsche's call for a Dionysian "aesthetic morals." Indeed its traces are evident in such twentieth-century extensions as the critical theory of Herbert Marcuse and Martin Heidegger's polis thought. Far from simply closing off the classical moment in European thought for civic justice, Shaftesbury opened up an entirely new area of contributions to ideals committed to the aesthetic and the political that need to be further clarified in terms fitting Murphy's narrative.[75]

---

[72] Shlegel [1956], and Weiser [1916].

[73] Details are in "Winckelmann: The Myth of the Aesthetic State," in Chytry [1989], 11-37.

[74] Frankfurt for Goethe and Biberach for Wieland. The third, Friedrich Schiller, was brought up in Württemberg, a modest state centered around Stuttgart and the single constitutional state in Germany during that period. Bruford [1962], 26-39; Elson [1913]; "The Legacy of Shaftesbury," in Witte [1949], 83-92.

[75] Although in other publications Murphy does write about this aspect of the German intellectual tradition, he clearly thinks it belongs to a mistaken "autochthonous" reading of the importance of the polis, and therefore he is equally dismissive of what he considers to be Martin Heidegger's recasting of "the romantic aesthetics of Schiller" and of "Herbert Marcuse's

Finally, *sixth*, Murphy's general scepticism toward American contributions to his model overlooks an area that he himself has favorably marked out, namely Thomas Jefferson's vision and creation of the University of Virginia. As studies of the history of the American university have confirmed, the extended American civic affair with the ideal of the college or university, more particularly with the remarkable set of experimentations that constitute the modern American university city as a physical, cultural and utopian space, has more often than not been driven by emancipatory goals that valorize these civic spacings not only pedagogically but also aesthetically and politically.[76]

Central to such studies is the argument that the creation of university cities is a distinctly American contribution to the history of the "concept of colleges and universities as communities in themselves—in effect, as cities in microcosm" captured in the social and pedagogical phenomenon of the *campus*,[77] a word that is traceable to the distinctive spirit of *campanilismo* once dominating the Italian city-republic.[78] In Paul Venable Turner's comprehensive account of the Campus, the richness of this tradition as an ongoing, educational, social, even political and utopian project is handsomely conveyed. His account helps to explain why even that influential historian of the City, Lewis Mumford, might detect clear analogies between the historical polis and the "university city," and also why the former president of the University of California, Clark Kerr, in coining the concept of "multiversity" should associate that phenomenon with the university becoming a "city" or "Ideopolis."[79] As network society presently expands at the pace and intensity recounted by Manuel Castells, it is clear that the university city, one of the central nodes within this technological universe, will become even more critical to future cultural and technological developments, possibly evolving into the cyber equivalent of the far-flung colonies of ancient thalassocentric Hellenic poleis.[80]

Schillerian aesthetic." Murphy [1998], 104. Some passing references to Hegel, Marx and Walter Benjamin notwithstanding, it would appear that only in the case of Heidegger has Murphy made any extended effort to sufficiently consider the appropriate texts. Murphy [1993], 57-59.

[76] See Chapter 8 below and Chytry [2003].

[77] Turner [1984], 3, who claims that the word was first used for "grounds" at Princeton University (then the College of New Jersey) in 1774 to replace the Harvard *yard* or *grounds* (4, 47). See also Gaines [1991].

[78] Waley [1969], 8.

[79] Kerr envisaged three stages in the history of the university as a civic reality, advancing from village (the early university and college) through town (Oxbridge) to city (Berkeley): the modern university is therefore "a system of government like a city, or a city state: the city state of the multiversity." Kerr [1963], 20, 91. Mumford himself pointed to the example of the campus and city of the University of California, Berkeley. Mumford [1961], plate 56 (432-3).

[80] Castells [2001], esp. "The Geography of the Internet: Networked Places," 207-46. Castells provides a useful e-linked bibliography of cybergeographies displaying the global coordinates of

IV

These six suggested adjustments might be more or less comfortably absorbed into Murphy's narrative. There remains, nonetheless, the task of assessing the general viability of Murphy's theory itself. In this final section, three recommendations are offered in consequence of such an assessment.

First, if Murphy wishes his theory of civic justice to enjoy a more global contextuality, he should consider the relevance for his model of "the theory of the central place" in urban and sacred geography.[81] Particularly the work of Paul Wheatley and Robert McC. Adams, drawing on the classic investigations by Fustel de Coulanges into the origins and character of urbanity, its intraneous affinity to ceremonial space as the city center, and the geomantic propensities underlying the "classical-magical basis of the traditional city,"[82] could be incorporated into a global theory of civic space and city-state which helps position Murphy's own Mediterranean orientation.

In this endeavor cross-cultural comparison could furnish extra help in light of the difficulty of raising testable hypotheses about the early history of the city tradition. Granted the improbability of any prior communication with the Mediterranean, one important area for such comparison might be the "ancient Mexican city-state" as "the center of life"[83] for a Mesoamerican urban tradition that starts with the exemplar Teotihuacán and passes through four intermediate capitals before culminating in Tenochtitlán, the vision of which city center awakened awe even among its ultimate destroyers, the Spanish conquistadores.[84] A second area is the rich literature on the "cosmic state" of classical Hindu-Buddhist kingdoms in South and Southeast Asia, based originally on the theory of Robert Heine-Geldern and subsequently applied to a wide variety of examples from Orissa to Angkor and Bali.[85] A third area would include studies of Chinese urban centers to which Wheatley himself has contributed an incisive set of readings of Chinese urbanity, the ceremonial

---

the internet universe (246). The similarity with Kerr's vision of a growing geographical cluster of university centers or "Ideopolis" is patent. Compare Kerr's geography of such "clustering universities" and "scientifically oriented industrial and governmental enterprises" in the Boston-Washington and California "plateaus." Kerr [1963], 91-94.

[81] This theory is associated primarily with Paul Wheatley. Other pertinent terms include "celestial archetypes" (Mircea Eliade), "astrobiology" and "bio-astrale" (René Berthelot).

[82] "The Ancient Chinese City as a Cosmo-Magical Symbol," in Wheatley [1971], 411-76; Adams [1966]; Coulanges [1956].

[83] Carrasco [1982], 2.

[84] Carrasco [1982], 1-9. For the conquistadores' astonishment at the size of the great arcaded space of the city market at Tlatelolco, see Thomas [1995], 296-8. Thomas provides references for the first European descriptions of Tenochtitlán as a "great Venice" (705 [note 12]).

[85] Heine-Geldern [1956]; Kulke [1978]; Tambiah [1976]; Geertz [1980].

center, and parallelisms of microcosm and macrocosm.[86] A fourth area might be the civic spaces of revolution, as in the case of the Czech Velvet Revolution of 1989 and St. Wenceslas Square in Prague/Praha.[87] In looking at these alternative patterns which share a common focus on the civic center and city-state forms, Murphy's theory would be enabled not only to entertain universal features related to the overall process of urbanity but also to demonstrate more effectively the uniqueness of his Hellenic-classical version.

Of course, once such comparisons, and their ramifications, are inaugurated, Murphy's model must face, *second*, the challenge of overall philosophical viability, for what Murphy is ultimately defending is the ontological priority of the concrete open space from which his poleis and their attendant (civic) justice emerge. Sadly (perhaps) for Murphy's own politics,[88] his most potentially helpful ally in this project is none other than Martin Heidegger, for among the major philosophers Heidegger alone has marked out an extensive discursive domain that both prioritizes openness as such for the experience of being or reality and attaches that openness to a more exact meaning for "polis" itself.

That Heidegger's controversial approach to *Da-sein* is not so much about "human being" or "being-there" as it is about "openness" has been explicitly confirmed by Heidegger himself to English-speaking translators of his thought.[89] This confirmation buttresses Heidegger's more general approach to truth as *aletheia* which he defines as disclosedness or revealing (*Entbergen, Unverborgenheit*), and with which he counters more conventional theories of truth as correspondence or coherence. *Aletheia* for Heidegger is akin to the lighting of a clearing (*Lichtung*), valorizing the sense of "lightness" from which *Lichtung* may be said to have been derived.[90] Such lightness entails, as the foundational verb *lichten* suggests: "to make something light, something *free*

---

[86] Wheatley [1971]. Wheatley has also written extensively on Japanese, Southeast Asian, and even Islamic cities.

[87] Kukral [1997]. See also Chapter 4 below for more details on this theme.

[88] While Murphy's antipathy toward Heidegger is clear in his article already cited (Murphy [1993], 57-59), *Civic Justice* contains no references to Heidegger in the text nor in the index; however, this reviewer found at least two references to Heidegger in the notes. Murphy [2001], 36, 89. On the other hand, Murphy does show appreciation for the thought of Heidegger's student Hannah Arendt (155).

[89] According to William Lovitt, "Heidegger has emphatically expressed his preference for 'openness' and his disapprobation of 'there' as a translation of *da* in *Dasein*." Heidegger [1977], xxxv (note 2).

[90] Derived from the French word "clairière," conventionally defined as "a place unencumbered by trees in a forest" (following the *Larousse* definition: "Endroit dégarni d'arbres dans une forêt"). It might be noted that this is a rare case of a Heideggerian etymological move that derives from the French and Latin rather than from the German and Greek.

and open."[91] The openness of *aletheia* is hence the clearing which *as* the "free and open" is coterminous with the manifestation and presencing of not only light (*das Licht*)—as illumination—but also darkness.[92] Accordingly, such "free openness" (*das freie Offene*), preceding and preserving both presencing and absencing, is that *in which* everything has its "place" (*Ort*). In effect it is the "heart" both of *aletheia* and of clearing as a "place of stillness" *(Ort der Stille)* that, to go back to Murphy's own philosophical sources, Parmenides originatively declared to be the perfect circle of the manifestable collected and preserved in its unhiddenness (*Unverborgenheit*).[93]

What gives this approach "political" potency is Heidegger's parallel effort to clarify the meaning of "polis" as something more primary than, albeit foundational for, the "political" as commonly understood.[94] Heidegger's original, and best known, definition of the polis describes it as "the site of history, the *Da*, *in* which, *out* of which and *from* which history happens [*Geschichte geschieht*]." This prior ground and "place" (*Ort*) of the "openness of being" is a crossroads wherein the work of the poet, the sculptor, the architect, the thinker, athlete and priest can be fashioned, and is therefore necessarily prior to the "political" which is its derivative.[95] During 1941-3 Heidegger extended this reading to emphasize that "the πόλις does not show itself to be determined as 'political.' The πόλις, and precisely it, is therefore no 'political' concept."[96] Instead, he added to his earlier definition of the polis the addendum that polis is "the essential site of history as determined by the holy."[97] Far from implying theological or religious priorites, the "holy" for Heidegger suggested an "originative wholeness" that characteristically only the poet could grasp and make into a site or "play-space" for celebrating the festival or feast. The festival is the connection between the polis as a dynamic settlement akin to a vortex or whirlpool around a still center (πόλος) and the

---

[91] Heidegger [1969], 72 (emphasis added). Indeed, Heidegger keeps close to the French meaning by using as his example a forest made "open and free" of trees.

[92] As well as other such phenomena as sounds and echoes.

[93] Heidegger [1969], 72-80.

[94] A full account of Heidegger's reading of polis and the relevant texts is provided in "The Timeliness of Martin Heidegger," in Chytry [2005], 74-92. See also Chapter 4 below.

[95] Heidegger [1966], 117 (emphasis in original), 147.

[96] Heidegger [1975-], ii-53,98, 99. These lectures, taking place around the general period of the battle of Stalingrad (1941-3), show the degree to which Heidegger attacked the "political" or power-state *(Machtstaat)* reading of the Greeks, for which he blamed Jacob Burckhardt, Nietzsche, and "National Socialist ideologues." It is in this sense that Heidegger polemically declared that the Greeks were the "apolitical people" par excellence. The connection between Stalingrad and these texts has already been argued by Heller [1997], 247-62.

[97] Heidegger, "Andenken," in Heidegger [1975-], i-4, 88.

greeting of the holy that is worded by the poet to establish the historicality of a true time in the eventing (*Ereignis*) of that festival. As a result of the priority of the holy and its attendant celebration in the festival, Heidegger's notion of the polis is shown to be originatively neither "political" nor "nationalistic;" rather, polis is the siting of the festival by which first and foremost humans partake creatively of the underlying freeness and openness that constitute the truth of things.[98]

Does Heidegger's speculative confirmation of the openness directing civic justice facilitate Murphy's challenge to alternate theories of justice on the academic landscape today? Answering this question leads to the *third* and final recommendation by touching on the relevance, already claimed by Murphy, of the category of beauty for a full account of the polis.

In *On Beauty and Being Just* Elaine Scarry has attempted to take seriously the double meaning contained in John Rawls' famous formula, justice as fairness, to argue the case for an intrinsic overlap between justice and beauty through the human demand for "fairness."[99] Scarry's point of departure is Rawls' reading of "fairness" as "the circumstances of the original position"—the "state of nature" of classical contractualist theory—which Rawls defines as "the symmetry of everyone's relation to each other."[100]

According to his most prominent rivals in critical theory, Rawls' original position already assumes too much. For Jürgen Habermas, the plurality of interests constituting modernity offers far too weak a reed for either moral (pace Rawls) or ethical (pace Rousseauean) solutions to the problem of fairness, instead of which Habermas argues the priority of the discourse principle that "just those action norms are valid to which all possibly affected persons could agree as participants in rational discourses."[101] For Jacques Derrida meanwhile, even a Habermasian discourse validation is already complicitous with the logocentrism of propositional narratives, against which deconstruction can only grant, and support, the view that the "idea of justice" proper is an "experience of the impossible," the "arrival of the Other as a singularity always Other," "a messianic promise."[102]

---

[98] The relevant terms are *das Feiern, festlich, das Fest*: the celebratory, festive, festival and feast. Heidegger [1975-], ii-52, 146, 91, 67, 94, 78.

[99] Scarry [1999].

[100] This passage has already been exploited on behalf of the aesthetic tradition by Chytry [1989], 491. Rawls [1971], 12. Other variants: "the parties are symmetrically situated in the original position," and "citizens' representatives are to be selected symmetrically in the original position." Rawls [2001], 18.

[101] Habermas [1996], 107.

[102] "Force of Law: The Mystical Foundation of Authority," in Derrida [2002], 254, 256. As might be expected, Habermas dismissingly classifies Derrida's effort as an example of "aesthetic

In this gallery of alternatives, Murphy's theory of civic justice most closely approximates Rawls' "symmetrical" moment and therefore Rawlsian justice as fairness, but only if it can satisfy both Habermas' and Derrida's concerns toward Rawlsian overdetermination. Symmetry is the decisive term because it raises the key notion of equality for both justice and beauty: as equality of relations, symmetry exploits the distributive element in justice, while in terms of beauty symmetry reinforces the equilibration of mutual enlivenment that, Scarry importantly suggests, operates between beholder and beholdee to encourage an ongoing expansiveness of reciprocal endearment. Such expansiveness serves the distributive in justice in those cases in which the latter has either not emerged or has been undermined. Moreover, even during the active operation of justice, the symmetry of "beauty assists us in our attention to justice." The cases that Scarry instances are relevant for Murphy's purposes, touching both on the occurrence of the political assembly and the rowing together by Athenians in defense of their ancient democracy. In both, a primarily sensory embodiment of justice that might be otherwise experienced only piecemeal or perhaps too conceptually is turned into the unique experience of "justice being sensorily present."[103]

Through her reading of the "aliveness" arising between beholder and beholdee that elucidates the reciprocity of aesthetic and juridical fairness in "a site of beauty," Scarry succeeds in recouping the original Platonic claim for beauty as incitement to procreation as well as for poiesis as the passage from "nothing" to "something."[104] Both experiences can be articulated in terms satisfying the kind of postmetaphysical insistence on "weak" claims for parties to just arrangements without overlooking the degree to which even the barest such requirements—whether as hypothetical original position, state of nature, discourse condition, or deferential waiting for the nonarticulable (messianic) other—presuppose humans who are potentially receptive to reciprocities that pertain universally to dwelling in the world. Nothing in this claim challenges the exigencies of pluralism; to the contrary, it is more frequently the case that art and related aesthetic attitudes furnish a more agreeable arena for shared exchange among representatives of differing religions and ideologies precisely in the loose dependence on the free play of the imagination and openness to

---

assimilations." Habermas [1996], xli and 522 (note 6).

[103] Scarry [1999], 86, 108.

[104] With regard to the relevance of "aesthetic" categories, Heidegger's account of the polis places great importance on this Platonic reading of "poiesis." Strictly speaking, however, Heidegger prefers to stay clear of the "aesthetic" and "beauty," both of which notions he interprets as consequences of a post-Cartesian metaphysics that demotes the poetic to a mere sensory appendage of thought.

difference that the aesthetic dimension sanctifies in comparison with formalized rational discourse. It is partly for such reasons that the classical German aesthetics of Friedrich Schiller concluded that beauty is in fact "freedom in appearance" or "the shine of freedom," that is (to merge his thought with Heidegger's): beauty is the sensuous experience of the openness by which poiesis, the leap from the hidden to the manifest, "happens"—and which, as a result, sustains polis.[105]

These broad recommendations—a more global approach to the themes of civic space and city-state; the relevance of Heidegger's philosophy for a more comprehensive thought supporting the priority of openness and celebration giving rise to, and sustaining, the polis; and a theory of justice that valorizes the fair play of both beauty and justice—are loosely offered to help Murphy on his important path. That path, as Murphy writes elsewhere, was taken, in opposition to the aporiae of professional and academic alternatives of the 1960s, by social thinkers who, like Murphy, deliberately sought out "the same dazzling phosphorescent light" of classical thought that gave birth to "the Mediterranean city."[106] For political and juridical thought, this "Mediterranean city" is always there to be discovered, and rediscovered. In the constancy of Peter Murphy's ongoing search, so ably documented and theorized in *Civic Justice*, both the polis and the poiesis of beauty (*Kallipolis*)—along with the "fair play" of (civic) justice—continue to be well served.

---

[105] "Kallias oder Über die Schönheit," in Schiller [1966], iv, 82, 93. Also: "Freedom in appearance is one with beauty" (92).

[106] Murphy [1998], 112, 113.

CHAPTER FOUR

Jan Patočka and Central European Polis Thought

From Phenomenology to the Czech Velvet Revolution

If Peter Murphy helps us espouse the "fair play" of polis or civic justice through his receptivity to the open frameworks of the "Mediterranean city," Jan Patočka's life and work epitomize the impact of polis thought on a thinker unfortunately confined to a "post-totalitarian" political system located in the heart of Central Europe.[1]

Jan Patočka is the most important modern Czech philosopher, not least for the range of his original and provocative contributions to a variety of philosophical and scholarly areas. Among those areas is that of the political, where Patočka's theoretical contributions meshed with his Socratic courage in helping to initiate the Charta 77 movement and in suffering for that participation.

This chapter clarifies an important element in the theory behind Patočka's participation and locates it within larger historical patterns of Central European thought and culture. It seeks to show how polis thought helps clarify the larger

[1] Earlier versions of this chapter were published in Simona Goi & Frederick M. Dolan (eds.), *Between Terror and Freedom: Politics, Philosophy, and Fiction Speak of Modernity* (Lanham, MA: Lexington Books, 2006), 119-172, and presented at the Jan Patočka Memorial Conference held in Prague/Praha, Czech Republic, on 21 April 2007. My thanks in particular to Dr. Ivan Chvatík, Director of the Jan Patočka Archives, Center for Theoretical Study, Charles University, Prague, Czech Republic, for granting me the privilege of two extensive discussions with him in Prague/Praha during August 2004 on Jan Patočka's philosophy and life as well as for his comments and suggestions on an earlier version of this manuscript. I am also grateful to Professor Erazim Kohák, translator of Jan Patočka's works into English, for providing me through electronic correspondence his stimulating interpretation of both Jan Patočka's and Václav Havel's influences on subsequent Czech politics. Granted the eminent status of both these major readers of the Jan Patočka legacy, the standard caveat that all interpretations in this article are the responsibility of the author is all the more applicable. I am also thankful to Dr. Ivan Havel, Director of the Center for Theoretical Study, for inviting me to give a lecture on 6 August 2003 at the Center which initiated my first contact with the Jan Patočka Archives.

ramifications of a philosophy that influenced a political transformation later dubbed the Velvet Revolution.

I

The origins of polis thought in Central Europe are first clearly detected in the eighteenth-century German cultural revival after mid-century. Central to this revival were the epiphanies of the archeologist-historian Johann Joachim Winckelmann whose Athens-oriented Hellenism blasted a prior unitary view of classical culture and replaced it with his uncompromising preference for the cultural Greeks over the martial Romans. Winckelmann's works and the epic nature of his life and death swept through Young Germany, becoming a bugle call for Sturm und Dränger poets, thinkers, and vagabonds to transform the Duchy of Weimar into a veritable "Athens on the Ilm" to be fashioned by Goethe, Schiller, Herder and Wieland in active cooperation with its young duke Karl August.[2]

The pragmatic grounds for such a reception may be attributed in large part to the confinements of eighteenth-century *Kleinstaaterei* under the shadow of French cultural hegemony. These factors had already encouraged a positive reception of the Hellenism of such liberal English writers as Shaftesbury and had linked up with the new interest in folk or popular culture as captured in the writings of the Swiss critic J. J. Breitinger. However Winckelmann's aesthetic evangelium on behalf of Hellas—a shrewd mixture of philological reasoning and archaeological rhapsodizing—sharply clarified the model that Goethe and his Weimar peers came to seek. They could be confident that there were material parallels between Athens and Weimar: both reflected populations of the same range, a similar organic character to their daily life, and Athenian cultural models were available to stimulate the court life of Weimar. Finally, as in the case of ancient Athens, Weimar encouraged its literary avant-garde to directly enter public life, from Goethe the privy counciller to Herder the general superintendent of school system and Wieland the publisher.[3]

In the long run Weimar "aesthetic humanism" impacted Central Europe on a scale far exceeding the modest size and population of the Duchy. Its Goethean message of Hellenizing classicism became the cultural standard for the pedagogical system at the University of Berlin set up by Goethe's admirer Wilhelm von Humboldt for future generations of German students and acolytes, and its more radical implications were carried forward by an impressive body of

---

[2] The classic account in English remains Bruford [1962].

[3] "Winckelmann: The Myth of Aesthetic Hellas" and "Wieland, Herder, Goethe: Weimar Aesthetic Humanism," in Chytry [1989], 11-69.

Weimar and Jena intellectuals and poets who under the driving force of revolutionary ideals carved out new ideals for a Germany of *Dichter und Denker*.[4] From the German Idealism of the Swabian colleagues Hölderlin, Hegel and Schelling to the political radicalism of the Young Hegelians including the Young Karl Marx, this influence may be detected in a litany of phrases such as the "aesthetic state," the "theocracy of the beautiful," and the "beautiful democracy" of the ancient Athenians.

The watershed for these ebullient ideals is the failure of the 1848-9 revolutions in Central Europe and the subsequent hegemony of the conservative Realpolitik of Bismarck and Wilhelm I in Central Europe during the 1850s and 1860s. Until the 1870s the Hellenic ideal with its image of classical Athens had still partly served as an ideal for a culture familiar with medium-sized states and political entities. Thus Hegel could seriously contemplate his "rational state" as conforming to the sizes of a modern Bavaria or Württemberg. Similarly the revolutionary Wagner could be driven by his image of the classicist Johann Gustav Droysen's account of ancient Athens to join the 1849 barricades in Dresden and become a political outlaw throughout the 1850s fighting for his revitalized aesthetic state via the Wagnerian *Gesamtkunstwerk*.[5] But after the foundation of the German *Reich* in 1870, these more familiar political landmarks in which Weimar and Hellenism had coalesced gave way to "blood,-and-iron" priorities. Not only the later Wagner, but also his one-time follower Friedrich Nietzsche reflect this concession to an imperialistic and increasingly brutalist cultural context.[6] Whereas in his readings of the "Greek state" the young Nietzsche continued to extend the Hellenism of the Weimar tradition however much radicalized, the later Nietzsche explicitly contended that the Greeks could no longer mean what imperial Rome promised to a future age of nihilism and his favored post-nihilist Caesars.[7]

Accordingly, the earlier Hellenism lost much of its humanistic flavor to the conservative revolutionary politics of the early twentieth century. Among major philosophers Martin Heidegger stood at the crossroads of such martial planetarianism insofar as he succumbed to support of, and membership in, the German National Socialist Party and espoused stances that clearly associate him with the conservative revolutionary attitudes of such "heroic vitalists" as Ernst Jünger.[8] Nonetheless, at the same time that he was assuming the position of

[4] Marchand [1996] and Chytry [1999b]. For the idealist reading of this Hellenism, see "Idealism" in Chytry [1989], 107-218.

[5] For more details see Chapter 6 below.

[6] See Chapter 6 below for more details.

[7] Chytry [1989], 198, 278, 326-327, 344-349.

[8] Rabinbach [1997]; Chytry [1989], 373-375. Heidegger remained a member of the National

rector of the nazifying University of Freiburg in 1933-34 (attended by Jan Patočka during the *Revolutionssemester* of 1933), Heidegger also plunged into an extended dialogue with Hellenic thought and the poet Friedrich Hölderlin. The eventual results turned out to be the first explicit modern articulation of polis thought. The writings that cover Heidegger's polis thought extend from 1934-5—when Heidegger turned away from direct participation in the National Socialist revolution by resigning his rectorship at the University of Freiburg—to 1942-3—the climax of his retrieval of Greek originative thinking simultaneously with the decisive battle of Stalingrad in which the fate of National Socialism was decided. If Heidegger can be seen in retrospect as the culmination of nearly two centuries of German Hellenism, he is no less the first formal adherent to the primacy of polis thought within what had conventionally passed for political theory or philosophy.

As pointed out in Chapters 1 and 3, Heidegger's basic definition in 1935 of the polis as "the history site, the Da, *in* which, *out of* which, and *for* which Da-sein as the historical is"[9] was one that he sustained throughout, only amplifying this definition with the 1942 addendum that this polis was to be "determined by the holy [*heilig*]."[10] The "holy" itself he came interpret as a "greeting" which could only be received by the "poet" whose subsequent words "named" the holy and opened out a space and environmentality for the world of humans. In bare terms, this is what Heidegger localized as polis, the siting for humans' relating to the "greeting" of the "coming" that the poet founds.[11] Yet, rather than thinking of this siting in terms of foundational institutions and practices that are normally called "political," Heidegger resorted to a more primordial set of communal phenomena to capture his originative sense of polis, a set that included the celebratory (*das Feiern*), the festive (*festlich*), and the festival or feast (*das Fest*). What is important to recognize here is that this is the only meaning that Heidegger was willing to ascribe to the idea of a "fatherland" (*Vaterland*).[12]

Socialist party until 1945.

[9] Heidegger [1966], 117 (emphasis in original).

[10] Heidegger [1975-], i-4, 88. Heidegger wished to title Plato's *Politeia*: "The 'Dialogue' about the Essence of the πόλις." "Platons Lehre von der Wahrheit" [1942] in Heidegger [1967], 119. Further details of Heidegger's polis thought are found in "The Timeliness of Martin Heidegger," in Chytry [2005], 81-91.

[11] Heidegger [1975-], ii-52, 193: "Das Stiften des kommenden Heiligen im Wort." The closing line of Hölderlin's "Andenken" reads: "Was bleibet aber, stiften die Dichter."

[12] For Heidegger, as the "fruit" of the "holy" the fatherland is never "political" in origin: "The turn toward the fatherlandish is however not also a turn toward the political." The fatherland is the highest aspect "only" in so far as it stems from the holy rather than from "political activity." Heidegger [1975-], ii-52, 141-142, 72-73.

After 1945 when Heidegger's complicity with National Socialism led to the stripping of his professorial post at Freiburg, Heidegger generally avoided any further development of his polis thought. In any event, even when compared with his poetic model Hölderlin, one of Heidegger's major weaknesses as a thinker had always been lack of concrete study of the political. Accordingly, it was rather Heidegger's students and other thinkers influenced by him who came to advance a more sophisticated reading of polis. As we noted in Chapter 1, these students included Hannah Arendt, Karl Löwith, and Herbert Marcuse. It is however the Czech philosopher Jan Patočka whose philosophy especially stands out in this respect. Patočka not only drew productively on Heidegger's polis thought but he also succeeded in making a significant original contribution that turned out to be directly relevant to the conditions of late twentieth-century Central European political reality and helped precipitate a set of movements called the Velvet Revolution.

II

A student of Edmund Husserl (as well as a good friend of Eugene Fink, Husserl's assistant during the 1930s), Jan Patočka also attended Martin Heidegger's lectures in Freiburg in 1933 and made original uses of the latter's thought particularly in his later years. Interpreters of Patočka's thought are content enough to grant that in his relation to these two major names of philosophical phenomenology Patočka was influenced not only by Husserl but also by Heidegger. They however would prefer to read the Heideggerian presence as an inconsistency in Patočka, one with which he spent his intellectual career grappling, and are above all unhappy with the increasing prominence of that thought in the final years of Patočka's own life, tending to regard such prominence as an unfortunate byproduct of Patočka's resigned state of mind after the defeat of the reformist Prague Spring of 1968-9 and therefore as far less important than his supposed lifetime allegiance to Husserl.[13] Unfortunately this reading—which itself generally prefers the admittedly revised rationality and humanism of the later Husserl of *The Crisis of European Sciences and Transcendental Phenomenology* of 1937-8 to the presumed "mysticism" and "irrationality" of the later Heidegger[14]—operates on the assumption that Patočka is primarily to be interpreted in terms of Husserl and

[13] On the other hand, Richard Rorty stresses the importance of Heidegger for Patočka. Rorty [1991].

[14] Thus Kohák refers to Patočka's last period as being "increasingly influenced by the dark romanticism of Nietzsche and Heidegger." "Translator's Postscript," in Patočka [1996b], 157.

Heidegger instead of considering the option that Patočka's *own* general intentions as an original thinker in his own right ought to be given priority.[15] Our reading of Patočka assumes the latter option.

What makes Patočka's own intellectual career of particular interest in this regard is the degree to which Patočka's early development grew directly out of the delicate relations between Husserl and Heidegger in the late 1920s and early 1930s. At this time Husserl's chosen heir Heidegger was not only breaking away from Husserlian phenomenology, but was also joining forces with German National Socialism in the *Revolutionssemester* of 1933. Patočka first met Husserl in Paris in 1929 through the introduction of the noted philosopher and historian of science Alexandre Koyré when Husserl gave the Paris lectures that were later expanded into his *Cartesian Meditations* (1931). In 1932-1933 Patočka received a Humboldt fellowship to study with Husserl in Freiburg during that same fateful summer semester of 1933. Although his time was spent mainly with Husserl (and Fink), it also included access to Heidegger's lectures,[16] even though, as Patočka later recounts, Husserl warned against any attempts to synthesize the Husserlian and Heideggerian positions. Notwithstanding this warning, Husserl seems to have continued acknowledging to Patočka Heidegger's "genial quality," and Patočka notes that in their serious labors both philosophers did not appear concerned with "the imposing political reality" of the moment.[17]

In 1934 Patočka received from Husserl the lectern that Tomáš G. Masaryk (1850-1937) had given Husserl many decades earlier when both men had been philosophy students at the University of Vienna under Franz Brentano. This gesture was apparently meant as the passing on of a "tradition" symbolized by Masaryk as social thinker and as the statesman who founded the Czechoslavak state in 1918, the homeland of both Patočka and the Bohemian-born Husserl.

---

[15] Kohák, the preeminent interpreter and translator of Patočka's thought in English, does argue that Patočka should be regarded as "an original thinker who has undertaken the daunting task of fusing Husserl's rationalism with Heidegger's romanticism." "Translator's Postscript," in Patočka [1996a], 175. But Kohák's admission that the "philosophy of the *Heretical Essays*— and the politics it entails—remain wholly alien to me" indicates the degree to which his own Husserlian and "Austro-Bohemian" proclivities prevent a full positive understanding of the Heideggerian dimension in Patočka. "Translator's Postscript," in Patočka [1996b], 159. Since these published comments, Kohák has amplified to me his serious misgivings regarding the conservative components to Patočka's thought. Personal and electronic communications, August 2004, Prague/Praha.

[16] Kohák notes that Patočka's first article on history, "Some Comments Concerning the Concepts of History and Historiography," in 1934 betrays a "distinctly Heideggerian" "tone." Kohák [1989], 27. Also Fink & Patočka [1999].

[17] Patočka [1976a], vii-xi.

Unfortunately a letter from Husserl to Masaryk which Patočka was to deliver never quite reached the elder statesman who in 1935 resigned from the presidency of the Czechoslovak state due to illnesses of old age that eventually brought about his death in 1937. Nonetheless, Patočka was instrumental in helping to invite Husserl to Prague/Praha in 1935 to give the important November lecture that became the basis for Husserl's final, albeit incomplete, work *The Crisis of European Sciences.*[18] By this stage Prague/Praha had become the center for intellectual refugees fleeing the conditions of Hitler's Germany, and Husserl, who as a Jew found himself an "inner emigrant" in Germany, was one of many notable figures who either visited or emigrated to the uniquely democratic Czechoslovak state for which the philosopher-statesman Masaryk had been mainly responsible. For Patočka meanwhile the following year 1936, characterized by German rearmament and occupation of the Rhineland as well as the outbreak of the Spanish civil war, began the collapse of these relatively favorable intellectual conditions for Prague/Praha and Czechoslovakia,[19] a year that for Patočka himself was marked by his academic habilitation at Prague/Praha with a thesis on the "natural world" (*přirozený svět*) that shared important affinities with Husserl's *Crisis* turn toward a more concrete reading of history and his new concept of the *Lebenswelt* ("life-world").[20]

Masaryk died in 1937 and Husserl followed in 1938, the year of the infamous Munich agreement in which Czechoslovak independence was sacrificed by the western powers Britain and France to the expansionist policies of the Third Reich. Patočka, who notwithstanding his qualifications for university teaching had been unable to secure an appropriate position since his habilitation, now found himself descending into the night of Nazi domination once German troops directly occupied the capital in 1939. For the duration of the second world war he survived intellectually with essays published in Czech periodicals that escaped the censor by the generality of their themes. These essays show his increasing efforts to shape a coherent understanding of the role of German thought in the philosophy of history simultaneously with the continuation of his habilitation struggle to clarify the meaning of the "natural world." During these fateful years when, as we have seen, Heidegger was confronting the world-historical issues of the battle of Stalingrad through an extensive dialogue with the poet Hölderlin and Presocratic thought, Patočka was similarly occupied with the Czech romantic poet Karel Hynek Mácha (1810-

[18] In 1934 it was Patočka who read Husserl's contribution to the Philosophical Congress in Prague. Kohák [1989], 9.

[19] Patočka [1976a], xv-xviii.

[20] See the French translation: Patočka [1976b].

1836) and a return to the Greeks. If Heidegger looked past the conventional reading of Hölderlin as a romantic poet to find in him the unique poetic voice of postmetaphysical thought, Patočka similarly avoided a romantic reading of Mácha's nature poetry by drawing from it a quasi-Heideggerian understanding of nature as the elemental relation of Sky and Earth—a reading not dissimilar to Heidegger's postwar "fourfold" (*Viertel*) of Men, Gods, Sky and Earth.[21] Moreover by the end of the war Patočka had amassed a formidable body of studies concentrating on Greek thought, both Presocratic and Socratic-Platonic to Aristotelian, that became the material for his postwar lectures to Czechoslovak students eager to regain access to the philosophical tradition after the drought of the German occupation period.[22]

Patočka actually taught only during two relatively brief periods in his life. His university position after Czechoslovak liberation from Nazi Germany (1945-9) was taken away after the Communist takeover of 1948, and a relative thaw after 1961 enabled him to return to publishing and teaching during the 1965-9 period that culminated in the Prague Spring of 1968-9, ending with a new crackdown that similarly deprived him of a university post. Between these two teaching periods Patočka had survived by working in centers associated respectively with Masaryk and the seventeenth-century Czech pansophist thinker Jan Amos Komenský (Comenius). Particularly the latter subject invigorated Patočka's lifelong inquiries into the break in European thought and culture of the sixteenth and seventeenth centuries from a perspective that highlighted the importance of Bohemian-Czech contributions.[23] After his second teaching period in the late 1960s Patočka reached an age enabling him to retire while remaining actively involved in his own writing and lecturing among private circles.

Accordingly, the 1965-1977 period of writing and teaching was the most prolific period of Patočka's production. In the works of this period Patočka carried Heidegger's polis thought into a direct involvement with the Charta 77 movement of 1977. This involvement eventually led to Patočka's own interrogation and death at the hands of police authorities in March 1977, but also, as a result, provided the Socratic inspiration for the dissident movement to be led by such students as Václav Havel and Václav Benda. Their success in creating a "parallel polis" (*paralelní polis*)[24] allowed these same dissidents

[21] *Symbol země u K. H. Máchy* (Earth as a Symbol according to K. H. Macha) (1944), cited and summarized in Kohák [1989], 34-35.

[22] E.g. Patočka [1990b].

[23] Patočka, "Komeniologické studie," in Patočka [1997-], ix.

[24] This term comes from the important dissident essay by Václav Benda, "The 'Parallel' *Polis*" (1978), translated in Skilling & Wilson [1991], 35-41. See also in the same volume the

to oppose and to eventually help overthrow the Czechoslovak communist government in the Velvet Revolution of 1989.

III

Jan Patočka's unique contribution as an original thinker begins and ends with the thematics of a "natural world" *(přirozený svêt)* that forms both the centerpiece of his habilitation thesis of 1936 and his last major work, the *Heretical Essays* of 1975. These thematics both link him with the Husserlian move associated with the *Crisis* arguments on historicity and *Lebenswelt* and with the Heideggerian motif of Truth as constituted by the opennness of human being in the unveiling and exposure of universal disclosure (ἀληθεια). In turn, "natural world," *Lebenswelt,* and the openness of disclosure converge on the central significance of polis (πόλις) as simultaneously "philosophical," "political," and "historical." As Paul Ricoeur puts it with regard to Patočka's priorities, the "public space" opened out by freedom for freedom means that the free thought of philosophy becomes, in its origins, inseparable from the conditions of the possibility of politics and history.[25] This, Patočka emphatically declares, is the epochal moment of the *terror* of a "shaking" by which history *as* history, for the first time, *is*—as precisely the "openness to the shaking" of "pre-historical" or "natural" (*přirozený*) humanity convulsed into an open and intrinsically questionable and questioning mode of being.[26]

What links this line of thought with the Husserl of the *Crisis* period is the latter's closing inquiries into the ramifications of the same western mode of rationality that for Husserl marked the distinctive character of European civilization. How was it, Husserl asked his 1935 Prague/Praha audience, that philosophy which had given birth to modern science (perhaps the proudest achievement in the western arsenal), became complicitous with a method of reading nature as objectivity in which inquiry itself was drained of meaning and turned into the "know-how" of technological thinking? It was a question that needed to be answered in such a way that what Husserl regarded as the rational core to the philosophical project—the centrality of the subject for an understanding of the nature of the phenomenal process prior to the kind of objectivizing that had led to the conundra of modern science—could be retained within what he came to refer to as "a transcendental-intersubjective

retrospective article by Martin Palouš, "Jan Patočka versus Václav Benda," 121-8.

[25] Ricoeur, "Introduction," in Patočka [1996b], viii.

[26] Patočka [1996b], 44.

consciousness" beyond "my individual self-consciousness."[27] This revision (albeit not entirely rejection) of his earlier Cartesian proclivities allowed Husserl to distinguish between the instrumentalism of objectifying modern science as a form of technocratism[28] and the genuine rationality underlying the philosophical project proper: the "difference," in Husserl's own language, "between objective science and science in general."[29]

The basis for this distinction rested on the primacy of what Husserl had come to call the *Lebenswelt*, or "life-world,"[30] for the very existence of those sciences themselves—along with the creators of science, their "scientific" communities, and their overall embeddedness. The *Lebenswelt* was the "actually experienceable" realm, the "subsoil" or "grounding soil" that remained prior to all objectivating; it was the "straightforwardly intuited world," the realm of "original self-evidences," that invariably situated subjects, as well as ultimately making possible the basic subject-object distinctions on which scientific thinking had emerged and prospered.[31] Husserl's counter to the draining of meaning in the modern sciences was therefore an attempt to formulate "a pure theory of the essence of the life-world" which would exploit the famous Husserlian bracketing step, or *epoché*, to encounter and understand the phenomena proper. This bracketing would be prior to the idealization and objectification processes by which science later succeeded in separating the "natural life," or "life within a universal unthematic horizon," from its own reading of the nature of reality as an infinite process of objectification.[32]

By injecting this *Lebenswelt* theme into philosophy, Husserl raised two issues that became pressing for Patočka. *First*, if the objectivating science of modernity which had become drained of meaning was itself grounded in a pre-scientific "life-world," how had it developed from those origins to ignore the priority of that same life-world that bestows meaning? This question was tantamount to resituating the Husserlian project of transcendental philosophy within human history, and in the Vienna lectures of May 1935 which would mark Patočka's future reflections, Husserl offered a dramatic account of the "birthplace" of the European spirit and culture that located it in "the ancient Greek nation [*die altgriechesche Nation*] of the seventh and sixth centuries

---

[27] Husserl [1970], 202.

[28] Patočka himself often refers to "technoscience" or "technologism." "The 'Natural' World and Phenomenology" [1967], in Patočka [1989], 245; also Patočka [1996b], 71.

[29] Husserl [1970], 123. That this latter science, or "science in general," is identical with true philosophy is explicitly affirmed by Husserl: "Radically presupposition-less and ultimately grounded science, or philosophy—this is simply another expression for the same thing" (195).

[30] Also "natural life-world." Husserl [1970], 154.

[31] Husserl [1970], 124, 131, 123, 127.

[32] Husserl [1970], 141, 145.

B.C." The overriding justification for considering "Europe" as a unity, namely its commitment to a "universal science, science of the universe, of the all-encompassing unity of all that is," was first grasped by "a single nation, the Greek nation" [*die griechische Nation*], due to its historical moment of experiencing the "outbreak or irruption of philosophy" in what Husserl dubbed the "theoretical attitude": "the attitude of θαυμάζειν," or "wonder."[33] From this stage on, the option of thinking theoretically, free of all practical interests, of man as a "nonparticipating spectator," burst upon world history. Indeed, in an important sense this event *constituted* world history through the figure of the philosopher and his communal circle of collaborative thinkers.[34] Such a process, according to Husserl, followed a complicated route to "ideal norms" on which the Greek philosophers eventually settled for their absolute standard of "ideal truth." The unfortunate result of this process was however that these same Greek philosophers helped commit the fatal error of separating the "ideal" from its life-world and encouraged the overall process of an objectification in which only the "ideal" was accepted as the "real," to be investigated by the "ideal" instruments of mathematics and geometry. Eventually Cartesian algebraic geometry encouraged the identification of the object of philosophical-scientific inquiry with that which was the most calculable and resulted in a world-view that carried the twin fallacies of "physicalism" and "naturalism."[35]

Whence emerges the *second* important consequence for Patočka. In this epochal process of objectivation the role of meaning that had resided in the subject and human being had also been undermined by the "psychophysicalism" of a modern psychology mimicking the objectivation processes of the modern natural sciences. It had thus helped to engender, according to Husserl's diagnosis, the very "sickness" of modern European culture *circa* 1935.[36] For Husserl himself, the solution was not however to abandon the subject but to engage in the project of a new "transcendental psychology" which would reclaim the true subjectivity that engaged in the same bracketing operation

[33] "The Vienna Lecture," in Husserl [1970], 276, 277, 273, 285. "Die Krisis des Europäischen Menschentums und die Philosophie," in Husserl [1962], 314-348 (esp. 321, 322).

[34] It is worth noting that other than providing a few vague allusions to ancient Greek curiosity and a playfulness made possible by occasional freedom from practical tasks, Husserl explicitly put aside the central question of how this Greek proclivity for "wonder" had *itself* emerged in the first place from its concrete life-world. Rather, he preferred to stress the more vital question "for us" of its further development from "mere" θαυμάζειν to *theōria.*

[35] The details of this stimulating argument are provided in the famous excerpt, "The Origin of Geometry," in Husserl [1970], Appendix VI, 353-78. It should be noted that "geometry" is here more broadly meant to cover all "shapes existing mathematically in pure space-time" (354).

[36] That this entire process was responsible for "the European sickness" is strongly affirmed by Husserl: "This is, indeed, my conviction." "Vienna Lecture," in Husserl [1970], 272.

through which philosophy and science could return to the starting point of the phenomenon and the life-world. This newer reading of subjectivity did not treat the spirit [*Geist*] as a mere "real annex" to the body or corporeality of dualistic psychophysicalist psychology. Rather, it recognized spirit as that which uniquely "exists in itself and for itself, is self-sufficient," and only to that extent is genuinely accessible to rational and authentically scientific treatment.[37]

Drawing on the priority of intentionality that had served to mark out the particular project of phenomenology since the work of Husserl's—and Masaryk's—teacher Franz Brentano, Husserl insisted on an "intentional psychology" that granted that the ego or subject was "an inward-being-for-one-another and mutual interpretation." It also granted that this "intentional mutual internality" accommodated itself to the fact that as transcendental ego the subject both "constituted" the world as such, including the "life-world," and also formed the human ego in that very same world which engaged in the inquiry that established the fact of such a transcendental ego. Any properly phenomenological inquiry therefore meant that the subject that inquired into the life-world itself—again, for Husserl the "grounding soil" from which all science and rationality had historically developed through the theoretical attitude—required a historical, if transcendental, understanding: "The universality of the absolute spirit surrounds everything that exists with an absolute historicity, to which nature is subordinated as a spiritual structure."[38]

By knotting the historical conditions of interwar Europe with the twin problems of the historicity of the theoretical attitude of philosophy (along with the subsequent career of rationality and science) and the larger impact of that attitude on the primacy of reflection and subjectivity, Husserl's *Crisis* readings proved pivotal for the subsequent philosophical career of Patočka. The themes that Husserl raised became even more central later, according to Patočka, when it became clear that although the particular nadir of "irrationalism" that marked the 1935 period—presumably the growth and success of European fascism at that time—had been overcome in the second world war, the characteristics of culture that Husserl had diagnosed had in fact intensified in the intervening period.[39] In this sense of sharing a common project and remaining committed to

[37] This entire passage is italicized by Husserl himself in the "Vienna Lecture" in Husserl [1970], 297; Husserl [1962], 345. Husserl stressed that as objectivism psychology could not successfully approach "as its subject matter the soul in its own essential sense, which is, after all, the ego that acts and suffers." Husserl [1970], 296.

[38] Husserl [1970], 298, 202, 297.

[39] Patočka specifically refers to 1935 as "a time when irrationalism was reaching its peak." Patočka, "Edmund Husserl's Philosophy of the Crisis of the Sciences and His Conception of a Phenomenology of the 'Life-World'" [1971], in Patočka [1989], 224.

the primacy of the phenomenon, Patočka continued an heir to Husserl throughout his own later philosophical career.

Nonetheless, Patočka found seriously faulty Husserl's own solution to the crisis that Husserl had so effectively articulated. According to Patočka, this "life-world" or "natural world" that Husserl had posited was mistakenly restricted to "the product of the common achievements of subjectivity for whom this world is nothing but a common link devoid of any genuine substantiality." Husserl's mistake, a product of his lingering commitment to the primacy of an "absolute subjectivity," had been to mix into his analysis of the life-world an "apodictic immanence given in a reflection of the stream of consciousness which presents itself to it with an absolute originality." If then subjectivity according to Husserl was basically "the natural world itself," it would appear that there was no need to posit another "infinite foundation" such as the phenomenon of the "natural" world in the first place.[40]

What was needed, Patočka insisted, was an account of the life-world or natural world that restored it to its intrinsic "physical, corporeal existence" through a more thoughtful reading of basic intentionality as an originary active factor foregrounding the "for the sake of which" or *pragmata* that drove action. Such an account would then be enabled to highlight the "world" itself as that which invariably transcended, while remaining foundational for, all such discrete objectivating actions. The natural world was therefore "the worldhood of the world toward which the human *Dasein* transcends himself" through experiencing that world as a world of good (and evil) in which the "for the sake of which" guides all structuring (the "good"). It was therefore equally a world composed of *finite* subjectivity invariably turning toward things and its understanding of them rather than the world made possible by Husserl's *absolute* subjectivity. As such, the natural world was meant to be lived in, containing indeterminate instantiations of embodiment which also included overriding orientations toward Sky and Earth, "the mystery of things and of life," "a good ever mysterious in its indispensable presence and accompanied by a no less mysteriously ambiguous shadow."[41]

---

[40] "Edmund Husserl's Philosophy of the Crisis of the Sciences" in Patočka [1989], 233, 234. Also: Husserl's life-world was "a sea of allegedly transcendental intersubjectivity surrounding objective unities constituted as unities of meaning by the common efforts of communicating consciousness" (233). For Patočka's critiques of Husserl's "absolute subjectivity," see 236 and "The 'Natural' World and Phenomenology" [1967], in Patočka [1989], 271. Patočka calls Husserl the "last great *diadochos*" in the lineage of the "philosophical ideal of life in truth" that began with "Ionian protophilosophy." Patočka [1996b], 82.

[41] "Edmund Husserl's Philosophy of the Crisis of the Sciences," in Patočka [1989], 234, 235, 236. While these strictures regarding Husserl's thought are found throughout Patočka's writings, this particular version is probably the most compact.

If Patočka's language and preferences sound Heideggerian, they were meant to be.[42] Since 1933-1934 Patočka had incorporated Heidegger's contributions to phenomenology[43] into his own more comprehensive approach to the life-world that Husserl's investigations had yielded. While Husserl was to be congratulated for stubbornly holding philosophy to the task of concentrating on the phenomenon and therefore of "manifestation," it was Heidegger, Patočka asserted, who had worked out the proper implication: since world belonged to manifestation, "the being of the manifestation is not human doing" and therefore "it is the manifestation, the being of phenomena, that phenomenology, in my view, sees."[44] Accordingly, in launching his final and perhaps most important work, the *Heretical Essays*, Patočka made it clear that Heidegger's philosophy was "better suited to serve as a starting point for philosophizing about history" and that his own *Heretical Essays* were to deal with problems "in light of motifs taken over from" Heidegger's superior reading of philosophy, history and freedom.[45]

IV

From the start the *Heretical Essays* makes plain what gives Heidegger's thought such relevance for Patočka's response to Husserl's *Crisis* challenge. If the phenomenon is the alpha and omega of philosophical inquiry, then, according to Patočka, Heidegger's approach alone—unlike Husserl's failure to grasp the originary perception of being-human as *Da-sein*—allows the phenomenon to manifest itself as what it is: "Every phenomenon must be understood as a lighting, a coming forth from concealment, and never otherwise." "Openness" that makes up the very possibility of being human prioritizes concealment proper in the sense that every manifestation needs to be understood as its own *un*-concealment, Heidegger's famous gloss of *aletheia* for truth.[46] Hence, while

---

[42] Patočka granted that "Heidegger anticipated by many years the questions which Husserl posed in *Crisis*." "Cartesianism and Phenomenology" (1976), in Patočka [1989], 316.

[43] In his 1973 comparison of Husserl and Heidegger Patočka refers to Heidegger regarding himself as a phenomenologist but adds the parenthetical comment: "at least for a time." "The Dangers of Technicization in Science," in Patočka [1989], 333.

[44] "Edmund Husserl's Philosophy of the Crisis of the Sciences," in Patočka [1989], 237.

[45] Patočka [1996b], 50-51, 51. "Most of all," Patočka asserts, Heidegger's philosophy "can shed light on the nature of historical action and open our eyes to what history is all about" (51). Also: "Heidegger is a philosopher of the primacy of freedom" (49).

[46] Thus Heidegger shows meaning as derived from "the concealment of what-is as a whole as the foundation of all openness and all uncovering." Patočka [1996b], 77. Patočka follows Heidegger in stressing the etymological implications of "ἀ-ληθεια." Patočka [1990a], 64. While the following citations to Patočka's work will continue to use this more generally available 1990 edition, the serious student will want to consult the more recent and far more scholarly edition

Heidegger does not entirely solve the problem of the *Lebenswelt* and "natural world," his "concept of openness is the most promising basis for a solution thus far."[47]

Nonetheless it is Heidegger's own historical shortcomings that provide much of the stimulus for Patočka's original contributions to polis thought. For Patočka "Heidegger's conception of history, insofar as it exists at all, appears to us to revolve around the 'rare and clear' decisive turns of history." Thus Heidegger dismisses any reading of history as gradual development in favor of his own vision of "an ever-repeated rising out of fallenness" attached to such turns.[48] For Patočka by contrast, Heidegger's ontological understanding needs to be refocused on a genuine history of openness, a history that operates through the more directed concept of a "region of openness" (*otevřená oblast*) "in a definite period" (*v určitého období*).[49] By the same token, Husserl's "life-world" and Patočka's concept of the "natural world" can then themselves be historicized in terms bringing out the greater truth of Heidegger's relation to being and freedom through openness.

Accordingly, Patočka turns the "natural world" into the "prehistorical" or "preproblematic" (or "nonproblematic") world of human development. It is still the natural world as essentially "an oriented, perspectival, situational world,"[50] but located in the evolution of human development it also takes on vital "futural" qualities that will help explain the more precise nature of "prehistory" and "history" proper within that evolution. Bearing in mind the centrality of Heidegger's concept of *aletheia* or truth as unconcealment, Patočka's statement of the manner in which such futurality is experienced in this prehistorical world proves particularly suggestive: "The nonproblematic world is one in which concealment is not experienced *as such*."[51] Instead, this nonproblematic world experiences modes of life that are increasingly related to family, work, household, even imperial strongholds—the "species" as the middle state "between the undifferentiated great Night and the autonomy of the

provided in *Sebrané Spisy Jana Patočky*, iii: 3, edited by Ivan Chvatík and Pavel Kouba (Patočka [1997-]). This edition contains important variants to the *Heretical Essays*, as well as including the particularly relevant 1974 lectures "Problém počátku a místa dějin" (283-300).

47 Patočka [1996b], 7, 8 10. See also the important study by Chvatík [2003].

48 "The Dangers of Technicization in Science," in Patočka [1989], 335. Patočka also describes the natural world as the "totality of fundamental modes of human comportment." Patočka [1996b], 10.

49 Patočka [1996b], 9; Patočka [1990a], 26. Patočka makes clear that openness "is ever an event in the life of individuals [*jako událost života jdenotlivců*]" and that "open comportment" is "of a temporal-historical nature; it is always in movement, coming out of the darkness and flowing into the darkness of concealment." Patočka [1996b], 9, 10; Patočka [1990a], 28, 29.

50 "The 'Natural' World and Phenomenology," in Patočka [1989], 251.

51 Patočka [1996b], 12 (emphasis added).

individual."[52] These modes betray the relation of the nonproblematic world to the overall concealment of truth (*aletheia*) as one of the mysterious, the secret, the sacred, indeed the "night." Philosophically expressed, this futurality may be described as "the character of a *that which is coming [jeho charakter příští]*;"[53] while for the prehistorical temper itself this same character is grasped as the "divine," something that is "always 'on the way' [*přichází*]" and which is turned into the indispensable distinction between the gods and mortals for the apparent balance and harmony of this prehistorical society. Evoking the flash of Nietzsche's famous *Nachtlied* or "night song" in *Thus Spoke Zarathustra*, Patočka strikingly notes that the prehistorical world is anticipatory precisely to the degree that it has not yet learned to distinguish between the night of regular experience and the "night as the darkness out of which the lightning of being [*blesk bytí*] strikes."[54]

"History" then properly speaking for Patočka occurs as the eventing of that same "lightning of being," since any authentic experience of the being of a thing "means to see the lightning of being [*blesk bytí*] over all that is, the open night of what-is." The enormity of this experience, only partially captured in the ancient Greek—as well as Husserlian and Heideggerian— identification of the philosophical vocation with an originary "wonder" or "astonishment" (θαυμάζειν) towards the naked fact of the what-is, is sufficiently catalysmic in itself to mark the cleft between "prehistory" and "history" proper. What was anticipated, coming, on its way in prehistory has "now" arrived *as* history and may be truly described as a "creative dawning,"[55] but Patočka prefers to underscore its effects of astonishment, terror, and (most important for the Patočkan vocabulary), a profound "shaking" and "shakenness." [*otřes, otřesenost*].[56] It is both the peril and greatness of this moment that constitutes the radical thrust to Patočka's polis thinking.

---

[52] Patočka [1996b], 22. This account owes a great deal to Patočka's reading of Heidegger's student Hannah Arendt.

[53] Patočka [1996b], 33 (emphasis in original); Patočka [1990a], 48. For Patočka this is the moment of "image, dance, and song" in humans' response to this coming of the "gods."

[54] Patočka [1996b], 32; Patočka [1990a], 47. Similarly prehistory cannot yet distinguish between the everyday earth of fruitfulness and the earth "that is the backdrop of all that is." Ivan Chvatík suggests that the importance of the theme of lightning or thunderbolt may well have been inspired by Patočka's reading of the publication of the seminar on Heraclitus that Heidegger and Eugen Fink held in Freiburg in 1966 that Patočka's old friend Fink later made available to Patočka. Chvatík notes a change of direction in Patočka's 1971-2 lectures on the Presocratics reflective of his response to this work. Personal communication, 23 August 2004, Prague/Praha. The seminar proceedings are translated into English as Heidegger & Fink [1993].

[55] Patočka [1996b], 42-43, 40: "'the first day of the creation,' mysterious and more pressing for enfolding and bearing with it the astonished." Patočka [1990a], 57.

[56] Patočka [1990a], 55, 56. These terms are strewn throughout the Patočka oeuvre and play a

This shaking is nothing less than the experiencing of the "world" proper as that which insofar as it makes all objects possible without itself being an object and allows for all manifestations without itself manifesting is ever the "transcending," that is, the transcending of the totality of the for-the-sake-of which, or *pragmata*, that confirms the concreteness of dwelling in the world. What has been "shaken" is the accepted everydayness of a nonproblematic or "natural" world which, while upholding the individual discrete meanings by which the everyday habitually perdures, has (not yet) faced the very question of meaning itself, a question for which the appropriate phenomenal language for its experience is that of astonishment, uprootedness, the "flashing" insight into the ungroundedness of all that appears grounded. It is on the basis of such terror and shakenness that "freedom" itself manifests. Freedom *presupposes* the terror of shaking, in the sense that freedom for Patočka is "being in its mystery and wonder: that being is [*bytí a jeho tajemství a div: že jsoucno jest*]."[57] Following Heidegger, Patočka defines this freedom as "letting being be what it is, not distorting being."[58] In the terror and shaking that confirms the eventing of being as the what-is in its transcending foundationality, humans experience freedom as a dynamic, if perilous, openness.[59]

For Patočka as for Heidegger and Husserl, the concrete individuals who first experienced this shaking are the ancient Greeks: "Here, in very specific conflicts on a modest territory and with minimal material means is born not only the Western world and its spirit but, perhaps, world history as such." For all his reluctance to idealize or localize, Patočka clearly means the polis, and in particular the "Athenian polis" (*obec*),[60] whence his philosophical hero Socrates will emerge. In this world of the historical polis the first clear Word for the

key role in his recommendations to his contemporary audience.

[57] Patočka [1996b], 49 (I do not, however, follow Kohák in capitalizing being in this passage); Patočka [1990a], 63.

[58] Patočka [1996b], 49. Also: freedom "is always a freedom to let what is be what and how it is" (142).

[59] Hence "the world opens itself" to human life "for the first time" once "the possibility of authentic life, that is, life as a whole," is glimpsed. Patočka [1996b], 39.

[60] Patočka [1996b], 41; Patočka [1990a], 55. Although Kohák's translations use "polis" throughout, Patočka himself tends to use both the proper Greek word "polis" and the Czech equivalent "obec." Often— but not always—Patočka uses "polis" when referring to specifically Greek factors, while "obec" is employed for more general reflections. H. Gordon Skilling points out that *obec* is often a synonym for *společenství,* which "means community or partnership." "Introductory Essay," in Skilling & Wilson [1991], 31 (note 1). *Obec* links with *občan*, "citizen," and *občanské*, "civic," whence *Občanské forum*, or "Civic Forum," the organization that helped precipitate the Velvet Revolution. Václav Benda's later reflections on his slogan, "The Parallel *Polis*," indicate that *polis* and both *obec* and *společenstvi* were interchangeable in the minds of the Patočkan dissidents. "Václav Benda," in Skilling & Wilson [1991], 50, 51, 53.

eventing of being is first pronounced as the Heraclitean *polemos* (Πολεμος), understood as "the flash of being out of the night of the world."[61] *Polemos* yields the conflictive and adversarial sense of a primordially experienced shaking while simultaneously retaining the spirit of unity or One premised by such conflict and battle. Thus *polemos* is the basic "law" or lawfulness behind this "lightning of being," justifying the view that Heraclitus was the first to grasp the inner unity of polis and philosophy at the outset, from which binding power "alone all laws and constitutions derive, however different they may be." Because this adversarial relationship marks the start and substance of shaking, Patočka agrees with Hannah Arendt that it presupposes "the mutual recognition of humans as free and equal, a recognition which must be continuously acted out" in order to manifest excellence, "demonstrating that in which humans can be in principle equal in competition with each other" through the pursuit of action and the realization of glory. Thus the polis necessarily bears "a mutual respect in activity significant for all its participants."[62] While this formulation does not fully posit a democratic basis for the originary polis as such, it is, like Arendt's own reading, far more participatory and collective than Heidegger's version. In any event, it shares with Heidegger the claim that the central event that makes history "happen" is the polis as "the proper site of history [*vlastní místo dějin*]."[63]

The "law" of this polis as *polemos* is therefore the origin of "politics"—its unifying agonistics—as well as "the primordial insight that makes philosophy possible." The combination of these two phenomena—politics and philosophy —*begins* "history" proper as the domain appropriate to the "freedom" henceforth available to humankind. Central to Patočka's reading is the position that not formal thought as such but the veritable "political" workings of adversaries identifies the original "life of the polis" which for a "short time" opens up the hitherto unknown domain of disclosure (*aletheia*) that will serve for the philosophical vocation.[64] Moreover, it is clear from this reading that in

---

[61] Patočka [1996b], 43; Patočka [1990a], 56.

[62] Patocka [1996b], 43, 42, 37-8, 63. Patočka also cites Hegel that consciousness of freedom requires that humans be in a "*community* of equals. For that reason, the beginning of history in the strict sense is the *polis*" [*polis*] (148). Also: "There is not only struggle but also solidarity, there is not only society, but also community [*společenství*], and community has other bonds besides a common enemy" (149).

[63] Patočka [1996b], 103; Patočka [1990a], 112. While Kohák prefers "proper place of history," one may also translate the Czech word *místo* as "site." See also "Problém počátku a místa dějin (1974)," in Patočka [1997-], iii-3, 283-300.

[64] "Since, however, philosophy and the spirit of the *polis* are closely linked so that the spirit of the *polis* survives ultimately always in the form of philosophy, this particular event, the emergence of the *polis*, has a universal significance." Patočka [1996b], 41.

an important sense genuine philosophy will become the only true *continuator* of the polis after the decay and fall of the historical polis by retaining, however inadequately, this original experience and spirit of the vertiginous nature of reality—that is, by acknowledging the permanence of the "Night" from which "Day" necessarily emerges and to which it necessarily returns. At the same time formal philosophy will soon lose that primordial link to the "darkness" or "obscurity" by preferring to see it only as "a lack of light" in relation to which philosophy then narrows its future tasks to an exclusive concern with "clarity."[65]

It is equally for such reasons that Socrates becomes Patočka's ultimate philosophical standard and guide, since his Socrates is the "most authentic thinker" for retaining the polis link with the phenomenon of openness through the Socratic commitment to a questioning practice and recognition of problematicity that preserves "the mysterious and the mystery" at the "very core of reality" central to the philosopher's vocation of seeking the truth.[66] The standard that Socrates establishes once and for all is "care of the soul," a care that retains the essence of the polis as the "site" for experiencing the openness of freedom and the responsibility of humans to hold freely to a "life in truth," itself taken to be the unconcealment inseparable from the permanence of concealment proper.[67] If subsequent philosophy and its progeny science have largely forgotten this vocation, the Socratic adherence to truth as aletheia can always be called upon to effect, at any historical moment, a total conversion or *metanoia* back to the priority of the polis and its site of freedom.[68]

V

For all his refining of Husserl's *Crisis* arguments, Patočka followed in principle the Husserlian—and to a lesser extent Heideggerian—account of the origins and progression of the objectivating sciences and the "draining" of meaning in modern "technoscience."[69] What distinguished the Patočkan version was a

---

65 Patočka [1996b], 44, 64-65. Patočka describes the subsequent career of philosophy after Plato as seeking the "continuous clarity of definitive certainty."

66 Already in 1953 Patočka described Socrates as a "special active, anthropologically oriented version of" the "knowledge" that is "a question," based on Socrates' own "absolute freedom." "Negative Platonism: Reflections concerning the Rise, the Scope, and the Demise of Metaphysics —and Whether Philosophy Can Survive It [1953]," in Patočka [1989], 180.

67 Patočka [1996b], 75, 82-3, 104.

68 Patočka [1996b], 134. In the Czech version the "metanoia" is spelled in Greek letters. Patočka [1990a], 141.

69 See in particular Patočka's useful elaboration of Husserl's arguments regarding the

greater concern for the specifics of not only the history of philosophy (or "being") but also of concrete material history. Notwithstanding the overriding patterns set down by Husserl and Heidegger, Patočka remained far more sensitive to alternative modes of thought summed up as a "natural philosophy" that combined the "cosmos of antiquity and the Renaissance" as represented by the works of Marsilio Ficino, Jacob Boehme, and Patočka's countryman Jan Amos Komenský (Comenius) in anticipation of the *Naturphilosophie* of German Idealism and its heirs.[70] In the nineteenth century the German-speaking lands therefore became a refuge of sorts for the struggle against the technoscience of industrial European society: the philosophy initiated by Kant and concurrent movements in poetry and music "made one more attempt to turn around the spirit of Europe." However, when transformed into the political structure of a unified Germany after 1871, this "spiritual Germany" went from the emancipatory elements of its critical attitude toward technoscientific civilization into a far more hegemonic version of political state rule over spirit and thus further reinforced the disintegration process.[71]

In the twentieth century this German relation to technoscientific civilization has remained ambiguous. For Patočka the century brought to a head the destructive underpinnings of this civilization by "its deep addiction to war" as summed up by the first world war, "the decisive event in the history of the twentieth century." "War" stripped bare the underlying logic of a millennial obsession with "the accumulation of building, organizing, transforming energy" through its unique function of "releasing reserves of energy accumulated over billions of years" in the "rapid release" of these accumulated forces.[72] In this sense war, revealing itself as the truth of technoscience, constituted the return of "the night." The German contribution to this process was its revolutionary pursuit of precisely the strength and power that gave "meaning" to the

idealization process begun by philosophy as a never fully provable hypothesis that "there always is a corresponding rational geometric structure for any qualitative datum," which gave birth to the "abstract physicalism" of modern science. For Patočka, however, the Greeks themselves still remained close to the "life-world," notwithstanding their use of "idealized forms." "Edmund Husserl's Philosophy of the Crisis of the Sciences and His Conception of a Phenomenology of the 'Life-World,'" in Patočka [1989], 230, 228.

[70] Patočka had already begun marking out the importance of these strands in the attempted "rebirth" of the ancient cosmos by the Renaissance and German Idealism in his 1942 essay, "Two Senses of Reason and Nature in the German Enlightenment: A Herderian Study" [1942], in Patočka [1989], 164, 173.

[71] Patočka [1996b], 88, 89.

[72] Patočka [1996b], 120, 124. This argument shares a great deal with those put forward by Walter Benjamin in his review of Ernst Jünger's work. See Hillach [1979], 107, 99-119, and Benjamin [1979], 120-8.

technoscientific identification with energy and force; hence Germany was closest to the "reality of the new techno-scientific age." Nonetheless, Germany remained confined to a "mechanical" understanding of this same truth, whereas such observers as Teilhard de Chardin and Ernst Jünger acutely realized the underlying meaning of the war "front" ("le front de la vague") as not only the experience of "absurdity par excellence" and the total meaninglessness of war (as well as the system that required it), but also as the glimpse by the few into the eschatological dimensions contained in the phenomenon of the front.[73] It is at this very "site," Patočka importantly suggested, that humans once again confronted "the shaken world [*otřesenému světu*]." The total meaninglessness produced by technoscientific civilization provided a first glimpse into the "night" of "absolute freedom" which had served the original creators and participants of the ancient polis. This "saving" element of the front has been subsequently universalized by its extension through "Hiroshima" to locate all humankind at the "front line" of possible total extinction, while it has been obscured by the "economic miracle" of post-war material growth which, notwithstanding its undoubted practical benefits, intensifies the possibility of war by expanding the gap between the rich and the poor.[74]

Ultimately, according to Patočka, this "saving" element suggested by the front experience must transform what was an individual event into the unified understanding of a collective "solidarity of the shaken" (*solidarita otřesenych*). The key to such solidarity is to exploit the wartime principle of "sacrifice." The wars of technoscientific civilization could not do without ultimate sacrifices by participants, but those sacrifices could not be themselves justified in accordance with the draining of meaning of the technoscientific project that produced such wars and thus inadvertently hinted at a something exceeding the motivations of that project. But whereas wartime sacrifice merely concerned itself with "sacrificial victims" who were unaware of the "metaphysico-mythological remnants" contained in the sacrifice principle, the solidarity of the shaken would include those who consciously gave themselves "for something" which nonetheless was "not objective:" "it is a sacrifice for everything and for all. In a certain essential sense, it is a sacrifice for nothing," this "nothing" to be

---

[73] Patočka [1996b], 122, 126. The importance of the front for Heidegger's philosophy of *Dasein* through Ernst Jünger's influence and the significance of Teilhard de Chardin's reading of the front as "the extreme boundary between what you are already aware of, and what is still in the process of formation" is also argued in "Heidegger: Ontological Anarchy, " in Chytry [1989], 373-5. At the time I wrote these passages I was unaware of Patočka's resort to exactly the same passages in Teilhard de Chardin as well as to Jünger.

[74] Patočka [1996b], 127, 132, 96, 132; Patočka [1990a], 134. This economic expansion has taken place in conjunction with the displacement of European supremacy by such superpowers as the United States.

understood as "no existing particular."[75] Since such a "nothing" was in fact coterminous with the openness inseparable from the freedom of the originary polis, it was no less a sacrifice on behalf of the siting of the polis proper.

At the end of his philosophical career, Jan Patočka therefore explicitly pronounced the return of the Heraclitean Word that had stood for the initiation of the polis and the dawning of history as freedom. Explicitly identifying his "solidarity of the shaken" with Heraclitus' declaration of *polemos* in the common experience of the "shaking of the everyday" that had driven the modern visions of Teilhard de Chardin, Ernst Jünger, and Martin Heidegger, Patočka proclaimed his politics to be "the realm of the discovery of freedom and the ground of truth" that had first emerged as the polis and survived in the distant recollections of a philosophy true to its polis origins.[76]

VI

For Patočka's successors this message fit effectively into the particularities of post-Reform Czechoslovakia in the 1970s. In what Václav Havel subsequently labeled a "post-totalitarian" age,[77] a society all the more brutal for no longer making direct use of totalitarian oppression in its encompassing control of the everyday, the sensitive issues of resistance and possibilities of "radical sacrifice" touched less on issues of party or governmental politics than on securing spaces and sites for human activity and experimentation.

As a result, the issues around which the first clear indications of dissidence grew after the enforced collapse of the Czechoslovak reform movements of 1968-9 turned out to be the rock musical scene of the Czech underground largely associated with the rock group The Plastic People of the Universe and its artistic director Ivan Jirous. Jirous himself had advocated the existence of a "second culture" (*druhá kultura*), a community made up of people who wanted to live life differently while seeking to turn life in society (*společenství*) into the eventual creation of a community (*obec*).[78] When Jirous and other members of

[75] Patočka [1996b], 134; Patočka [1990a], 141. "The Dangers of Technicization" in Patočka [1989], 338, 339. With regard to specific goals, Patočka states: "Without ignoring or making light of certain concrete historical social goals," the sacrifices of which he speaks "have another focus," namely "something like a light or a clearing which makes manifestation possible" (338, 339).

[76] The *Heretical Essays* ends with the reminder that the Heraclitean *polemos* "is the father of the laws of the *polis* [*obec*] as of all else." Patočka [1996b], 136; Patočka [1990a], 142. Also Patočka [1996b], 148.

[77] Havel [1978], 131.

[78] Skilling & Wilson [1991], citing Jirous' essay and that of Zdeněk Vokátý, 6-7.

the rock underground were brought to trial in 1976 for their "negative effect on the lifestyle of young people," Jirous' meeting with dissident playwright Havel persuaded the latter that Jirous' arrest was more than totalitarian politics as usual since it was directed against young people not otherwise involved in the political process, "who wanted to live in their own way, to make music they liked, to sing what they wanted to sing, to live in harmony with themselves, and to express themselves in a truthful way."[79] Accordingly, the Prague trial of September 1976 at which the accused were finally convicted became an occasion for the gathering together of dissident elements from 1968-9 who were only just gradually recovering from the crackdown of the 1970s: "a community of people who were not only exceptionally considerate, communicative and trusting of one another, but also a strangely democratic one" whose common denominator became the defense of elementary human rights.[80] From this original recognition of basic association, the group decided to broaden itself into the citizen initiative of Charter 77 of January 1977 that called for the Czechoslovak government to follow in practice the Helsinki human rights convention that it had recently ratified in law.[81]

If Charter 77 was not necessarily the precise words of Jan Patočka, it is generally agreed that the Charter "by its entire substance and significance was (and is!) the work of Jan Patočka." Indeed it has been strongly claimed that a special affinity existed between Patočka's *Heretical Essays* and the Charter.[82] That Patočka was the key philosophical figure for the Charter's ideals and effects may be inferred from at least two factors. *First*, since 1968-9 Patočka had held small discussion groups that played out the classic Socratic commitment to challenging ("corrupting") youth. Moreover, in 1975 he apparently compared the available alternatives for his "solidarity of the shaken" with either the Platonic path of withdrawal, the Sophist path of compromise—*or* "the path of Socrates," which led to conflict and, "if followed consistently, to death." Patočka signed the important public letter of 16 August 1976 to German writer Heinrich Böll apprising a sympathetic outsider of the stakes at the Prague trial, and his comments of December 1976 sympathetically regarded The Plastic People of the Universe as akin to a separate society of pure aliens symbolizing

[79] See the account of "The Musical Underground" as the "Origins of the Charter" 77 movement in H. Gordon Skilling [1981], 7-16, 11; also Havel's later account of his meeting with Jirous in Havel [1990a], 125-38, 128, and the play *Rock'n'Roll* by Tom Stoppard dedicated to Václav Havel. Stoppard [2006].

[80] Havel, "The Trial" (11 October 1976), in Skilling [1981], 204.

[81] In his later recollections, Havel stresses the direct link between the Prague trial and the articulation of Charter 77. Havel [1990a], 133.

[82] Zdeněk Pinc, March 1977, cited in Skilling [1981], 20, 22.

"a guest, arriving from the unknown to begin life anew."[83] Thus Patočka easily qualified as one of the three main spokesmen—along with Havel and reform communist Jiři Hájek—of Charter 77. According to Havel's later reminiscences, Patočka seemed to be sensing at the moment "that one day he would have to put his thinking to the test of action, as it were, that he couldn't avoid it or put it off forever, because ultimately this would call his whole philosophy in doubt."[84]

And *second*, among the youth supposedly "corrupted" by Patočka, the most significant candidates were the ones to creatively develop and expand on the implications of Patočka's polis thought in a post-Charter 77 world. This is particularly true of the student who turned out to be the key figure of the Velvet Revolution of 1989. Václav Havel, who first read Patočka's dissertation on the "natural world" in the 1950s before avidly seeking out the rest of Patočka's writings, met Patočka through the director of the Theatre of the Balustrade in 1960 where he himself was developing his lifelong work in the theatre, and then assiduously followed Patočka's "unofficial seminars" all the way to a closing Socratic discussion with Patočka on human immortality and responsibility in the prison waiting room shortly before Patočka's death in March 1977.[85] Thus, although Patočka himself contributed important explications of the Charter 77 movement right up to his death,[86] it was after Patočka's departure that his ideas were relentlessly and effectively pursued by such students of his thought as Václav Havel and Václav Benda. Benda's "The Parallel Polis"and Havel's "The Power of the Powerless," both dated 1978, represent the most fruitful extensions of Patočka's polis thinking and helped shape the atmosphere and experiments that eventually paid off in 1989.[87]

---

[83] Zdeněk Pinc's recollections of a seminar in 1975, cited in Skilling [1981], *77*, 22, also 21; Jaroslav Seifert *et al.*, "Letter to Heinrich Böll (16 August 1976)," and Patočka, "On the Matter of The Plastic People of the Universe and DG 307 (December 1976)," both in Skilling [1981], 199-200, 205-6.

[84] Havel [1990a], 135. Havel goes on to point out that once he had decided, Patočka was fully committed to the cause, especially during the period when Havel himself was incarcerated and Patočka and Hájek had to push the Charter 77 project themselves.

[85] Havel, "Last Conversation (1 May 1977)," in Skilling [1981], 242-4; Havel [1990a], 26. Also Havel [2007], 304. Havel draws on Patočka's concept of the "natural world" in his own presidential reflections on "home" in Havel [1992], 30.

[86] Patočka's comments of 3 January 1977 and 8 March 1977 are in Patočka [1989], 340-7. Skilling also mentions an interview with a correspondent of *Die Zeit* held on 9 March 1977 which was published 1 April 1977. Patočka died on 13 March 1977. His funeral on 16 March 1977 included a crown of thorns placed on his grave by two members of The Plastic People of the Universe. Skilling [1981], 22, 23.

[87] Benda, "The Parallel 'Polis,'" called Patočka "unquestionably the *spiritus movens*" behind Charter 77 (77), while Havel, who dedicated "The Power of the Powerless" to Patočka, later claimed that the Charter 77 movement would not have developed "had Patočka not illuminated its

Actually it was Benda—himself a succeeding spokesman for Charter 77 which like Havel cost him several years in prison—who first explicitly transformed Jirous' "second culture" into the goal of the "creation of a parallel polis." This parallel polis, like the "second culture," was meant to develop parallel institutions and structures that nonetheless did not ignore the "official" structures, but aimed at influencing the latter in the direction of "the growth, or the renewal, of civic and political culture."[88] Accepting Benda's suggestion, Havel broadened it to encompass Jirous' earlier recommendations into a full-scale political theory for a "post-democratic" system. Far more than Benda, Havel insisted that "the parallel *polis* points beyond itself" to the true polis—beyond both "the main *polis*" of post-totalitarianism and the "parallel *polis*" in relative autonomy from it—to "a way of discovering the most appropriate *locus*" for lives lived in responsibility toward truth as "proud and responsible members of the *polis*."[89] In his early enthusiasm Havel even suggested that "these informed, nonbureaucratic, dynamic, and open communities that comprise the 'parallel *polis*'" might be regarded as "a kind of rudimentary prefiguration, a symbolic model of those more meaningful 'post-democratic' political structures that might become the foundation of a better society."[90]

In these reflections Havel was no less driven by his own extensive experience in an ostensibly different kind of space: the "electrifying" realm of the theatre to which he had been drawn as a young man and in which he, along

beginnings with the clarity of his great personality." Havel [1990a], 136; Havel [1990b], 4. Attempts at creating an "anti-university" or alternative academy in 1978 were called the "Patočka University." Skilling [1981], 115.

[88] Benda [1991], 36; Benda in Skilling and Wilson [1991], 55. Benda explicitly presented the "second culture" as "the most developed and dynamic parallel structure" (38) and called for initiatives in the direction of parallel educational structures. He also noted the existence of a parallel economy in the black market (37).

[89] Havel [1978], 196, 204; Havel [1990b], 57. Throughout, Havel uses the Greek word *polis*. Havel reminded his reader of Patočka's injunction to carry responsibility everywhere and to accept suffering for the truth (157, 195). In this work Havel provides a clear account of the development of the idea of the parallel polis from Jirous through Benda to his own formulations (192-8).

[90] Havel [1978], 213; Havel [1990b], 63. In this essay it is not perfectly clear whether Havel believed that a typically western parliamentary democratic system was the "normal" alternative to post-totalitarian society and that the concept of the parallel polis was merely intended to deal with the anomalies of a society lacking such institutions until these were gained (or regained), or, as his closing thoughts suggest, that the development of a parallel polis might actually point beyond the model of parliamentary democracy to what he here called a "post-democratic" order. Havel's view of "traditional parliamentary democracies" was influenced at this time by Alexander Solzhenitsyn's critiques of their shortcomings (208-9). Havel's later more muted explanation of the term "post-democratic" was that it was "something like 'nonpolitical politics.'" Havel [2007], 328.

with a host of sympathetic experimenters, had hoped to create "a new poetics" within "that special magnetic field that comes into existence around the theatre."[91] From rock band performances of the late 1950s to attempts at capturing "theatre in a state of birth" in the 1960s, Havel was a charter member of a wide range of theatrical realities which aimed at "the joy of performance" and "freedom, pure humor, and intelligence."[92] Particularly after his release from prison in 1983, Havel committed himself to the expansion of the spirit of a parallel polis in a manner that was alternatively political-cultural and dramaturgically-theatrical.[93]

This mixture, graphically demonstrated by the lead role of Havel's Magic Lantern theatre as the gathering point and site for the dissident movement in the crucial period of 1988-9,[94] turned out to be remarkably relevant for the preconditions of revolution in Czechoslovakia.[95] If on the one hand Czechoslovakia in 1988-9 lagged behind other East Central European countries in its lack of a clear political opposition and maturated "civil society," it had developed, on the other hand, a far more extensive set of civic movements

[91] Havel [1990a], 41, 40. Havel often refers to "that special conspiratorial sense of togetherness that to me is what makes theatre" (43); also: "an inseparable part of the kind of theatre I've been drawn to all my life is a touch of obscurity, of decay or degeneration, of frivolity .... I think theatre should always be somewhat suspect" (43). See the excellent study by Robert Pirro [2002] in which he quotes Havel in 1986 as stating that the theatre must become "a living spiritual and intellectual focus, a place of social self-awareness ... *an area of freedom*, an instrument of human liberation" (237, emphasis added).

[92] Havel [1990a], 42-3, 46. Ivan Vyskočil, director of the Theatre on the Balustrade in the 1960s, was responsible for Havel's first meeting with Patočka in 1960. Subsequently it was at the Theatre that Patočka "would talk to us late into the night about phenomenology, existentialism and philosophy in general. Listening to him was bliss." Havel, "Last Conversation" (1 May 1977), in Skilling [1981], 242.

[93] Future research might wish to compare the political and theatrical in Havel's work with the Greek notion of "theatrocracy." See also "Landfall: Theatrocracy" below. Robert Pirro provides a vital study of the importance of tragedy for Havel, particularly with regard to the role of "catharsis." Moreover, specifically citing Havel himself, Pirro notes that in stressing the importance of catharsis for political change, Havel asserts his "interest in public matters, i.e. in matters of the polis [*zajímám o věci obecné, tj. o věci polis*]." Pirro [2002], 239. John Keane meanwhile provocatively claims that Havel was inspired by the German romantic poet Novalis' vision of the "poetic state," "a state that resembles a vast stage performance watched by the public and directed by the playwright monarch and a cast of citizen-actors" (379). In line with his claim, Keane even cites Clifford Geertz's study of the classical Balinese "theatre state." Keane [1999], 381-383 and 383 (note 2); Geertz [1980].

[94] As Havel more recently stressed, "theater people played a very important role at the time." Havel [2007], 75. See also Timothy Garton Ash [1990].

[95] The contributory role of western academics, starting with members of the sub-faculty of philosophy from the University of Oxford, who visited and lectured in Czechoslovakia is ably recounted in Day [1999].

reflective of, and including, the original Chartists of 1977. Moreover, Havel's polis thinking, deeply affected by the openness of theatrical spatiality and gathering, had learned from the Reform movement of 1968 the important lesson of the power underlying "the plurality of social association from below."[96] Now in 1989 it was precisely this large number of independent groups which under the suddenly propitious conditions of October-November 1989 quickly materialized to form the umbrella group Civic Forum and, negotiating directly with the government, displaced the Communist Party as the main political force, and in 1990 produced a new governmental and institutional system under the formal presidency of playwright Havel. This background also helps explain the lingering tone of miracle and euphoria that left its distinctive resonance over the later recollections of the participants.[97]

In light of the deflation of the Velvet Revolution around 1991-2, the preceding interpretation of that revolution as largely reflective of the tradition of polis thought of Heidegger and Patočka through such "parallel polis" students as Benda and Havel may prove more apposite in helping to account for that deflation. Following in principle Patočka's politics as evolved primarily by Havel, the Revolution opened out a theatrical site for the "lightning of being" to strike a moribund society caught in "post-totalitarianism." The parallel polis, itself the conceptual product of a "second culture" reflecting the theatrical-musical life of the underground, had promoted the standard of a polis whose very openness to being was most compatible with a pluralistic network of decentralized forces, clubs, organizations and associations with a wide variety of aims and purposes—what Havel called "authentic social self-organizations" *(autentické společenské 'samo-organisace')*—whose characteristics were to remain "open, dynamic, and small."[98] This "post-democratic" system of the future polis was itself predicated on the experience of openness itself that miraculously took place in the euphoric moments of the Velvet Revolution. In that Revolution, particularly in such spaces as St. Wenceslas Square, site and theatre united to ignite a veritable "theatre of revolution," perhaps the most fitting political confirmation of Heidegger's and Patočka's polis visions of a veritable "site of history."[99]

---

[96] Havel claimed to have been taught this lesson by Czech exile Ferdinand Peroutka who "considered the relentless defiance of those small social units to be more important for the future than all those sensational political revelations of the Prague Spring." Havel [1990a], 21.

[97] Following the analysis in Skilling & Wilson [1991], 19-29.

[98] Havel [1978], 211, 210; Havel [1990b], 62; also 50. Although there is an acknowledged affinity with T. G. Masaryk's recommendation to "small-scale work" (*drobná práce*), Havel noted its vulnerability to cooptation by a post-totalitarian system. Havel [1978], 172-3.

[99] See the analysis by Michael Andrew Kukral of this "theatre of revolution" in the "place" and "siting" of St. Wenceslas Square in Prague/Praha in Kukral [1997], 1, 2, 8, 176, 188. As

By the same token, such an interpretation suggests that the ideal which the Revolution made momentarily concrete may not have been so much the ethnico-cultural unity of Czech, Czechoslovak, or Czech and Slovak history—let alone issues related to a multicultural "Bohemia."[100] It was rather the *primacy of the polis* as manifested by the concrete city and region of Prague/Praha proper. At this given moment—"the siting of history where history 'happens'"— Prague/Praha temporarily reconstituted the historic poleis of the past (e.g. Athens, Florence, Venice) as the opening for an experiment in political cooperation grounded in what President Havel in 1991-2 still envisaged as his "utopia" of "a highly decentralized state with confident local governments" crisscrossed "by a network of local, regional, and state-wide clubs, organizations, and associations with a wide variety of aims and purposes."[101] If the realities of 1992-3 brought an end to the Velvet Revolution by reinstituting the classic parliamentary struggle of conventional political parties, the increasing prominence ascribed to "free-market" economic politics that were to be associated with Havel's future presidential successor Václav Klaus, and the permanent split of Czechoslovakia into the new states of the Czech and Slovak Republics of 1993, they also implicitly underscored the unique achievements of 1989-90 as the opening up of a polis reality—however temporarily—conforming to Patočka's ideas.[102]

In Ivan Chvatík's important formulation this reality means "the establishment and preservation of an open forum for competing political views .... the preservation of the *agora* of a really functioning democratic regime."[103] For the new Czech Republic founded in 1993 largely on the experiences of the Velvet Revolution and on the philosophical inspiration of Patočka's polis thought, this remains no mean legacy for the future.[104]

Kukral argues, "for a brief time in the late autumn of '89," Wenceslas Square was transformed "into a dramatic and powerful Theater of Revolution" (103). If then Husserl's and the young Patočka's Prague/Praha of 1935—the scene of Husserl's *Crisis* thoughts—was betrayed by the events of Munich 1938 and repeated in 1948 and 1968 to constitute a kind of "death of Europe" according to the interesting study by Jürgen Serke, the Velvet Revolution may indicate an important new turn for that reading of the significance of Prague/Praha for Europe. "Europa starb in Prag," in Serke [1987], 7-85.

[100] Patočka's own thoughts on the meaning of "Czech" are best recorded in Patočka [1992].

[101] Havel [1992], 103, 104.

[102] Havel as president continued to emphasize that the theatrical dimension of politics included what conventional politicians tended to overlook, namely that the world is also "governed by a mysterious order." Robert Pirro, citing Havel's address to the Academy of Performing Arts in Prague on 4 October 1996. Pirro [2002], 248.

[103] Chvatík [1992-3], 166. Chvatík recognizes the Patočkan (and Heraclitean) basis of the identification of "nothingness" with "the possibility of manifestation, the *agora*," in which one "defeats" but does not "destroy" opponents if one is not to destroy the *agora* itself.

[104] It should be noted that both Ivan Chvatík and Erazim Kohák have retained misgivings, for

VII

At a certain stage Plutarch's *Life of Pericles* raises the question of the origin of Pericles' nickname as "the Olympian". After considering several obvious candidates (including Pericles' responsibility for the construction of the fabled Acropolis complex), Plutarch himself settles on the most likely account: Pericles' style of public speaking. According to contemporary comedic sources, Pericles would orate to the people in the Olympian-Zeus register of "thundering" (βροντᾶν) and "lightning" (ἀστράπτειν), "carrying a terrible thunderbolt in his tongue" (δεινὸν δὲ κεραυνὸν ἐν γλώσσῃ φέρειν) which shook them.[105]

Granted that Pericles' rule over the Athenians was never based on a hegemonical institutional office and that the Athenian citizenry of the Periclean period could hardly be described as passive or excessively pliant, Plutarch's little anecdote is like a flash of ancient truth about Pericles' idiosyncratic relation to, and influence on, the original democratic polis that Jan Patočka uniquely intuited and himself largely articulated for the modern world. In Patočka's formulation the problematization which *founds* history and the character of the real is inseparable from the Heraclitean illumination within the "night as the darkness out of which the lightning of being [*blesk bytí*] strikes." Marking genuine democratic discourse in the agora and the assembly, it comes forth in the phenomenological shape of truth, illuminating even as it shakes and thunders. This is neither hegemonical force nor power-politics as usual: it is the homology of thunderbolt and truth that Pericles apparently first set off among some 40,000-50,000 citizens of the Athenian democratic polis and that Jan Patočka has both recapitulated and rewielded for the Czech public spaces of its contemporary citizenry.

---

different reasons, regarding the larger question of the positive influence of both Patočka and Havel on post-Velvet Revolution Czech political realities, a theme that will receive separate treatment in a future study. Chvatík believes that Patočka's thought never entirely freed itself from the "history of onto-theo-logical metaphysics" and questions what he considers to be Havel's naive understanding of political realities and party politics especially for the 1990-1992 period. Chvatík [2003], 26, and personal communication, 17 and 23 August 2004, Prague/Praha. Kohák concludes that both Patočka and Havel have had a deleteriously conservative effect on Czech thought and politics by not doing enough to reinforce elements of "its radically democratic tradition." Personal and electronic communications, 13 August 2004, Prague/Praha.

105 Plutarch [1914], viii.3. Plutarch himself thinks that the sobriquet is deserved due to Pericles' mildness of demeanor even under the most pressing circumstances (xxxix.2-3).

PART TWO

THE ARTFUL FIRM

CHAPTER FIVE

Organizational Aesthetics

The Artful Firm in Organization and Management Theory

If Part I dealt primarily with our efforts to legitimate and further develop polis thought on behalf of cytherics, Part II turns to what appears to be the very different "apolitical" subject-matter of management, organization, and firm analyses.[1] Yet the two parts are at least linked by certain features intrinsic to both polis and organization.

To think the polis is to think the assemblage or gathering together of a populace upon a site, the site of and as "history" for that populace. It is precisely such a siting—the very "happening" that is "history" (*die Geschichte geschieht*)—which merits the designation "polis," along with its distillation, the "political." This summary is of course strongly Heideggerean, but it finds, surprisingly perhaps, an echo of sorts in the conventional modern definition of formal organizations. Organizations, assert James G. March and Herbert Simon in their classic text, are "*assemblages* of interacting human beings and they are the largest assemblages in our society that have anything resembling a central coordinate system."[2] Regrettably students of the polis and of the political have often overlooked these domains of the modern organization as well as the entrepreneurial firm, largely perhaps for reasons of ideological distaste. Yet the story of contemporary society and economics has been no less about the growth and increasing sophistication of these institutions.

Meanwhile, since the 1990s formal organization theory has for its part taken an increasing interest in the role of the aesthetic. True, aesthetics traditionally hovered at the edge of the product and the commodity.[3] Yet the allure of

---

[1] For an earlier version of this chapter published in *Aesthesis,* see Chytry [2008b].

[2] See Chapter 8 below for more details.

[3] To mark out our subject matter, I resort to two terms. The first, "organizational aesthetics," is derived from the chapter heading and references in "Organizational Aesthetics, Experience and Plausibility," by Strati [1999], 9, the title of which book is however "organization and aesthetics." The second, "the artful firm," is my amalgamation of "art firm" by Guillet de Monthoux [2004] and "artful making" by Austin & Devin [2003]. The term "aesthetic firm" by John Dobson [1999] is also relevant. I am grateful to Lee Devin for his comments and tips on an earlier version of this article.

aesthetics proved generally more seductive to those critics of the overall system of capitalism who hoped for an age of the product that, freed from the constraints of commodity-formation, would resemble the oeuvres generally expected from the professions classified as arts, crafts, and design. In turn, these professions long regarded the language of aesthetics as the official judge of value-claims. Although those judgments have become in time far more attenuated since the formal origins of "aesthetics" in the eighteenth century, they have left behind exemplars which the theorists of business and management apparently at long last intend to exploit.[4]

Two questions immediately arise. Why? And, what is the "aesthetic object" that is being groomed on behalf of the answer to that "why"? The works that have primarily stimulated the thinking behind this chapter have all come up within the last half-decade or so. Prior to them there was already a growing literature in the late 1970s and 1980s that sought to add an aesthetic seasoning to the managerial dish, in some cases possibly reflecting crossovers between systems theory and management concerns.[5] Still, granted a time-lag of one to two years from completion to publication, it is highly probable that these more recent works represent the crest of the dot.com prosperity of the 1990s. Yet to make them the chance product of a passing decade would be to mistake the significance of these works, and indeed their worth. For the most part, these are intelligent ventures at finding bridges between the world of aesthetics and the world of the corporation. If "beautiful corporations" and the coming of the "aesthetic manager" and "art firm" as well as "artful making" for an "Age of Aesthetics" and "Aesthetic Universe" are probably not in the cards, it is no rebuke to these efforts that they have striven to imagine how the future might be so. After all, even a failure to predict that future can help tell us why aesthetics and business might not be automatically such potential marital partners as these authors keenly hope. To that extent, such works might have something to say to the need for business itself to metamorphose into something substantially different if it wishes to draw on the "authentically" aesthetic.

At the core of the difficulties in much of this literature is the unproblematic confidence with which that literature often moves between categories belonging

---

[4] Largely because concern has moved to the relation and opposition between the "aesthetic" and the "anti-aesthetic." Foster [1983].

[5] See the useful introductory comments and references in Strati [1999], 4-7, regarding the early literature which seems to have come to a head in the late 1980s. Also Strati [2000], 25-26. Rafael Ramirez's Ph.D. dissertation at the University of California, Berkeley, concerning the "beautiful in social organization" was completed under the supervision of C. West Churchman, a Berkeley philosopher linked to systems theory. Churchman's institute, the Center for Research in Management at the University of California, Berkeley, became the Institute of Management, Organization and Innovation (IMIO) under the directorship of David J. Teece. Ramirez [1991].

to the aesthetic in general and those directed more closely to art and the artwork. While it might be helpful at times to minimize such distinctions in order to encourage innovative readings of the phenomena under consideration, it might be no less helpful at other times to clarify the differences involved in these two related areas of discourse. In the following survey of the relevant literature, this chapter will try both to highlight unique features of those works and keep to the overriding purpose of an overall critique attached to issues involved in the distinctions between the aesthetic in general and the artwork. Following the criterion of focusing on settings "where aesthetics is the operative management theory for the enterprise,"[6] our inquiry will be guided by the sort of narrative that has made organizational aesthetics into a subject of some viability, as well as one that, as presently articulated, could still do with some fundamental correctives and refinements—something we try to provide at the end with a consideration of the philosophical implications of art and the artwork.

I

John Dobson's *The Art of Management and the Aesthetic Manager* sets out probably the most comprehensive overview of both the historical and the prescriptive priorities behind these texts. Dobson helpfully posits a theory of three stages of development from (1) the "given" of the conventional twentieth-century firm with its fixation on a technicity geared towards standards of maximum aggregate wealth and shareholder wealth maximization, through (2) the challenge of business ethics that sets up the "enlightened agent" for "the moral firm," to, finally, (3) the manager "as artisan" reconfiguring as the "aesthetic manager" who generates the "Aesthetic Universe" at the *telos* of Dobson's particular reading.

For all the stimulating case studies with which Dobson peppers his text—from Pepsi Cola in Burma, Shell in the mid-Atlantic, to Nike in Vietnam—the key influence to his project is the "virtue ethics" of Alasdair MacIntyre and its indebtedness to classical Aristotelian philosophy.[7] Without MacIntyre's

---

[6] Guillet de Monthoux [2004], xi. In terms of my arrangement, it should be noted that although Pine & Gilmore [1999] belongs chronologically to this earlier stage, I shall be treating it under the later heading of theatrics as developed in a more sophisticated manner by Austin & Devin [2003].

[7] Admitting that this term can mislead, Dobson also suggests: "the ethics of excellence or the ethics of living" (127). The latter clearly resembles Michel Foucault's "aesthetics of existence," which Stephen Cummings invokes as an "alternative" to conventional business ethics. Cummings, "Resurfacing an Aesthetics of Existence as an Alternative to Business Ethics," in

encouragement, Dobson would probably never have dared go so far as to posit "the aesthetic firm as a *polis*" and to underscore that "this aesthetic pursuit of personal excellence is only possible within an organization that approximates a *polis*."[8] Not that Dobson is under any illusions that MacIntyre's ethical philosophy has much of direct import to offer business theory. Dobson simply seeks to capture McIntyre's far more comprehensive sense for ethicality by invoking as his own standards for the firm an "all-inclusive excellence" and "a holistic quest for excellence."[9] Clearly such standards, formally anyway, trump the business ethicists; and the moment that such wording joins the discourse we find ourselves flirting with "pre-modern"priorities of the Renaissance where business, management and art presumably conspired to fashion far more "creative" organizations and productivities.[10]

Dobson's optimism is catchy and the attentive reader would hope that he comes up with answers to two central concerns. The first is whether his teleology in fact provides sufficient empirical support for what he claims to be a descriptive, and not just a prescriptive, statement regarding an inevitable union of aesthetics and business.[11] Unfortunately Dobson does not provide sufficient evidence of such inevitability, or for that matter of sustainability. The prediction itself seems to depend on a general recognition of what the technical literature labels the M-form type of firm transforming itself into far less vertically-oriented operational structures (of which the 1980s adulation of Japanese firm structure was but one passing phase). To argue, as does business historian Alfred D. Chandler in his studies of the evolution of the American firm, that due to massive internal growth as well as increasing international competition the modern firm since the 1960s and 1970s has had to restructure simpler versions of the M-form through diversification, divestiture, mergers and acquisitions is certainly to acknowledge the significance of strategic corporate restructuring in the recent course of firm history.[12] But perhaps a "technical" problem—the

---

Linstead & Höpfl [2000], 212-227.

[8] Dobson [1999], 159. Also: "The firm becomes a nurturing community, a *polis*" (132).

[9] Dobson [1999], 143. The aesthetic manager "as artisan" is "one motivated primarily by a desire to achieve excellence" (157). His/her *telos* is also described as "the absolute Quality" (160).

[10] As Dobson states, "to the extent that they both represent the absence of modernity, the premodern and the aesthetic are one" (144).

[11] Dobson [1999], 149, 175, 156. The crisis in the Technical and Moral Universes "will result in the Aesthetic Universe becoming the dominant management paradigm of the twenty-first century" (167). Dobson still holds to these phrasings in Dobson [2006].

[12] Besides the major body of Chandlerian contributions (Chandler [1977], Chandler [1990]), see Alfred D. Chandler, Jr., "Corporate Strategy, Structure and Control Methods in the United States during the 20th Century," in Dosi, Teece & Chytry [2005], 381-401.

manner in which the modern firm is to remain viable and competitive—can be, and is being, dealt with technically without needing or presupposing intervention from the ethical.

And, second, how far are Dobson and MacIntyre themselves to be counted on the side of the aesthetic—and the polis? Even if he himself does grant the primacy of the "aesthetic" for any final solution, Dobson seems far too generous to MacIntyre. Notwithstanding MacIntyre's strategic invocations of the polis against the technicists, MacIntyre's own thought remains closer to what Dobson labels "Thomistic business," that is, a business ethics that however much nurtured in classical Greek and Aristotelian philosophy took Christian leave through Augustine to formulate Scholastic priorities that were never more than tangentially sympathetic to the pre-Christian classical world of the polis.[13] MacIntyre, who is in fact quite honest about his preferences for the scholastic revaluation of classical ethics, in no way upholds the aesthetic or the artistic, nor for that matter does his philosophical hero Thomas Aquinas. Dobson, by contrast, is drawn to the civic humanism of Renaissance thinkers and practitioners for whom Thomistic solutions, along with medieval Scholasticism in general, were anathema in the distinctly artisanly and business environments of Renaissance Florence and Venice.[14] Lacking MacIntyre's theoretical support for this very different alternative, Dobson is reduced to rather bare approaches to the "essence" of the aesthetic as he argues "that there is no absolute criterion" and that "there is no single answer, no rule, no dictum that can be applied"—formulations that are basically, as Dobson himself admits, little more than variants on an increasingly outdated postmodern ideology. Dobson is to be congratulated for providing the literature with a most stimulating narrative and historical framework, but if there is to be "the birth of beautiful business"—the

---

[13] Dobson [1999], 151. As MacIntyre himself puts it, "Aristotle's conception of justice and practical rationality articulated the claims of one particular type of practice-based community, partially exemplified in the *polis*, while Acquinas', like Ibn Roshd's or Maimonides', expressed the claims of a more complex form of community in which religious and secular elements coexist within an integrated whole." MacIntyre [1988], 389. Unfortunately, this reading also betrays MacIntyre's pro-Christian (and even pro-Islamic) refusal to recognize the religiosity intrinsic to the Hellenic polis.

[14] A vivid contrast to Aquinas and the scholastic tradition would be the positive contributions by the civic humanist and Florentine chancellor Leonardo Bruni to the new valorization of wealth-creation within the explicitly polis-committed ethos of the early Florentine Renaissance. This combination of wealth-creation and polis priorities is what distinguishes the Florentines no less from contemporary entrepreneurial ideologies. Bruni [1987], especially the editors' introduction, 3-46.

last words literally of Dobson's book—something in addition to Dobson's version à la MacIntyre of an aesthetic universe is needed.[15]

II

On its face, Antonio Strati's *Organization and Aesthetics* would seem to be that indispensable supplement. Clearly saturated in the literature of philosophical aesthetics, Strati has no hesitation in correctly claiming that the eighteenth-century revolution in aesthetics is "one of the greatest upheavals in the paradigm that defines humankind."[16] Strati's "aesthetic approach to organizations" means to prioritize the "aesthetic" element in organizational life. He defines as "aesthetic" the entire range of "sensory and perceptive faculties," "sensible" experiences, indeed "all the human senses," thus stressing the pathic, *em*-pathic forms of understanding not only with regard to the object proper but also to the researcher or investigator who is expected to refine "his or her own perceptive and sensory abilities" in the course of any such inquiry.[17] Traditionally the aesthetic approach has celebrated "beauty" as the "principal aesthetic category," and Strati himself admits that his own research has been empirically guided by the category of the beautiful, but he quickly denies that it is intrinsically more important than a host of other aesthetic categories. Strati himself provides the following list in addition to the beautiful: the ugly, sublime, gracious, tragic, pictaresque, ironic, and holy (or "sacred").[18] This broader canvas for the topic of the appropriate "object" of the aesthetic approach intends to encourage a much more pluralistic respect for the wide-ranging role of the aesthetic in human and organizational life, and could even be said to be follow the spirit of the larger trajectory of the aesthetic as originally formulated in the eighteenth century.[19]

---

[15] Dobson [1999], 173, 174, 175.

[16] Strati [1999], 119. Indeed its roots, Strati is quick to add, extend back to Ancient Greece (75). "It is in fact the origins of this category [of the beautiful] in the pre-Socratic thought of ancient Greece and of Magna Graecia, in the polemics waged against Pythagoras, Plato and Aristotle by the sophists and sceptics, and in the transformation of beauty from the equivalent of aesthetics into one of the numerous categories of aesthetics in late eighteenth- and early nineteenth-century European philosophy, that constitutes both the mainstream and the cultural *humus* in which the contemporary aesthetic approach to organizations has developed" (122, emphasis in original). In the following analysis, I shall also cite Strati [2000] since the latter is often a more succinct summary of Strati's positions.

[17] Strati [2000], 20, 14, 24, 29, 30-31.

[18] Strati [1999], 115; Strati [2000], 20, 24-25.

[19] The outsider to the history of aesthetics is often unaware that besides the categories of the beautiful and the sublime, aesthetics was also originally concerned with the pictaresque. Cf., e.g.,

Difficulties, however, arise when Strati wishes, on the one hand, to underscore that the aesthetic approach to management is due to the philosophical tradition of aesthetics and art rather than to organization theory proper, but, on the other hand, wants his "aesthetic" researcher to accept at face value the "aesthetic" comments of his interviewees rather than attach them to some overriding formal aesthetics. In point of fact, Strati's "empirical"data consist of inferences drawn from a series of impressionistic summaries offered by organization participants bracketed within the conditions and premises of their own discursivities.[20] From Strati's perspective a fully evolved "organizational aesthetics" would reflect the formalized results of such free-wheeling—and "empathic"—inquiries into the variety of ways in which the minds and bodies of organizational participants articulate—both verbally and non-verbally—their unique sensory and imaginal experiences as members of an organization. Ultimately Strati hopes to turn his agenda into an academic revival of what he calls the "mythical thinking" that he traces back to his *mezzogiorno* compatriot Giambattista Vico, mythical thinking being understood as presumably everything that post-Cartesian cognitivist and rationalist thinking is not.[21]

Yet Strati's specific agenda only fitfully accords with the priority of the aesthetic and the artful firm. The choice of test cases may reflect Strati's aesthetically ecumenical standards but, at least as communicated through Strati's summations, these test cases offer little more than a sequence of narrations on which very little theoretical substance can be forged. Strati dismisses any call for control factors and a modicum of statistical patterns as vestiges of an outdated "cognitive-rationalist" modeling, but his own characters remain restricted to their own articulated pathos.[22] Indeed, Strati's reiterations

---

Hipple [1957].

[20] Thus, in the core chapter of his book called "The Beautiful in Organizational Life," Strati insists that when one of his businessmen sources talks of the "beauty" of his organization, he should not be taken as making any artistic claims "in the sense that he never declares that his organization is as beautiful as a work of art" (127). Rather, he is giving us expressions in "ordinary language" that he habitually uses to evaluate the lived present; and interpretations of such language should stick to its imbeddedness, that is, the interpreter must not seek out "objective" claims proposed on behalf of a given organization but should treat comments as manifestations of the imagination and synaesthetic capacities of his interviewee (as well as his own).

[21] Strati [1999], 151-155.

[22] Strati's example of the two questions he consistently asks his interviewees in organizations connected with art photography—"Do you do beautiful things?" and "What is beautiful about the organization?" (140)—confines the range of empirical information to individuals who are primarily associated with activities touching on the arts and artisanship, thus leaving untested the presumed applicability of his approach to *all* organizations.

that he is not looking for a "rational explanation of organizational phenomena"[23] may betray something of an ideological bent behind this entire line of inquiry: like Dobson, Strati's text seems methodologically committed to postmodern discursivities. Yet, although this commitment to the celebrated democratic randomness of postmodern narrations would suggest a healthy skepticism toward *any* possible set of theoretical priorities, Strati is quick to take sides in favor of postmodern hostility toward "strong ontology" and the latter's presumed "assumptions of rationality and normativity."[24] The organization, however, which might follow Strati's critiqued "cognitive-rational" bent could legitimately claim its own "aesthetic," namely, the minimalist and functionalist aesthetic of radical modernism in the early decades of the twentieth century—even if such "aesthetics" are unpalatable to Stratis' postmodern priorities.[25] Strati may not wish to recognize such readings in the chasm he has hewn between the "sensuous" and the "cognitive-rational," but his approach has after all committed him to the discovery of the aesthetic element *wherever* any organization as such exists.

Despite these qualifications, Strati has added considerably to the level of theorizing on the artful firm. Still, in the long run the theme of the artful firm calls for something perhaps more effectively normative than his particular variant of organizational aesthetics. On the one hand, the key aesthetic object, "beauty," which Strati prefers to relegate to an equal status with a host of other such objects, deserves its own centrality in theory, since what makes this signifier "beauty" (or: "belleza," "Schönheit," "καλά") worth entertaining—both "imaginally" and "synaesthetically"—is the degree to which proximity to the adventus of the foam-born Beloved is being promised.[26] If that promise is broken or, for that matter, not even under consideration, the entire verbal sophistication to which Strati's "organizational aesthetics" is committed will yield rather flimsy dividends. And, on the other hand, instead of just taking for granted the existence of the aesthetic among members of any organizational structure and activity, it might make more sense to highlight exactly those organizations, or elements within organizations, which, at least on the surface, are purposefully engaged in the formation of art-, aesthetic- or artful firms.[27]

---

[23] Strati [2000], 31.

[24] Strati [1999], 178, 192.

[25] The subject-matter of extensive aesthetic and cultural studies on such themes as Ludwig Wittgenstein and Adolf Loos, Cubism and the Bauhaus. An easy introduction is Janik & Toulmin [1973].

[26] As an advocate of ancient Magna Graecia thinkers, Strati might wish to recall the primacy of "Aphrodite" or "Kupris" for such predecessors as Parmenides and Empedokles. Chytry [2005], 143-144.

[27] Such a strategy is perhaps hinted at by Strati's empirical dependence, notwithstanding the

Both conditions are met by a work that in its aesthetics, art-firm empirics, and sheer *brio* of personal and objective narration sets a new standard for this genre of work.

III

Pierre Guillet de Monthoux's *The Art Firm* is in important ways a realization of Strati's call for the new researcher who both widens and embodies a synaesthetic approach to the aesthetic element in organizations. The author's flair for the occasional rhetorical grand gesture should not put off the conventional academic reader since Guillet de Monthoux is, in his own right, a considerable producer of "aesthetic energy," as he himself coins it, whose work furnishes a matchless body of sheer information in the number of historical candidates potentially qualifying as embodiments of the "art firm."[28] Backed by an original and incisive reading into perhaps the most salient tradition of aesthetic thinking—the German theorists Schiller, Kant, and their post-Kantian heirs—*The Art Firm* makes up the one necessary text for our theme.

Guillet de Monthoux writes as a man with a vision: "Dionysus Inc.", an art firm grounded in what he calls "aesthetic philosophy" and its unique "metaphysics." Inspired to this vision by what he correctly sees as the increasing prominence of art and aesthetics in management literature, Guillet de Monthoux makes directly for the most promising fusion of the aesthetic and the social, indeed political, in classical aesthetics: the German poet-philosopher Friedrich Schiller's *Letters on the Aesthetic Education of Man* (1794-1795).[29] According to Guillet de Monthoux, "Schiller awakened my desire for a learned kind of management": Schiller's account of human drives prioritizes what Schiller dubbed the "play drive" (*Spieltrieb*) inherent in all humans, inspiring Guillet de Monthoux to forge a management aesthetic based on what he himself describes as the "oscillation" or *Schwung* central to this play drive. For both Schiller and his epistemological guide Immanuel Kant,[30] the redemptive feature

formal affirmations of his method, on art and artisanly operations.

[28] Guillet de Monthoux occasionally familiarizes his canonical figures as "entrepreneurs" with such gestures as describing Arthur Schopenhauer as "Nietzsche's and Wagner's management professor" (97), Robespierre as "management scientist of the Revolution" (154), "Kant and Company" (325), as well as "Fred Nietzsche" (xi), "Freddy Schiller" (274) and "Arty Schopenhauer" (353). There is also an unfortunate tendency to overpopulate his text with branding neologisms. Thus, while his reference to Joseph Beuys' "social sculpture" is relevant, it seems far less applicable to Tony Blair's British Labor politics (273).

[29] Guillet de Monthoux [2004], xii; Schiller [1967].

[30] Guillet de Monthoux [2004], 20. Guillet de Monthoux correctly calls Kant "the founder of

of the aesthetic was its liberation of human faculties into an open play in which no single faculty gains domination over the others. Both Schiller and Kant valorized the moment of this "free play" of faculties as encouragement for developing the multiple dimensions of human thought, sensibility and imagination. Taking what he learned from Kant, Schiller then applied such speculation to human drives which he summarized into a basic "form drive" and "sense drive," the solution to which one-sidedness must be found in a "play drive".[31]

Armed with these provocative ideas, Guillet de Monthoux wades through a thick body of supportive theory—the German Idealist F.W.J. Schelling's concept of genius, Friedrich Nietzsche as the "technician of speed" whose "Dionysian" reading of art supports Richard Wagner's theatrical experimentations, and even (to step momentarily outside the German ambit) the democratic aesthetics of the American pragmatist John Dewey[32]—all the while testing his Schillerian intuition that *Schwung* can furnish the most effective, while malleable, aesthetic standard for his "art firm." He points out that what these writings have added to the basic aesthetics of Kant and Schiller is a "network of players" that enriches the so far bare account of *Schwung,* thus showing that—following the hermeneutic thinking of Hans-Georg Gadamer—art is about the dynamics of social action imbedded in the production of art. For Guillet de Monthoux, art must be "managed," indeed some kind of "organization" is always necessary, but mere organization is not enough. Accordingly the "network of players" must widen to embrace both market and audience to yield a "Gadamerian" truth-table made up of the interaction of the four essential "players" for "art": the technician, artist, audience, and critic.[33]

Art seen as simultaneously management and creation nevertheless runs two major risks. The first is *totalization*, in which art activity is collapsed into the totalitarian demands of a cause, ideology, political monolith, such as fascism, nazism, or soviet communism, along with their apologists such as Martin Heidegger and Jean-Paul Sartre. The second—the apparent escape from such totalization—is the "big bang of *banalization*" in which all four "players" break off into their private realms of narcissism to generate "infantocratic" art worlds

---

aesthetic philosophy" (97).

[31] Schiller [1967], 214-219 (letter 27). Cf. also Chytry [1989].

[32] Guillet de Monthoux [2004], 59. Indeed, for all his apparent Germanophilism (excepting the perhaps unfairly pilloried G. W. F. Hegel), Guillet de Monthoux confesses that it is Dewey's "aesthetic philosophy that is a grounding for the management perspective of this book" (44).

[33] Guillet de Monthoux [2004], 75, 79 and diagram.

of the modern scene, such as Andy Warhol and comparable "continuous celebrity" campaigns.[34]

Concentrating on examples drawn from the "theatrical enterprises of the last two centuries" in France, Germany, and Sweden, Guillet de Monthoux comes up with what he regards as *five* authentic versions of the art firm: *avant-garde enterprises, artistic companies, art corporations, flux firms,* and *postmodern performances.*[35] *Avant-garde enterprises*, indeed the launching of the art firm as a whole, owe everything to the inspiration of Richard Wagner, "the pioneer of the modern art enterprise," and are all about the creation and maintenance of his Bayreuth temple to art: fan clubs, spa atmosphere, unique auditorium, educational seminars, all directed toward bringing together the experience of the arts into a single collective art-work (*Gesamtkunstwerk*).[36] *Artistic companies* are organizations as "regular" private companies, often public joint-stock, with largely didactic aims ideally suited for capturing surplus value from the space (the "subtext") between original scripts and actual stage events.[37] *Art corporations* constitute the "incorporation of art as a socioeconomic institution" into "state-financed networks of public theaters and art space," an option that obviously works best in those European state systems geared toward social democratic political practices.[38] *Flux firms*, as the name implies, represent the kind of

[34] Guillet de Monthoux [2004], 91-93. Guillet de Monthoux's Gadamarian truth-table changes accordingly: in the totalizing case, all four players "arrow" in to the center ("art") in visual confirmation of the collapse of interaction, while in the banalization case, the arrows point outward toward each player in visual confirmation of narcissistic patterns of banalization.

[35] Guillet de Monthoux [2004], xiii, 318. It is not perfectly clear whether Guillet de Monthoux is claiming that these five forms are terms applicable to the varied historical shapes taken by the one art firm over different periods—starting with the avant-garde enterprises initiated by Richard Wagner's Bayreuth project and ending up with the postmod performances of Frank Castorf's Berlin Volksbühne—or that these five are in principle heuristically available options of the art firm, notwithstanding their sequential historical manifestations. At the very least this listing helps clarify a variety of enterprises to which Guillet de Monthoux rightly wishes to draw our attention.

[36] Guillet de Monthoux [2004], 121. Also the Parisian theatrical enterprises of André Antoine's Théâtre Libre and Aurelien Lugné's Théâtre de L'Oeuvre as well as art dealer Daniel-Henri Kahnweiler with his stable of modernist artists: "in this laboratory-art firm, Braque and Picasso worked as contracted research-artists for a dealer-critic, their gallerist Kahnweiler" (135). For Wagner as business manager and entrepreneur, cf. 117 and also Chytry [2007]. Regarding the importance of Wagner, Guillet de Monthoux calls the art firm "today's bastard child of Greek tragedy" (94).

[37] Examples include French painter Jean-Louis David's ventures in Jacobin festivities as well as Stanislavski's (Constantin Alexeyev) joint-stock company and Sergei Pavlovich Diaghilev's Russian Ballet.

[38] Guillet de Monthoux [2004], 37. Examples include the Berlin Freie Volksbühne and such

event innovations associated with the postwar fluxus avant-garde movement and the antics of one of its cult-heroes Joseph Beuys,[39] from whose frenetic activity emerges a number of associations, parties, and groups, the most prominent of which was perhaps the invention of the German Green Party in 1979.[40] Finally, *postmodern (postmod) performances* encapsulate the theatrical-performative experiments beginning in East Germany under the direction of such theatrico-entrepreneurs as Frank Castorf who turned its Volksbühne into an arena for infiltrating traditional (if radical) drama with the peculiar "Dionysian" flare of rock concerts as well as the postmod multimedia reservoirs of movies and records and the glitz of modern marketing and advertising techniques.[41]

Eventually Guillet de Monthoux thinks he has found his "2002 update of the Gadamerian model" in a *Cittadellarte* founded by the Italian artist Michelangelo Pistoletto in the latter's home town of Biella (near Turin) where an old factory compound has been transformed into UNIDEE, "a university for ideas." Drawing on art students engaged in "socially responsible art" projects, UNIDEE confirms the author's intuition of a future in which the art firm will act as the "middle position" for the mixing of media, finance, management, and culture—the "open space" afforded between "media-culture and finance-management"—under the aegis of the artist as aesthetic philosopher.[42]

This closing vision is inspiring indeed, and it is good to note that Pistoletto himself points back to the Renaissance *botteghe* for his inspiration.[43] Still, it does not follow that *Cittadellarte* is (as yet) its actualization—certainly not from the sparsity of the somewhat euphoric-pilgrimatory rhetoric of Guillet de Monthoux's conclusion. In order to supply additional pragmatic content, it is

original directors as Max Reinhardt and Erwin Piscator, as well as the "Swedish art corporation" and its Stadsteatern starting with Alf Sjöberg and continuing with Suzanne Osten—through the new CEO Vivien Bandler (202, 214, 218. 239, 242, 246).

[39] Since Guillet de Monthoux's only concrete example is Beuys' own career, this category is the least transparent for analysis. Apart from a somewhat separate treatment of the sociology of Georg Simmel in this section, there is only the single passing reference to "the work of socially engaged artists such as Hans Haacke" (267).

[40] Guillet de Monthoux calls these composite results a "socially engaged flux firm" (253). Fundamentally though, the "flux firm" is little more than Beuys as a consciously "living brand" (255), "brand manager," or "concept developer" whose artwork is meant to function as "flux-firm models for aesthetic power plants" (262).

[41] Eventually such events spilled out beyond the traditional auditorium to encompass squares and housing blocks. Also included are the GDR playwright Heiner Müller and the American mise en scène "star" Robert Wilson. Guillet de Monthoux was himself an active witness to much of this part of his account.

[42] Guillet de Monthoux [2004], 351, 354.

[43] Guillet de Monthoux [2004], 353.

all the more necessary to push the author's optimism in the directions he provides. These directions may be listed under the following headings: (1) the theatrical metaphor and (2) the open-space metaphor, the former inclining toward the performative, while the latter inclines toward the designal and architectural.

IV

Joseph Pine and James Gilmore's *The Experience Economy*—along with Bernd Schmitt, David Rogers and Karen Vrotsos' *There's No Business That's Not Show Business*—and Robert Austin and Lee Devin's *Artful Making* prioritize theatre and the stage for their management recommendations.[44] Between these two sets of works, Guillet de Monthoux seemingly prefers the latter, since he relegates Pine and Gilmore to an example of banalization and includes among his colleagues one co-author of Austin and Devin.[45] Still, Pine and Gilmore—as well as Schmitt, Rogers and Vrotos— make good sense by stressing the historical emergence of what they dub the "experience economy" and "experience culture." What rightly strikes Pine and Gilmore is the proliferation of enterprises which are not simply concerned with consumption of goods and services, but with the offer of a total experience, as exemplified by theme parks of which the exemplar remains Disneyland/Disney World. This "fourth" economic offering—after commodities, goods, and services—provides (for a price) "a series of memorable events that a company stages—as in a theatrical play—to engage" the consumer "in a personal way." What is key to the "experience" is the degree to which it is "memorable" for the individual through his or her immersion and interactive participation. This "experience economy" has become increasingly central as a result of technology, rising affluence, concomitant changes in the sense of economic value, and the increase in competitive intensity. Although connected with entertainment, experience as understood by Pine and Gilmore transcends it through stressing not only an entertainment component, but also education, escapism, and explicitly aesthetic rewards, the purpose being to let one's "guest" (the authors' gentle term for the consumer) be free to be in the experience and thus undergo that personalized intensity which makes experience memorable.[46]

---

[44] Pine and Gilmore's subtitle is in fact: "Work is Theatre & Every Business a Stage."

[45] Guillet de Monthoux [2004], 317-318. Co-author Rob Austin is a participant in Guillet de Monthoux's CD "Liedership: Franz Schubert Schwungsongs for Aesthetic Management." Guillet de Monthoux [2006].

[46] Pine & Gilmore [1999], 2, 5, 31-40.

Hence Pine and Gilmore's punchline: if these four realms are brought into a single setting, then any plain space turns into a space appropriate for "staging an experience."[47] This sense toward a generic and "mnemonic space" explains why for the experience economy "work is theatre," since theatre captures the dramaturgical character of the enterprise; accordingly, it is to the practices of drama and dramaturgy that the experience manager should turn in order to create—following formal drama—the memorably staged experience. Ultimately there is no clear line for distinguishing between an exemplary two-hour performance of King Lear and a FedEx "overnight performance."[48]

Pine and Gilmore's exploitations of theatrical performative clues for management practices contain some stimulating insights and tips, but, as we shall see, Austin and Devin furnish a more developed management understanding of the theatre metaphor. What remains worth noting regarding the peculiarities in the Pine and Gilmore approach is the degree to which they regard the experience economy stage as itself merely a transition to a more sophisticated—and desirable—stage. This ultimate level they call a "transformation economy" to be presumably guided no longer by "experience stagers" but by "transformation eliciters."[49] Instead of paying for a single experience as in the case of the experience-economy level, customers are given a "*series* of experiences" designed to elicit self-transformations. If the experience economy was exemplified by Disneyland and Rainforest Cafes, the transformation economy resembles the long-term offerings of the martial arts, nutrition management, reading transformations, and higher education. Indeed, at this visionary summit Pine and Gilmore drop all timidity and reveal "transformation eliciters"—and themselves—to be engaged in something far more comprehensive: a life of service for which the true key is to be found in the teachings of Jesus and Paul. Once we are about transformations and inner selves, then commerce becomes a matter of universal moral choice and knowledge is designed to produce a "wisdom technology." To be perfectly frank: transformation is inevitably "spiritual transformation" and our "purpose is to glorify God and to encourage others to do the same." After all, where have

---

[47] Pine & Gilmore [1999], 42. The reader of management literature may wish to compare this resultant "sense of space" (42) with the Zen concept of "ba" promulgated by Nonaka & Konno [1998] and Ikujiro Nonaka, Noburu Konno & Ryoko Toyama, "Emergence of 'Ba': A Conceptual Framework for the Continuous and Self-Transcending Process of Knowledge Creation," in Nonaka & Nishiguchi [2001], 13-29.

[48] Pine & Gilmore [1999], 101, 161.

[49] Pine & Gilmore [1999], 186. According to the authors we need to move beyond the comparatively simple "work as theatre" of the experience-economy level to "an important shift" in which customers themselves learn to "act" and the customer becomes "the product" as such (194-195).

we come to but the call of Jesus to "preach the gospel" as the ultimate in "strategic intents" in our concern for the care of ourselves and of others?[50]

Fortunately for the theme of an "experience economy," Schmitt, Rogers, and Vrotsos provide some secular relief to Pine and Gilmore's excesses by extending the more salient aspects of the concept into their more professional reading of an "experience culture." Schmitt, who already contributed in an earlier book to the understanding of aesthetics for marketing,[51] argues, along with his co-authors, that show business practices can augment management's exploitation of the range of experiences available for marketing products in this emerging experience culture, and provides a heady set of examples. Besides some fascinating looks at the business of cooking and the art business, the authors single out Las Vegas as the most striking example of an entire municipality functioning according to the precepts of such an experience culture. Indeed, Las Vegas, they aver, is "the real capital of the United States." The usual model of a modern democracy, the United States "is now quite clearly the worldwide source of entertainment ideas. Entertainment is, in fact, one of the great democratic experiences the U.S. has to offer."[52]

Still, it is with Austin and Devin that one is furnished a more forthright and ultimately practicable account of the relevance of theatre for management.[53] Although modest for not only warning that "artful making"—in contrast to the more conventional "industrial making" — is not the best option in every case but also that the prerequisites for choosing either option "are firm, no 'ifs' or 'maybes' about them," Austin and Devin do see something fundamentally topical about artful making for the present stage of economic development. If their basic proposal is that the "activities of a wise manager...need not be much different from those of a theatre director" because "the collaborative art of

---

[50] Pine & Gilmore [1999], 165, 182-183, 189, 195, 202. Thus: "perfecting people falls under the province of God, the Author and Perfecter of our faith rather than in the domain of human business" (206). This Pauline telos to Pine and Gilmore's particular "story" should have been detected at the very outset—the dedication of the book is after all "To the Author and Perfecter of our faith"—but the articulations of their concluding raptures, anchored in their "personal belief" that even "transformations are only temporal states for the eternalities they glorify," at least underscore for us the transient commitment of their book to the entire thesis of work as theatre (206). The connection between the theme of caring or care and management has been already made by management interpreters of the philosophy of Martin Heidegger to the extent that the latter is grounded in the thematics of Care (*Sorge*). See Spinosa, Flores & Dreyfus [1997].

[51] Schmitt & Simonson [1997], esp. "Aesthetics: The New Marketing Paradigm," 3-25.

[52] Schmitt, Rogers & Vrotsos [2004], 239.

[53] One of the authors is a practicing dramaturg, actor and playwright with extensive experience in a theatre company while the other author is a Harvard management professor. The company is the People's Light and Theatre Company of Malvern, Pennsylvania (Lee Devin informs me that the theatre has recently dropped the word "Company" from its name).

theatre, and particularly rehearsal, as an enabling metaphor," is the most apt one to this level of development, artful making can be expected to play a growing role in the age of information economy, granted the latter's strategic making and agile software development.[54] Drawing on a three-stage history marked by agricultural, industrial and now information or knowledge phases, the authors see artful making as uniting "industrial making's" advantages of working through cheap and rapid iteration transactions with "ancient making's" capacity to customize.[55]

If Pine and Gilmore extracted Drama, Script, Theatre, and final Performance from their dramaturgical gambit, Austin and Devin in their turn come up with: Release, Collaboration, Ensemble, and Play. Instead of conventional restraints on original thinking and fluid collaboration by workers, the rehearsal process of theatre can teach business managers to stress "emergence," allowing product thinking to "emerge" spontaneously from the process of making. Rejumbling familiar business vocabularies, the authors insistently downplay even such apparently "innovative" themes as "experimentation" and instead model behaviors resembling what really happens in theatre rehearsals where ambiguity, iteration, and exploration sustain the kind of "high uncertainty" which generates "creation" and "reconceiving." Willing to risk the prospect of matters spinning "out of control," Austin and Devin call for a "control through release" where all parties achieve an almost simultaneous sense of release and focus.[56] Given that artists and actors are famously unresponsive to coercion, it behooves this "artful manager" to give free rein to "reconceiving" and "spontaneity"—just as the theatre director does—in treading the fine line between such "control through release" and an "anything goes" policy.[57]

Once "emergence"occurs through the management equivalent of "rehearsal," we advance to "collaboration"—a state in which participants have been released from the usual constraints of vanity, inhibitions, and preconceptions. We then move on to the conception of "ensemble," the quality of collaborative work in which the whole becomes greater than the sum of its parts and inspires a level of productive interchange which the authors do not hesitate to label "a kind of artwork." Finally, the level of "play," a concept

---

[54] Austin & Devin [2003], 45, 162, 167. The authors subscribe to this particular way of designating present computer technology priorities. See the Manifesto for Agile Software Development (38).

[55] Austin & Devin [2003], 54.

[56] Indeed they bring up helpful breathing exercises to urge along the process of concentrated relaxation, a familiar move in conventional Buddhist practices.

[57] Austin & Devin [2003], 95, 97, 98. Aware of the obvious objections, the authors repeatedly deny that they are endorsing an "anything goes" agenda (89, 97).

invaluable for suggesting both a quality and an event, is seen through the conventional theatrical metaphor that the "act of making a play *is* the play," suggesting that a business product should be analogously "redefined as the experience of its action with customers, an interaction in which both product and customers vary over time."[58] The authors close with the final promise that like actors, workers who have achieved such a "play" level of awareness will share with artists an identification with their work "for the sake of doing their work." In other words, they will have discovered the "ultimate purpose" and the "final cause" of artful making as such, namely, "the joy of working for the sake of doing the work, of *work as Play*."[59]

In reviewing Austin and Devin's enterprise as a whole, one cannot but hope that the authors are on the right track given the attractions of a "work-as-play" vision for the economic and product-making future. Nonetheless, it is worth voicing some concerns. First, Austin and Devin's theoretical dependence on an economic dialectics that assumes the return of more originative patterns within newer configurations may be unsustainable. While they see ancient making as furnishing the model of the craft manufacturer, the "art" metaphor they regard as more relevant to the information economy is dramaturgy and the theatrical arts, a shift that is not backed on the authors' part by a comparable genealogy of its origins and development throughout human history. Second, the authors' version of the theatre vocation depends on "ideal" accounts of what theatre, actors, and directors habitually do to such an extent that the authors themselves must occasionally intervene in their own narrative to admit that in practice theatrical professions will fall short of such ideal practices. But if that is the case, why should business management not invoke its own "ideal" standards of honest product-making and exemplary firm performances in the more traditional manner?[60] And third, the authors are unclear on the implications of their

---

[58] Austin & Devin [2003], 128-129, 131, 170 (emphasis added). Lee Devin emphasizes that this act is *not* a metaphor, "it's the fact." He adds: "This feature of drama, which it shares with dance and music, is a key to understanding. It's also a feature of any service....Delivering a car to me when I need a rental—that service exists only as executed." Personal communication, 2007.

[59] Austin & Devin [2003], 180 (emphasis added). Of course, the authors continuously emphasize how practical their project really is. A whole chapter on the "fiscal responsibility" of artful making presumably will reassure more rigid mentalities that theatrical enterprises are like venture capital planning and investing since both ultimately depend on "casting," securing the appropriate people for effective risk-sharing (149-160). Moreover, rehearsal and theatre financing have never been separate from firm performance deadlines and profit results, at least in principle. Thus, even in their final paeans to the vocation of work as play, the authors make sure to note that beyond the intrinsic rewards to artful makers, there will be external results which are "yes, highly profitable" (180). Profit may arise through newer, econometrically more updated, categories of "innovation and real value creation," but it will remain profit nonetheless.

[60] Austin & Devin [2003], 119, 134, 177-178. This seems particularly the case when the

approach for the meaning of "profit" as such. They seem confident that a process that has culminated in their version of Play for workers unleashes a state of felicity, collaboration, and good feelings which should surmount any particular shortcomings of the success of their resultant product on the market, but then they want to promise an ultimate "profit" at some stage to keep that felicity and creative spirit going. On its face this seems as difficult to accept as it would be in any realistic assessment of the professional decisions by directors, actors, and sundry other participants in the formal theatrical process and vocation. More clarification in this respect is needed, and the odds are that it will be furnished through the standard vocabulary of formal economic and management theory.

Still, any theorizing about value creation in general should benefit greatly from drawing on the theatre metaphors so ably championed by Austin and Devin —as well as, to a lesser extent, by Pine and Gilmore and Schmitt, Rogers, and Vrotsos. Such theorizing will also want to look into our final area of aesthetic readings of management and business enterprises, namely, the spaces opened out by design and architecture.

V

Of our final two selections, it must be forewarned that Paul Dickinson's *Beautiful Corporations* is replete with propositional embarrassments.[61] Nonetheless, appraisal of this intimate collaboration between author and designer can serve as focus for a tendency among the contemporary design industry to claim as its own the presumably coming age of "a new beauty." As in comparable cases, its argument for an historic alliance between aesthetics and organization comes down to the critical role that design is playing today in competitive advantage, particularly as it addresses "corporate identity" and "brand."[62]

---

authors start bringing in practices like breathing exercises and rehearsal tips. Such suggestions can be accommodated within more conventional management approaches as at best an occasional relief from the more pressing demands of workmanship and innovation in such fast-paced industries as agile software development.

[61] Statements presumably grounded in the author's "atheist, Darwinist perspective" range from such evolutionary cretinisms as: "those that did like spending time interacting with idiots all died," to the deliciously inane: "Nature has equipped us with instincts that can, eventually, snuff out Nazis." Dickinson & Svensen [2000], 8, 9.

[62] Dickinson & Svensen [2000], 98. In fact the best part of the book is the inset of color illustrations of various exemplars of contemporary corporate design.

For Dickinson the "beautiful corporation," certainly the beautiful corporation of the future, will be driven by Dickinson's key direction: "sustainability product marketing."[63] Dickinson envisages this futuristic firm to be committed to care, environmentality, a humane attitude toward employees, the assumption that customers are intelligent, and the maintenance of a "higher" tone overall. Put together such a world of beautiful enterprises should yield a "Mozart economy." To this purpose his companies will exert all their resources in design, advertising, tone and even ergonomics to further the standard of sustainable development, defined as "meeting the needs of the present without compromising the ability of future generations to meet their own needs." Dickinson advocates Peter Downing's "sky-blue corporate social reporting" which measures economic performance not only by the usual economic indicators but also by the inclusion of environmental performance and social impact reports for the company's "stakeholders," the latter term covering the entire panoply of groupings—not just shareholders—involved in company production all the way to the community in general. As a result the company which pursues such sustainable competitive strategies deserves to be labeled "beautiful," since "beauty is the essence of sustainable competitive advantage."[64]

There is certainly nothing wrong with these estimable goals demanded—but also predicted—of Dickinson's dream corporation. However, Dickinson's most extensive confirmation, the case of IKEA and its founder Ingvar Kamprad, hardly delivers confidence.[65] Kamprad's putative "democratization" of furniture stylistics to the Greater Number is certainly worth assessing, but might be approached with a touch more skepticism regarding this occasionally richest man in the world. The embarrassing facts of Kamprad's own dalliance with earlier Swedish Nazi movements have wrung from Kamprad the obligatory mea culpa; but even without such revelations, Dickinson, intrepid fan of stylistics and moral tones, should have been a bit more sensitive to the "tonalities" of such *völkisch* lines as he himself cites from Kamprad: "What we want, we can and will do. Together: A glorious future!"[66] *Marschieren wir*?

---

[63] Putting aside the question of whether the author thinks that this has always been the case or that the beautiful corporation is a new phenomenon; certainly he regards it as a "new" beauty (98).

[64] Dickinson & Svensen [2000], 98, 100, 103.

[65] After a perfunctory description of IKEA operations that could have been penned by an IKEA publicist, Dickinson simply ends up quoting at length from Kamprad's soporific 1976 manifesto The *Testament of a Furniture Dealer* without bothering to draw on third-person evaluations and studies of both Kamprad and IKEA.

[66] Dickinson & Svensen [2000], 114.

If there is nothing in Dickinson's work to guarantee the fiscal practicability —let alone, as he claims, the inevitability—of the "evolutionary" turn to his beautiful corporation, a similar concern must be expressed about Virginia Postrel's *The Substance of Style.* Nonetheless, notwithstanding her tendency to pursue her stated aim—"examining afresh the nature of aesthetic value and its relation to our personal, economic, and social lives"—through phrases (from "look and feel" to a rousing "smart and pretty") whose cloying pertness actually obscures her more serious reflections, Postrel's work is theoretically more substantive and her overriding thesis that we are entering an "aesthetic age" in which the "aesthetic imperative is here to stay" worth further scrutiny.[67]

By "aesthetic" (or "aesthetics") and "aesthetic age" Postrel definitely does not intend a "philosophy of art," nor does aesthetics include the "meaning" even of poetry (although the "sound" of poetry is "arguably" acceptable), nor finally is aesthetics about beauty, since that would make it "too limited."[68] Rather Postrelian aesthetics concerns direct sensory, emotional reactions to precognitive stimuli that more often than not provoke pleasure. Central to her revision of aesthetics is a demotion—or democratization—of its bounds in order to bring in a multitude of features that in her view were prematurely excluded by the snobbism of a traditionalist aesthetics tied to high culture.

Postrel posits three marks of the new aesthetic age: the coexistence of different styles in our pluralistic, liberal, and formally tolerant culture; the primacy of environment or "place" for focalizing the world of designs, brands and commodities (best exemplified by the Starbucks coffee chain); and the increasing stress on personal appearance.[69] Particularly the easy availability of credit cards in the early 1970s followed by computerized data streamlining the consumption process and the burst of high tech and internet innovations of the 1990s that are "particularly friendly" to aesthetic criteria has facilitated the cross-over to "a new economic and cultural moment" ever since the 1980s.[70]

Given this importance of the "aesthetic imperative"—as she labels its admonitory component—it turns out to be not so surprising that Postrel's apparently minimalist approach toward the aesthetic gives way soon enough to acknowledgment that even an aesthetic limited to "sensory elements that move

---

[67] Postrel [2003], xi, 164.

[68] Postrel [2003], 5-6.

[69] Postrel [2003], 9, 19, 24. Postrel later repeats: "places, the touchstone of our aesthetic era" (123). Her invocation of "immersive environments" (123) recalls the language of Pine & Gilmore. Postrel does grant that such factors were present earlier—interestingly citing a 1927 article by Elmo Calkins called "Beauty the New Business Tool" to this effect—but contends that what is different today is their pervasiveness (34-35).

[70] Postrel [2003], 39, 49, 45, 52. Also: "a major ideological shift" (11); a "turning point" and "critical mass" (39).

or delight" must bring in the fact that humans are not only "visual-tactile" but also "social, pattern-making, tool-using creatures." This, in turn, entails the injection of "meaning" into her calculus. If "aesthetic value" is "intrinsic," and "meaning" is the source of such aesthetic value, it turns out that it is "identity" which constitutes the very meaning of that source. Identity according to Postrel stands for a sense of the self which manifests itself; hence the "aim of aesthetic meaning" is "to turn our ineffable sense of self into something tangible and authentic."[71]

It is at this point that Postrel's argument, reflecting the author's overlooking of much aesthetic philosophy since Kant, becomes jumbled in evocations of standards of "what seems *right*" and demands that "others"—society or other individuals—should "see something *true* about who I really am." Alas for further clarification, Postrel's contentions immediately get tied up with her confused reading of "authentic" or "authenticity,"[72] and having abandoned any interest in the master category of beauty or the beautiful, Postrel has no alternative in facing the overall issue of genuine meaning within aesthetic value other than to resort to the familiar dichotomy between the "shine" of aesthetic value and the "substance" of moral value: "aesthetic pleasure and moral virtue are independent goods."[73]

Yet throughout this same text Postrel's own passing comments serve to unsettle her stated parameters. Designs, she grants, can be "comparatively attractive in some universal sense;" "making things beautiful can also make them work better; "all other things being equal, we prefer beauty, just as we prefer intelligence, charm, eloquence, or talent." What Postrel wants to appropriate is nothing less than the Renaissance which fused art, science and personal refinement, a "renaissance attitude" combining technology, science

---

[71] Postrel [2003], 33, 75, 95, 102, 104, 108-109.

[72] Postrel [2003], 116, 108 (emphasis added). Postrel denigrates the "authentic" as an "objective" category, overlooking that its original introduction into the philosophical literature by Martin Heidegger as *Eigentlichkeit* aimed precisely to bring an "ownness" *(eigentlich)* or individual owning up into philosophical discussion, thus giving rise to subsequent existentialist thought. Postrel insists that the authenticity literature had removed the "subject" (113) and she eventually provides her own presumably original reading of the "authentic."

[73] Postrel [2003], 90. Also: "Rhetoric that treats aesthetic quality as a mark of goodness and truth—or as a sign of evil and deception—is profoundly misleading" (89). Not surprisingly Postrel therefore comes up with the postmodernist version of the moral conundrum of the "beauty" of acts of destruction which carry nefarious human consequences. If the older version invoked the "pleasurable" sights of air bombings, Postrel brings up the spectacular case of 9-11 images (91). That the theoretical problem might be lessened by a different—less impoverished—reading of aesthetic value eludes Postrel (no less than traditional "aestheticization of politics" critics), even though such readings are at the origins of the aesthetic philosophizing launched by Kant and Schiller. See Chapter 2 above for more details.

and beauty: "Can we recapture the wisdom of the Renaissance, learning again to accept a world that is smart *and* pretty?"[74] This is all admirable, but there is no chance of even approaching a Renaissance profundity in these matters if one takes Postrel's otherwise dismissive and reductive approach toward the higher levels of aesthetic value that necessarily raise—as they certainly did for the original Renaissance—the theme of beauty.[75]

It would be unfair not to mention at the same time that notwithstanding such shortcomings, Postrel can be stimulating on a variety of empirical themes when she balances competing claims.[76] Yet an approach that remains content to locate the aesthetic "on the margin" cannot but raise misgivings. Indeed, in the final analysis Postrel even contradicts her own earlier contention of the permanence of our aesthetic age by claiming that this "aesthetic age won't last forever" as her "age of look and feel" is topped by "something else." Such turnabouts can only be explained by Postrel's consistent failure to sufficiently appreciate the depth and range of the aesthetic in the first place. If the "paradox" of aesthetics is, as she puts it, that it is "at once trivial and eternal," then it is clear that she has not sufficiently considered its "eternal" component, just as she earlier failed to accommodate her thought to the "truth" and "rightness" of the "self" which aesthetically manifests, at least in part, as something "true" also for others.[77]

Postrel is learned enough to know that in different epochs even "poor people" built European cathedrals and constructed Tibetan sand paintings, and she rightly wonders whether in contrast our "aesthetic age" may leave posterity nothing more substantial than "Rashid's curvy plastic trash cans." However, she does not draw the obvious inference that maybe this contrast simply accentuates the fact that we are not in an aesthetic age at all—unless, of course, we follow her lead of depriving the aesthetic of almost everything that gave it transcendent and luminous importance to less deliberately commodifying epochs.[78]

---

[74] Postrel [2003], 89, 178, 179, 182 (emphasis in original). In giving content to her standard of "smart and pretty," Postrel even takes the giant step of invoking Galileo Galilei himself: apparently "his work was smart *and* pretty" (170, emphasis in original).

[75] That such profundity does not reject but easily absorbs the Postrelian "look and feel" approach toward the aesthetic can be confirmed by Schiller's own extensive approbation and account of the ongoing human "delight in semblance (or shine)" *(die Freude am Schein)*. Schiller [1967], 193 (Letter 26). A theory such as Schiller's that celebrates play as the key to being human can hardly be regarded as oblivious to Postrel's concerns.

[76] I mention Postrel's treatment of "design boundaries" as a refreshing adjudication between excessive regulation and no control in "The Boundaries of Design," Postrel [2003], 122-163, as well as her speculation that increasing investment in aesthetics can be difficult to gauge in conventional economic measurements, culminating in her sensible recommendation to conceptualize an economy where sources of value "are also sensory and expressive" (174-176).

[77] Postrel [2003], 167, 168, 171, 190.

[78] Postrel [2003], 45, 191.

VI

Hey! People! Listen Up! Ya gotta Schwung![79]

The preceding body of works carries one overriding virtue: if it does not necessarily prove that we are in a privileged age with regard to the ubiquity of the aesthetic for management and commodities, it does raise important problematizations that might have something worth offering in time on the relationship of management to the aesthetic dimension. Yet, while such literature is therefore encouraging, it is essential to build on the more serious theoretical formulations within them.

For this effort what must be equally recalled is that the aesthetic dimension is a wider and looser category than the categories of art and the artwork which largely helped give birth originally to the development of aesthetic discursivities. The artwork, embodying the universal play that is responsible for the very existence of the human activity of play, encompasses the entire range of human production or productivity. Formally, however, a simple typology of different kinds of such products would include at least the following: (1) the artwork proper (the work of the artist), (2) the craftwork (the work of the artisan), and (3) the commodity (the work of the enterprise). Most of our contributors to an organizational aesthetics remain really concerned with the commodity level since it is the kind of product that is thoroughly embedded in an ongoing entrepreneurial or innovative process, and no matter how radically the commodity stretches its essence in directions extraneous to its character, it can never quite constitute the next level, that of the craftwork or artisanship. For what makes a commodity a commodity is its membership in an industrial-productive system and process that cannot do away entirely with its own incentives of profit. Even if the presumably generous notion of value-creation is substituted for profit, very little if anything will have been conceptually achieved to free the commodity of its inner constraints. This is not to impugn the role of the commodity, especially in contemporary life; after all, the commodity process has been responsible for an unprecedented provision of resources, comforts and luxuries to at least a substantial portion of the global population.

Nonetheless, what immediately distinguishes the craftwork from the commodity is the former's imbeddedness not so much in profit or value-creation motivations as in what used to be celebrated as a "calling" (*Beruf*) or vocation, something particularly well described by Austin and Devin in their account of

[79] From the inside jacket of the musical CD by Guillet de Monthoux [2006].

"ancient practices."[80] The craft ethos is a guild ethos that minimizes, even where it cannot entirely do away with, profit concerns in its commitment to quality of production, to "craft" in the full meaning of the term. We are certainly not in an age prioritizing such standards over production, although we can hope and expect, as do Dickinson & Svensen and Postrel among others, that some of these craftly qualities will attach themselves to the commodity process.

But even the "calling" of the artisan and the standard of guild practice are not the final, constitutive layer. The artwork—or the artist—is bound neither by profit/value-creation, nor by the dignity and moral ethos of the craftsperson, but by the simple spontaneity of a play that is content to justify itself precisely as such play.[81] To further understand the implications of this level we turn again to Guillet de Monthoux's work, the only project among those we have considered which has taken on the explicit task of developing an effective and relevant aesthetic theory related to play and artwork.

Guillet de Monthoux has built on Schiller's and Kant's insights into the aesthetic as focused on the "free play" of human faculties whenever understanding and imagination are in a state of spontaneous openness or "indeterminability" prior to being "constrained" toward adopting either a cognitive or a moral stance, and on the centrality of this state of play for the standard of genuine humanness.[82] In turn the hermeneutic philosopher Hans-Georg Gadamer has widened the scope of Kant's and Schiller's insights to cover the very character of reality proper,[83] his formulations actually more in the spirit of Guillet de Monthoux's reading of the play drive (*Spieltrieb*) as a "swinging bridge between form and substance," a "weightless condition of Schwung, where the individual balances in the aesthetic seesaw between form

---

[80] My inclusion of the German word is meant as a reminder of Max Weber's classic sociological readings of the function of vocation.

[81] It should be noted that claims of a hierarchy ruling the productive trinity of artwork/ craftwork/ commodity are not simultaneously claims on behalf of hierarchy in society proper. As in the case of classical Athenian culture, the supremacy of the artwork and craftwork (over the commodity) may often go with a greater social equality *(demokratia)*.

[82] Although it is true that Guillet de Monthoux's inspiration for Schwung is Schiller, the latter did not in fact generally employ the word itself. Instead, he regularly invoked "free movement" (*Gang*), "reciprocal action" (*Wechselwirkung*), and "oscillation" (*Schwankung*); above all he is rightly renowned for introducing to the philosophical literature the related notion of "play" (*Spiel*): "Man only plays when he is in the fullest sense of the word a human being, and he is only fully a human being when he plays." Schiller [1967], 106, 107. German scholars studying the late medieval concept of "impetus" are prone to translate it as *Schwung* in order to highlight its "liveliness" or "vivacity." Blumenberg [1987], 151.

[83] Gadamer's reflections on the "way of being of play" (*Seinsweise des Spieles*) are located in the section "Play as Indicator of the Ontological Explication" in Gadamer [1972], 97-127, the most important part for our observations being "The Concept of Play," 97-105.

and substance."[84] Within this context the specific purpose of *human* play, according to Gadamer, is "the ordering and shaping of the play-space" as such (*die Ordnung und Gestaltung der Spielbewegung*). Such "ordering" allows the "hither and thither" of the play movement to be released as if from itself, explaining the commonly-noted self-generation of play. It also means that whatever the specific ordering or shaping, the play movement tends to repetition and a continued, punctuated self-renewal (*Sich-Erneuern des Spieles*) which engraves its form on the specificities of the play movement.[85]

At this stage Gadamer himself defers to the speculations of his own teacher Martin Heidegger's "ontological exposition of the horizon of time." Thus the priority of the Schwung of nature becomes in effect an inquiry into the very meaning of time since, as the title of his magnum opus *Being and Time* promises, Martin Heidegger is famed for the degree to which his interpretation of human being (*Dasein*) necessarily attaches to the horizon of time as the key toward raising the ultimate philosophical question of being (*Sein*).[86] What is less commonly recognized is that Heidegger's stubborn pursuit of a new reading of originary time as timeliness (*Zeitlichkeit*)—versus the commonplace notion of time as a sequential series of "nows"—culminates in exactly the same priority of Schwung that Guillet de Monthoux and Gadamer—themselves following in the wake of Kant and Schiller—have formulated.[87] If originary time or timeliness is the "original unifying unity of the three ecstases of expectance [future], retention [past or has-been], and enpresenting [present]," as Heidegger exhaustively argues, it is because time as such invariably temporalizes (*zeitigen*), since it is in its essence the *ekstatikon*, that is, the "outside-of-

[84] Guillet de Monthoux [2004], 19-20. The author even provides an illustration of someone on a swing. His first use of the word Schwung occurs in his account of the sculptor Joseph Beuys' *The Crucifixion* regarding the "Schwung" between its two poles of energy of "idea" and "substance" (6).

[85] Gadamer [1972], 103, 100. For Gadamer human play simply belongs to an overall process in nature (*Naturvorgang*), and this process lacks any underlying substrate or subject preceding play as such: in other words, play is the execution of the movement (*Vollzug der Bewegung*) characterizing *all* nature and reality. Like Guillet de Monthoux, Gadamer then pinpoints the precise character of this movement as the "hither and thither of the movement of play" (*Hin und Her der Spielbewegung*) which opens up a play-space (*Spielraum*), the boundary and shape of the particular site of the specific play which is itself bound by a universal outside that Gadamer calls "the limits of free space" (*die Grenzen des freien Raumes*). Gadamer [1972], 102. Sometimes Gadamer describes this "hither and thither" as "tense" or "taut" (*spannungsvoll*) (101).

[86] Gadamer [1972], 116. Cf. also Gadamer, "The Timeliness [*Zeitlichkeit*] of the Aesthetic" (115-122).

[87] Heidegger's students included not only Gadamer but also his assistant Eugen Fink who subsequently wrote at length on "play as symbol of the world" (*Spiel als Weltsymbol*), drawing partly on the play reflections of Friedrich Nietzsche. Cf. Fink [1960] and Fink [2003].

oneself" as such, the (non-spatially meant) stretch of tense or tension proper.[88] For Heidegger the "being" of such "ecstases" "lies exactly in free ecstatic Schwung."[89] Temporalizing "is the free oscillation [*Schwingung*] of the original entire timeliness; time reaches [*erschwingt*] and contracts [*verschwingt*] itself."[90] Thus at the very limit of originary reality Schwung is in fact the essence of time in its "ecstatic unitary oscillation" [*Schwingung*].[91]

This complex account forms perhaps the most far-reaching philosophical justification of Schwung as the core, so to speak, of originary time. Its relevance for our theme is that, just as Schwung culminates in time or timeliness, Schwung no less lays out the originary basis for the *aisthesis* that serves as the lexical grounds for the modern word "aesthetics." If *aisthesis* as such derives from the Greek verbs *aistho*/*aisthomai*/*aisthanomai* (ἀΐσθω/αἴσθομαι/αίσθάνομαι) meaning: "breathing in, gasping," then the cosmic Schwung translates most effectively into the primordial human phenomenon of ongoing breath: of breathing-in and breathing-out as the human "play" of liveliness without which there is, to be obviously frank, no life, let alone vivacity or *élan*.[92]

Phenomena which manifest or appear with the impact of a prominent or memorable emergence (characteristically labeled *Adventus* or *Parousia* in the relevant literature) provoke the involuntary intake of breath ("gasp") that corresponds to the proper translation for *aistho* (ἀΐσθω).[93] A gasp of this order "stops," as it were, time itself—one is invariably "breathless" before the emergence of the authentically beautiful—only to reconfirm through the very same register of that apparent stoppage the pulsating, palpitating nature of pure time itself: as the play of the Aion, the play of time's plenitude—its "foreverness" (εἰς τοὺς αἰῶνας τῶν αἰώνων). The Beautiful is that, in short,

---

[88] Heidegger [1978], 264. Intrinsically "outside" any possible object or sets of objects, timeliness is no less intrinsically open as such, its horizon necessarily making up the "open expanse" (*offene Weite*) toward which its own carrying-away or remotion is as such outside of itself.

[89] Heidegger [1978], 268. He specifically likens this notion to Henri Bergson's concept of *élan*.

[90] Heidegger in fact links the primordiality of Schwung to his key existential notions of throw, thrownness (*Geworfenheit*) and projection (*Entwurf*). Heidegger [1978], 268.

[91] Indeed, such oscillation carries an upswing" (*Überschwung*) that "swings in" the very possibility of "world" or "worlding" (*Welten*) for humans (*Dasein*). Heidegger [1978], 269, 270.

[92] Following Onians [1988], 74-75, in his penetrating move between the meanings of a later "I perceive" (thus the commonplace philosophical reading of *aisthesis* as perception or senses) and an earlier "I breathe (in), gasp," both meanings centered on the Homeric and Attic Greek verb *aio* (ἀΐω). The emphasis on breathing in or gasping is unique to Onians; generally Greek lexicons simply translate the verb as "breathing" or "breathing out".

[93] And its middle voice *aisthanomai* (αίσθάνομαι).

on behalf of which gasp (hence *aisthesis*) occurs. It goes without saying that such provocations to our everyday are more than just "smart and pretty"; at the very least, they launch a thousand ships.

If, then, nature shows itself precisely as this purposeless, non-intentional, continually self-renewing play that is manifested in humans as the "hither and thither" of *aisthesis*, it becomes no less, at least according to Gadamer, the "model for art" (*Vorbild der Kunst*).[94] This is why the artist is often seen as irresponsible when compared with the craftsperson or entrepreneur. Yet that apparent irresponsibility reveals the full superiority of the artwork and the comparative freedom intrinsic to its operations. The most direct human manifestation of the ontological priority of the Aion as universal play, artwork must invariably surpass and bracket both the craftwork and the commodity. For:

> All holy plays of art are only distant imitations of the eternal play of the universe, of the eternally self-creating artwork.[95]

[94] Gadamer [1972], 101.
[95] Friedrich Schlegel, cited by Gadamer [1972], 101.

CHAPTER SIX

'Aphrodisian Bliss' for the Artful Firm

Wagner, Nietzsche, and the Idea of Bayreuth in Relation to Organization and Management Theory

> Nietzsche's break with Wagner, this last event of the German spirit over which greatness broods ...
>
> Oswald Spengler, *The Decline of the West*[1]

> zerging' in Dunst
> das heil'ge Römische Reich,
> uns bleibe gleich
> die heil'ge deutsche Kunst![2]
>
> Richard Wagner, *Die Meistersinger von Nürnberg*

> *On the genesis of art*—That making perfect, seeing as perfect, which characterizes the cerebral system bursting with sexual energy (evening with the beloved, the smallest chance occurrences as transfixed, life a succession of sublime things, "the misfortune of the unfortunate lover worth more than anything else"): on the other hand, everything perfect and beautiful works as an unconscious reminder of that enamored condition and its way of seeing—every perfection, all the beauty of things, revives through contiguity this aphrodisian bliss [*die aphrodisische Seligkeit*].
>
> Friedrich Nietzsche, *The Will to Power* [805]

Not only did Pierre Guillet de Monthoux's theory of Schwung encourage our speculations closing the last chapter. His choice of the Bayreuth music drama festival created by composer Richard Wagner as the first "art firm" forms the

---

[1] Spengler [1969], 475.

[2] "Were the Holy Roman Empire to vanish into mist, there still would remain to us the Holy German Art."

inspiration behind the following investigation on behalf of the concept of "the artful firm."[3]

Among the more effective predictions of Friedrich Nietzsche was his stated confidence that future generations would forever entwine his name with that of composer Richard Wagner.[4] Nietzsche had been one of the most enthusiastic younger supporters of Wagner's cause of promulgating a new music drama and theatrical-cultural site for its reception—the so-called "Idea of Bayreuth"—that would regain for the German spirit the standards and pathos of classical Hellenic tragic drama. The break between Nietzsche and Wagner proved a crucial element in the matured Nietzsche's formulations of an "aesthetic morals"[5] that would supersede Wagner, Wagernianism, and the gathering of Wagnerian acolytes in Bayreuth.

"Bayreuth": a town in northern Bavaria, a "temple of art," "art-Washington," "Grail city of art"—among its many accolades. In point of fact the siting of a whole body of theory and practice perpetrated through a lifetime of musico-dramatic experiments by that "Red Composer," that "Marat of Music": Richard Wagner, himself the very embodiment of the *Gesamt-kunstwerk*, "total artwork," no less than *Gemeinsam-Kunstwerk*, "collective artwork."[6]

How is such a phenomenon to be classified: The coming to fruition of the most flamboyant wing of European Romanticism? Breakthrough to a world promised by the total revolutions of 1848? Quantum leap onto the "aesthetic utopia" anvilled on a century of German Hellenism and nostalgia for the Hellenic polis? Manifestation of the *décadence* of triumphal "theatrocracy"?

Perhaps most simply: the first sustained venture in an "artful firm"—that is, the first exemplar of the "art firm," "aesthetic firm," "artful making," terms that have come into increasing prominence and currency among a contemporary generation of post-Schumpeterian management, organization, and business theorists eager to converge aesthetics, management, and community.[7] Without

---

[3] The original version of this chapter was presented as part of a panel on the "Aesthetic-Political" at the Southern Political Science Association meetings in Atlanta, Georgia, on 6 January 2006. I am grateful for the comments of the other panelists, especially Robert Pirro, in helping me to formulate the present version, as well as the suggestions of an anonymous reviewer for *Aesthesis,* in which a slightly earlier version of this chapter appeared (1:2 [2007], 43-53).

[4] *Ecce Homo*, in Nietzsche [1966], ii, 1092. When the heirs of Wagner and Nietzsche met in Weimar in 1926, "Politisch waren die Wagner- und Nietzsche-Verwandten und ihre Vasallen einer Meinung." Hamann [2002], 152.

[5] See Chytry [1989], 317.

[6] For further references, see "Wagner: The Communal Artwork," in Chytry [1989], 274-317.

[7] For the non-economist it may be worth noting that Joseph Schumpeter is regarded as the father of contemporary institutional and evolutionary economics. Schumpeter was a key

denying the more aesthetic-political-spiritual readings of The Idea of Bayreuth, this chapter considers such an option. In the first part it traces the important two phases in Wagner's own career as the context for applying such a reading. The second part then calls upon the help of Nietzsche's closing revaluation of Wagner and Wagnerianism in terms of Nietzsche's own project of a "physiological" aesthetics. Finally, the third and fourth parts look at the phenomenon of Bayreuth itself as an entrepreneurial enterprise located within the standards of the radical Wagner's and later Nietzsche's aesthetics.

I

What was Richard Wagner getting at with what eventually became known as the Idea of Bayreuth? The answer is woven into Wagner's career and its division into two phases, separated by his encounter with the philosophy of Arthur Schopenhauer around 1854-56. This division is itself deeply marked by Wagner's relation to the politics of his age and to his search for a distinctly German renewal of the arts and of what he came to call the "purely human" (*das reine Menschliche*).

The first phase is marked by Wagner as the total revolutionary, increasingly imbibing radical ideas from anarchist and socialist circles regarding the need for a complete transformation of society through political revolution. By his own confessions Wagner began as a child of the Revolution of 1830—"with one blow I became a revolutionary"—convinced that every striving person should become "exclusively occupied with politics;"[8] and by the time of the Revolutions of 1848, Dresden *Kapellmeister* Wagner had become a full-fledged ally of such unquestioned radicals as the Russian anarchist Mikhail Bakunin in the Dresden revolution of 1849. After the failure of the latter, Wagner was lucky to escape to Switzerland and became the most famous outlaw of music for European political conservatism over the next decade, producing a steady stream of radical-revolutionary works—both programmatic and musico-dramatic—that famously brought together the themes of art and total revolution.

In the second phase, chastened by Napoleon's coup of 1851 in France, Wagner was redirected to take an interest in Schopenauhauer, which after 1854-6 grew into a lifelong, if idiosyncratic, devotion to Schopenhauerian world

economist of the twentieth century for the emphasis he gave "innovation" and "creative destruction" in his analyses of the factors promoting growth in modern technological and capitalist societies. Schumpeter [1976] and [1997]; also Freeman & Louçã [2001].

[8] "Autobiographische Skizze" [1843], in Wagner [1967], i, 98

renunciation.[9] Subsequently, personally saved from his immense debts by the timely intervention of that "perfect Wagnerite" King Ludwig II of Bavaria in 1864, Wagner embarked on the pragmatic realization of his hopes for a theatre and cultural space specifically capable of producing and understanding his grandest musico-dramatic projects—from the *Ring* cycle to the body of works that culminate in the one musico-dramatic work, *Parsifal*, shaped and staged with his concrete Theatron of Bayreuth in mind.

An understandable, but incorrect, reading of this evolution would claim, as does Bryan Magee in his study of Wagner and philosophy, that the first-phase Wagner was politically inclined, whereas the second-phase Wagner had freed himself from such adolescent expectations in favor of a more matured and profound reconciliation with the limits of politics as such. In truth however, the second-phase Wagner was even more driven toward ensuring political change after his Schopenhauerian "conversion." What had changed was quite simply that whereas the original plan foresaw the cooperative alliance of radical political movements and theatrical revolution, the later strategies, having given up on the equality between the political and the theatrical, aimed rather at effecting political change directly *through* the impact of the musico-dramatic works themselves while subordinating any remaining political fellow-travelers to this one overriding objective. It is in the transition between these two approaches that something like the "artful-firm" reading of the Idea of Bayreuth then becomes salient.

Let us accordingly reconsider the central features of the *first* phase. Like his Leipzig university peers, the Young Wagner of 1830 was bowled over by the revolutionary tide. That August in Brussels the most striking conjunction of opera and revolution took place when a crowd attending the French composer Daniel Auber's opera *La Muette de Portici* was so overwhelmed by the patriotic duet "Amour sacré de la patrie" sung by the renowned tenor Adolphe Nourrit that it poured forth into the streets shouting out patriotic slogans against the ruling Netherlands government, seized the *hotel de ville* and other governmental buildings, thus launching a revolution that ultimately founded the Kingdom of Belgium and the establishment of a Belgian constitution in 1831.

This is as transparent a connection between "opera" and "revolution" as one might wish, and not surprisingly, in his later reminiscences of Auber in 1871Wagner was lavish in his praise of *La Muette de Portici* as an explosive event for German audiences in 1830—and of course himself—in terms of the future possibilities for genuine music drama.[10] This opera, he averred, "became

---

[9] Ironically perhaps, Wagner was directed to Schopenhauer by his political revolutionary allies such as Georg Herwegh.

[10] Wagner spent many occasions conversing with Auber in Paris cafes during his Paris years.

recognized as the manifest theatrical predecessor of the July Revolution and seldom has an artistic manifestation had such an exact relation to a world event."[11] Not surprisingly, Auber's presentation of the crowd scenes in revolutionary conditions formed the model for Wagner's early opera *Das Liebesverbot* (1836) that similarly exploited revolutionary possibilities based on a theme culled from Neapolitan history. Similarly, *Rienzi, der Letzte der Tribuner* (1837), Wagner's first extensive foray into "grand opera" in the contemporaneous Parisian tradition, was based on the historical figure of Cola di Rienzi whose temporary fame in 1347 as the Tribune of the Roman *populus* refounding the Roman Republic had long received the approbation of such canonical European authors as Petrarch.[12] This same opera, performed with dazzling effect in Dresden in 1842, actually launched Wagner's career beyond a local German context onto the wider European stage, whence emerged Wagner's explicit embarkation, starting with his *Die fliegende Holländer* (1843), toward the ideal of a superior "music drama" to supplant mere entertainment opera and work hand-in-hand with the political-revolutionary transformation of German and European landscapes.

Critical to this ambition was Wagner's absorption during precisely this 1847-9 revolutionary period of the image of ancient Athenian democracy and its commitment to dramatic tragedy as a political, spiritual, and religious celebration that Wagner drew from his readings of the German classicist Johann Gustav Droysen. Droysen's main claim that the tragic poet was the ultimate educator for bringing together the first genuine democracy by a "Volk" proved the catalyst for Wagner's project. From now on—unlike his German Romantic peers—the meaning for Wagner of the standard of "Volk" was inseparable from this model of the Athenian polis,[13] allowing Wagner to evoke for the first time "the great total art-work [*Gesammtkunstwerk*] of [Aeschylean] tragedy" for his ideal of the music drama as the union of all the arts in service to the creation of a people's self-understanding.[14] Accordingly, in terms of the revolutionary movement, this model of the Athenian polis meant for Wagner that the music dramatist's task *during* the revolutionary stage proper must be to cultivate this same standard in conjunction with explicit political revolutionary change. Such

---

[11] "Erinnerungen an Auber" [1871] in Wagner [1914], vii, 141.

[12] And was apparently a critical influence on the young Adolf Hitler according to his childhood friend August Kubizik, a claim heavily exploited in the Peter Cohen film *The Architecture of Doom* (1989). Kubizek [1955], 98-101.

[13] See the important conclusions of "Polis-Verständnis," in Bermbach [1994], 146-167. As Bermbach stresses, not German myths but "die griechische Polis" was for Wagner the "Modell, in dem das 'Volk' als der eigentliche soveräne Akteur selbst bestimmt auftritt, als creator communitatis, beratend und entscheidend zugleich" (146).

[14] See the references in Chytry [1989], 278, esp. note 15.

a dramatic standard would arouse an "authentic" sense in the audience of how a people should live and identify themselves, thus undermining the deleterious effects of industrial civilization on modern individuals (more particularly, it would also undercut the continued dominance of French cultural standards over German self-identification). *After* the success of the revolution, this same model of the Athenian polis would then help suggest the kind of role that music drama should play in a society like the Athenian, for which commercial considerations had been excised in favor of the religio-spiritual event of the festival and public participation in drama and music.

Turning to the implications of the *second* phase in Wagner's evolution, what had markedly changed around 1854-56 was Wagner's loss of confidence in explicit political revolution for effecting a total transformation in society. Moreover, Wagner's Schopenhauerian "turn" provided the first (and final) clear philosophical legitimation of what Wagner thought that he was doing dramaturgically. Together however, these changes, far from removing Wagner from the political arena, reinforced his single-minded commitment solely to himself and the Wagnerian *Gesamtkunstwerk* for his prime agent of change.

Thus Wagner began the long, and fascinating, turn in his dramaturgy which, while continuing to rely on the priority of the total artwork of all the arts, placed music front and center in a manner that undermined his earlier theory of the balance of (poetic) word and music for drama. It was still to be the artwork of all the arts—but music was the mistress, since Wagner now understood from Schopenhauer that music was the single artform that directly manifested the universal/noumenal Will. Put in non-Schopenhauerian terms, music revealed the underlying nature of all being, and as a result, transformation through the music drama became all the more pivotal for transforming human beings directly. Accordingly, the deliciously naive musings of the revolutionary Wagner during his Zurich exile of a special temporary theatre to house the four events that would freely perform the *Ring* cycle before that theatre was consigned to the "flames" gradually evolved during the 1850s into the more sober recognition that he would somehow have to build his special temple for the kind of performances that his works metaphysically demanded.

With Ludwig's miraculous entry into this process in 1864, Wagner immediately began rhapsodizing with his royal admirer that they should transform Bavaria's capital city of Munich into an "Athens of the Isar" crowned "with a monument to all the Muses, the temple of the *Gesamkunstwerk.*"[15] More practically, Wagner hastened to bring a mixed bag of old radicals, barricadeurs, and young experimental musicians—August Röckel, Julius Froebel, Gottfried

[15] See the reference in Chytry [1989], 297, esp. note 82.

Semper, and Heinrich Laube among others—to Munich in service to the common cause. Nor did he himself hesitate to "instruct" his young ward of the political theories—Ludwig Feuerbach, Constantin Frantz, and Ferdinand Lasalle—that he regarded as trenchant to their project. In fact, the first genuine productions of Wagnerian music drama, from *Tristan und Isolde* in 1865 to the first parts of the *Ring* cycle in 1869 and 1870, did confirm that Ludwig would stop at nothing to ensure appropriate performances in his capital, including the construction of the ideal Wagnerian theatre.[16] Yet, partly because of the reaction by Catholic Bavaria to Wagner's new liaison with Franz Liszt's illegitimate daughter Cosima—the cause of Wagner and Cosima leaving Munich during 1865-8—Wagner recast his gaze upon an entirely independent site of pilgrimage for his temple of the arts, finally discovering in 1870 a Brockhaus encyclopaedia account of the north Bavarian (and Protestant) city Bayreuth that seemed perfect for his purposes.[17] As it turned out, the original baroque theatre in Bayreuth that Wagner had planned to update proved completely useless; but once the die was cast, Wagner's single-mindedness succeeded, as of 22 May 1872, in transforming the Idea of Bayreuth into the inauguration event of setting the foundation stone for the literal building of his own specified *Gesamtkunstwerk* theatre. From this point on, it is fair to say that the Idea of Bayreuth had become a permanent aesthetic-political fact of modern German life.

But what exactly did the Idea of Bayreuth suggest to Wagner himself at this later stage of his career? We suggest as the most appropriate terminology: "religion of art" (*Kunstreligion*), a term originally coined by the German philosopher G. W. F. Hegel to refer to the epoch of classical Greek society, politics and spirituality in which "art" served as the focal point for the highest manifestations of spirit (*Geist*). This term *Kunstreligion* is particularly useful because it pinpoints Wagner's purposes through its conjunction of "religion" and "art." Wagner, it seems clear, sought out a musico-dramatic experience that required an "island" or refuge from daily demands, its center a veritable "temple" to the experience of an ultimate or grounding reality that was only accessible to music, and that then needed to be incarnated into dramatico-figural shapes to access an audience or acolyte. Thus contemporary descriptions of attending Bayreuth as a "pilgrimage" or even a "hadj" are not necessarily mistaken, or for that matter automatically blasphemous. Something comparable

---

[16] See Gottfried Semper's plans for a theatre in Munich, a model of which Semper presented to King Ludwig on 11 January 1867. Spotts [1994], 37.

[17] In his letter to a banker, Wagner stressed that he wanted a small town with no competing theatre or fashionable spa attracting an unsuitable public; it should be in the center of Germany and in Bavaria (in order to enjoy the protection of Ludwig). Cited in Spotts [1994], 40.

to the experience of a kind of religiosity does reward the undeterred Bayreuth pilgrim.[18] Indeed, Wagner finally resorted to the term "Bühnenweihfestspiel" (a "stage dedication play") to further distinguish *Parsifal*—the one work specifically composed with the Bayreuth Festspielhaus in mind—from the common run of operatic works and traditions.[19]

The trouble of course with such formulations is that it threatens to remake Wagner himself into a quasi-divine figure, a "messenger" as he saw himself, or prophet for modernity. Such a reading would then drag in his more prosaic fulminations covering the insalubrious subject-matter of his inveterate anti-Semitism. Still, it is worth noting that Bayreuth has had only a century for deepening, or chastening some of, its effects. Comparable times marked for such long-lasting religions as institutional Christianity and Islam indicate similar teething pains toward something that would in time grow into pragmatic sustainability. Even so, far more relevant for us is the question of what exactly this "religion" entails. The hasty answer: "art," only begins the process of unraveling the extent to which the domains of the aesthetic and artistic creation have increasingly preempted zones of traditional religiosity since the early nineteenth century. It may be argued that such a religiosity requires no "God" (Buddhism is not dependent on one) nor "Artist-God" (as the later Nietzsche put it teasingly), but rather the originating reality of *Poieisis* proper: the deeply poetic origination to all things that past cultures have expressed through the idea of primordial vibration, of the ontological "non-sound" (*anahata/shabda*) that first makes possible proper Sound itself—and consequently *mousiké,* or "music."[20]

Granted that this slant on Wagner's goals is helpful, how then did the later Wagner plan to make practicable the siting of his distinctive religion of art? Here we enter into the "commercial" Wagner, a feature of the composer's prodigious energy that is often overlooked or misread. To plan out the Temple, to line up support for it, to ensure appropriately exemplary performances of the music dramas, is surely not the least of Wagner's lifetime accomplishments.[21]

---

[18] Frederic Spotts refers to Wagner's "desire to transform theatre into an essentially eschatological experience." Spotts [1994], 51. Spott's general account provides the outsider to Bayreuth with the best introduction to the "experience" of the Bayreuth pilgrimage, one which this author can confirm from his own attendance of the 1968 performances.

[19] The groundplan of the Festspielhaus of 1876, along with the 1882 addition of the royal annex, is reproduced in Spotts [1994], 49 and back cover.

[20] For an excellent philosophical inquiry into *mousiké*, see Goehr [1998].

[21] The original Munich project had not only included the sanctuary of a Wagner theatre proper, but also a supportive journal, societies of patrons, and a musical school developing training in naturalness of voice and gesture presumably akin to classical Greek tragedy. Newman [1976], ii, 318; "Bericht über eine in München zu errichtende deutsche Musikschule [1865]," in

Since he had managed to gain autonomy over the whole "festival" project of Bayreuth, Wagner's original financing strategy depended on privately raised funds through a large number of small donors. Wagner first tried patrons' certificates, purchasers thus securing seats at forthcoming performances, and he supported the founding of Wagner societies which might secure patrons through fund-raising. These fiscal sources would hopefully allow Wagner to retain his ideal of a festival without charge for genuine devotees. However, the schemes failed and ultimately Wagner had to resort to ticket sales and to turn the enterprise into a joint stock company.[22] Even then, Ludwig himself was called upon for a timely loan, and the first Ring festival in 1876 proved a financial failure; it took two decades before Bayreuth worked as a commercial enterprise, and not till 1913 did Cosima and the Wagner family manage to pay off all outstanding debts.

For all that, Wagner did succeed in establishing the first modern musical festival. The Shakespeare festivals at Stratford were founded in 1879, the Mozart Salzburg festivals in 1920, while the first such family enterprise, Glyndebourne, came much later in 1934. Indeed, it could be argued that Bayreuth is the first truly "classical" theatre since the Roman odeions; parallels between its Festspielhaus and the ancient Hellenic theatre at Epidauros have been noted. Above all, the tradition of serious opera (or music-drama) attendance begins with Wagner and his admirably stubborn commitment to exalted standards of performance and audience. For all the subsequent permutations of the Bayreuth enterprise, it can be argued that Wagner's "festival" today remains perhaps the most impressive exemplar of artistic commitment to the performance of music drama on the part of performers and audience alike.[23]

II

Enter the Young Nietzsche.[24]

Wagner [1914], viii, 125-176.

[22] Following Spotts [1994], 45.

[23] As K. H. Ruppel notes with regard to New Bayreuth: "In Bayreuth allein gibt es noch den Begriff der 'Festspielgemeinde', d.h. einer Versammlung von Menschen, die nur um des künstlerischen Ereignisses willen zusammenkommen." "Bayreuth—Alte Idee in Neuer Form," in Wieland Wagner [1962], 207.

[24] See "Nietzsche: Aesthetic Morals," in Chytry [1989], 319-358. In light of more recent Nietzsche scholarship that explores in further detail—and in some cases opposes—the positive significance of art and the aesthetic dimension for Nietzsche's thought, it may be worth stating here our commitment to the aesthetic or "artful" Nietzsche, that is, the Nietzsche who, emerging

The tale of Nietzsche's early infatuation with Wagner, and the Wagners, at the Tribschen "Asyle" has become a commonplace of intellectual history. Unexpectedly meeting up with Wagner in Leipzig in 1868, the philological student had the good fortune shortly thereafter to receive a teaching post in Basel within commuting distance of Tribschen. In a short period he had become a favored member of the Wagner household and was engaged in extensive discussions with Wagner on their special topics of Schopenhauer and Greek tragedy. Tribschen gave Nietzsche a unique first contact with Wagner's many friends in politics and the arts and his first concrete image of what the Athens of Aeschylus and Sophocles might have been like. Indeed Nietzsche was among the first to be told of the Bayreuth enterprise, and his early participation in what he called the "Temple" (or "Gralsburg der Kunst") included a manifesto to the Germans on behalf of Wagner's fund-raising schemes.[25] Above all, Nietzsche gave new respectability to the Wagnerian enterprise by his unalloyed praise of Wagner's cultural mission as the modern equivalent of the Dionysian ethos informing classical Athenian tragedy according to Nietzsche's maiden work *The Birth of Tragedy* (1872). Not only his formal dedication to Wagner, but also the last ten sections of the entire book were devoted to a rather shameless Wagnerophilia.[26]

It is however no less true that as early as January 1874 Nietzsche was privately beginning to raise serious misgivings about Wagner as musician and cultural phenomenon. Attending the Bayreuth rehearsals of 1875 and planning to attend the 1876 inaugural cycle, Nietzsche found himself burdened by second thoughts about what he subsequently dubbed Wagnerian "theatrocracy," the Bayreuth gathering of Wagnerian acolytes who represented less a new spirit than the "cultural-philistinism" (as Nietzsche coined it) of the new post-1871 German Reich. Nietzsche's *Richard Wagner in Bayreuth* (1875) is both a final praise and subtle critique of Wagner as artistic tyrant, and it was not long before the very different flavors of Wagner's libretto for *Parsifal* and Nietzsche's first

---

from the critical attitude toward art and the artist of his "positivist" writings, produced a final body of works—as well as relevant *Nachlass*—that promulgated a "revaluation of all values" geared toward the primacy of the paradigm of artistic creativeness.

[25] "Mahnruf an die Deutschen," associating Bayreuth with "der Wohlfahrt und die Ehre des deutschen Geistes und des deutschen Namens" (303), in Nietzsche [1966], iii, 303-307. However Wagner did not use the manifesto, preferring a softer sales pitch.

[26] Nietzsche's own contribution to cultural renewal was to be his version of something like a "monastic-artistic cooperative" (*klösterisch-künstlerische Genossenschaft)* with his friends somewhere in the Alps as part of Wagner's regeneration of the German spirit. See his letters to his friend Erwin Rohde in Nietzsche [1975-2004], 2:1 (15 December 1870), 166, and 2:3 (22 March 1873), 135-137.

post-Wagnerian work *Human, All Too Human* (1878) hastened the closure of their friendship.

During his prolific writing decade of the 1880s, Nietzsche accordingly settled on Wagner as embodiment of a variety of illnesses that Nietzsche attributed to modern society. These writings, often characterized as the "positivist" phase of Nietzschean thinking before it arrived at the set of revaluations rhapsodized in his most singular work *Thus Spoke Zarathustra*, have proven a subsequent boon to postmodern readings of Nietzsche which valorize his ironic, decentering, aphoristic moves that sit somewhat uneasily beside his subsequent prophecies of the superman, will to power, and eternal recurrence of the same.[27] Above all, such "positivist" writings unfold an unremitting critique of conventional veneration and valorization of art, the artist, the aesthetic, and the poetic and musical genius—critiques that more often than not are launched with the target of Bayreuth and the later composer of *Parsifal* in mind but also contain far wider implications regarding such veneration of art. To the degree that this suspicion of the stratagems and ideology of the cult of art and artist can be traced even to the final Nietzschean oeuvre, let alone his voluminous *Nachlass*, perceptive readers of this feature in the Nietzshean project of revaluation are right to wonder whether any room is left for a favorable Nietzschean view of the role of art—certainly of "art as work of art."[28]

Yet even such comprehensive doubts about the extent of Nietzsche's devotion to art and the aesthetic dimension are willing to grant his continued sponsorship of something vaguely labeled "artisticality" (*Künstlertum*) and of art "as meaning a notion of activity, creativity, or organization in the most basic sense," of "an ambiguous kind of art, an art of deeds."[29] In the final analysis Nietzsche may well have felt that the most consummate genre of art, tragic drama, still fell short of its originating dynamics in the Dionysian mysteries, the spectacle, and the festival.[30] Nonetheless, his final efforts during his final year of sanity of 1888 to sum up Wagner and Wagnerianism do include what he considered an effective antidote, one which might well help launch an alternate

---

[27] The idea of a "new Nietzsche" was announced as early as the 1977 collection of essays in Allison [1977]; also, more recently, Allison [2001], along with the bibliography in Pothen [2002].

[28] "Die Kunst der Kunstwerke." *Menschliches, Allzumenschliches*, ii [174], in Nietzsche [1966], i, 804-805. This passage is cited and exploited most effectively by Pothen [2002], 38, 190.

[29] Even if such a venture would appear "as undefined and elusive as possible." Pothen [2002], 6, 195, 200.

[30] In *Ecce Homo* Nietzsche envisaged a future in which "the most select" would be set for "the greatest of all tasks": "Die Vision eines Festes, das ich noch erleben werde." Nietzsche [1966], ii, 1112.

and post-decadence mode of creativeness. Accordingly, not only did Nietzsche bring out two small works that dealt solely with Wagner—*The Case of Wagner* and *Nietzsche contra Wagner*—but Nietzsche assured a correspondent that a third work, *Ecce Homo*, was completely concerned with the theme of Wagner.[31]

Thus, at the same time that Nietzsche was ready to release his own final cannonades under such portentous titles as *The Will to Power* and *Revaluation of All Values*, he was no less concerned with Richard Wagner: as artist, man, and cultural phenomenon. Upon originally hearing of Wagner's death in 1883 Nietzsche had declared himself heir to the "authentic Wagner,"[32] for central even to Nietzsche's final accounting is less a savaging of Wagner than a clarification of his earlier cooperation with the composer in service to a philosophical revaluation of modernity that he thought the latter shared. This meant a return to the area of philosophical aesthetics, the subject of Nietzsche's prime concern during his early years with Wagner. Indeed "aesthetics" is the one area in which the early Nietzsche would still regard himself as a formal philosopher (*The Birth of Tragedy* being taken as above all a work belonging to "aesthetics"). Prior to making his stylistic and substantive turn toward the "positivist" Nietzsche of 1876-8, Nietzsche had been preoccupied with formally working out a genuine "tragic" philosophy corresponding to his account of tragic Greek culture. Nietzsche sought to legitimate his famous early claim that "only as an aesthetic phenomenon is the universe eternally justified" by arguing in a subsequent fragmentary work called *Philosophy in the Tragic Age of the Greeks* that the Heraclitean vision of "the artistic play of the cosmos" was basically correct: the universe is indeed a continually dynamic play, the play of the artist and child, the play that the Aion (Zeus) plays with itself.[33]

Nietzsche originally thought that this important conclusion—basically what Nietzsche would henceforth call a "Dionysian" vision of the universe meant to challenge both Wagner and Schopenhauer—was the philosophical fulfilment of the vision that he had earlier shared with the *Tribschen* Wagner—and, incidentally, one which in due course also undermined the young Nietzsche's commitment to the final truths of Schopenhauerian metaphysics. Thus when Nietzsche finally returned to the project of an appropriately formal

[31] In a letter to Heinrich Köselitz (Peter Gast), Nietzsche mentions his work *Nietzsche contra Wagner* before adding immediately: "Das 'Ecce' enthält alles Entscheidende auch über diese Beziehung." Nietzsche [1975-2004], 3-5 (22 December 1888), 545. Also: "W(agner) ist durchaus der erste Name, der in E(cce) h(omo) vorkommt." Nietzsche [1975-2004], 3-5 (31 December 1888), 567.

[32] Nietzsche [1975-2004], 3:1 (19 February 1883), 334.

[33] A more detailed presentation is found in "Cosmos as Līlī: Nietzsche's Dionysian Cosmology and the Problematic of the Postmodern," in Chytry [2005], 32-35.

philosophical aesthetics in his last year, it was this philosophical alternative that he had in mind when undercutting Wagner, Wagnerianism, and the metaphysics behind the entire Idea of Bayreuth.

Starting with *Toward a Genealogy of Morals* (1887), Nietzsche announced the prospect of a forthcoming "physiology of aesthetics"—a subject, he claimed, "which is practically untouched and unexplored so far."[34] Although such a project was never completed, bits and pieces of it float through the production of that final year.[35] By "physiology" Nietzsche showed his primary concern with the state of plenitude which art either fosters or reinforces. Beauty as the master category of aesthetics should therefore not be read in Kantian-Schopenhauerian terms as a matter of "disinterest" but, on the contrary, as a matter of greatest "interest." This alternative view was underscored by Nietzsche's resort to the French writer Stendhal's definition of beauty as "a promise of happiness": "*une promesse de bonheur.*"[36] Far from constituting the beginnings of a turn *away* from the world—and the unmoral metaphysical will of Schopenhauerian vintage—beauty for Nietzsche was to mean "the highest sign of power, namely power over opposites; moreover, without tension." Thus beauty—Nietzsche's aesthetic punch line—was really the "aphrodisian bliss" (*die aphrodisische Seligkeit*) that rewarded the state of intoxication (*Rausch*) which had reached a sense of self-perfection. Idealism was therefore not opposed to sensuality; rather, it was the heightening, magnification, transfiguration of the intoxication called "love"—an immense sexual, "aphrodisiac" surge—into the perfected replications made possible through the formalities and technicalities of the varied arts.

Accordingly, Nietzsche's objection to the Idea of Bayreuth carried a critique of the evolution of Wagner and Wagnerianism in terms of the two phases that we have already described and that Nietzsche himself was perhaps the first to explicitly clarify. Wagner succumbed to Schopenhauer, Nietzsche asserted, because Schopenhauer gave him a metaphysical justification for the priority of

---

[34] *Zur Genealogie der Moral*, ii [8]. "Aesthetics is nothing else than applied physiology" (*Nietzsche contra Wagner*). Also a "psychology of the artist," so long as this is understood as based on the "physiological precondition" of "intoxication" (*Rausch*). *Twilight of the Idols*, "Expeditions of an Untimely Man" [8]. See Nietzsche's formal plan for a section entitled "Toward the Physiology of Art" containing 18 parts which (minus the 18th part) receives an extensive commentary from Martin Heidegger in the latter's analysis of "Nietzsche's aesthetics-art physiology." Heidegger [1991], 93-95.

[35] These would include relevant sections in *Twilight of the Idols*; the "small aesthetic work" *The Case of Wagner* (plus *Nietzsche contra Wagner*); and the section of *The Will to Power* notes called "The Will to Power as Art." Also his letters in Nietzsche [1975-2004], 3:5, to Jacob Burckhardt (13 September 1888), 420-421, and to Paul Deussen (14 September 1888), 425-427.

[36] *Zur Genealogie der Moral*, ii [6-8]; *The Will to Power* [802-810].

music; but that priority was itself based on Schopenhauerian metaphysics that unlike all the other arts—which for Schopenhauer were quasi-Platonic Ideas of the will—music was the direct *expression* of the will. True, such a position elevated the ontological status of the musician, but it still tied the priority of music to a thoroughly renunciatory metaphysics. If music directly expressed the will—itself the unmoral, striving essence of being—then an entire Festival ideal for culture committed to such music (the later Wagnerian music, particularly the renunciatory ethics of *Parsifal*, as well as the turn taken by the *Ring* theme in Wagner's final version) could not but be nihilistically directed in the straightforward sense that its purpose was to preach "redemption" *from* the world and reality.[37] Since Nietzsche did not really believe that Wagner meant to instill such an uncompromisingly renunciatory ethics, he could only conclude that, like Baudelaire, Wagner had become the summation of the décadence of a modernity that was capable at its best of lingering over niceties and miniature experiences—Wagner "as our greatest *Miniaturist* of music"[38]—but incapable of forming values that might supersede the implicit nihilism of his own time. Wagner in effect was the "playactor" (*Schauspieler)* par excellence, a tyrant of the theatrical experience who enjoyed the pseudo-Christianizing, pseudo-Buddhistic posturings of a *Parsifal* without actually embracing the values of either religion. Nonetheless, the consequences for his theatrical experience and his "theatrocracy" were nefarious, producing neither a sublime experience of the "true" nature of reality—the priority of the cosmos as play, as a "Dionysian" reality—nor the equivalent of past religio-theatrical modes of solace as sustained over time by formal institutional practices. Only a theatre freed from the tyranny of Wagnerianism could hope to renew the liberatory experiences that Greek tragic theatre had once offered and that the more radical Wagner himself had once presumably sought to regain.[39]

---

[37] This point should be considered quite apart from the additional fact that Nietzsche saw Wagner's and Schopenhauer's very concept of "redemption" (*Erlösung*) as incoherent. When Nietzsche called Wagner's operas "die Oper der Erlösung," he was in effect blaming Schopenhauer, particularly the account of redemption in Book IV of Schopenhauer's *The World as Will and Representation*. Nietzsche [1966], ii, 908, 911.

[38] Nietzsche [1966], ii, 918 (emphasis in original).

[39] It should be noted that if Nietzsche was deeply disappointed by the original Bayreuth Festival in 1876, so too was Wagner. Indeed, reading Thucydides, Wagner compared the 1876 Festival to the fall of Periclean Athens. Westernhagen, *Wagner*, 513.

III

It is no part of this chapter to consider a reading of Wagner that would take seriously the latter's Buddhism and show its differences with Schopenhauerian renunciation.[40] Such a reading would need to distinguish characteristic accounts of Buddhism as a "pessimistic" world-view and religion, a position to which Nietzsche in his limited understanding of Buddhism was liable, and show how Wagner, at least for this one work, achieved the kind of contemporary tragic experience to which Nietzsche, even in his last polemics against Wagner, seems to have deferred.[41]

In this third and the following fourth sections the aim is rather to indicate how Nietzsche's more "aesthetic" metaphysics of the universe as play and his reading of beauty as "aphrodisian bliss" supplements our understanding of the meaning of the Idea of Bayreuth as it has unfolded since its inception by Wagner and how a reading of the Bayreuth project as an "art firm" aids in this endeavor.

As a family operation, Bayreuth has remained under firm—if less direct—control of the Wagner family. Thanks both to an excessively literalist reading of the works and festival idea by Wagner's wife Cosima and son Siegfried, and to Siegfried's wife Winifred Wagner's embrace of, and apparently even love for, Adolf Hitler,[42] Bayreuth became almost fatally identified with the Third Reich during the 1930s and 1940s.[43] Indeed Hitler very probably saved

---

[40] Particularly with regard to what Wagner called his "metaphysics of sexual love" and which he may have expressed in his most "Nietzschean" work, *Tristan und Isolde.* See the reading of this music drama in Chytry [1989], 290-296.

[41] The term "pessimism" came into vogue precisely in the 1850s at a time when Schopenhauer and Buddhism were also growing in popularity. Indeed it was the French orientalist Eugène Burnouf who apparently coined the word "nihilism" as a translation of the Buddhist concept of "nirvana." Cited in Poggioli [1968], 61. More sophisticated contemporary understanding of Buddhism has had to contend with this automatic equation of Buddhism with pessimism that its original European vogue established. Govinda [1991] provides a cogent critique of this identification from the perspective of a contemporary "Western Buddhist" thinker.

[42] "Hitler in Bayreuth (1923-1924)," in Hamann [2002], 73-100. Brian Magee claims that Winifried Wagner personally informed him that she had fallen in love with the Young Hitler during the early 1920s and wanted to marry Hitler after her husband's death in 1930. Magee [2000], 367. At the time foreign minister Gustav Stresemann found himself asking how "the old democrat Wagner" could end up being taken for a "modern *Hakenkreuzler*." Cited in Hamann [2002], 142.

[43] See especially "The Perfect Wagnerite" in Spotts [2002], 221-263, supplemented by Hamann [2002]. In fairness to Wagner, it should be noted that he left absolutely no statement that he expected Cosima to continue his mission; rather, he hoped for Siegfried to become his successor.

Bayreuth itself by becoming its greatest patron,[44] and it has been argued that, in turn, the Bayreuth reception of Hitler from 1923-1924 on by Houston Smith Chamberlain and the Wagner clan led by Winifred transformed Hitler himself into the Führer-type of the future.[45] While it is true that the henchmen of National Socialism were not in the least interested in four-plus hours of serious Wagnerian fare, it is no less true that the lynchpin of the system, Adolf Hitler himself, remained a genuine and informed Wagnerite, proposed a new plan for an expanded Festspielhaus, and even forced his lieutenants to attend the festivals until their beer-guzzling propensities finally discouraged even the *Führer.*[46] German defeat in World War II meant the disgrace of the Wagner family and temporary control of the Festspielhaus by the U.S. Army. In 1950 however, thanks to the ebbing of de-nazification programs, the Festival's assets were turned over to Siegfried's sons Wieland and Wolfgang, and in 1949 the Society of the Friends of Bayreuth began the old Wagnerian ploy of selling memberships in exchange for donations.[47]

The immediate results of this turnabout were that Bayreuth and the Wagnerianism of National Socialism escaped serious accountability—nor has it occurred since.[48] Still, as a result of these Nazi associations, foreigners avoided Bayreuth, and since this included the all-important potential legions of foreign performers, conductors, theatrical experts, and audience, such avoidance could

[44] Hitler guaranteed "the Festival's finances for the first time in its history." Ironically, thanks to Hitler's patronage, the Bayreuth Festival ("the Bayreuth Republic") "was the only cultural institution in the Third Reich independent of Nazi control." Spotts [2002], 258.

[45] Wagner's home Wahnfried became in effect the "home" that Hitler "had not known since childhood." Spotts [2002], 250. "Bayreuth believed in him as he believed in Wagner." Köhler [2000], 197; also 191-208. Still, it is worth heeding Ian Kershaw's warning not to reduce the Third Reich to the relation of Hitler to Wagner as Köhler does. As Kershaw's own prodigious two-volume study of Hitler shows, a great deal more is involved in the political reality and aims of the Third Reich than Wagnerianism. Kershaw [1998], 617 (note 121). See Chapter 2 above for more details.

[46] For the details, Spotts [1994], 159-204, including a reproduction of Hitler's own proposed new Festspielhaus designed by Rudolf Emil Mewes (197). Similarly Hitler failed to interest his henchmen to performances of *Die Meistersinger* to precede the Nuremberg Rallies of the 1930s. In fact, "Hitler's passion for Wagner aroused great anguish inside the party." Spotts [2002], 256. It should be noted—a point however that Brian Magee in his defense of Wagner overstresses—that in general Third Reich ideologists were unhappy with the actual messages of Wagner's works, particularly *Parsifal.* For them, there was an intrinsic difference between their ideology and the Wagnerian "religion of art." *Die Meistersinger* was criticized in 1943 by the *Frankfurter Zeitung*: "Der darin mitschwingenden romantischen Primat der Kunst über die Politik kann der Deutsche unserer Zeit nicht mehr mitvollziehen." Barth (ed.) [1973], 117.

[47] Hamann [2002], 498-567.

[48] Winifried Wagner's continued anti-Semitic faith in her Führer to the end of her life is narrated in Hamann [2002], 635-639.

have permanently sunk Bayreuth. What in effect saved Bayreuth for the highly successful commercial enterprise that it has since become were two factors. First, the concept of the "Temple" of Bayreuth had to be changed into that of "Workshop" or *Werkstatt.* That is, instead of being a temple to the worship at the altar of "'ce dieu Richard Wagner'," as even the structuralist anthropologist Claude Lévi-Strauss once celebrated,[49] it should become the scene for countless artistic and artisanly experiments in theatre that could maintain variety and outside interest in a format and venue that after all were rather limited (to the main Wagner music dramas).[50] Second, starting in 1951, Wieland Wagner embarked on a wholly new way of reading the Wagnerian experience, instituting what became known as New Bayreuth.[51] Even if the "post-New Bayreuth" of his brother Wolfgang after Wieland's death in 1966 has been somewhat less successful in establishing historic readings of the Wagnerian oeuvre,[52] Wieland entirely turned around the general view of what to expect from Bayreuth and achieved the modern connection with ancient Greek tragedy that his grandfather—and the latter's erstwhile young friend Friedrich Niezsche—had once hoped for.[53]

Technically the Festival was turned over by 1973 to the German government with the Wagner estate becoming the "Richard-Wagner-Stiftung Bayreuth," to be run by a board of directors of eight members representing the federal government, the government of Bavaria, members of the four lines of the Wagner family, and other elements. This board was entrusted with the responsibility of choosing the director of the Festival, whose autonomy would be "guaranteed." Not surprisingly, the board chose Wolfgang. Thus, although by 1973 the Festival was no longer strictly a private dynastic institution, it remained under the direction of Wagner's grandson.[54]

---

[49] Lévi-Strauss [1964], 23.

[50] This would also include opportunities for renowned scenographers such as the Czech Josef Svoboda. Burian [1983].

[51] Wagner [1962]. Some interpreters regard Wieland Wagner as the founder of a specifically operatic or lyrical scenography and regret how quickly his innovations have been forgotten: after his death in 1966 "Bayreuth meurt pour la second foi." Lust [1969], 26-30.

[52] Hamann [2002], 595-611.

[53] Spotts [1994], 200, 202, 273. Also Wolfgang Wagner's own general account in Wagner [1994].

[54] Spotts [1994], 263-264. Overall Wolfgang Wagner, attaching his own achievement to his brother Wieland's, expresses satisfaction for having brought "in und für Bayreuth eine Stabilisierung—und zwar künstlerisch, juristisch, finanziell und materiell" as a basis for the future—this stated with a disapproving glance at "das gigantomanische Grossprojekt Hitlers auf dem Grünen Hügel." Wolfgang Wagner [1994], 434-435.

This in effect is the institution that Guillet de Monthoux in his pioneering work in aesthetic management theory has tried to appropriate for his concept of the "art firm."[55] For Guillet de Monthoux, Wagner was an absolute original in conceiving of an art firm or "art enterprise" as a project working within commercial boundaries while still committing itself to the kind of aesthetic experience of the ancient Greeks that escaped modern dangers of commodity cooptation and banality. Guillet de Monthoux's account of Wagner is rich in demonstrating Wagner's pragmatic commercial understanding of the obstacles the serious music dramatist had to face in a modern capitalist reality and the steps he took to mitigate some of those obstacles in order to awaken what Guillet de Monthoux labels—following the aesthetic writings of Friedrich Schiller—the "swing" or "oscillation" (*Schwung*) essential to aesthetic experience as such.

Chapter 5 has already offered some details on the relevance of Guillet de Monthoux's theorizing for the further development and sophistication of contemporary interest in links between aesthetics and management. Behind such theorizing stands the acknowledgment that modern organizational and entrepreneurial developments, particularly in the areas known as knowledge-creation primarily connected with fast-moving digital technologies, have raised important competitive issues that are increasingly related to aesthetic considerations, from simple design to the running of the (successfully competitive) firm as a quasi-theatrical operation. Indeed one student of the contemporary commercial landscape argues that we have entered an "aesthetic age," an "aesthetic universe"—evident in such highly successful commercial chains as IKEA and Starbucks—which more traditional managers ignore at their peril.[56] Wagner's originality is to have anticipated such contemporary developments by his many-sided invocation of theatre, entrepreneurship, and the Event that crystallizes the "experience economy."[57]

---

[55] Guillet de Monthoux [2004], 110-121.

[56] "The Aesthetic Imperative," in Postrel [2003], 1-33. Another index is the rapid growth of industrial design programs in burgeoning art colleges.

[57] On the "experience economy" and its relation to Event and theatrics, see Pine & Gilmore [1999]. Interestingly enough, Pine & Gilmore foresee a further stage in which such an "experience economy"—confirmed by such enterprises as Disneyland and Disneyworld—will be supplanted by one in which spiritual-religious factors become more explicit. See also the work of Philip Hancock regarding an "aesthetic economy" that gives more emphasis to the conceptual importance of a Hegelian-Marxian dialectical approach for the "inter-subjective process of 'becoming' a subject" in organizations. Hancock & Tyler [2001], 211.

IV

It would be premature to grant speculative legitimacy to this body of works before it reaches further theoretical sophistication. Nonetheless, at least as a symptom, theorizing about the "artful firm" provides a useful perspective with which to read the Idea of Bayreuth and its Festival. If the latter cannot serve—and should not, if it wishes to avoid unnecessary controversy—as a "spiritual" equivalent to the ceremonies and liturgies of established formalized religious institutions, Bayreuth should also not be dismissed as a mere commercial enterprise tied to the successful sale of tickets to a theatre-going public. A century of survival and prosperity has shown Bayreuth to be what Wagner hoped in his less "redemptive" days that it might become: a serious occasion for the experience and reflection of the aesthetic dimension for the lives of individuals otherwise restricted to the everydayness of advanced industrial society. The category of "art firm" provided by Guillet de Monthoux saves the Idea of Bayreuth from methodologies limited to interpretations of capitalistic cooptations of "art," and the growing body of empirical and theoretical work that we call the "artful firm" shows the variety of ways in which this "art firm" might be regarded as aiding the practical functions of the modern business firm according to metaphorics of theatre and design.

Indeed as these connections are further explored, it may even prove possible to relate such management literature in the "artful firm" to corresponding academic work in the "aesthetic-political" as such. If the original impetus behind the "aesthetic-political" is less the de-masking of a fascist "aestheticization of politics" (*die Ästhetisierung der Politik*)[58] and more a modern attempt to regain some of the constructive elements of the ancient Greek polis without succumbing to historical nostalgia, then clarification of Bayreuth as an "art firm" and its relation to management literature on the "artful firm" and "organizational aesthetics" will inevitably have to face its further connections with the political dimension as such. In this endeavor the "aesthetic age" of the management theorist and the "aesthetic-political" of the academic theorist may fertilize one another—perhaps eventually to the extent of taking more seriously the radical Wagner's own commitment to the polis.[59]

---

[58] As some misguided interpreters of the canonical passage in Walter Benjamin's classic study *The Artwork in the Age of its Technical Reproducibility* have held. Cf. Benjamin [1963], 51.

[59] In such early essays as "The Greek State," Nietzsche himself began as a proponent of the Hellenic polis, but in his final writings seems to have shifted to advocacy of imperial Rome—at least as a tactical move on behalf of his campaign against Christian morals and its undermining of the "noble" morals underlying the construction of the *Imperium* in the "grand style."

Any such moves will remain thankful to Nietzsche's rereadings of the proper function of music drama in favor of a philosophy preferring "aphrodisian bliss" to Wagnerian "redemption." In the final analysis Bayreuth is about providing a space for the particular virtues of the music drama, vaguely based on the revival of the communal experiences of ancient Greek tragedy. Accordingly it will be about the liberatory elements contained in the communal-spectatorial experience made available by "music." Although little can be done about changing Wagner's "music" as such, a great deal can be done about the manner of interpreting and dramatizing it. If, according to Wagner, the music that legitimates music drama is the very core of the universe, then Nietzsche's reading of that core in terms of the universe *as* a continual, dynamic play would seem far more "musical" than Wagner's own Schopenhauerian stance. Indeed, Niezsche himself conceived of such music as ideally "*la gaya scienza*; light feet; wit, fire, grace, the great logic; the dance of the stars, wanton spiritedness; the light-shudder of the South; the *glossy* sea—perfection ..."[60]

Still, notwithstanding Nietzsche's *theoretical* calls for a "mediterreanization of music," it is after all Wagner who provides us with the actual *practice* of music and the musico-dramatic Festival. In the hands of a master interpreter such as his grandson Wieland Wagner, this music and the drama it entails were successfully transferred to the domain of secular concerns that highlighted the archetypal truths contained in them.[61] Accordingly Wieland Wagner first gifted Wagnerian music drama with that "Greek tragic" quality which its original creator had used as his guide and which his immediate heirs had largely wasted with their redemptive cult of Wagneriana (partly reinforced by the later Wagner himself).[62]

Significantly enough, Wieland Wagner claimed that he was inspired by his readings of the radical Wagner's prose works and aims to undertake this vital "Greek" turn in the stagings of his New Bayreuth.[63] As Wagnerian music drama

---

[60] *The Case of Wagner*, in Nietzsche [1966], ii, 925.

[61] See Wieland Wagner's brief account of the process of weaning Bayreuth from the Cosima cult of piety to newer scenographic standards represented by Adolphe Appia in order to produce "Wagner's archetypal musical theatre" for contemporary audiences. "Denkmalschutz für Wagner," in Wagner [1962], 233-235.

[62] According to K. H. Ruppel, Wagner sought out not simply an artistic effect but "auch sittlich erhebende, reinigende Wirkung (wie bei der antiken Tragödie)." "Bayreuth—Alte Idee in Neuer Form," in Wagner [1962], 207. 208

[63] For Wieland Wagner pivotal influences included Mozart, the Greek dramatists (especially Aeschylus, Wagner's own hero), and Homer (Wieland called himself "a Homer fan, if you like"). The discovery of the Greek dramatists, Wieland was delighted to find, took place for him at the same age as it had for his grandfather Richard. Spotts [1994], 209.

has become genuinely universal for the first time thanks to such stagings,[64] it has thus fulfilled the radical Wagner's—as well as the young Nietzsche's—highest aspirations: to produce profound experiences within a modern contextualization of the human condition that music drama—post-Renaissance successor to Greek tragedy—seems uniquely equipped to convey.

[64] Following Spotts, the defining characteristics of the stagings of New Bayreuth are: a circular acting area, use of light to link music to movement and color, the simplification of costumes without suggesting a specific time or place, the transformation of characters from pseudo-human beings into symbols, and the stripping away of sets and gestures inessential to the conceptual core of the work. Apparently Wieland was inspired by his discovery in Cosima's diary of Wagner's statement that besides having created the "invisible orchestra," he wished he could invent "the invisible theatre." Spotts [1994], 216.

CHAPTER SEVEN

Cosmo-Polis: Cine-Città

Italian Neorealism and the Roman Film Studio Cinecittà as an Artful Firm

To step from music drama or opera to cinema is not much of a stretch, certainly not for a filmmaker of the operatic and melodramatic sensibilities of Luchino Visconti, a central figure in the movement of cinematic history known as neorealism.[1] In both cases a siting of the art experience and the institutions necessary to its production in an economic system prone to underplay that experience in favor of consumer entertainment generates problematizations intrinsic to the notion of an artful firm. This chapter extends our inquiries into that notion by investigating the influential cinematic siting of Cinecittà.

At the same time the coincidental location of Cinecittà in Rome—the one "city-state" to conquer the whole world, as Machiavelli once noted—provokes a deeper questioning. Since Rome is no less the home of "Cosmopolis," might one risk the following analogy: if "polis" fits, more or less formally, with "città," perhaps "cosmos" matches "cine" or "cinema"? At least this is what is urged at the outset by the cinematic works of the epoch of Italian neorealism and its immediate successors, covering not only the classic neorealism of Luchino Visconti, Roberto Rossellini, and Vittorio de Sica (with Cesare Zavattini) (1945-1956), but also the putative "second neorealism" of Federico Fellini, Michelangelo Antonioni, and Pier Paolo Pasolini (1959-1964).

This chapter suggests an intrinsic link between the neorealists' Rome as both the site for neorealism's original brand of postwar humanism and for the replication and cultivation of Rome in the construction of the critical Roman film studio appropriately named Cinecittà. Rome, the exact "polis" for the original coining of the notion "cosmo-polis" by its most erudite emperor, Marcus Aurelius Antoninus, turns out to be the home of a "cinecittà" manifestation of whatever "cosmo-polis" might realistically entail for a distinctly modern, post-world war II mode of life. Closing with a reading of a

[1] An early version of this chapter was presented as an invited paper at the Conference on Film and Literature, Florida State University, Tallahassee, Florida, on 5 February 2007.

body of cinematic works that transcends neorealism—Federico Fellini's so-called "Roman trilogy"—this chapter shows how a tradition that began with *Roma, città aperta* closes, appropriately enough, with *Roma*, Open City for the Director's unbridled imagination through the studio phenomenon of Cinecittà.[2]

I

"Rome" is the site of the first true articulation of the concept of "cosmo-polis." Although the term was associated with Cynic philosophers, it is Marcus Aurelius, last of the great Antonine emperors, who made the classic claim that the cosmos (ὁ κόσμος) is "as it were" a polis (πόλις) (IV.3) and that man should recognize his "citizenship in this great world-polis" (XII.36). Yet the Emperor certainly did not mean by that affirmation to deny his Romanness. On the contrary, a less well-known comment by him affirms both: "I have a polis (πόλις), and I have a country (πατρὶς); as Marcus I have Rome (ἡ Ῥώμη), and as a human being I have the universe (κόσμος); and consequently, what is beneficial to these poleis (τὰ ταῖς πόλεσιν) is the sole good for me" (VI.44).[3] If there is a single localization of "Rome" as capital of a world empire, indeed of the entire "world", it is surely atop the Capitoline hill upon which the statue of the first influential advocate of "cosmo-polis", Marcus Aurelius, still imperially stands.[4] To utter "cosmo-polis" is therefore to utter, at least historically: "Roma."

Between Marcus' "cosmo-polis" attached to the Imperium Romanum and the Risorgimento later founding the Italian state with Rome as its capital, the most important commentator on "Rome" is the Florentine patriot and classical republican Niccolò Machiavelli. Machiavelli's commentary on the first ten books by Roman historian Titus Livius recounting the origins and expansion of Rome uses as its point of departure the unique phenomenon of the res publica of Rome as the only city-state to successfully conquer the "world."[5] If Machiavelli's own polity Florence was to survive and flourish as such a city-state, it must emulate the Romans and their unique cultivation of *virtù*. Obsessed with the humiliating status of the Italian polities under the heel of larger and more powerful European security-states such as France and Spain

---

[2] As has been noted regarding Rome: "With its unique ability to mobilize myths of history and power, it is a potent source of connotative power, allowing the filmmaker to move from the familiar to the conceptual." Wood [2000], 220.

[3] Marcus Aurelius Antoninus [1916].

[4] This is apparently the only bronze statue of a non-Christian Rome emperor which has survived, apparently because it was mistaken for the pro-Christian emperor Constantine.

[5] Gilbert [1965], 181-182, 183-184.

("this barbarous domination stinks in the nostrils of every one"), Machiavelli called for an alliance system and virtuous leader to reverse the political fortunes of Italy but did not necessarily conceive of a unified single Italian state or empire: rather, he set up the ancient Romans as the standard which would suffice to save Italians.[6] Above all, Machiavelli spoke unsparingly of his contempt for an organization, the Papacy, which was neither sufficiently political nor spiritual, which was large enough to prevent cooperation among Italian states, but not strong enough to be the leader itself.

Faced with the challenge of the Papal States, the nineteenth-century Risorgimento failed to come to a satisfying settlement with regard to the relation between Italian national sovereignty and the universalistic if still territorial pretensions of the Holy See. Envisaged as the eventual capital of a unified peninsula under republican auspices, the Rome of the Young Italy proponents Giuseppe Mazzini and Giuseppe Garibaldi sought a "Rome of the People" to replace the former "Rome of the Caesars" and "Rome of the Popes."[7] Mazzini and Garibaldi in fact helped in the seizure of the city itself in the 1848-9 revolutions to create the short-term *Repubblica Romana.* Although these radical republicans sent out feelers to the pope who had fled the Vatican, the latter disclaimed the Revolution, and supportive French troops from then republican president Napoleon Bonaparte (the future Emperor Napoleon III) retook the city by June 1849. Even the unification of Italy in 1860, along with additional territories gained in 1866, failed to encompass Rome so long as the Papacy was protected by French troops; however, as those troops were withdrawn when France fought the Franco-Prussian war of 1870-1871, takeover of Rome was ensured by the armies of the new Italy proclaiming Garibaldi's slogan: "Roma o morte!" Considering himself a "prisoner" within the new secular capital of Rome, the pope rejected this new Italy until his successor Pius XI came to a Concordat with the Fascist government of Mussolini in 1929 which created the present independent postage-stamp state of Vatican along with specified privileges for the Roman Catholic religion in Italy.

Yet this "solution" was effected by a regime which soon launched its own universalistic ambitions and indeed attached those ambitions to a burgeoning ideology of *Romanità*, the cult of ancient Rome, invoking particularly those military imperialistic successes as the standard for the new Order of Fascism—the very term *fasces* itself being derived from the Roman icon of power and authority.[8] Not that the intervening Italy of liberalism had not also called upon the model of Rome for its imperialistic ventures in the Mediterranean and

[6] Machiavelli [1950], 98.
[7] Mazzini, cited in Bondanella [1987], 160.
[8] Bondanella [1987], 173.

African regions, but Mussolini applied a far more systematic exploitation of the Roman theme for his visions of a renewed Mare Nostrum.[9]

It is noteworthy that the fate of early Italian cinema is juxtaposed to the two major phases of this Italian fascism. In the first phase, more or less between the 1922 "March on Rome" and 1929, Mussolini generally played within the rules of the formal constitutional system since he had been called to form his government by the king himself who in principle could retract that invitation. But between 1929-1934 and particularly after 1934, Mussolini grew far more aggressive in his attempts to fashion a new order of "Italians" and a much more militaristic internal and foreign presence, a process that, unfortunately for him and notwithstanding the peaking of his popularity with the taking of Abyssinia in 1936, had degenerated by the early 1940s into a general collapse of the Italian military machine and economy.

In terms of these two phases, the fascism of the first phase did very little with the film industry. That industry had enjoyed a remarkable start in the first two decades of the century by establishing itself among the foremost film nations by 1914, partly through cultivation of Italian mythology films such as Enrico Guazzoni's *Quo Vadis?* (1912) and Giovanni Pastrone's *Cabiria* (1914) celebrating the heroic deeds of ancient Rome, but then fell on hard times in the postwar recession. Unable to establish an effective production, distribution, and movie-house system, Italian film succumbed to a major domestic-consumption shift in favor of the far more industrially effective system inaugurated by Hollywood in California (1915-1920). Given the serious drop in Italian film production during 1920-1928, concern was indeed felt by the new fascist government but few practical steps were first taken by Mussolini. In 1924 the regime formed the Istituto LUCE to produce documentaries and newsreels as well as to establish censorship rules, and in 1926 Mussolini took over the UCI (Unione Cinematografica Italiana), but generally revival of the film industry was passed on to private initatives.

After 1929-30, however, partly spurred by the continued inroads of Hollywood as well as by the relative success of the Russian filmmakers in supporting the ideological cause of Soviet socialism, the regime embarked on a major program of revitalizing the Italian film industry.[10] This revitalization went hand-in-hand with Mussolini's cult of Rome, since a work like Carmine Gallone's *The Last Days of Pompey* (1926) had already shown how Caesar's and Mussolini's Rome could be intermeshed—a conceit dear to the Duce who

---

[9] Bondanella [1987], 172.

[10] See Mussolini's concession to Emil Ludwig in 1932 that the Russians were "vorbildlich" in film and film propaganda, along with the promise: "Wir werden auch bald mehr Geld dafür haben. Der Film ist heute die stärkste Waffe." Mussolini [1932], 212.

proclaimed himself: "Civis romanus sum." Besides, in 1925 fascist Italy had already established the Institute for Roman Studies devoted to investigations into the history of the Eternal City, and by 1932 Mussolini could predict a future Europe to be made increasingly fascist "with the doctrine and wisdom of Rome."[11]

This program turned more aggressive starting in 1934 as the regime became committed to the active spreading of fascist ideas through its Ministry of Press and Propaganda.[12] Not surprisingly, this included the new adventurist militarism that only ended with Mussolini's unceremonious hanging in a Milan square in 1945. In 1935 the Centro Sperimentale di Cinematografia was formed to improve the quality of film production. In 1936 a new journal *Cinema* provided space for vigorous discussion on film which eventually became an important venue for the ideas of such neorealist thinkers as Luchino Visconti and Giuseppe de Santis. By then, not only Mussolini himself, but also his sons, particularly Vittorio who took over the running of *Cinema*, were actively involved in promoting Italian cinema. Finally, in 1937 fascist Italy and Mussolini personally gave birth to Cinecittà.

Cinecittà, to be exact, was founded on April 21—the mythical date for the foundation of Rome proper in 753BCE and commonly used by the fascist regime for regime-sponsored inaugurations. With the Duce himself in attendance, the founding of Cinecittà was meant to serve as Italy's answer to the Hollywood studio system. Set up on 99 acres of rural land located 5.6 miles southeast of Rome, it became the physical heart of the revival of Italian cinema and has since served as site for some of its most imposing achievements—as well as for some of the most prominent examples of Hollywood's own appetite for the blockbuster film, from literary classics like the Tolstoyan *War and Peace* to the century's most memorable vistas of ancient Rome in *Ben Hur* and *Cleopatra*. Whether or not Cinecittà is in fact the largest film studio in the world, it certainly belongs among the top ranks—in size, productive capacity, and legendary reputation.[13]

What is the conjunction between Rome and Italian cinema—between "cosmo-polis" and "cine-città."? For the founders themselves of Cinecittà, the connection was transparent. Cinecittà existed: "So that Fascist Italy may spread more quickly through the world the splendor of the civilization of Rome."[14] In short, an actual site had been set up to transmit the ancient mission of Rome

---

[11] Cited in Bondanella [1987], 176, 181.

[12] Landy [1987], 10.

[13] Savio [1979], Fellini [1989].

[14] "Perché l'Italia Fascista diffonda nel mondo più rapida la luce della civiltà di Roma." Cited in Fellini [1989], 8.

toward universality and eternality via the ideological priorities of fascist Italy and the cinematic skills of its creators and technicists.

How exactly that mission meant to be expressed is the subject of extensive studies of the relation between fascist cinema and fascist ideology. The general conclusion is that Italian fascism (unlike German Nazism) was far less concerned with pushing a single message, or set of messages, than improving the box-office results of its sponsored efforts. It has been noted that film during the Italian fascist era concentrated on comedy and family drama, and only a small number of films clearly stressed fascist political and military ideological themes.[15] This certainly does not mean that there was no interest in indirectly pushing the cause of reinforcing a sense that things were better under fascist rule. Censorship made sure not to encourage disconcerting and disturbing aspects of everyday life that might be productive of disillusionment and cynicism. Nonetheless, it is noteworthy that the censors reacted far less strongly to direct criticism of the regime than to exposure of everyday crime.[16]

The early proponents of what became "neorealism" have been associated primarily with contributors to *Cinema* in the late 1930s and early 1940s who were acting against such overstress on genre films and calling for models, particularly American and French, which might increase exposure to a more "real" reading of facts of the everyday, individual psyche, and family and social pressures—all pushed under the surface by fascist censors' horror of commonplace reality.[17] Thus, strictly speaking Luchino Visconti's *Ossessione* (*Obsession*) (1942)—based on the "hard-boiled" stylistics of Californian James M. Cain's *The Postman Always Rings Twice* (1934)—and Vittorio de Sica's *I bambini ci guardano* (*The Children are Watching Us*) (1942)—already in collaboration with former "white-telephone" scriptwriter and future neorealist heavyweight Cesare Zavattini[18]—may be classified as full-bodied harbingers of neorealism.

---

[15] See the important study by Landy [1987].

[16] Cf. Giacomo Paulucci de'Catholi, "La Città del Cinema" (10 July 1936), in Mostra Internazionale del Nuovo Cinema [1985], 237-243.

[17] Thus the commonly recounted story of Vittorio Mussolini's scandalized reaction to Visconti's *Ossessione*: "This is not Italy!" On the other hand, Mussolini himself approved the film.

[18] The highly popular "white-telephone" films which Zavattini scripted for Mario Camerini and in which Vittorio de Sica starred were comedies along the lines of Hollywood's Frank Capra; highly admired in Italy, Capra was even invited to help the Italian film industry with his practised knowledge. "White telephone" refers to the always ubiquitous telephone ready to ring in new twists to the fashionably comedic plots.

Nonetheless *Rome, Open City* "is widely regarded as the most important film in Italian cinema history."[19] Accordingly something more than the previous account of political and filmmaking convergence in the fascist era is needed to mark out the burst of original Italian filmmaking that is associated with the label "neorealism." For this we turn directly to its apparent founder: Roberto Rossellini (1906-1977), a Roman.

II

Far more than the other major names conventionally associated with neorealism, Roberto Rossellini was a true Roman—through family, birth, values, and habitation: as one biographer puts it, "he was a Roman through and through."[20] Born in the Eternal City to wealthy parents, Rossellini all his life enjoyed the amenities of wealth: from not having to work, which allowed him to maintain a purity throughout his filmmaking ambitions (not available to, for example, the more limited prospects for Vittorio de Sica born in modest circumstances in nearby Sora) to drawing on the intellectual and practical resources his father made available to him, from early contact with highly intellectual discussions of his father's friends saturated in the aesthetics of Italian philosopher Benedetto Croce, to the availability of the first important cinema houses in Rome, the Corso and the Barberini, actually built by his father—who also later built the housing project for Mussolini which was to be the actual domicile for the working-class Roman families graphically depicted in *Rome, Open City*. Like his fellow Romans as seen by outsider Italians, Rossellini might well have been regarded as unserious, cultivating the unique Roman trait known as *trasformismo*—bending to the winds of change and opportunity—that found him working without apparent problems of conscience in the fascist film industry, including very probably collaboration with his friend Vittorio Mussolini's prize-winning film *Luciano Serra, pilota* (1938).[21]

Everything changed, however, when Mussolini was arrested and imprisoned by the king in the summer of 1943 at the time of the first Allied invasions of Sicily and south Italy. The Germans reacted by seizing Rome directly and ruthlessly controlling the city between September 1943 and June 1944. The brutality of this occupation forms the immediate conditions for the sudden turn taken by Rossellini and other fascist collaborators toward a new anti-fascist

---

[19] Brunette [1987], 41.

[20] Brunette [1987], 37.

[21] The title was in fact thought up, while shaving, by Vittorio's famous father.

politicization.[22] Rossellini's film was made immediately after the German forced departure (and the coming of the Allies, as recorded in the third episode of Rossellini's subsequent film *Paisà* (*Paisan*) (1946)); with the facilities at Cinecittà bombed out and appalling material conditions reigning in Rome, the director was forced to find tools and materials simply to put together a functionally viable film.[23] These factors help explain a great deal of the use by Rossellini's film of the purportedly unique technical signs of cinematic neorealism (as later formalized by Zavattini): non-professional actors, on-location shooting, post-synchronous sound and moderate improvisation, and cinematic simplicity.[24] Such a pragmatic explanation also explains why those priorities shifted and/or vanished as those conditions changed in the postwar era.

Even if the more minimalist definition of neorealism as a genre concerned with actual problems, employing contemporary stories, and focusing on believable characters taken from Italian daily life is utilized, more is needed for an adequate account of Rossellini's purposes in this, the putatively first neorealist work. Ultimately room must be made for the assertion that for the film, "in many ways, Rome is its chief protagonist, standing synecdochically for the rest of Italy."[25] Certainly it is obvious that Rossellini juxtaposes the eternality of Rome to the temporary presence of the Nazis: from the start it is evident that the Germans, utilizing what was called the "Schroeder system," can only think of the city as schematically identical with every other city they organize for purposes of control and surveillance.[26] In contrast, the "Roman" answer to their lethal rule comes forth in a series of admirably animated Roman figures covering the gamut of social classes, not least of whom is the priest Don Pietro reflecting Rossellini's accommodationism of leftist politics—in deference to the Communist partisans at the heart of the Resistance movement—with a generously interpreted Christian charity. "I am a Catholic priest," asserts Don Pietro in a revealing passage, "and I believe that a man who fights for justice and liberty walks in the pathways of the Lord—and the pathways of the Lord are infinite." Meanwhile the noblest resistance fighter Manfredi, tortured by an unrelenting Gestapo, provides the film with one of its most striking images in

[22] Brunette [1987], 38.

[23] Ironically with regard to the theme of Rome, while the founding of Cinecittà had led to the domination of Rome over other sites in the fascist period, bombing of its studios allowed production to emerge in other studios and regional centers—as in the silent film era. Wood [2005], 12.

[24] Zavattini, "Some Notes on the Cinema." Zavattini [1970] and Overby [1979].

[25] Brunette [1987], 51.

[26] My thanks for this information to Sophia Chytry, "Italian Neorealism and Civic Contexts: Tragedy and Comedy in a Roman Robe" (unpublished paper).

suggesting his death as a veritable crucifixion. Even the fabled *coralità* (from "chorus") of Rossellini's concern for the group over the individual seems rooted not so much in the class solidarity of Marxism or socialism as in Christian love.[27]

Underplaying both the Italian fascist and the Roman Church's complicity with Nazi rule, Rossellini concludes his film with a memorable image of the Roman skyline.[28] Although the Dome of St. Peter is an important element on this skyline, Rossellini's closing scene gives equal emphasis to the overall contextuality of the entire city of Rome, not just the Church; and his human participants are boys who, having fought for the resistence and lately weighed down by the martyred execution (by Germans, not Italians) of Don Pietro, make their painful way, physically supporting each other, down the hill toward Rome and the future that they alone can fashion. If it seems permissible to regard this denouement as the Roman Rossellini's faith in what has been called "the myth of Rome" understood as "a form of secular religion,"[29] then it may be equally acceptable to see the work as a vitalization of that myth to serve ecumenical interests in binding together partisans (Risorgimento) and Christians (Papacy) in a uniquely new cinematic confirmation of the Roman "cosmo-polis".

In contrast to Rossellini, Vittorio de Sica (1902-1974)[30] was not a Roman. Although born in the nearby town of Sora, he was brought up Neapolitan and throughout his life identified with the Napolitano—and, in his sponsorship of the Pozzuolo-born Sophia Loren, Napolitana—ethos. Nonetheless, it was actor-director de Sica who immediately followed up on Rossellini's first two neorealist triumphs of 1945 and 1946 with his own Roman masterpieces *Sciuscià* (*Shoeshine*) (1946) and *Ladri di biciclette* (*Bicycle Thieves*) (1948). If to these works are added *Umberto D* (1952) and *Il Tetto* (*The Roof*) (1956)—these last products considered the final members of the conventional canon of Italian neorealism—there results a body of work that carries forward Rossellini's more generalized themes for a Roman humanity, rather than social class, tinged with a kind of hope and goodness in which—notwithstanding the dangers of sentimentalism—de Sica revelled.

---

27 Already reflected in his pre-*Rome, Open City* works, as recounted by Brunette [1987], 29.

28 The Italian fascists are only seen as passive figures under the thumb of cruel and sexually sadistic Nazi rulers and collaborators, and the Church generally takes on the contours of the sometimes clownish but impeccable Don Pietro (his role in fact played by an Italian actor famed for his clown roles).

29 Bondanella [1987], 4.

30 Although 1901 is commonly used as the date for de Sica's birth, I follow Cardullo's preference for 1902. Cardullo [2002], 3.

Most important, *Shoeshine* and *Bicycle Thieves* pick up where *Rome, Open City* left off. In effect de Sica takes up the closing image of Rossellini's street children and places them in the postwar Roman world of poverty, magistrates, thieves, and prisons.[31] In *Shoeshine* he unfolds the tragedy of vagrant orphans incarcerated by the adult world, but his purpose is not so much to accuse this society on the fate of its children as to unfold the drama of a society divided against itself in the exhausted conditions of a Rome "bereft of its pride."[32] Indeed there are plausible reasons for the specific actions of much of this adult society under pressures from a collapsed civil society, but the grief that ensues exposes, in de Sica's perspective, the overall human tragedy of lack of communication and solidarity. It is then all the more poignant that the horse purchased by the two young protagonists as constituting their happiness against these circumstances takes flight instead of riding "triumphantly throughout Rome and its environs" as testimony to their earlier love.[33]

In turn, *Bicycle Thieves* is largely about "a (Roman) world inextricably interrelated through perverse economic ties" which the film brilliantly exposes by treating its struggling father-and-son team as the rule, not exception, in a world of quantities of people and things.[34] Again, de Sica does not move toward suggestions of popular revolt against these conditions so much as he sustains his humanist themes of the absence of human ties and sympathies. Yet in the end the film propounds the message of the echoes of human solidarity and empathy at least within the family and the father-to-son relationship in a Rome that is shown through a lyrical cinematic account of "their scouting expedition through the city." This Rome is far from the tourist's Rome with its spectacular sights; rather, the expedition passes through the contemporary realities of drab streets, ugly houses, and deserted embankments along a morose Tiber River. Even so, this rendering of "a visually austere rather than picturesquely lush Rome" makes its mark in identifying de Sica's neorealist humanism with the variety and realism of Roman life at that postwar moment, one which even includes its moments of solidarity.[35] As de Sica later notes: "All my films are about the search for human solidarity. In *Bicycle Thief* this solidarity occurs, but how long does it last? Twenty-four hours. One experiences moments, only moments

[31] As already shown in his prior work *The Children are Watching Us* (1942), de Sica displayed remarkable sensitivity toward the world of children and directing non-actor children.

[32] Cardullo [2002], 34.

[33] Cardullo [2002], 36. As de Sica put it regarding his intentions in *Shoeshine*, "I intended to emphasize a phenomenon that has always deeply saddened me—the indifference of humanity to the needs of others." Both he and Zavattini were struck by "the melancholy poetry of that generation of children led astray by the war" (168).

[34] Cardullo [2002], 40-41.

[35] Cardullo [2002], 38, 43, 44.

of solidarity."[36] This statement may seem dispiriting; in fact it saves de Sica's work from sentimentalism by anchoring it in a distinctly contemporary Roman "cosmo-politanism."

Umberto D (1952), which de Sica considered his best film, continues de Sica's reading of postwar Rome by presenting a retired administrative clerk—typical for a bureaucratically-populated capital—increasingly incapable of surviving the high costs of sustenance. Based partly on de Sica's own bourgeois father, it is a deliberate effort to widen neorealism's concern for the working poor to now include "the poor middle class." Yet, again, de Sica wishes not only to focus on the indifference of society to this considerable minority, he also continues to stress that the tragedy of Umberto D is no less that of his isolation and lack of connections with others—even, in Umberto's own case, his failure to pay attention to the plight of the pregnant maid who is a similar discard of the new postwar conditions: "The economic condition of Umberto is not what concerns us. What concerns us is his moral and human relationship with society."[37] This relationship not only exposes "the egosim of all of us" indifferent to each other's plight, but also that of Umberto himself.

Finally, de Sica's *The Roof* (1956) narrates the difficulties of the new generation of young Roman couples attempting to survive chronic crises of housing and employment. Although less known than his other neorealist films, this work—which de Sica, again in collaboration with Zavattini, regarded as "one of my best"—brings de Sica's efforts to record "a way of life" characteristic of his oeuvre right to the mid-1950s when the original neorealist project of humanistic optimism had evaporated under the more recent effects of the first postwar "economic miracle" of the early 1950s.[38]

III

Umberto D carries another, increasingly significant feature. By making use of studio facilities available at Cinecittà, it highlights the degree to which the "open-air" priorities attributed to neorealism's tenets were giving way to more conventional concerns for directorial control over setting and acting.[39]

---

[36] Cited in Cardullo [2002], 182.

[37] De Sica notes that "All the neorealist films were made in favor of the proletariat, always forgetting the poor middle class." Cited in Cardullo [2002], 185. Also 175.

[38] Cited in Cardullo [2002], 181. A fuller survey would include the collective neorealist project organized by Zavattini that became the film *Amore in Città* (*Love in the City*) (1953) and focused on a variety of readings of contemporary Rome by Carlo Lizzani, Michelangelo Antonioni, Dino Risi, Federico Fellini, Cesare Zavattini, and Alberto Lattuada.

[39] Moreover, Cinecittà in this period "offered delayed payment facilities, which made it a bank

Revitalized after its wartime bombing by the new Christian Democratic government, Cinecittà was to become central not only to a revived Italian popular film industry but also to the emergence of "Hollywood-on-the-Tiber," the new tendency by Hollywood producers to employ Cinecittà facilities for fiscal, and in some cases political blacklisting, reasons, as well as in order to draw on the extensive Italian experience for putting together blockbuster "mythology" films.[40]

Since this epoch corresponds to the changed Italian economic and political conditions of the mid-1950s, it also marks what is generally regarded as the end to classic neorealism.[41] The accepted view of this change is that the immediate postwar optimism of a "common front" among the different elements of the anti-fascist resistance in which neorealism found its early program had broken down after 1947-1948 into the extended struggle between the conservative parties in power and the changing left alliances on the periphery, all the while that measures reinforcing Italian incorporation into a new Europe fed new patterns of growth and configurations of power.[42]

From these factors emerged what Roman author Pier Paolo Pasolini in 1957 labeled as the "vital crisis" in neorealism. This term has subsequently become the basis of the title of a cinematic study of the relation between this "classic" neorealist period of 1945-54 and the remarkable burst of Italian filmmaking creativity around 1960-1964 for which, as the author of this study notes, no "comparable blanket term" exists.[43] In our study we shall regard this later period as the very culmination of the neorealists' vision of a Roman "cosmopolis" humanism, augmented by the new factors of the mild "economic miracle" of mid-1950s followed by the more accelerated "economic miracle" of 1958-1963 that conveniently corresponds to the later burst of works.[44]

Into this cauldron emerge three further contributors to our theme: Federico Fellini, Michelangelo Antonioni, and Pier Paolo Pasolini. The continuity between these two stages is confirmed by the fact that the first two had worked with the earlier neorealists and the third, known in the 1950s as a poet and novelist of the Roman "subproletariat", advised Fellini on his Roman film, *Le*

---

to its own clients" —basically a level of subsidy, as Wood states. Wood [2005], 17, citing Champanier [1989], 67.

40 Campari [1980]; Kaufman & Lerner [1982]. Cf. also Time Magazine [1954].

41 By 1954 this was even being reported by popular newsmagaziness like *Time*. Time Magazine [1954], 61-62.

42 See Ginsborg [1990] for the single best account.

43 Sitney [1995], 1.

44 The growth rate per year for the mid-1950s was 5.5%; for 1958-1963 it was 6.3% per year. Figures are from Ginsborg [1990].

Notti di Cabiria (*The Nights of Cabiria*) (1957), before turning to filmmaking himself with *Accattone* (1961).

An adoptive Roman from Ravenna, Federico Fellini (1920-1993) is probably the filmmaker most universally identified with the great era of Italian cinema; equally he is the one most closely associated with the image of "Rome" in the modern cinematic imagination, an association that he has gone to great trouble to affirm in his work and countless interviews. Although listed as part of the second of two cycles of trilogy by the early Fellini, *The Nights of Cabiria* also marks an early "Roman" setting of shooting character to environment. As Pasolini, Fellini's collaborator for material on Roman prostitution life, asserts, Fellini developed a technique of repeating patterns of relating his main character, a working-class prostitute, to her environment. Cabiria and her attitudes are closely attached to her varied workstations, from the Passeggiata Archeologica to the more sophisticated Via Veneto, as well as to her proudly maintained shanty home eighteen kilometers outside Rome. The result is that Fellini's account, far from drawing on the traditional prostitute figure of melodrama, is shown freed of bourgeois morality and content with her profession. If Cabiria suffers, it is because of the lingering element of grace and love to which she is still vulnerable. Even here Fellini offers the characteristic Roman escapes of religious pilgrimages (the shrine of Divino Amore at the Via Ardeatina) and variety theatre before closing with the fleeting hope promised by music and procession that sustains in her (and presumably in us)—as Fellini once told a Jesuit priest—"a note of grace."[45]

With *La dolce vita* (1960) Fellini raised Italian cinema to a status among the world cinematic public that has probably never since been equalled.[46] Indeed perhaps there has never been a film that has produced such a universal image of the "sweet life" as Fellini's depiction of late 1950s Rome.[47] But *La dolce vita*

---

[45] Following Bondanella [1992], 121-130.

[46] It is also worth mentioning Rossellini's return to neorealist themes with a new film *General della Rovere* (1959) concerned with the Resistance and starring de Sica. Rossellini then followed up with the sequel *Era Notte in Roma* (*It was Night in Rome*) (1960) in which continued use of the icon of St. Peter's Dome was exploited as part of Rossellini's overall intention to remind a young generation of fascism. (According to Brunette [1987], 221, Rossellini had been struck by the ignorance of the younger generation upon hearing of an Italian high school student who thought that Mussolini was a neorealist film director.) For his part, de Sica used a 1957 novel by Alberto Moravia regarding a wartime Rome widow to film *La Ciociara* (*Two Women*) (1960) in his home town of Sora and as part of his sympathetic treatment of a mountainous region to the south of Rome caught in the coils of war. Yet these works differ from earlier neorealist efforts for being retrospective gazes at a recent past rather than observant treatment of the present.

[47] Not merely the title, but even the name of one of its characters "Paparazzo", has become a commonplace of public media discourse. See Fellini's own sketch in Fellini [1989], 35.

embarks on familiar neorealist attentiveness to the specific conditions of the Rome of Fellini's time in order to furnish a set of promises that are even dimmer than the vague suggestion of grace in his previous cinematic trilogy.[48] Indeed, strictly speaking "la dolce vita" may be translated as the "economic miracle" itself of the 1958-63 period: that is, the moral atmosphere succeeding the end of reconstruction with the emergence of a new consumer society oriented toward media influence, motorization, and the shrinkage both of the importance of the Italian family and of the Church. At the same time, Fellini's alternative title for such a film—"Babylon 2000 Years After Jesus Christ"—is a reminder of more eternal Roman considerations for his exacting gaze, through the eyes of a journalist working for possibly crypto-fascist newsmagazines, at the Rome of the postwar republic. If "Hollywood on the Tiber" is an evident source for scandalized interest—as personified in the character of Anita Ekberg, itself based on the Swedish actress' earlier frolics in the Trevi Fountain—along with the hub of activity on the Via Veneto, Fellini frequently slips in alternate imagery and symbolism to suggest more permanent elements to the bittersweet search for happiness and possible equanimity. Nonetheless, unlike his previous trilogy of "grace," *La dolce vita* remorselessly if sympathetically closes the door on the search for meaning, whether in religion, sexuality, or intellectuality. The promise of grace, if such there is, will be found elsewhere.

That "elsewhere" stems from one of the more striking features of the making of *La dolce vita*. For a film which ostensibly took extra care to depict the Roman cityscape, it remains remarkable that the studio facilities at Cinecittà were used almost entirely for its eighty-odd locations, the first time that Fellini completely committed himself to the studio process for his films.[49] From now on Fellini was able to visualize each specific location, character, and ambiance for the total control offered by the eventually legendary Studio 5 in Cinecittà. Instead of the promise of spectacle, procession, and music that he had referenced in his earlier films as residues of human and divine "grace", Fellini now found such "grace" in the Director's very capacity to create Cinema itself as Spectacle, as—eventually—the phenomenon of "Meta-cinema." From this date on originates the "Fellini myth" of the Director himself as "Superstar," creating out of nothing (*ex nihilo*) in a manner resembling none other than Our Lord: "God the Father."[50]

---

[48] *La strada* [1954] *Il bidone* [1955], *Le notti di Cabiria* [1957].

[49] The entire set of sequences localized in the Via Veneto was filmed using a perfect replica of the real street, Fellini himself becoming so used to this simulacrum that later on whenever confronting the genuine street he found himself irritated by its sloping in contrast to the perfectly horizontal Cinecittà version.

[50] Thus Fellini: "Film is a divine way of telling about life, of paralleling God the Father.... For

IV

Before however Fellini's step toward the supra-reality of Cinecittà was fully enacted, two cinematic contemporaries continued to exploit the "real" Rome for their strikingly diverse readings of the cosmo-polis of Rome. Each managed idiosyncratic readings of aspects of the economic miracle that are worth recounting.

Michelangelo Antonioni (1912- 2007) responded to the themes of *La dolce vita* with *La notte* (1961) which depicted the "sweet life" of industrially progressive Milan, urban piston to Italy's "economic miracle", and *L'eclisse (The Eclipse)* (1962) which was centered on Rome. Already noted as a documentarist and filmmaker of sparse individuals, Antonioni chose a remnant of the fascist era urbanscape to assemble his particular version of Rome. If Fellini moved from the open neorealist landscape of Rome as exploited by Rossellini and de Sica to the director's dream of a Cinecittà simulacrum of Rome, Antonioni headed directly south to the former Esposizione Universale di Roma (E.U.R.). Originally set up by Mussolini to create a Rome of new Fascist buildings to serve as open museums of presumably living history, E.U.R. had been intended to serve as the site for a world fair in 1942 to celebrate twenty years of fascist rule. Obviously prevented by the war from serving such a function, E.U.R. was nonetheless developed by the postwar Christian Democratic Party as part of its campaign for a civic expansion toward the sea, and in fact functioned among the sites for the 1960 Rome Olympics.[51] Seen as a showpiece of the economic miracle, this curious remnant of fascist planning now served as an apparently attractive home and business area for a range of groupings extending from the international community to middle-class intellectuals and affluent Italians without access to traditional Roman apartments held by the older classes, a change of venue made easier by the fact that Mussolini himself had favored bold modernist architecture to emphasize the novelty of fascism.[52]

---

me the ideal place—I have said this many times—is Theater 5 in Cinecittà when it's empty. Total emotion, trembling ecstasy is what I feel there in that empty studio—a space to fill up, a world to create." Worried lest this confession might remind us of another Duce, Fellini's foremost American interpreter Bondanella immediately adds another, more sobering quote from Fellini: "the cinema has always been the same thing: a rickety camera with someone behind it filming a clown moving in front of it." Bondanella [1992], 211, 213.

[51] Bondanella [1987], 190-205. Both E.U.R. and Cinecittà, although respectively south and southeast of the city of Rome, are easily accessible through the Metro lines B and A.

[52] The link between modernism and fascism is the early twentieth-century manifesto and art movement of Futurism with its emphasis on newness, speed, and destruction of ossified nineteenth-century tastes. The Futurist poet Gabriele d'Annunzio played a key role in advancing

For Antonioni, E.U.R. served as part of his continuing exploration of the social contradictions of the economic miracle. Not surprisingly *The Eclipse* became the immediate object of international leftist conferences drawing on the works of such Marxists as Gramsci and Lukács to explore the favored theme of reification. No doubt the director was not loathe to play with contemporary political and even Armaggedon worries during the height of the Cold War threat of possible thermonuclear exchange (the Cuban Missile Crisis of 1962 was on the horizon), and his camera play with the apparently cold, solitary, even alien spaces of E.U.R. facilitates such referencings. From the opening image of a mushroom architectural shape suggestive of the nuclear cloud as seen through a formal modernist interior (the mushroom structure was in fact a popular restaurant in the district) to his tracking caress of its one important modernist building from the fascist era, the Palazzo della Civiltà Italiana (now "del Lavoro" rather than "Italiana"), Antonioni played up the difficulty of human communication and contact in the bare and often empty carrefours of the district. Augmented by his simultaneous use of the Roman Borsa, as contrasted with the Piazza di Pietra which had been the traditional center of Roman public life through its access to the Hadrianeum, Antonioni highlighted the petty nature of its exchange with middle-class players of small capital and a generation without a proper sense of home. Not surprisingly, it is a cityscape that adds little encouragement to the ostensible narrative of an affair between an observant but passive woman whose mother is addicted to the Borsa and an aggressively successful young stockbroker who is apparently enjoying the usual bachelor amenities—sports car and dames included—of the economic miracle.

Yet, even here with what would seem to be clear links to political motifs, Antonioni's intentions proved far broader. As the subtitle of a study of Antonioni has underscored, Antonioni, at least during his immediately post-realist works between 1960 and 1964, was primarily concerned with "the surface of things."[53] That is, his works sought a fully "secular" reality freeing humans from a former atavistic panic in front of what he called the "face" of nature. Since for Antonioni all past language—the language of gods and demons and other collective objects of fear—had been motivated primarily by this panic, relief could only come when humans became reconciled to nature and to space as their true background.[54] Accordingly, for all the sparseness of

---

the role of cinema as well as in showing through his temporary rulership of the city-state of Fiume (1919-1920) a pre-Mussolini set of militant gestures (including possibly the fascist salute, itself possibly stemming from a Roman mythology film of that period). See also Chapter 2 above for further details.

[53] Chatman [1985].

[54] Cited in Sitney [1995], 154.

the evident narrative of the film, the astonishing beauty of Antonioni's camerawork, even down to the gentle running of water that Antonioni's Japanese admirers have compared to a contemplative Zen sense for nature, sought to elicit a delayed exhilaration for the specificities of objects, light, and pure spatiality—the stuff of, if not a "redeemed" nature, at least of a nature seen for the first time—without presuppositions. Even granted that these scenes are located with painstaking deliberation in a Rome as apparently "alien" as E.U.R., the general effect—as highlighted by the closing extended scene which is nothing if not an elaborate set of photographic stillwork on this cityscape—may almost be regarded as a promise of purely secularized grace

In contrast to Antonioni's Roman cosmo-polis, Pier Paolo Pasolini (1922-1975), an adoptive Roman like Fellini, brought to his new Roman life after 1950 a preoccupation with pre-industrial modes of humanity that attach him both to earlier neorealist as well as to Gramscian leftist concerns.[55] Like such neorealists as Luchino Visconti in *La terra trema* (*The Earth Trembles*) (1948), Pasolini took extra interest in language and the tendency of political and economic hegemony to favor one dominant language at the cost of other living languages (demoted to the category of mere "dialects"), something Italian fascism had sponsored in its campaign against all local resistance to its hegemony. The early Pasolini had been fascinated by the Friulian language of his home region and even sought to write in that mode. Later, however, he came to recognize that his relation to that language had been merely "aesthetic" in the sense that he had failed to incorporate its living daily operations. Henceforth, upon moving to Rome and coming into contact with its impoverished suburbs (*borgate*), Pasolini learned to partake of a living language, that of the Roman "subproletariat," the body of Romans who were being discarded as losers in the economic miracle(s) but who retained a direct relation to reality with its mythical and poetic features.[56] This "dialect" Pasolini first employed in his Rome poems and novels *Ragazzi di vita (Children of Life*) (1955) and *Una vita violenta* (*A Violent Life*) (1959) which, as we have seen, brought him to the attention of Fellini for collaborative work on the latter's *The Nights of Cabiria*. Subsequently, in 1961 Pasolini himself entered the filmmaking fray with *Accattone*.[57]

Accattone helps form a body of works that some critics have read as a sort of "second neorealism" and associate with Pasolini's "Roman period."[58] It is

---

[55] See Pasolini's "Gramscian" poems in Pasolini [2003].

[56] Pasolini [1969], 15, 17, 26-27.

[57] Pasolini [1969], 31. Sitney suggests that in a sense "*Accattone* is a critique and revision of *Le notti di Cabiria.*" Sitney [1995], 176.

[58] Oswald Stack, in Pasolini [1969], 8. The other works listed under this heading are: *Mamma*

perhaps the most deliberately leftist body of efforts in the neorealist or quasi-neorealist canon while at the same time its meta-secular gestures condemn it from a purely secularist point of view. Like Antonioni Pasolini is obsessed to get to the nature of things without the prior history of tags and categories,[59] and his Roman subproletariat is among the last vestiges of a humanity which contains, despite itself, the clues toward such an arrival.

One of the first semi-historians of the original neorealism, Pasolini claimed that the latter reflected "all our hopes for a new kind of society," which sadly had been subsequently crushed under the hegemony of the new bourgeois classes of the economic miracle. Accordingly, instead of holding on to elements of middle-class values as he thought that other filmmakers like Fellini continued to display, Pasolini utilized without apology the values of the Roman subproletariat and its criminal elements.[60] *Accattone* constitutes "a refashioning of neorealism" by bringing in a cinematographic rawness in tandem with burning *borgate* cityscapes that result in a "vision of an unknown Rome" in which Gospel allusions, Renaissance iconography (especially Masaccio), and the music of Bach are juxtaposed into the daily environment of the Rome subproletariat.[61]

The resulting "technical sacredness" (*sacralità tecnica*)[62] then becomes the hallmark of Pasolini's immediately succeeding works. His "accattone"— a Roman word that can be roughly translated as panhandler or vagabond—ends up suffering humiliation in a kind of *imitatio Christi* insofar as his diffuse rebelliousness brings on a variety of punishments from this brave new world of Italian economic progress. Pasolini continues to pursue this obsessive concern with the *via crucis* in his *Mamma Roma* (1962) where a valiant attempt to break free of the despairing circumstances of an "accattone" means at best to fit into blank housing projects mimicking middle-class values that are arising along the suburbs to accommodate aspiring former prostitutes like Pasolini's main lead (played by the legendary neorealist star Anna Magnani).[63] Appropriately the

---

Roma (1962), *La ricotta* (1963) and *Il vangelo secondo Matteo* (*The Gospel According to St. Matthew*) (1964).

[59] "I see everything in the world, objects as well as people and nature with a certain veneration." Pasolini [1969], 14. Also Pasolini refers to "my tendency always to see something sacred and mythic and epic in everything, even the most humdrum, simple and banal objects and events" (77).

[60] Pasolini [1969], 39; Sitney [1995], 179.

[61] Sitney [1995], 180.

[62] Patrick Rumble, in Bertellini [2004], 109.

[63] Interestingly Pasolini blamed himself for his choice of Magnani who, he realized too late, remained "a woman who was born and has lived as a petite bourgeoise and then as an actress and so hasn't got those characteristics" of "a woman of the people [*popolana]* with petite bourgeois

film closes with the stunning image of the death of its main male lead incarcerated and bound on a slab in a manner easily recalling the famous Dead Christ of the Renaissance painter Mantegna.

Thus it is not surprising that Pasolini's "Roman period" works culminate in an effort to render the story of Christ itself through the account narrated in the Gospel of Matthew. Although not strictly speaking a "Rome" film, *The Gospel According to Saint Matthew* was carefully filmed in the equivalent of subproletariat settings throughout South Italy and was in fact greatly inspired by the pontificate of John XXIII (1958-1963) then taking place in the Vatican. For perhaps the first time in centuries a pope ruled Christian Rome in a manner that promised considerable reform and a papacy sensitive to the poor and subproletariat. Certainly without John's brief reign, it is difficult to imagine the advent of the Second Vatican Council as well as the emergence of liberation theology within the Church. Pasolini himself was apparently inspired by the topic of *The Gospel* while awaiting the arrival of the pope in Assisi, and he would fulsomely dedicate his film to John a year after the latter's death. As he later noted, "everything was made easier by the advent of Pope John XXIII who objectively revolutionized the situation."[64]

For Pasolini who resolutely continued to insist that his cinematic "style was religious"—adding that he actually preferred the word *sacrale* ("reverential")—the Italy following the 1958-1963 economic miracle was finally closed to the possibilities he had envisaged from his Rome subproletariat. Increasingly Pasolini looked to Third World cultures as well as to other exotic historical periods for his candidates. With Rome and Italy themselves now fully part of the industrial West, the Italian peasantry and non-industrialized minorities of the Roman *borgate* (as in the earlier cases of their English and French counterparts) were vanishing permanently from the face of history—along with Pasolini's unique vision of a subproletariat Roman "cosmo-polis."[65]

V

What then marks the final curtain on the theme of a Roman "cosmo-polis" originally set off by Italian neorealism? Federico Fellini's evocation of Rome

aspirations." Pasolini [1969], 49. See also the analysis in Wood [2000], 215, on the role of the Roman "periphery—not-Rome and not-suburbs."

[64] Pasolini [1969], 75.

[65] Pasolini's own later brutal murder in the Roman coastal town of Ostia at the hands ostensibly of members of this same subproletariat is perhaps as Pasolinian a commentary on this closure as one might invent. However Pasolini's legacy has been recently revitalized by Roberto Saviano's non-fiction *Gomorra* (2006) and Matteo Garrone's film (2008) of the same name.

had already abandoned the lingering influence of neorealism still traceable in *La dolce vita*; but just as that film ends the first phase of Fellini's filmmaking, it no less begins the second and final phase of Fellini's own forays into "metacinema." Now that "Rome" had in effect become its own simulacrum in Cinecittà—itself a literal, physical district of the Roman region—the possibilities for rendering its "cosmo-politan" lessons turned endless. Their implications may be discerned through a closing survey of Fellini's group of films on Rome—*La Dolce Vita* (1960), *Fellini Satyricon* (1969) and *Roma* (1972)—called "the most original and most complex variation on the mythology of Rome in the modern world."[66]

If *La Dolce Vita* belonged at least tacitly to the neorealist concern for readings of the contemporary cityscape and its participants in given material circumstances, *Fellini Satyricon* and *Roma* move freely between ancient and modern Rome through the transformers of dream and imagination. As "metacinema," neither of the latter films gives much credence to narrative integrity; instead, they furnish a set of discernible tableaux. These operate in conformity with Fellini's stance that straightforward archaeological or sociological approaches to the meaning of Rome will inevitably come up against fatal obstacles, whereas the relatively free flow of imagination might render insights that transcend the problems of time and space in the eternality that is presumably "Rome." Indeed, the scenes for both films are almost entirely shot within Cinecittà, and even that ultimate portentous edifice representing ancient Rome, the Colosseum, is in fact not the original but Fellini's Cinecittà reconstruction.[67]

Given that for Fellini access to the "truth" of Rome comes through the imagination, it is Fellini's own imaginative reading of "Rome" which provides the appropriate entry. Convalescing from a serious illiness in 1967 which threatened his creative instincts, Fellini turned to the Roman author Petronius' *Satyricon* which he identified with his own youthful memories of ancient Rome through the silent cinema of Guido Brignone's *Macist all'inferno* (1926) and the tradition of Rome-mythology silent films going back to Pastrone's *Cabiria* (1914). The ancient Rome which results in *Fellini Satyricon*, a film driven largely by preliminary sketches and images rather than written script, reinterprets the Petronius text, often exploiting gaps in the original manuscript that has survived to produce the Fellini version of a Petronian reality which confirms analogies between the ancient and modern world in terms of the theme

---

[66] Bondanella [1987], 257. Elsewhere Bondanella refers to Fellini's "Roman trilogy." Bondanella [1992], 205.

[67] The following account largely follows the exemplary analyses in Bondanella [1987] and [1992]; also Foreman [1980].

of "decadence." This theme of loss of values among Petronius' fellow Romans and Fellini's contemporary Rome "points unequivocally to the period of the late 1960s, the time when the film was made."[68] Thus, even if imagination (rather than collected "facts" of archaeology and history) is the point of entry into the "past" of the mythology of Rome, this entry still has direct relevance for the specificities of contemporary Rome. For Fellini himself, the implications were "exhilarating": breakdown of stable values on the part of both ancient and modern Rome meant that "the young are aware that a new world is beginning," and a work like *Fellini Satyricon* confirmed, at least for the director himself, that the key lies in giving oneself the right to free use of the imagination in creating one's reality, a reality anchored, in Fellini's case, in the transformer of Cinecittà.

With *Roma* Fellini dives directly into his imaginative reading of Rome in order to create "a new and daring Roman mythology of his own, combining the older and familiar elements with novel images."[69] As confirmed by his many writings on the subject, Fellini's Rome is "a completely feminine city, combining qualities of the ideal mother and the mistress."[70] This turns out not to be entirely healthy since Romans, certainly males, end up immature and unprepared for dealing with actual realities of life. Vaguely bringing himself into this cauldron, Fellini projects something of his own entry into Rome in 1939 and links it with both his adolescent sense for sexuality and for cinema. Yet this phantasmal sense that maternal Rome induces can also be exploited by an artist—in this case, a director of an entire cinematic reality through Cinecittà—to celebrate one's imaginative capacities. Hence the most striking tableaux in this work include those taking us to the remarkable variety show at the Barafonda theatre where performers and audiences are equal participants, to a trattoria of gluttony and familiality, and even to an astounding papal fashion show. Appropriately Fellini closes with two central images for the "Rome" he invents for us. The first shows a brief exchange in the Trastevere with Anna Magnani herself, the central female icon of classic neorealism, who embodies Fellini's Rome as "both vestal and tramp, the perfect female embodiment of the Roman she-wolf or *lupa*."[71] Her message to the persistently inquiring Fellini is to tell him to go to bed by shutting her door in his face. There then follows the spectacle of a gang of motorcyclists—the new "barbarians," as it were, of modern Rome—thundering through the classic highlights of ancient Rome toward its heart at the Colosseum—itself a Cinecittà construction—before

[68] Bondanella [1992], 251.
[69] Bondanella [1987], 257.
[70] Bondanella [1992], 196.
[71] Bondanella [1987], 247.

heading out to the infinite possibilities of new realms as promised by the name of the avenue: "Christopher Columbus":

> Fellini's humanistic vision seems to promise the possibility of infinite transmutations of this complicated mythology. The future may well be renewed by its link to the presence of ancient Rome in the modern world, just as Fellini's poetic vision was liberated by its presence in his films.[72]

VI

Fellini's penultimate project, *Intervista* (1987) (*Interview*), is in many ways his closing homage to Cinecittà proper, to the Roman "world" which had sustained him throughout his metacinematic redemption of reality. Today Cinecittà continues to prosper, although increasingly its workload is committed to television rather than films, a transition that the later Fellini deeply regretted since it was the cinema and its social-fantasy reality for a collective theatrical audience that had in large part sustained his grand projects in metacinema.[73] Particularly since 1997 when the Italian government turned over its controlling interest in Cinecittà, the private companies which are running it have tried to attract American productions while explicitly underplaying the former affiliation of Cinecittà with Fellini. The upshot has been to minimize Italian productions since Italian films cannot offer the profitable level of desired clientele.[74]

Yet Cinecittà is also the surviving material and symbolic site for the thread of our theme. Neorealism took on its distinct contours in reaction to the fascist project of globalizing what fascist Italy called the "civilizing mission" of Rome, that is, the fascist version of Rome—one which increasingly and fatally celebrated the militaristic and imperialistic traditions of the ancient Romans. In important ways nurtured by the fascist environment of underscoring the importance of cinema for propagating the universal civilization that "Rome" embodied, the neorealists shifted their focus toward the living particularities of this universal site for some of their most evocative and significant projects. From the hopeful "cosmo-politanism" of the classic humanist neorealist works of 1945-1954 to the more skeptical reflections of their immediate successors of

---

[72] Bondanella [1987], 251.

[73] The recent TV HBO series "Rome" was filmed in Cinecittà. For an account of a visit to the studios and photographs of the "Rome" set, see Muschamp [2007]. In 2007 Cinecittà was seriously damaged by fire.

[74] Horowitz [2003]. Since this change Hollywood films at Cinecittà have included Martin Scorcese's *Gangs of New York* and Mel Gibson's *The Passion.*

1960-1964 concerned with the tribulations brought about by a series of "economic miracles" through which Italy became a functionally effective modern industrial state, this tradition highlighted the living reality of Rome for its more universal "humanist" visions via the cinematic experience. Once however Italy had moved past this transition phase to full industrialization and permanent membership among the advanced nations, the age of neorealism and its "cosmo-polis" came firmly to an end.[75]

In Federico Fellini's resolve to find humanist experiences—via "Rome"—through the creative acts made possible by the grand potentials of Studio 5 in Cinecittà, the tradition was transfigured into Fellini's call for the individual's creative fantasies of incorporating ancient and modern Rome through the facsimile of Fellini's own retort of Cinecittà. The implications of Fellini's project will no doubt outlast its creation in propagating the imaginative life as one of the few viable answers to what Fellini himself positively read as the state of modern "decadence."

At the same time Fellini leaves cinematic history a tradition that began with Rossellini's *Roma, città aperta*—"Rome, [a truly] Open City"—and ends with Fellini's own *Roma*. Among its lasting images are the younger Anna Magnani being shot to death by Nazis while rushing to defend her fiancé (and future "humanist" Roman family) in *Roma, città aperta,* and the older Magnani impatiently (albeit sympathetically) slamming the door on a pesky director (Fellini himself) in *Roma*. It is a tradition that furnishes one of the more memorable contemporary versions of the universal benefits to be derived from that distinctively Roman invention, "cosmo-polis," within that characteristically "cosmo-political" cinematic retort called Cinecittà:

> I have a Polis, and I have a Country; I have Rome, and I have the Cosmos.

[75] I do not here treat the somewhat separate, albeit related, theme of the end of cinematic use of Roman antiquity during the 1960s, for which see Wyke [1997], esp. 183-192.

CHAPTER EIGHT

The Castles of Kafka

Organization, Polis, and Poetry in the Oeuvre of James G. March

> Everywhere there is organization, everywhere bureaucratization; like the world of feudalism, the modern world is broken up into areas dominated by castles, but not the castles of *les chansons de geste*, but the castles of Kafka.
>
> Sheldon Wolin[1]

> *Yo sé quiem soy.*
> I know who I am.

> For a knight errant to make himself crazy for a reason
> merits neither credit nor thanks.
> The point is to act foolishly without justification.
>
> Miguel de Cervantes, *Don Quixote*[2]

And so we are left with two remaining overriding questions: What is the Political? And what is its connection with Organization?[3]

For American political philosopher Sheldon Wolin the two are entirely incompatible. Author of the classic *Politics and Vision* (1960), Wolin has brought out more recently an updated edition (2004) in which the first part more or less reflects the original publication while the second part shows Wolin's evolution since that period toward a position that he describes as moving from "liberalism to democracy."[4] In either case, both in the original and in the expanded version, he is clear that the *bête noir* to both remains "organization" or the large-scale business corporation which has closed the door on the

---

[1] Wolin [2004], 317.

[2] Cited in March [1999], 377, 378. Compare: "The tears of spring/Have dried their salts/Around our roots;/And we are what we are." "A Day in September," in March [1980], 3.

[3] An earlier version of part of this chapter was published in *Industrial and Corporate Change*, 12:4 (2003), 943-960. A first version was presented as an invited paper at Institutions and Organizations: A Conference in Honor of James G. March, Lucca, Italy, on 6 July 2002. I deeply appreciate the kindnesses of James March and Thierry Weil in looking over this chapter.

[4] Wolin [2004], xv.

"political" through a "postmodern power" that has replaced the "political" with an inchoate "regime" that Wolin labels "Superpower."[5]

Putting aside for a moment the validity of Wolin's prognostications, what remains noteworthy is Wolin's early recognition of the importance of organization and the corporation for the overall phenomenon of the "political" in modern life. Already in the tenth chapter of his first version of *Politics and Vision* called "The Age of Organization and the Sublimation of Politics," Wolin engages organization thought on a level that is surprisingly sophisticated given his overall message of concern and even repugnance. Strewn throughout his analysis is a reasonably extensive referencing of some classics of organization theory up to that period, including Chester Barnard, A. A. Berle, Peter Drucker, Elton Mayo, Philip Selznick, and Herbert Simon. The relative ease with which Wolin absorbs this managerial literature is due in fact to his own expertise recounting the history of political thought proper, particularly at that pivotal juncture of early industrialization when thinking about the political began to split into advocates of "organization" and those of "community" or "solidarity."

Standing squarely at this juncture are the writings of Henri Comte de Saint-Simon.[6] More than any other observer of the post-French Revolutionary scene, Saint-Simon set the agenda for a future rule of *les industriels* consisting of scientists, industrialists, engineers, and artists—an elite, and elitism, of modern efficiency that forms the logical counterpart to that other invention of the industrial age: the "vulgar masses." Meanwhile, the "community" side, represented most effectively by the earlier writings of Jean-Jacques Rousseau, evolved into an emphasis on solidarity and groupism that were to be reflected in the thinking of Saint-Simon's contemporary Charles Fourier and later on in the sociology of Émile Durkheim. To no ostensible avail, since organizationists were driven by "power" while communitarians were inspired by "fraternity," and needless to predict, "power" has won out.[7]

It has done so nevertheless in a surprising fashion—with momentous consequences for the very survival of the concept of the "political." Even radicals of leftist vintage such as V. I. Lenin came to espouse organization over democracy, and ultimately the triumphant forces of capitalism ensured the monopoly of power by the business corporation as it relentlessly expanded its capacities throughout the twentieth century and ultimately even helped shape a new state form, a quasi-imperialist hybrid that Wolin labels "Superpower,"

---

[5] Wolin [2004], 594. Wolin even coins the label "inverted totalitarianism" to refer to this hybrid (561).

[6] See also Fay [1975], 47, 58, for whom Saint-Simon's writings mark the fusion between the rise of industrial social organization and the idea of a policy or social science.

[7] Wolin [2004], 326.

epitomized by the contemporary United States of America, in alliance with which the corporation continues its invincible drive toward "totality."[8]

Such is the ubiquity of this large-scale organizational genre that it has absorbed both "organization" and "community" into its own expanding body of structures and loyalties. For organizationists, the pulsation of community that the Rousseauist communitarians passionately espoused can be recouped—but within the organization itself.[9] Accordingly, the old debate has been apparently renewed within managerial thought as one of "rationalists" against "organicists." Such renewal is nonetheless entirely illusory, according to Wolin, since both accept and seek to further reinforce the most damning element in the overall victory of organization over community or solidarity: "the belief that the world created by organizational bureaucracies is and should be run by elites."[10] In effect, what formerly belonged to the "political" has been pre-empted by organizational life through dismissing former elements of the political as pointless ornaments and ceremonies and ultimately claiming (in the words of one influential managerialist): the "corporation is the *Contrat social* in its purest form."[11]

What then remains of the "political" as such? This question raises of course the very theme and subject-matter of political philosophy proper, which Wolin approaches from a frankly historicist angle by pointing out that the idea of the political has changed over time and owes much of its cogency to different priorities in different historical periods. Even so, Wolin goes against the grain of these implications by suggesting the persistence of a set of terms that invariably reappear whenever the political has been discussed, terms like general, public, common, community. In short, the political inevitably will be about the most comprehensively "common" or "general" set of concerns and goals affecting humans in their social and communal context. Historically this has implied some sort of limited geographical space, or what Wolin calls a "political space" circumscribed by an outside in relation to which that space has formulated its sets of self-identities and culture. Given, however, the presumed ubiquitous threat to the political as such, Wolin seems willing to fall back to the more modest strategy of rereading the (genuinely) political in terms of a "fugitive democracy," the range of local, spontaneous or at least formally unplanned acts and gatherings by which individuals today might attenuate some

[8] This drive toward totality is never consummated in Wolin's view because it is "periodically interrupted by the dislocations that accompany it." Wolin [2004], 605.

[9] Wolin himself is clear that Rousseau's concept of community remains "a specter haunting the age of organization." Wolin [2004], 336.

[10] Wolin, [2004], 370-371.

[11] Cited in Wolin [2004], 375.

of the maleficent consequences of the totalizing push behind globalizing Superpower.[12]

In his catalogue of the manageralists, Wolin sees fit to compliment Herbert Simon as "one of the most brilliant and original writers in the field of administrative theory," citing at least two of Simon's publications of 1957.[13] At more or less the same time Simon was also collaborating on a work that Wolin does not mention and yet that is considered the founding text in the modern theory of formal organizations. That text, *Organizations* (1958), was written with James G. March and it inaugurated March's own entry into the guild through a body of work that over time would cover a variety of subjects extending all the way to education, political science and theory, and even poetry. In effect, it brought into managerial play a mind and theorizing that, in principle at least, might serve as a possible control device on Wolin's set of mistrusts. This chapter considers March's contributions to organization theory in light of Wolin's concern for the political in the age of Superpower, and it widens the discussion, fully in the spirit of March's own efforts, by also considering how that theory lines up with March as political theorist, as poet—and as "quixotic" fool.

I

The original edition of *Organizations* begins with what seems a clear-cut working definition of organizations: "Organizations are assemblages of interacting human beings and they are the largest assemblages in our society that have anything resembling a central coordinate system." Since this is a broad definition, the authors understandably qualify it with the proviso that they are discussing "the theory of *formal* organizations."[14] The 1993 edition of the same book provides meanwhile a somewhat different definition: "Organizations are systems of coordinated action among individuals and groups whose preferences, information, interests, or knowledge differ"[15]—a concession perhaps to some thirty-odd years of subsequent communications theory and vocabulary, as well as a possible reluctance to continue invoking the quasi-biological metaphors evident in the earlier definition. In any event, the body of the later text proper proves almost exactly the same as the original.

---

[12] Wolin [2004], 10, 8, 602-603.

[13] *Models of Man* (1957) and *Administrative Behavior* (1957). Wolin [2004], 340.

[14] March & Simon [1958], 4, 1 (emphasis added).

[15] March & Simon [1993], 2. The original definition is however restated without qualifications in the text proper of the second edition.

That text is mainly structured and driven by an almost Hegelian reading of organizational responses to the givens of the production and consumption environment. In these responses three main stages mark out a progressively more sophisticated set of formulations and understanding of organizational operations. The first, and least sensitive, is summed up by the "scientific management" or Taylorian accounting of the physiological and psychological dependabilities inherent in human routines to be exploited on behalf of increased performance. For March there is much in fact to say in favor of the Taylorian sensitivity to what makes for optimal performance, including the need to recognize and adjust to periods of human rest and recuperation. This "classical" organization theory nonetheless needs to be supplemented by a superior understanding of unanticipated consequences through study of how motivations and goals deeply affect organization behavior—March's second stage.[16] Instead of mechanistic accounts, March underscores the importance of roles and their coordination which, while amenable in many cases to organizational control and direction, may also reflect extraorganizational forces at play. Besides, decisions on whether or not to participate in an organization cannot be adequately accounted for by utility considerations, since the individual's preferences bring in a host of outside alternatives. Finally, the classical account fails to incorporate sufficient recognition of the conflictual elements that form an enduring feature of organization practices.[17]

Beyond such important amendments to the classical theory deriving from motivational factors, March also calls in a further third stage that raises the overall theme of what it means to be a rational being for an organization member. Questioning conventional models of human rationality, March endorses the concept of "satisficing"—"the requirement that satisfaction levels of the criterion variables be attained"[18]—to argue for a reading of action as goal-oriented, adaptive, approximating and fragmented. This approach transforms the meaning and intentions of organizational planning and innovation by reinforcing preferences for what March and Simon label "bounded" or "limited" rationality and of humans as "adaptive, reasoning beings."[19]

In thinking about organizations in these ways, March's narrative aims to replace hierarchy with decision making, stressing that even decision making should be taken less as a theory of choice and more as a theory of "attention." Another way of expressing the perspectival change he endorses is to replace a

---

[16] March & Simon stress that the classical theory needs to be "supplanted" rather than "totally displaced." March & Simon [1993], 53.

[17] For March's concept of "organized anarchy," see Weil [2000], 42-47.

[18] March & Simon [1993], 191, 157.

[19] March & Simon [1993], 233.

"logic of consequences," or actions driven by expectations of their consequences, with a "logic of appropriateness," or actions shaped by the set of rules and the roles of self-identity that actors take on in organizations.[20] The latter, as already noted, not only helps give emphasis to ambiguities and indeterminacies in explaining decision making, or "limited rationality;" it also pays increasing theoretical attention to the larger social contexts influencing such role-playing. Thus, for example, procedural rationality in modern society forms a key feature that might not be so apparent in other societies: for such a modern society decision making is a "sacred ritual" which other societies might otherwise express through consultation with oracles.[21]

March himself does not take the next more radical step of shifting priority from his limited-rationality decision making to that of interpretation proper, and he admits that his treatment understates the importance of a potential fourth stage that would place increasing emphasis on the social and historical contexts for such decision making.[22] March's cautions are not however simply the result of an agenda still in fluid process; rather they reflect March's own continued commitment to restrict the study of organizations to standards of serious theoretical and empirical analysis. Instead of changing organization theory itself, the larger implications suggested by his greater respect for interpretation and the social-historical context should be sought in the more comprehensive areas of political theory and, beyond that, of a global philosophical-poetic reflectiveness.

II

March's most substantive application of his insights to the political realm proper forms a more recent work in collaboration with Johan P. Olsen.[23] Like *Organizations*, *Democratic Governance* (1995) is a deceptively nontechnical discussion of the workings of its subject-matter.[24] Yet its aims carry the critical

[20] Appropriateness is defined as "a match of behavior to a situation." March & Olsen [1995], 30.

[21] March & Simon [1993], 18.

[22] March & Simon [1993], 18, 16.

[23] Far from being a late development in his theorizing, March's concern with the political begins with his Yale doctoral dissertation on the role of autonomy in group organization and draws on a rich body of anthropological material pertaining to native American organizations. It was completed in the political science department under the supervision of Robert Dahl. The dissertation begins by citing Plato's *Laws* and defining the study of politics as "the study of the means by which men are governed" (1). It was later published under the title *Autonomy as a Factor in Group Organization: A Study in Politics*. March [1980a].

[24] Governance is "a way of thinking about how things happen in a polity." March & Olsen

task of questioning contemporary accounts of modern democratic processes as being little more than negotiation and competition to the detriment of "an autonomous public virtue and collective purpose." As March and Olsen put it, such "exchange metaphors" need to be challenged by "an institutional perspective." To this extent March extols a visionary approach that "is romantic in its imagination of governance" and committed to the classical standards of "a good life" and "ways in which human beings can live together with civility and grace."[25]

Indeed March clearly recognizes the source and continuity of the democratic tradition he espouses: "Democratic governance first arose in a small city-state"—undoubtedly March means classical Athens—and took on modern forms in a few countries with similarly modest demographic, wealth, and geographic structures.[26] On the other hand, the democratic ideal has been also formally adopted within entirely different global contexts. Many of the classical virtues of democracy have had to be adjusted to these newer frameworks, and in the process a great deal of the civility and humanity of the original modes of democratic governance has been either overlooked or buried.

As in the case of his treatment of organization theory, March does not deny the importance and relevance of the ruling "exchange" paradigm in political theory. Rather he seeks to supplement it with his own more comprehensive "institutional" approach which he thinks builds more effectively on the relevance of identity concepts and the teachings of modern organization theory. Put in a nutshell, the key difference with the exchange approach that the institutional approach celebrates is that "life is organized by sets of shared meanings and practices that come to be taken as such."[27] Accordingly the institutional approach sponsors four main themes which are listed under the heading of the "craft of governance." In the first place, the institutional approach stresses the need to develop identities for cultures and groups within a political environment that explicitly supports civic institutions. Secondly, it develops capabilities for political action compatible with such identities. Thirdly, it shapes and articulates accounts of political events in order to provide sustaining stories and histories. And finally, it seeks to develop a political system that is adaptive to what March calls the "meandering" nature of historical patterns which, while "comprehensible" in principle, are "difficult to predict."[28]

[1995], 7.

[25] March & Olsen [1995], 5, 6, 241.

[26] March & Olsen [1995], 4.

[27] March and Olsen [1995], 30. By "institutional," March emphasizes that he does not simply mean formal institutions but also systems of social organization, law, identities and roles (27).

[28] History is "a path-dependent meander." March & Olsen [1995], 40; also 43, 248, 251. The overall arrangement of *Democratic Governance* is divided into these four major tasks of

Given his premise that the institutional approach actively tries to “mold” social and political life, March is at pains to distinguish it from other available approaches to the task of democratic governance. He grants that these other approaches all have plausible objectives but that the institutional approach is superior for using all those ways as well as knowing how to “fit” them together into a more pragmatically effective and prescriptively preferable vision. Thus the “minimalist” approach—representing in toto the overall “exchange” paradigm that the institutional approach is at pains to challenge—is simply concerned to establish rules for voluntary exchanges among aggregates of autonomous individuals, a standard that the institutional approach respects but then transcends by also including three far more activist approaches. The “redistributive” approach of the progressivist or socialist agenda that is committed to equal distribution of goods and capabilities, the “developmental” approach of the communitarians that hopes to build a political culture of common beliefs and shared purposes, and the “structuralist” approach (possibly redolent of the Habermasian school of communicative action) with its priorities toward explicitly constructing political processes and rules all help the institutional approach in its “attentiveness” to aspects of each, thus serving the common premise that “citizenship or membership in the polis is the most important and inclusive identity” and that the standard of civic virtue remains the ultimate goal of a polity driven by the democratic spirit and vision of a “self-considered life.”[29]

Of course any approach committed to furthering an “open society,” however broadly envisaged, still faces the perturbing task of properly defining the criterion of civic virtue itself. In *Democratic Governance*, March and Olsen conclude somewhat cautiously that trying to “do good” can only be “an assertion of faith” rather than a “claim of significance.”[30] March however has a couple of further dimensions which can help this process along, all the while granting the epistemological impossibility of coming up with a formal theory of civic virtue that simultaneously preserves this open dimension of political thinking and acting.

“democratic governance.”

[29] March & Olsen [1995], 242, 37, 251-252. In this regard the text makes an interesting distinction between communitarianism, which it locates under a logic of consequences, and civic identity, which belongs to a logic of appropriateness. Although this manner of distinction might lead the reader to infer that March rests his hopes on the latter, in fact March warns that often the dangers to a democratic polity arise from the civic identity side with its proneness to encourage hostilities grounded in group-based identities. March & Olsen [1995], 38-39.

[30] March & Olsen [1995], 252.

III

The first such dimension is the broadly conceived category of "leadership." Written with Thierry Weil, March's *On Leadership* (2003) is the most succinct and, compared to the standard leadership literature of managerial ideology, the most radical expression of March's willingness to challenge conventional idols.[31] Much of March's empirical findings operate to undermine grand heroic images of the leader. Not only are the only solid constants toward becoming a leader that one should be born of successful parents and be born a male, but the general evidence also severely questions whether leaders have much practical-technical effect on the successful running of organizations.

Behind such iconoclasms lie March's more serious intentions. His purpose is not to deflate the role of leaders as such but to relate that role to more serious questions of living a "proper life." Appreciating leadership is, for March, "an aesthetic of experience" much like poetry, art and expertise, and it requires having some sort of sense for the condition of humans in "the nature of things," social organization (technical, political and moral), social action, and, finally, the "self" as such.[32] Accordingly, March's exemplars are drawn not so much from the narrow terrains of management literature as from the great literature of the world, particularly Shakespeare, Tolstoy and Cervantes.[33] Such literature is primarily concerned with "the great conflicts of life" and the task of creating "attractive human beings or an attractive human existence" which it is the responsibility of the leader to acknowledge and to actualize.[34]

Colorfully put, March's leader must be capable of meeting the standards of both "plumbing and poetry." Plumbing covers the effective application of human techniques—down to the dependable operation of toilets—which any organization must fulfil in order to be minimally and efficiently functional. March rounds up these operations under the four headings of competence, intuition, identification, and "unobtrusive coordination" which he thinks essential to proper administration, but he sees his exemplary leader as actually having very little to do with their specific effectiveness beyond practical overseeing.[35] Poetry, meanwhile, makes up

[31] The original version is in French (March & Weil [2003]) but I shall use the more commonly available English version which is somewhat different: March & Weil [2005]. See also the important interpretation of March's work by Weil [2000].

[32] March & Weil [2005], 6, 7-10.

[33] Even here March has a polemical purpose. Noting that the secret of management literature is to be found in its dependence on the great works of military strategy such as Sun-tzu or Clausewitz, March counters with his alternate diet of *Othello*, *Saint Joan* (by George Bernard Shaw), *War and Peace*, and *Don Quixote*.

[34] March & Weil [2005], 10.

[35] March & Weil [2005], 96-100, 115.

the other indispensable task of the leader: "Leadership also requires ... the gifts of the poet." Having managed the mundane aspects of organizational efficiency and routinization, March's leader is no less expected to produce "pieces of managerial poetry" and things "that could be read and interpreted as poetry."[36]

March's text is replete with nuanced interpretations of a variety of literary classics that help articulate the leader's vocation.[37] Nonetheless, the crucial work for March remains Cervantes' *Don Quixote*. Here March takes his greatest interpretive risks by invoking a leadership model which is "self-obsessed," parasitical, and (to be frank) somewhat mad.[38] At the core of March's admiration for Cervantes' peculiar hero Quixote is the latter's protestation: "*Yo sé quiem soy*" ("I know who I am.") which March not only frequently quotes, but no less locates next to Quixote's related insistence that the aim of a knight errant is "to act foolishly without justification."[39] For March what these two claims epitomize is the importance of leading "a proper life—one that realizes the concept" Quixote has of himself. Acting according to such a concept of oneself is to hold to an identity through the role one has embraced for oneself. In Quixote's case it is the self defined as knight errant—a role with socio-historical legitimations. Having embraced this role, Quixote acts in such a way that he creates a world consonant with what March calls his own logic of appropriateness: "his sense of himself and his identity and the obligations associated with it." Quixote can be so persuasive that others are drawn, not necessarily to the truth of his image of the world but to his joy in living such a life. Throwing himself uncompromisingly into such a role, Quixote "turns his life into a work of art."[40]

March is certainly equally quick to mark down Quixote's anti-social actions, his loss of contact with reality, his failure to maintain minimal common sense. But what he wishes any appropriate theory of leadership to retain is the desirability of not overlooking the poetic vision which, whatever his "plumbing" skills, must attach to the true leader. Sometimes March speaks of this aspect as a kind of "romanticism" in which life is acted in a playful manner, a "technology of foolishness" is celebrated, and the art of the leader is something akin to "a sculptor" molding clay" with board meetings resembling

---

[36] March & Weil [2005], 98, 121. Indeed, for March managerial memoranda can be a form of poetry (43).

[37] March's proclivity for such influences reflects his more general call as an organization theorist for modeling that reflects the spirit of "playfulness." See Weil [2000], 68-69.

[38] March & Weil [2005], 80, 83.

[39] E.g. March & Weil [2005], 86, 88, 92, 99. In his recent poetic collections March has Quixote reaffirm: "And I do what knight errants do,/Not because of the consequences/That I expect to follow,/But because that is what I am." "Quixote's Code," in March [2005], 73.

[40] March & Weil [2005], 90; also 85-90.

"theatrical performances." Such an outlook valorizes beauty and grace, and may seem "much too romantic for a cynical age," but March wants to go on record that no concept of leadership is complete without this creative component.[41]

At the same time, particularly with the sadly comic elements of Quixote's story in mind, it is a concept far removed from the artificial "heroic" mold of managerial literature. March's more considered evaluations of the characteristic managerial leader remain highly skeptical and his texts are full of admonitions to be careful with the power that comes with leadership functions. As he puts it aptly, such power should be at best used "as a means of encouraging other people to blossom."[42] At this point the poetic moment in March's thought begins to exceed formal theory as such. In order to understand March's own accommodation to his standards of a logic of appropriateness, it is therefore necessary to take a final step in his oeuvre, for only in and through poetry proper can this final, and encompassing, level of "a proper life" find its appropriate articulation.

IV

> Are not all words made for the heavy? Do not all words lie to the light?
> Sing! speak no more!'
>
> Friedrich Nietzsche, "The Seven Seals,"
> *Thus Spoke Zarathustra*

Thus, the second dimension—superseding even the theme of leadership— belongs to the utterance of the poetic proper. For poems, as March elsewhere points out, "claim exemption from the rules of coherence and resolution of dilemmas that managerial discourse imposes." They allow for articulation of "life's confusions without requiring that awareness be reflected in managerial thought."[43]

The explicitly poetic work of James G. March consists of eight moderately sized collections of poetry. Their titles—*Academic Notes* (1974), *Aged Wisconsin* (1977), *Pleasures of the Process* (1980), *Slow Learner* (1985), *Minor Memos* (1990), *Late Harvest* (2000), *Footprints* (2005), and *Quiet Corners* (2008)—bear all the subdued charm of a Wisconsin native son who is not loath to tout the legacy of reliability, modesty, occasional suspicion toward what the author labels "smartness" or "cleverness," and admiration for those midwestern

[41] March & Weil [2005], 42-43, 121.

[42] March & Weil [2005], 98.

[43] Also: "Poetry is a voice of an incoherent truth." These comments belong to a rare text by March that considers the managerial and the poetic simultaneously with regard to the politics and poetics of the Irish revolutionary movement. March [2006], 72.

women—from Iowa and about—with their milky attributes.[44] The reader is often struck by a remarkable consistency of mood and ethos over a body of work extending from 1974 to 2008; every few years, it seems, James G. March must put down enough poetic thoughts to justify a publication of generally 100-130 pages made up of poems of mostly less than a page.[45] Even if some of these works originate from March's youth, the fact of their being collected and organized in these versions after 1970 reminds us that March's poetic career coincides with his permanent move to Stanford, California, in 1970. All share a single dedicatory object bearing the name of "Jayne" (March's wife), all but the last three were published by the same London Poets' and Painters' Press,[46] and—perhaps most to the point—all share the same organizational structure of following the alphabetical order of poem titles.[47]

The content of these works is a rich familial, social, and academic life devoted to wife, children, grandchildren, peers, friends, weddings, mountains and spring flowers—and, inevitably, the "klikety-klick" of the eternal-feminine.[48] Their "wisdom" rests in the almost imperceptible reaffirmations of a man from Wisconsin whose "proper life" cannot ultimately be exposed for all to see and read, since that same "proper life" is more a matter of the "right of an unimportant man"[49]—as March graciously puts it—than the well-known object of awards, respect and, in many cases, profound admiration.[50] Here is the midwesterner who speaks early like a blushing Walt Whitman: "I am the white son/Of conventional parents, .../If I were a play/I would have closed/In New Haven;"[51] someone who polished his shoes on "my girlfriend's mother's sofa'"[52] who confesses he is "not native/In this place" called "academe" where he remains "A grateful immigrant/Far from home."[53] Someone who is "not/A son of the city" but claims prior natality in a Wisconsin whose "thoughts/Are

---

[44] "Surprises," March [1985], 98. A fuller account of March's poetry—minus *Footprints* (2005) and *Quiet Corners* [2008]—is found in Chytry [2003].

[45] Not surprisingly, the largest time gap between 1990 and 2000 also led to *Late Harvest* as his largest collection of 146 pages.

[46] *Late Harvest* [2000] , *Footprints* [2005], and *Quiet Corners* [2008] were published by the Palo Alto Bonde Press.

[47] Such arrangements for poems resemble the basis of the Persian poetic genre called *Rubbaiyat* associated with the Victorian translations of the work of Omar Khayyam. See March's own poems titled "Persisk Ekteskap" and "Persisk Idyll," March [1980], 71, 72, and Yarshatar [1988].

[48] "Noise Pollution," March [1974], 69. Compare "Santa Cruz," March [2005], 82-84.

[49] "Plea from a Cripple," March [1980], 76.

[50] Cf. "Wisconsin Rules," in March [2000], 146: "Where I come from,/A man doesn't say what he wants,....Lives are better when dressed/In the fabrics of silence."

[51] "Critic's View," March [1974], 31.

[52] "Shoe Polish," March [1974], 89.

[53] "Immigrant," March [1977], 48.

weighed/By the strength/Of their silence;"[54] indeed, someone willing to call himself a "Yokel,"[55] whose "family's fathers knew/Not to expect affection ..../They were willing to wait/Among rules of civility/Without inventing promises/Or making plans."[56] Very occasionally these same roots provoke a patriotism and attitude toward social change—particularly regarding gender relations—that betray the conservatism of the great American heartland: "Yes, I am, indeed, American;/And you must shoot me so."[57] More commonly they seem to recall the aging author of, if not timeless, at least long-term virtues of kith and kin: "Dullness has its rewards."[58] At best these solid virtues produce a direct, and admirable, credo: "I believe/In sympathy, dignity,/And the grace/Of simple decency."[59]

Yet this is also a man who has tasted the fruits and "costs" of, as he admits, the "good life:" "beauty, power, and wealth."[60] After all, how could one not be "corrupted/by an easy life and a clever wife"? So on to the realms "among the lotus blooms" where one meets "some nice folks," and learns to be seduced by haute cuisine. Forget the Wisconsin "world/in which soup was served hot,/but beer was not,/peas and beans/and potatoes were fine,/rice was for mice,/and only the winos drank wine." Bring on the "genuine treat:/quails with snails,/and pigeon breasts/wrapped in vest of tarragon;/and parmesan on ptarmigan,/with lemon on the side." We have left our midwestern kin far behind, even though "I know damn well my father would say/I should forget the poulet au jardiniere/and return to the comforts of turnips and beer."[61]

It is easy to make light of such slidings by acknowledging the permanent effects of class advancement. March neither succumbs to the facile self-justifications of the parvenu nor simply parrots puritan concerns over loss of innocence. "Every cardiologist," he recognizes, knows that propriety could do with "a little bit of sin/...for keeping the arteries open," even if admittedly it "can lead/To an awful lot of trouble."[62] But he also recognizes that rituals of public confession over moral lapses serve the upper class far more than "the poor, the

[54] "Oral Facility," March [1977], 74.

[55] "Yokel," March [1977], 134.

[56] "My Family's Fathers," March [1990], 75.

[57] "Fair Judgments," March [1985], 30. Other examples include: March [1974], 71; March [1985], 42, 69-70, 89. Also see March [1990], 27, for March's antipathy toward talk therapies and confessionals.

[58] "Toy Builder," March [1985], 107.

[59] "Resistance Movement," March [1974], 81.

[60] "The Cost of a Good Life," March [1980], 102.

[61] "Refinements of Taste," March [1985], 77-79. See also "Asian Invitation," 11, and "Spatulas," 94, in which the utensils of cuisine become the objects of meditation.

[62] "Public Office," March [2000], 93.

honest, and/The insistently intelligent." The former will go to church and maintain their propriety, "Reciting a catechism of rectitude/Without too serious an illusion/That their recitations are close/To reality." The latter, alas, "haven't practiced/The skills of mock contrition/And the art of manufacturing/Tears of repentance that/Sustain a moral code."[63] Yet perhaps indulgence is itself indicator of a culture and civilization that may be peaking: "Signs that the American empire nears its ends,/Joining Spain and Rome in sure decline" by bearing the hallmark symptoms of "unjustified arrogance,/A distinctive cuisine, neuroses of indulgence,/And a copious capacity for denying/The inconvenient demands of hard work," but also perhaps containing the divine sign that it may be time for others to "have a turn."[64] Such grand vistas are not meant, however, to absolve James G. March, beneficiary of such power, for there is also always an underlying "hypocrisy" in pontificating to others (including especially one's children): "However content I am/With my life today,/It is, in the end,/Indefensible."[65]

If such two-sidedness speaks well for March's sensitivity to the stratifications of his time, it is also deeply ingrained in his more formal manner of thought. March's poems are replete with phrases redolent of ambiguities and ambivalences: the "ambiguity of affection" or the "ambiguities of experience" are not simply hesitations within earlier texts but are mirrored in the later "ambiguities of judgment," "ambivalence of indecision," "ambiguities of truth," and even the "thickets of maybe."[66] Perhaps there is little surprise in this for students of his formal thought. March, it is commonly recognized, made ambiguity topical for decision theory, and the importance of ambivalences is central to his ambitious work in redirecting contemporary democratic political theory.[67] What the poetic oeuvre brings into clearer focus is the man who dwells in, and is responsive to, that region of ambiguities, ambivalences, hesitations, not so much as a weakness but as further confirmation of a self-identity, an adaptiveness, that echoes classical models of the whole personality: "A wise man hides/The sounds of experience/In the white noise/Of his reticence."[68] Yet James March is not classical, and perhaps in that absence lies a web of issues that may be worth highlighting.

For the author of these poems often seems ultimately discomfitted by thought in general and its pretensions. Sometimes his laments are the understandable

---

63 "Rituals of Confession," March [2000], 105-106.

64 "Decadence," March [2000], 30.

65 "Reminders," March [1980], 83.

66 "Maps," "To a Girl Friend," March (1974), 64, 97; "Mistakes of Harmony," March [1977], 62; "Greater Evil," March [1990], 55; "Speaking Clearly," "Brave Philosophies," March [2000], 123, 22.

67 March [1999], 17-18; March & Olsen [1995], 168-181.

68 "Sounds of Experience," March [1980], 94.

complaints about the familiar games that professors play: to win, to gain tenure, to reap the material and status benefits of being "smart" and "clever." Sometimes it would appear professors, these "appertifs of life," are not even men: "When a man is not a man/But a professor..."[69] Not that March himself is immune to these games: "As willing tribute to/The ministers of pretense,/I perform/Learned conversations/With consenting adults/in Private./But not among strangers/Not where/The agents of honesty/Hide."[70] Yet it seems that not even wisdom helps in the end. Controlling ambition and forgetting (dubious) desires may finally produce "real wisdom", but: "you probably won't like it."[71] And were one to prefer "the pretenses of experience," March can only confide to us that "life runs lousy experiments,/And that we grow older, not wiser."[72]

It is not that March has not enjoyed the benefits of a formidable intellect. He has gone forth in battle, has punished the weak and the corrupted in the public arenas of the academic combat: "I will/Chop up your ideas/Stuff them into an old condom/And hang them in my trophy room."[73] Yet there is another domain in which one simply begins to do without thinking of consequences, for the true standard of judging a man is to "Ask whether he can act/Without assurances/Of good consequences." And quite often such an attitude is not all that different from the spontaneous foolishness of children, or, for that matter, of kittens. It means to free joy from "justification/Within a calculus of consequences."[74] It means to join forces with the "realists of happiness."[75]

Has March himself joined these mysterious and beguiling legions? Although reticent to go beyond the virtues of prudence, March will have nothing to do with "the pale preachers of self-denial"[76]—even if March himself measures freedom more by what one must do than what one simply wants—and is the first to declare: "I'm not ashamed of instincts/For enjoying the syrups of life."[77] Such syrups, as every successful male academic knows, are always floating through the classroom and lecture hall, threatening the pious instructor with temptations

---

[69] "Appertifs," March [1974]; "Sponsors," March [1980], 95.

[70] "Learned Conversation," March [1974], 54. Also: "Doctor, councillor, and/Endowed professor/Of almost anything,/You give names/To the parts I play/In order to conceal/Weaknesses in their scripts." "Indian Chief," March [1980], 46.

[71] "Finding Wisdom," March [2000], 46.

[72] "The Pretenses of Experience," March [2000], 134.

[73] "One More Time," March [1974], 72-73. See also, e.g., "On Being a Patsy," "Rivals," March [1974], 71, 82; "Without Reason," March [1977], 133; "Warning," March [1980], 115-116. More gently, see "Job Description," "Monuments," March [2000], 60, 65.

[74] "Beginnings," "Essential Things," "Proper Authorization," March [2000], 16, 41, 90.

[75] "Realists of Happiness," March [2000], 95.

[76] "Complications," "Measures of Freedom," March [1990], 29, 69.

[77]"Marshmellows," March [1990], 67.

to act or at least engage in profound calculations on the ratios available for pedagogical seduction.[78] After all, what is one to do before this barrage of brassieres, of "a nylon flounce/Hiding breasts that bounce,/And a belly that's broken in," "softness dancing" under skirts, those "buttons on a blouse/Opened without reluctance." James G. March, we are amply forewarned, is no angel: "Professors aren't heroes./But they are convenient,/Curious,/And often have softer beds/Than the nearest competition."[79] In any event, these are not foibles that one can just abandon with age: "Old advisors aren't blind,/Or immune to perfume,/Just because they're harmless."[80]

At the same time the author of these works is a genuine lover, and the object of his love is inevitably capable of undermining all these outside allurements—those "laws of lechery."[81] Whether during those long moments in the airport or on the airplane, in foreign hotel rooms, or within the incitations of the conjugal bedroom, his one and only Beloved focuses the poet's love, devotion, friendship and faith with a completeness that obliterates her potential rivals. So much so that March himself will occasionally drop literary intentions to simply declare his love with unwonted unambiguity.[82] March may be proud of his "manliness,"[83] but he is no less absolute in his devotion: "Ask me if/I am faithful/And I will answer/Yes./And you will know/I am."[84]

V

The body of James G. March's writings is indeed a "work," an "oeuvre," in the sense of a distinct identity emerging throughout with its developments, its emotions, its pretensions, its contexts, its wisdom, even its failures. But does it match up to the challenge posed by Sheldon Wolin?

---

[78] "Student/Faculty Ratio," March [1977], 108. See also, e.g., March [1974], 51, 70; March [1977], 18, 107; March [1985], 47.

[79] "Incest," March [1974], 51. These themes of "The bouncing of/Impatient breasts/In silken packages" continue in the later collection by March [2005], 71, and March [2008], 54.

[80] "Reprise," March [2000], 101.

[81] "Glass Houses," March [1977], 35.

[82] "Authenticity," March [1980], 16; "Stuck in Heathrow," March [2005], 93.

[83] "Testimony," March [1974], 94. Compare the lament: "Must I really stop being a man/To be a professor?/Whatinhell is bad/About whisky and women?" "The Research Ethic," March [1974], 95.

[84] "Obiter Dictum," March [1977], 69. Also: "All the rest," March [1985], 8; "Maslow's Maxim," March [1990], 68; "Audit Exception," March [2000], 8. Even if sometimes the dynamics of consummation run up against new complications of age: "But most of my life/I assumed the risks/Were connected to/The exuberances of sex,/Not the plumbing/Of the prostate." "Sexual Surprises," March [2000], 114.

Throughout his life March has been a university professor (as has Wolin), and the setting of his work and influence, certainly since 1970, has been Stanford University and its environs of the Californian city of Palo Alto.[85] March's decision to relocate to this environment was an emphatic one and is reflected in countless references found particularly in his poetry. March himself has never been timid about professing his love and reverence for the university as indeed a kind of secular "temple"—a "temple of education" or " institution of learning as an object of beauty and an affirmation of humanity." For March its students are not "customers" but "acolytes," its teaching not "a job" but a "sacrament," and its research not "an investment" but a "testament."[86]

Chapter 3 delineated the importance of the American campus and its "Ideopolis" as an extension of the life of the polis in contemporary society, and drew analogies between the historical polis and the "university city." Within this process Stanford and the development of its campus have played an exemplary role.[87] That development has transformed the city of Palo Alto to such a level that, recognizing its centrality for the technological and cultural phenomenon of Silicon Valley, Stanford rooters have even seen fit to call Stanford the "Florence" of the high tech age. As venture capitalist John Doerr points out, it may well be "the greatest legal accumulation of wealth in the history of the world."[88] Small wonder that Stanford is often regarded as "a self-contained republic unto itself," the "Fortune 500 University," with Palo Alto as "a new form of civilization" meriting the description of "virtual city," or indeed "the invisible city."[89]

James G. March is the poet and thinker, the "leader," for this counter-Florence, this "invisible city" to the historic "visible city" of the original polis of Florence. Central to the more enlightened niches of its university arms, March's poetic oeuvre combined with his more analytical products offers entry into some of the perturbations, satisfactions, contradictions, and whatever passes for wisdom within its virtual age. This is far removed from Wolin's particular fears of the "age of organization," but it is also a far more realistic rendering of the benefits and losses of the priorities that such an age empirically carries. When Saint-Simon listed the members of his favored *industriels* of the future, he made sure that his list not only included entrepreneurs, engineers and

---

[85] See in general Weil [2000].

[86] "A Scholar's Quest," in March [1999], 378, 379. See also Weil [2000], 139-145.

[87] See Turner [1984], 169-174; also Gaines [1991], 122-126.

[88] For all the following facts and quotes on Stanford and Palo Alto I am indebted to the study by Kātz [1998].

[89] Still, as Kātz [1998] asks: if one is to grant Stanford and Palo Alto the status of a genuine world city, where is its Parthenon, its Pitti Palace, its Louvre, its British Museum? Of course there is always the Barbie Hall of Fame, as Kātz wryly notes.

scientists, but also the creative "artists."[90] In this redemptive gesture, the Father of the "age of organization" legitimated the saving grace of a March.

VI

According to James March, his "hero" Quixote provides the literature on leadership with, not an ideal social order, but "a proper life of beauty and harmony." Among the elements inspiring that proper life March lists the virtues of chivalry, the pleasures associated with being a leader, and the assertion of self-identity. But there is also a fourth virtue. Quixote for March teaches the need to embrace a beauty ("Dulcinea") that, strictly speaking, does not exist at all, but must be "created" by the striving imagination of the "knight errant."[91] If this admonition is to be taken seriously, it means nothing less than recapitulating in each leader's psyche the priorities of a knightly vocation inseparable from devotion to the Lady. But what can that possibly imply for "organization" and "politics," the starting-points for our inquiry?

The first step toward an answer is to revert to March's original definition of "organization": "Organizations are *assemblages* of interacting human beings." What, then, are "assemblages"? The standard lexical response is that an assemblage is "a bringing or coming together," a "gathering" of "a number of persons."[92] Behind such simplicity rests a much richer suggestiveness. As the theologican Hans Küng has stressed when discussing the conciliar movement in Christianity, the Latin *con-cilium* is an exact equivalent for the Greek *ecclesia*: both point back to a "calling," or "summons" (*con-calare*, *ek-klesi*a, from *kalein*). The original Christians used the Greek assembly/ekklesia, as already utilized by the Athenians and the Greeks in referring to their political assemblies, when they spoke of "the assembly of those who believe in Christ."[93] The key reference here, central for Athenian democrats no less than for these early Christians, was the "calling" itself, the *kalein*. As Irwin Panofsky importantly adds with regard to the Italian Renaissance response to these ideas, Platonists (both ancient and modern) "liked to derive the Greek word for 'beauty', κάλλος, from the verb καλεῖν, 'to call.'" In short, the Call was inseparable from "a beauty which, by its very nature, 'calls the soul to God.'"[94]

---

[90] Wolin [2004], 318.

[91] March & Weil [2005], 82, 92.

[92] Following the Oxford English Dictionary, the etymology is: Latin *ad*, "to", and *simul*, "together".

[93] Küng [2002], 228.

[94] Panofsky [1972], 185.

Freeing these readings from theological priorities, we are left with the primacy of the Call as something coterminous with the experiencing of Beauty. For the philosopher Martin Heidegger such primacy is really the "call" from Being proper. But even a more mundane "political" reading by Jean-Jacques Rousseau gives primacy to sounds particularly favorable to "liberty": "sonorous, prosodic, harmonious, whose discourse one distinguishes from far away."[95] Listening to the Sound in their incomparable public sites, the ancient Greeks, founders of the polis, of democracy, of the cult of "beauty," were enabled to access a language uniquely appropriate for a people "continuously *assembled* in the public place" — compared with impoverished modern languages which, Rousseau complained, cannot even make themselves heard *en plein air*.[96]

The complex thrust of March's oeuvre thus reaches its apogee in its "quixotic" receptivity to the "call" wherein is borne the "beautiful"—for thought, spirit, and the politics of public assemblies and democratic orders. From that reception there follows the political as the democratic and the authentic as the beautiful.

The man who registers such a reception, satisfied to have fulfilled his role without leaving a trace, may surely account his life a "Success:"

No one needs him
After he's gone.
No one who stays
Depends on him.
If he has done it right;
No one asks
Why flowers grow,
Or how a summer ends,
Or notices long
That he has gone, quietly
Into the dark.[97]

---

[95] Rousseau [1990], 144.

[96] Rousseau [1968], 142 (emphasis added).

[97] "Success," March [1980], 98. Compare the final words of March's latest collection: "In cosmic history/There are no endings,/Just reconstitutions/Of matter. But lives end,/And so do wishes/For novelty." "Zen", March [2008], 108.

LANDFALL: THEATROCRACY

A little polis living orderly in a high place is greater than block-headed Nineveh.
Phocylides[1]

The city fosters art and *is* art; the city creates the theater and *is* the theater. It is in the city, the city as theater, that man's more purposive activities are formulated and worked out ...
Lewis Mumford[2]

Our inquiries closed within the rigorous contextualities of contemporary management and business theory. But for an appropriate "landfall" on Cythera something beyond the welcome political and poetic affirmations of James G. March's brand of organization theory is still needed. To advance to the more visionary levels of cytherics, we therefore make a first transition from management to polis. True, some effort is required to recognize an underlying affinity between inquiries into contemporary broadening of the workplace and organizational routinization in postmodern configurations, the increasing importance of newer management categories such as knowledge-creation to supplant older conventional notions of profit pursuit, and—the crucial insight—the possible lessons afforded by classical Athenian democracy as a supreme polis model of self-governing citizens. Fortunately a recent provocative study by Brook Manville and Josiah Ober proposes to do just that.[3]

I

In their admonitions to the modern corporation, Manville and Ober take from Athenian democracy the operating values of a "company of citizens"—"an organization in which people are treated as citizens." Uniting democratic values, governance structures, and participatory practices, the Athenians according to the authors managed with reasonable efficiency and innovativeness to keep going their "technology of self-governance" over a period of some two hundred years—something few if any Fortune 500 companies can claim.[4] While granting the substantial differences between ancient and modern "hypercompetitive"

---

[1] The sixth-century poet Phocylides, cited in Kagan [1991], 96.
[2] Mumford [1938], 480 (emphasis in original).
[3] Manville & Ober [2003].
[4] Manville & Ober [2003], 17, 55, 176.

environments, the authors persuasively push for an Athenian "*politeia*-building in action" based on a "people centered" revolution that they think would be singularly appropriate to a modern "knowledge-based" body of "worker-citizens."[5]

To be sure, Manville and Ober also point out the Athenians' greater success in fostering a self-conscious explicitness in their practices, a more holistic system—the polis—for those participatory functions, and a scale of membership—the figure of 30,000 Athenian citizens is commonly cited—that easily dwarfs the workings of the typical modern corporation. But simultaneously the authors are encouraged by two modern features eluding the ancient Athenians: the cultural recognition of universal citizenship rights denied by the Athenians and the technological innovations of modern interactive communications that easily surpass the limits to the "unamplified human voice" restricting ancient participatory gatherings.[6]

To their credit Manville and Ober at the same time remain sanguine about the extent to which technological innovation as such ("teledemocracy") can ever match the "human dimension" of personal face-to-face contact.[7] Such welcome skepticism leaves unsettled the global inferences to be legitimately drawn from their advocacy. What seems lacking in any attempted analogy of this order are certain features essential to the Athenian experience. If replicated, these features would transfer the lessons of the Athenian model from the limited arena of the modern corporation to the more directly transformative one of the properly political.

The first such feature is the engine for the Athenian success, one on which all interpreters are agreed: the realpolitik variation on the amalgam of cultural, economic and political factors that we earlier identified as thalassocracy. For Thucydides' hard-headed account of Hellenic global history, the underlying motif of sea power had reached its culmination in Periclean Athens. A "natural development, inherent in the character of naval power," it was "realized for the first time in the Athens of his day."[8] Indeed, one of the few available contemporaneous accounts of Athenian democracy even utilizes the term "thalassocracy" (θαλασσοκράτορές)[9] in accounting for this sea-power basis to Athenian hegemony.[10]

---

[5] Manville & Ober [2003], 55, 57, 116, 175.

[6] Manville & Ober [2003], 149, 154-155.

[7] Manville & Ober [2003], 158.

[8] Kagan [1991], 112, stressing Thucydides, *Histories*, i-4-19.

[9] Xenophon [1966], ii.2 (more typically the author uses the language of hegemony (τὴν ἀρχὴν τῆς θαλάττης) to describe Athenian sea power [ii.7]). The author of this work, dated around 424, who is not actually Xenophon, is often identified as the "Old Oligarch" or as "pseudo-

The second feature concerns the larger ramifications of the revolution in Athenian *demokratia* first set off by the reforms of Cleisthenes in 508 BCE and then presumably completed by the reforms of Ephialtes in 462 BCE. What Athenian thalassocracy brought to this revolution was the ultimate political victory by the greater number of citizens—the class of *thetes* who manned the oars and cultivated the seamanship for which Athenian naval power became justly famous—over farming and landowning interests in Attica. As a result, a sequence of steps to full-scale democracy can be followed from the emphasis on *isegoria* and *isonomia*—equality before the law—that Cleisthenes' reforms legitimated to the newer language of *demokratia* which had become more commonplace by the period of Ephialtes' reforms around mid-century, by which time the naval orientation of Miltiades' and Themistocles' policies had borne fruit in the Athenian hegemony over the Aegean Sea.[11] After that stage, and throughout the Periclean ascendancy (443-429 BCE), the task of Athenian radical democracy became the conservative one of preserving these gains, which might be summed up as perhaps the most extensive participatory democratic system in history.[12]

The limitation to such a conventional account (the account generally utilized by Manville and Ober) is its moderately static reading of Periclean democracy. While understandable in terms of Manville and Ober's overall strategy of utilizing an ancient paradigm to back their proposals for improving the modern corporation, it underplays Athenian dynamics in the Periclean era which might have contained a further stage beyond those of *isonomia* and *demokratia*, one which was thwarted thanks to the crushing Athenian defeat in the Peloponnesian War (431-404 BCE), nor revived during the more restrained

---

Xenophon."

[10] It should be noted that scholars' frequent use of the term "empire" to designate Athenian thalassocratic hegemony is historically unsound. "Empire" or "imperial" stems from the later Roman success in harnessing the lessons of the great land empires of Assyria, Persia, and the Hellenistic dynasties. Typically (true also for the cases of Chinese empires from Han to Qing) it presumes an effectively universal bureaucracy capable of reliable collection of taxes and exercise of provincial rule from the center as well as a large-scale standing army which can regularly expect to receive its salaries from these same sources. Neither condition is met by the operations of the Athenian hegemony. The best account of this "Athenian empire" remains Meiggs [1972].

[11] The first actual record of the use of the word *demokratia* (τὴν δημοκρατίην) is Herodotus [1960], vi.131, usually dated around 430BCE.

[12] Through Pericles the Athenian constitution became "as thoroughly democratic as the world has ever seen." Kagan [1991], 47. Stockton describes it as "one of the most open societies known to history." Stockton [1990], 50. This "conservative" reading is stressed by Forrest [1970], 221. Cf. also Kagan [1991], 47. In light of the limited range of the Athenian concept of citizenship, it is worth heeding A. H. M. Jones' reminder that Athenian democracy was not meant to consist of all the inhabitants of Attica, but "was the democracy of the Athenian people." Jones [1969], 10.

post-thalassocratic period of Athenian democracy 403-322 BCE. For this might-have-been of Periclean possibilities, we propose the term *theatrocracy*.[13]

II

Theatrocracy (θεατροκρατία) is a term coined by Plato in his final dialogue the *Laws*, composed around 350 BCE.[14] Plato intended the term as a pejorative designation for what he thought Athenian democracy had come to after the heroic period of the Persian Wars (490-479 BCE). The placing of theatrocracy at this particular textual juncture carries however major implications for reading this most extensive Platonic attempt to deal with what Plato saw as the fatal shortcomings to the Athenian experiment. Only after he had identified, and dismissed, this Athenian turn to "theatrocracy" was Plato (the "Athenian" in the dialogue) ready to embark with his Spartan and Cretan friends on the delineation of an ideal polis, Magnesia, to be founded by Knossos on the historically fertile Messara plain of Crete, island home—as we already depicted in our opening remarks—to the originative thalassocracy.[15]

For Plato it was proper that the Athenians of the Persian Wars period had been "enslaved" (ἐδούλευε), as it were, to "the laws" and therefore showed respect and self-control; subsequently, however, presumably during the Ephialtes and Pericles periods, they had been granted freedom from all "authority." When asked what "laws" exactly were meant, Plato's Athenian answered: the laws concerning "music" (περὶ τὴν μουσικὴν), playing, as does the work's title, on the fact that the same Greek word implies both juridical laws and musical melodies. Thus the crucial turning point for Athenian history

---

[13] The following narrative is in sympathy with the work of Jacques Rancière toward theatrocratic priorities in art and politics. Hallward [2006], esp. 113 (note 12), and "Theatrocracy; or, Surviving the Break," in Weber [2004], 32-39. Weber's reading is commendable for recognizing a distinction between *demokratia* and theatrocracy (33-34); unfortunately he uses the term also to refer to the "modern theatrocracy" which he associates with contemporary technological and media developments (52). It is also worth comparing theatrocracy with the notion of "theatre state" formulated by anthropologist Clifford Geertz for his account of the nineteenth-century Balinese political state. Geertz [1980] and "Spies: Theatre State," in Chytry [1989], 448-481.

[14] Plato [1962], 701a.

[15] Willetts argues for a close connection between Plato's *Laws* and the Cretan polis in Plato's time. Willetts [1962], 301. Morrow points out that Plato, who also composed the short dialogue *Minos*, was aware of Minos' sea power and saw him as a wise legislator instructed by his father Zeus. Plato regarded the Crete of his day as representing archaic institutions and lawfulness; the 600 BC Gortyn inscription on Crete is in fact "an early source of the polis type of constitution." Morrow [1960], 17, 19, 20, 23.

according to Plato takes place in the theatrical setting of Athenian cultural life where judgment and performance shift from control by firm rules and recognized musical judges to composers breaking those musical rules and audiences appropriating judgments on musical and performative standards.[16] This apparently mild rebuke then expands soon enough into Plato's larger criticism. Once such behavior extends beyond "music," and *demokratia* is no longer limited to rule by the better sort of individual presumably still operative after Cleisthenes' reforms on behalf of *isonomia*, all respect for standards and one's elders collapses, and the crisis of the Athenian polis becomes that of the multitude and the individual setting themselves up as final judges of taste and pleasure, a condition of constant change and instability that flouts all standards of excellence.

As Plutarch notes in his life of Pericles, Ephialtes granted the multitude just such "undiluted freedom," in Plato's words, and Plutarch's own account confirms the degree to which Pericles, the younger acolyte of Ephialtes, made it his policy to radically encourage the demos in this regard.[17] What is strikingly ironic is that Plato himself cites Pericles' own teacher Damon on behalf of the general principle that "music"—that is, patterns of rhythm and harmony—can help shape positive and negative effects on the desired style of life.[18] The question that then arises is, granted that both Plato and Pericles in effect agree on the primacy of the "musical" shaping of the culture of a polis, what was it that Damon—and his student Pericles—pursued which would provoke such Platonic rancor against "theatrocracy"—this, in effect, ultimate Periclean vision for Athenian *demokratia*?

Plutarch presents Pericles' Damon as a teacher of music who was simultaneously a sophist (σοφιστὴς) concerned with real political power, indeed who was later ostracized by the Athenians.[19] Granted the other pedagogical names that are brought up with regard to Pericles' early formation — Pythocleides, Zeno, Anaxagoras—such information suggests that from the start Pericles was indoctrinated into a conception of political ideals integrated with musical-aesthetic philosophical standards. Pericles' subsequent steps into the political realm easily confirm this reading. Pericles' first intervention took place as *choregos* on behalf of the winning Aeschylean tragedies of 472 which

[16] Plato [1962], 698-701. The young Nietzsche grasped this link between Plato's ideal Cretan polis and the role of music when referring to "der kretische Staat als Musikstaat," Cited in Chytry [1989], 347 (note 100).

[17] Plutarch [1914], vii.6, citing Plato's *Republic* (viii.562c).

[18] Plato [1902], 400b. Elsewhere Plato notes that Damon linked musical and political change (424c). See also Podlecki [1998], 210-211, 25, 31.

[19] Plutarch [1914], iv.1-2.

included the extant play *The Persians* treating of the great Athenian victory of 480-479 over the Persian Empire.[20] Pericles also committed himself in particular toward the building of the Odeion, an auditorium for musical performances. Finally, attending performances with great regularity, Pericles campaigned for yearly contests in musical skill at the Panathenaic Festival and was chosen judge on the specific rules for the competitions in singing and playing the flute and harp.[21] Indeed "it was Pericles who created a more permanent theater" on the acropolis by moving the site slightly and constructing stone walls for the ongoing development of the theatre of Dionysos.[22]

As Ephialtes' younger ally and successor after 462, Pericles is credited with supporting the demos by providing the people with subject territories for occupation and by beginning a policy of payments for performance of public duties through jury service.[23] A very suggestive facet of this approach is the later view that Pericles also brought in payments for attendance at shows and theatre performances (θεωρικά). While this claim is not confirmed by contemporary accounts and the ancient sources are considered "contradictory," there does seem to be a reliable tradition that Pericles may have introduced a law that polis funds "should be theoric money for the citizens."[24]

What is not in doubt is that Pericles pushed hard for measures to furnish shows, banquets, processions, and performances for the demos. Thucydides' Pericles in fact makes this accomplishment a point of special pride: "We celebrate games and sacrifices all the year round," and the "Old Oligarch" confirms that the Athenians held far more festivals than any other Hellenic polis, adding that such public events were paid for at public cost by this "beautiful and large polis" (πόλιν...καλὴν καὶ μεγάλην).[25] Of course the climacteric to these Periclean measures was his adamant sponsorship of the creation of the remarkable body of buildings atop the acropolis of which the Parthenon remains the pearl of classical architectural and sculptural

---

[20] Kagan [1991], 36-37; Podlecki [1998], 11-16.

[21] Plutarch [1914], xiii.5-6; also Podlecki [1998], 157.

[22] Aylen [1985], 88. Rabinowitz mentions a street lined with monuments marking theatrical victories leading to the theatre. Rabinowitz [2008], 44.

[23] Plutarch [1914], ix.1. Payment for assembly (and council) attendance was introduced during the 390s, confirming the Athenians' commitment to participatory democracy even without an "empire."

[24] Plutarch [1914], xiii.4-6, ix.1-2. Following the commentary on these passages by Stadter [1989], 116. θεωρικοῖς refers to "festival monies", or funds for festivals (θεωρίαι). Cf. Rabinowitz [2008], 45.

[25] Plutarch [1914], xi.4; Thucydides [1992], ii.38; Xenophon [1966], ii.9, iii.2, iii.8. The Old Oligarch estimates twice as many Athenian festivals as any other polis. Stadter notes that "almost half of the days of the year were regular festival days at Athens." Stadter [1989], 137.

expression.[26] This cluster of masterpieces of Athenian polis architecture was supervised by Pericles' colleague Pheidias with the clear intention of shaping an Athenian civic consciousness as memorably expressed by Thucydides' Pericles: "We cultivate beauty (φιλοκαλοῦμέν) with moderation and philosophize (φιλοσοφοῦμεν) without weakness."[27] It served as a further theatrical environmentality (κατασκευή) for the unveiling of the Athenian body politic along the Parthenon friezes and for a standard of "power and splendor" in which the rapidity of execution helps explain what Plutarch would perceptively describe as the resultant "bloom of perpetual newness" which preserved these works "from the touch of time."[28]

The crown of this theatricality was Pericles' own exceptional abilities as an orator. Having learned from Anaxagoras to help raise the level of the content of public speaking, Pericles exploited his own sensitivity toward the musical to cultivate an art of rhetoric that in Plutarch's account reads more like that of a musician. Playing on the affections and passions as the veritable "strings and keys of the soul" (τόνους και φθόγγους ψυχῆς), Pericles displayed an unerring "touching and striking" (ἁφῆς καὶ κρούσεως) in his utterances.[29] Armed with such rhetorical skills and maintaining contact with a remarkable body of culture-makers which included Anaxagoras, Herodotus, Sophocles, Euripides, Pheidias, Aspasia, Hippodamus, and Protagoras, Pericles was regularly elected one of the ten Athenian generals, the only formal executive basis for his forty-odd years of guidance of the Athenian polis.

III

For all the importance of Pericles himself in unfolding this "Periclean age," the admonition that the word "Pericles" should be taken as "an elision for 'the assembly, guided by Pericles'" bears repeating.[30] That Pericles was able to lead

---

[26] Plutarch [1914], xii.1-2; also "Comparison of Pericles and Fabius," iii.5.

[27] Thucydides [1992], ii.40.

[28] Plutarch [1914], xii.1, xiii.13. The conventional complaint that Pericles exploited the treasury of the Delian League (first brought to Athens from Delos around 454) to pay for the building of this monument to the polis ideal has been sufficiently answered by Plutarch and other commentators: Pericles pointed out that the allies paid for protection provided by the Athenian navy in exchange for their payments and were not otherwise expected to furnish ships or forces. What Athens did with those payments was her own business so long as those obligations were met—as apparently they were with regard to the ever-present Persian threat. Plutarch [1914], xii.3-4.

[29] Plutarch [1914], xv.4-5; also vii.1, viii.1, viii.4.

[30] Kagan [1991], xiii.

Athens toward his vision of the theatrocratic polis was only made possible after all by the more general approbation of his policies by the demos as well as larger tendencies of the period in which Pericles operated as an important, but not the only, factor. By the same token, the specifically Periclean element that was realized needs to be contrasted to, on the one hand, the input of those Athenians whose reading of such visions would turn out to be far more pedestrian and, on the other, the level of thought and vision that he probably shared with only a small minority of similarly acute participants. These three points will be considered in turn.

For theatrocracy the most important larger factor preceding and enclosing the Periclean stance was the simultaneous growth and unprecedented achievements of Athenian drama during the fifth century. That *demokratia* and the Dionysian festival drama of tragedy and comedy converge during these crucial decades remains one of the more intriguing features of Athenian polis history.[31] Frequently cited as particularly suggestive moments of actual connection are the Oresteian cycle of Aeschylus with Ephialtes' reform of the Areopagus in 462, Sophocles' Oedipus cycle with the "tragedy" of Pericles in the plague of 429, and Aristophanic comedy with the contortions of Athens at war during the 420s and 410s. Ultimately both Periclean democracy and the final theatrical products of classical Athens as epitomized by Euripides' *Bacchae*, Sophocles' *Oedipus at Colonnus*, and Aristophanes' *Frogs* came to a head in the final years of the century exactly prior to the epochal Athenian defeat of 404, nor were such dramaturgical accomplishments to be ever successfully challenged in the subsequent canons of Hellenic and Hellenistic repertoires.[32]

In considering this remarkable efflorescence, two facts are worth taking into account: in the first place, Athenian *demokratia* did not create theatre (and drama), and, second, theatre and drama were not confined to the Athenian experience.[33] Rather "theatre" *(theatron)* proved a feature of general Hellenic development in which existence of the polis necessarily entailed both the "aesthetic" (*theatron*) and the "political" (*agora*), with both institutions traceable back to a cultural space later called the *orchestra* but originally termed

[31] In the following section I concentrate more on tragedy. For comedy as a critical outlet for the demos, see McGlew [2002] and Wohl [2002].

[32] Although composed prior to their respective deaths in 407 and 406, Euripides' *Bacchae* and Sophocles' *Oedipus in Colonnus* were first presented after the fall and recovery of Athens in 404/403. Aristophanes' *Frogs*, the plot of which presupposed the deaths of both Sophocles and Euripides, was first presented in 405/404.

[33] In his exhaustive study of Hellenic poleis and theatres, Rune Frederiksen concludes that "the theatres are found in the urban centres and territories of only some 17% of all *poleis*." Frederiksen [2002], 66.

the *choros* (χορός) or "sacred circle" (ἱερὸς κύκλος) of a dancing site generally consecrated to a polis deity or hero.[34] This concrete and specific geographical location which held together the celebratory, the agonal, and the assembly functions of polis life can already be found in the Homeric account of the Phaiakaians that we earlier delineated which highlighted the agonal pre-eminence of the dance for the island's agoric celebrations.[35] It confirmed the centrality of "one and the same sacred place [*Ort*]" from which both the explicit theatron and agora of Hellenic polis life first emerged.[36]

It is a hearkening fact for theatrocracy that both the Athenian drama and the Athenian political assembly would eventually take place at the very same site, the theatre of Dionysos. However, such locating seems only to have fully occurred after the reforms of Lykourgos in 355. During the Periclean period itself, the assembly had been slowly transferred from the agora to the Pnyx hill. Nonetheless, at least two political gatherings, one related to pragmatics of the Festival of the Dionysia taking place in the existent theatre, the other related to naval matters taking place in the Piraeus theatre, attest to the attraction of overlapping theatrical and assembly sitings.[37]

To this more general Hellenic pattern, increasingly marked in fifth-century Athens but not necessarily specific to it, the theatrocratic significance of the emergence of *tragic* drama in Athens, and *only* in Athens, can be given all the greater prominence. Whatever the extensive efforts to relate that emergence to mythical or ritualistic origins, the most directed interpretation would have to grant primacy to the dialogical dramatics and poetic-political articulations of

---

[34] I follow the important work of Kolb [1981], esp. 3-15, 101-106 (which provides suggestive neopalatial Cretan Minoan evidence for these links). Like Martin Heidegger, Kolb stresses that his use of the word "political" in these contexts means simply: "Alles, was die Polis betrifft" (5, 5 [note 2]). Kolb also notes that whereas "agora" is linked from the start with a relevant institution, this is not the case with "theatron" which only means a gathering place *(Versammlungsort)* as late as Herodotus, before it comes to carry the added meaning of specific architectural structures in Thucydides (3). Although its cognates were widely used in earlier periods, the specific word *orchestra* does not appear to have been in use before the fifth century but its implications were generally covered by *choros*.

[35] "Der Zusammenhang zwischen Agora und Agonen war folglich kein rein topographischer, sondern ein kultischer und damit auch politischer." Kolb [1981], 8. Kolb adds that for the Phaiakaians "ist der Tanz offensichtlich der wichtigste Agon, die Orchestra die bedeutendste agonale Kampfstätte auf der Agora."

[36] "'Heiliger Kreis' und 'Orchestra' (bzw. 'Choros') erscheinen somit als nur funktional differenzierende Bezeichnungen für ein und denselben sakralen Ort." Kolb [1981], 101. Frederiksen qualifies Kolb's arguments by noting that the agora was not only the political center but also "the commercial and religious center." Frederiksen [2002], 85 (note 101).

[37] Following Hansen [1987], 12-14. Hansen credits Lykourgos with installing marble benches and dates the reserving of the theatre front seats to 346-345 (48).

Solon, the sixth-century creator of at least Athenian *isonomia*, if not *demokratia* proper.[38] During the sixth century both Solon and the tyrant Peisistratus contributed to the founding, by 534, of the venue proper to the first tragic and (after 487) comic drama, the Festival of the Dionysia, meant to serve the general sense of unification of the Attic citizenry and celebrating Dionysos as the god of the demos. Between Thespis, the presumed creator of *tragoidia*, and Aeschylus, the true creator of tragic *drama*, a set of crucial metrical, visual, and dramaturgical experiments wound toward the unquestioned voice of tragic drama during the last fifteen years of Aeschylus' own career (472-456). The intimate link of these dates with the emergence of Athenian *demokratia* from Cleisthenes to Ephialtes is patent. Genuine tragic drama, starting with Aeschylus' *Agamemnon* (458), is then polis drama carrying forth the very spirit of this newly formed *demokratia* capable of raising to the level of the whole citizenry the heroic standards of the Homeric epic, first against the Persian invasion of 490, and second as confirmed by the unprecedented victories of 480-479.[39] Indeed the "specifically Attic religiosity of Solon" already contains in embryo the classic features of the Aeschylean world-view of shared pathos between the striving flawed hero and the responsive mass of the chorus, to be resolved in a catharsis exhibiting the ultimate retributive "justice of Zeus."[40]

If this is the religiosity emblematic of the tragic vision that Solon passed on to Aeschylus, it is no less that of Pericles. Yet Pericles' own vision has been confused with far more straightforward—and pedestrian—expressions of Athenian expansionist sentiment.[41] That many common—and some well-placed—Athenians exploited the surge in Athenian self-confidence after the Persian Wars to push avidly for conquests and adventures to the extent of fantasizing about territorial acquisitions in Sicily, Tuscany, and even Carthage, reflects one unquestioned aspect of the story of Athenian extremism leading to the Sicilian expeditionary disaster of 415-413. Pericles, however, is on record as relentlessly resisting such adventurism, particularly after the so-called First Peloponnesian War of 460-445, and adamantly favoring a moderate

---

[38] Generally following Else [1965]. Also Linforth [1919], 46-90.

[39] Else [1965], 76-80. The theatrical festival was "explicitly political" in the straightforward sense that "it was sponsored and funded in part by the city of Athens." Rabinowitz [2008], 44.

[40] Else [1965], 36. As the poetic admonitions of Solon put it: "For the works of unprincipled men do not continue long. Zeus watches all things to the end." Generally following Linforth's translation in Linforth [1919], 165 (fragment XL). The passage goes on to describe the purity brought about by the wind to earthly matters, adding: "Like such a sudden wind is the justice of Zeus."

[41] Kagan in fact compares the enthusiasm of these new Athenian democrats with "those of the young French and Russian revolutions" for believing that "free men inspired by a noble cause would sweep all before them." Kagan [1991], 73.

thalassocratic version of Athenian power that had renounced foreign land acquisitions.[42]

Far more symptomatic of this lethal variant of Athenian ebullience were Alcibiades' fulminations during the Peloponnesian War that "we have reached a position in which we must not be content with retaining but must scheme to extend [our empire], for, if we cease to rule others, we are in danger of being ruled ourselves"—the same politician who would proclaim soon enough to his Spartan hosts that *demokratia* itself was a "patent folly" (ἀνοίας).[43] At the core of the literal tragedy of the Sicilian expedition was the degree to which, following Alcibiades, "all alike fell in love" with the Sicilian enterprise with its promise of foreign adventures, land, and continued public funds.[44]

At the same time such adventurism may be regarded as the most problematic and facile variant on something more fundamental to the Athenian experience. The speeches Thucydides attributes to as varied a set of spokesmen as the Corinthians, Spartans, and Syracusans, as well as the Athenians themselves, tried to spell out exactly what that element was. Not surprisingly, granted the novel qualities of the latter combined with the perspectival prejudices of these spokesmen, no single clear account emerges. Innovation (νεωτεροποιοὶ), swiftness (ὀξεις), restlessness are characteristically brought up to demean the presumed Athenian tendency to "take no rest for themselves" and give "none to others."[45]

Less pejoratively, such traits are sometimes also framed as the "daring spirits" (ἄνδρας τολμηρούς) and "dash and enterprise" (οἱ ... ὀξεῖς ... καὶ οἱ ... ἐπιχειρηται) of the Athenians, qualities found only in such democratic poleis as their eventual nemesis Syracuse.[46] In Pericles' famous oration these traits even become transformed into a contemporary collective equivalent of the ancient heroic boldness (τόλμη) toward honor and everlasting glory.[47] Certainly Pericles

---

[42] Thucydides [1992], i.143-144; Plutarch [1914], xviii.1, xix.1, xx.2, xxi.1, xxii.1. As Kagan puts it, Pericles "put an end to imperial expansion and moderated Athenian ambitions." Kagan [1991], 92; also 115.

[43] Thucydides [1992], vi.18, vi.89.

[44] Thucydides [1992], vi.24. Thucydides notes that in general the young—not just on the Athenian but also on the Spartan side—were prone to military adventurism during this period (ii.8). This commonly shared hubris is all the more accentuated in Thucydides' searing account of the "beauty" and "splendor" of the doomed fleet as it set off that fateful dawn from the Piraeus harbor. Thucydides [1992], vi.32. For Thucycides and the tragic model of literature, see Finley [1963], 221, 267, 312, 322-325; also Connor [1984], 249.

[45] Thucydides [1992], i.70; also i.71.

[46] Thucydides [1992], vii.21, viii.96. The Syracusan Hermocrates agreed that the Syracusans were also rarely at rest (vi.38, also vii.55).

[47] Thucydides [1992], ii.41.

did not mean to identify such audacity with narrow territorial imperialism, which he opposed. This is a point perhaps best underscored by the irony that Pericles' flamboyant successor Cleon (who had fiercely opposed Pericles) berated the Athenians for being insufficiently cold-hearted imperialists during the famous Mytilene debate.[48] It is of even greater significance that at this same debate Cleon turned vociferously against the theatrocratic propensities of post-Periclean Athens by roundly upbraiding the demos for wanting "to see an oration as you see a spectacle" (θεαταὶ), "more like the audience of a rhetorician [σοφιστῶν θεαταῖς] than the council of a polis"—charges eerily reminiscent of Plato's later attacks on Athenian theatrocracy.[49] In contrast, Cleon's opponent Diodotus quietly pointed out the importance of good speaking and fair debate in settling the central issues of politics, a key gift of the theatrocratic culture that Pericles had helped inaugurate.[50]

This contrast between Cleon and Diodotus is a timely reminder that the "new politicians" of Athenian politics in the 420s were not necessarily "more" democratic in their anti-Periclean leanings. In fact, Pericles' own legacy is connected with a very different circle of culture-makers. Together, alongside Pericles, they almost helped realize the transition from democracy to theatrocracy before the disasters of 413 and 404.[51]

IV

To list such culture-makers as Anaxagoras, Herodotus, Sophocles, Euripides, Pheidias, Aspasia, Hippodamus, and Protagoras as colleagues, in some cases friends, and in one case the lover, of Pericles is not necessarily to argue for their subordinate status to Pericles' guidance, but rather to recall the higher levels of

---

[48] Cleon puts it unambiguously: "a democracy is incapable of empire." Thucydides [1992], iii.37.

[49] Thucydides [1992], iii.38.

[50] Thucydides [1992], iii.42. Fortunately for Athens' reputation, it was Diodotus' arguments rather than Cleon's which won over the demos to withdraw its earlier death sentence on the Mytilenians (iii.49). Perhaps the most important legacy of such an innovative temperament is the later Athenian "attraction for intellectuals" and its evolution after Alexander into a kind of university city. See Habicht [1997], 105, and compare with accounts of the modern American university city and Ideopolis in Chapter 8 above.

[51] While Kennedy [1971] provides a balanced view of the new politics initiated by Cleon and his peers, he does grant that "one problem, growing out of the style developed by Cleon and others, contributed to the deterioration of Athens' public life": a flamboyance that repulsed more established members of Athenian society to either avoid politics or in time seek dominance by the "better" sort (196, 197).

thought and vision pervading the inner circles within which Pericles operated.[52] These trendsetters in tragedy, history, rhetoric, city planning, and democratic culture clearly influenced Pericles in directions far removed from the flamboyant ambitions of a Cleon.

Of these, Anaxagoras has long been recorded as the principal intellectual influence on Pericles.[53] In his thought philosophy and politics merge to furnish a final justification for the Periclean vision that we identify with theatrocracy. One modern summary of this vision describes it as "a place for the development of the aesthetic and intellectual greatness inherent in humanity and especially in Greek culture," and even: "the greatest political community the world had ever known."[54] How does this claim vie with our more precise assertion that the best terminology for Pericles' vision is "theatrocracy' and that such "theatrocracy" can be accounted for in terms largely of the Anaxagorean influence?[55]

Anaxagoras is generally regarded as the revival of Ionian Milesian thought after the intrusion of Parmenidean ontological motifs into philosophy. The Ionian school was primarily concerned with the nature of a basic stuff, such as water or even the infinite, that accounted for the universe as a whole; Anaxagoras' particular version was to posit a "universal mixture" (περιχώρησις) through which everything contained everything else.[56] Anaxagoras' radical pluralism required, in its turn, an original impetus to which he ascribed the name of *Nous* or "mind," an original force, itself probably also corporeal but remarkably fine so that it remained unmixed, which imparted a rotary movement releasing an immensely rapid revolution giving rise in due course to all things.[57]

If Socrates and Plato later drew from Anaxagoras' Nous an ordering and rational principle ruling the world of change and politics from above, Pericles' inference proved quite different. Like the Anaxagorean cosmos, Pericles' *demokratia* let members of the polis work out their fate in freedom and unpredictability, risking instability in exchange for the ability to release the full energies of all members, "thereby creating a polis of unprecedented potential."[58] Moreover, it was *theatrocratically*-inclined through its intrinsic affinity with

---

[52] For an overall account of Pericles' relation to these important figures in Athenian culture, see Podlecki [1998].

[53] Isocrates coupled Anaxagoras with Damon as the principal pedagogical influences on Pericles. Cited in Podlecki [1999], 25.

[54] Kagan [1991], 111, 136.

[55] As nicely captured in reports of Anaxagoras' nickname as *Nous* or "mind," the central category of Anaxagoras' philosophy. Plutarch [1914], iv.4.

[56] Podlecki [1999], 23-25.

[57] Following Kirk & Raven [1969], 362-394, esp. 374, and fragments [503-505].

[58] Paraphrasing and following Kagan [1991], 64; also 24-25, 63.

central features of fifth-century Athenian practices. During the period 560-460, and more particularly after 510, largely as a result of the widening of the citizenship after Solon, Athens significantly extended the range of citizens' participation in a variety of competitive events. This blossoming of competitive festivals was especially marked in the dramatic competition where political issues were brought into public prominence, but it also included other competitions by unfolding a "critical openness toward government."[59] For the tragic festival, this extension meant celebration of Dionysos as the divinity of "illusion and change, paradox and ambiguity, release and transgression," all bound within the primacy of the polis: the tragic festival "both lauds the *polis* and depicts the stresses and tensions of a *polis* society in conflict."[60] Its tragic hero, "a bearer of contradiction," allowed those contradictions to unfold "without thereby compromising the unity of the social institution of theater."[61] More generally, competition became "a basic element of the workings of the gods of Athens," filling up the yearly competitive calendar with a variety of non-dramatic festivals, as Athenians exploited the notion that "the advantages of the competition to the city outweigh the disadvantages."[62]

Through this extensive range of competitive festivals, the Periclean application of the workings of the Anaxagorean cosmos to those of the Athenian polis was powerfully buttressed. Pericles' vision for his "greatest political community the world had ever known" became, in short, inseparable from the theatrical metaphorics appropriated by a political community emboldened to launch the Anaxagorean principle of the cosmic whirl (περιχώρησις, *Wirbel*) as theatrocracy.

V

Among his favored etymologies for the word "polis" Martin Heidegger on one occasion brings up "polos": "The πόλις is πόλος, that is, the pole, the whirl [*Wirbel*], in which and around which everything turns."[63] Heidegger's polis archetypally "whirls" around the "site of history" (*Geschichtstätte*), holding

---

[59] Robin Osborne, "Competitive Festivals and the Polis: A Context for Dramatic Festivals at Athens," in Rhodes [2004], 221.

[60] Simon Goldhill, "The Great Dionysia and Civic Ideology," in Winkler & Zeitlin [1990], 128, 129.

[61] Oddone Longo, "The Theater of the *Polis*," in Winkler & Zeitlin [1990], 19.

[62] Osborne, "Competitive Festivals and the Polis: A Context for Dramatic Festivals at Athens," in Rhodes [2004], 211, 217.

[63] Heidegger [1984a], 100.

together its "gods, temples, priests, festivals, games, poets, thinkers, ruler, council of elders, people's assembly, the military, and the ships."[64]

In a provocative study of the Presocratics and Anaxagoras, the young Friedrich Nietzsche amplified Heidegger's insight by driving it toward an explicit celebration of play and the artwork.[65] Heidegger's "whirl" (*Wirbel*) here becomes Nietzsche's "Whirl" (*Wirbel*) and "swinging" (*Schwingung*) with which Nietzsche interprets Anaxagoras' vision as that of an "artist" teaching the lesson that "becoming is no moral, but only an artistic phenomenon," with the cosmos itself functioning as "the monstrous artwork." The polis implications of this vision are further underscored by Nietzsche's claim that "the greatest Anaxagorean is however Pericles" for being the "abbreviation of the Anaxagorean cosmos, the image of Nous," through Pericles' memorable "Olympian" speeches to his people that resounded with the full suggestiveness of a cosmology based on the primacy of cosmic "play" (*Spiel*).[66]

Whatever the idiosyncracies to Nietzsche's youthful reading of Anaxagoras and Pericles, it holds to some important truths that we have already derived from our own brief overview of Athenian polis practice and thought during the fifth century: namely, during this period Pericles and a sympathetic group of culture-makers helped carry *demokratia* toward a mode of governance and culture that we dub "theatrocracy." Yet Nietzsche himself recognized the risks to such a theatrocracy when he elsewhere noted that there are ages when humans develop a faith in taking on a variety of roles that they can play, becoming in the process "actors." Such ages are characteristically "democratic" ages—Nietzsche explicitly cites "the Athenian faith that first becomes noticeable in the Periclean age" as one such prime case—and he contrasts them to those ages which are capable of building for distant futures by holding humans to the role of a mere "stone in a great edifice."[67] Admittedly, these "democratic" ages carry enormous risks endemic to an open, experimental attitude. Thus, to prevent them from getting entirely out of hand, it is essential to retain a sense of punctuation, of "a certain habitual groundedness." For this "theater of politics," as Nietzsche's reading has been recently described, manifests itself as an age without limits: "the age of actors encompasses the maddest and most interesting of all ages."[68] In any event, Nietzsche himself is

---

[64] Heidegger [1977], 117.

[65] "Die Philosophie im Tragischen Zeitalter der Griechen," in Nietzsche [1966], iii, 349-413.

[66] Nietzsche [1966], iii, 409, 410, 411, 412. Also: the "type of the child's play or the artistic play-drive" (*Art des Kinderspieles oder des künstlerischen Spieltriebes*) (413). See also Chapters 4 and 5 above.

[67] *Die Fröhliche Wissenschaft* [356], in Nietzsche [1966], ii, 224.

[68] Following the reading by Ronell [2008], 302, 303, 304-305. Ronell refers to Nietzsche's

clear that whatever misgivings one might hold about such ages, the Periclean striving toward theatrocracy is undoubtedly a leading candidate. His account helps us understand some of the excitement accompanying the Athenian experiment, felt even by her rivals, as Pericles and his fellow culture-makers supported and contributed to precisely those theatrical institutions and characteristics which drove the democratic polis to its historic moment of epiphany as a theatrocracy in the making.

In turn, this unprecedented convergence of politics and theatre reflects, as was earlier argued, the distant legacy of an originary siting. That siting was identified as the "dancing-place," the χορός, traceable all the way back to thalassocratic features of Cretan neopalatial civilization. Here, if anywhere, we may find the closest earthly and social analogue to the cosmic whirl of Anaxagoras: if the entire universe manifests as a swirling rotation from which all beings emerge and develop, the χορός—along with the related χῶρος for "place," or even "temple" and "grove"—is its human and theatrical equivalent. χορός denotes not only the "dancing-place," but "is consistently used of those dances ... which take place within a prescribed outdoor area, often surrounded by spectators," performing dance and song to the "goddess."[69] That "goddess," as cytherics is grateful to register, is more often than not identified with the "Aphrodite" who has taken over the functions of the Minoan sea-goddess "Ariadne" for whom the Homeric craftsman Daedalus once apparently built a χορός.[70]

Thus a steady if distant motif carries us from the sacred spaces and public arenas essential to the practices of Cretan neopalatial civilization—located in such temple- and civic-complexes as Knossos, around which the first thalassocratic realm of governance has been recorded—all the way through the agoras of sixth-century Crete to the full burst of dramatic and theatrical practices in classical Greece, ultimately converging into the sea power and tragic dramatic festivals of Periclean Athens to briefly promise the realization of *demokratia* as theatrocracy. The heritage of this legacy may be most concisely summed up as: *thalassic theatrocracy*. Since future millennia have failed even to approach the level of Athenian *demokratia* in terms of the latter's actively participatory democracy—Rousseau's modern *theory* of the social contract serving as perhaps the most imposing standard legitimating such practices—it is hardly surprising that this vision of a mode of governance aiming to surpass

own "unquestionably Californian invention of lifestyle" (303). Also Weber [2004], 33.

69 Boedeker [1974], 57. Also Lawler [1064], 28-39.

70 Following the evidence in Boedeker [1974], 43-47, 85-87, particularly: "Aphrodite and the χορός" and "Appendix: χῶρος and χορός." More generally, see the bold reading by Kittler [2006].

even the classical Athenian polis model has been largely forgotten—or, at most, vaguely glimpsed through intervening practices largely relegated to artistdoms (*Künstlertum*, *artistisme*), bohemias, and countercultures.

Cytherics recoups this "thalassic theatrocratic" moment by speculative thinking that links such moments to the aspirations surrounding the signifier "Aphrodite" or "Cytherea." Sustained reflection on the political standards entailed by thalassocracy and theatrocracy is intended to help this project along, in conjunction with the concepts of polis thought and artful firm drawn from contemporary political reflection and from organization and management analysis that are advocated in this volume. Joining the notions of "labor of love," "aphrodisian logic," and "paradisics" proposed in a previous volume, these perspectives thus enrich the harvest to be reaped by continued development of a faculty of thought called cytherics.[71]

VI

In a larger sense this volume is no less about embarkation (*embarquement*), even if within the formalities of scholarly inquiry—an embarkation (*Unis vers Cythère*) directed toward the "isle" that mythographers have labeled "Cythera."

Cythera: the environmentality of a bounteous and fecund isle bearing the cluster of aesthetic, erotic, and politically emancipatory aims summed up through deference toward the "works" of an oceanic (Mediterranean) sea goddess of love and beauty.

For the themes of thalassocracy and theatrocracy proper the most portentous previous such embarkation—the one welding together these themes into the single cauldron of myth—is that bearing the Athenian hero Theseus from the shores of Attica to the capital of Minos at Knossos on Crete where Theseus succeeded in slaying the Minotaur and in abducting Ariadne, thanks, it must be said, to the help of Aphrodite in solving the problem of the labyrinth. In this in itself labyrinthine tale of adventure, glory, and ultimately unresolvable issues of thalassic hegemony and theatricality on behalf of a sea goddess presiding over the sacred χορός, these two themes have become inseparably and permanently entwined.[72]

Thus, in so far as it entails a voyage—*unis vers Cythère*—our own embarkation must finally acknowledge the risks intrinsic to oceanic

[71] Details of these notions are provided in Chapters 8-10 in Chytry [2005].

[72] See in general Walker [1995] for the original sources on the myth of Theseus and the "paradox of a democratic king."

undertakings of this order.[73] For no cytherean venture can ultimately expect to arrive at its landfall if it ignores the admonitory resonances floating across the seas from that last, intrepid votary of the "philosopher" Dionysos:

> ...thus does a god suffer, a Dionysos. The reply to such a dithyramb of a sun's solitude in light would be *Ariadne* ... Who knows besides me what *Ariadne* is! ...[74]

Světovina, Czech Republic &
Berkeley, California

[73] For Aphrodite as provider of "calm seas" (γαληναίη) and happy arrivals of ships in harbors, see the references provided in Kittler [2006], 49.

[74] *Ecce Homo*, in Nietzsche [1966], ii, 1138 (emphasis in original). Cf. Nietzsche's allusions to the "celebrated dialogues on Naxos" between Ariadne and Dionysos in *Götzendammerung* and *Der Antichrist* [39]. Nietzsche [1966], ii, 1001, 1201.

BIBLIOGRAPHY

Adorno, Theodor W. [1952]. *Versuch über Wagner* (Berlin: Suhrkamp).
——— [1965]. *Noten zur Literatur* (Frankfurt: Suhrkamp).
Alberti, Leon Battista [1966]. *On Painting* (New Haven, CT: Yale University Press [956]), transl.
——— [1988]. *On the Art of Building in Ten Books* (Cambridge, MA: The MIT Press), transl.
Allison, David B. (ed.) [1977]. *The New Nietzsche: Contemporary Styles of Interpretation* (New York: Dell).
——— [2001]. *Reading the New Nietzsche: The Birth of Tragedy, The Gay Science, Thus Spoke Zarathustra and On the Genealogy of Morals* (Lanham, MA: Rowman & Littlefield).
Ankersmit, F. R. [1996]. *Aesthetic Politics: Political Philosophy beyond Fact and Value* (Stanford, CA: Stanford University Press).
Archibugi, Daniele (ed.) [2003]. *Debating Cosmopolitics* (London: Verso).
Arendt, Hannah [1958]. *The Human Condition: A Study of the Central Dilemmas facing Modern Man* (New York: Doubleday Anchor).
——— [1963]. *On Revolution* (New York: Viking).
——— [1982]. *Lectures on Kant's Political Philosophy* (Chicago, IL: University of Chicago Press).
Aristotle [1967]. *Politics* (Cambridge, MA: Harvard University Press [1944]), Greek text & transl.
Armitage, John [2006]. "From Discourse Networks to Cultural Mathematics: An Interview with Friedrich A. Kittler," *Theory ,Culture & Society*, 23: 17-38.
Arnason, Johann P. & Peter Murphy (eds.) [2001]. *Agon, Logos, Polis: The Greek Achievement and its Aftermath* (Stuttgart: Franz Steiner Verlag).
Ash, Timothy Garton [1990]. *The Magic Lantern: The Revolution of '89 Witnessed in Warsaw, Budapest, Berlin, and Prague* (New York: Random House).
Austin, Rob & Lee Devin [2003]. *Artful Making: What Managers Need to Know About How Artists Work* (New York: Prentice-Hall).
Aylen, Leo [1985]. *The Greek Theater* (Cranbury, NJ: Associated University Presses).
Bachofen, J. J. [1967]. *Myth, Religion, and Mother Right* (Princeton, NJ: Princeton University Press [1954]), transl.
Barocchi, Paola (ed.) [1960]. *Trattati d'Arte del Cinquecento: Fra Manierismo e controriforma* (Bari: G. Laterza & Figli), vol. 1.
Baron, Hans [1955]. *The Crisis of the Early Italian Renaissance: Civic Humanism and Republican Liberty in an Age of Classicism and Tyranny* (Princeton, NJ: Princeton University Press).
Barth, Herbert (ed.) [1973]. *Der Festspielhügel: Richard Wagners Werk in Bayreuth* (Munich: List).
Benda, Václav [1991]. "The Parallel 'Polis' [1978]," in Skilling & Wilson [1991], 35-41.
Benjamin, Walter [1973]. *Das Kunstwerk im Zeitalter seiner technischen Reproducierbarkeit* (Frankfurt: Suhrkamp [1936]).
——— [1979]. "Theories of German Fascism: On the C*ollection of Essays* War and Warrior, edited by Ernst Jünger" [1930], *New German Critique*, 17 (Spring), 120-128, transl.

Benoit, Fernand [1965]. *Recherches sur l'Hellénisation du Midi de la Gaule* (Aix-en-Provence: Editions Ophrys).

Berenson, Ruth [2002]. *The Operatic State: Cultural Policy and the Opera House* (London: Routledge).

Berghaus, Günter [1995]. *The Genesis of Futurism: Marinetti's Early Career and Writings 1899-1909* (Leeds: The Society of Italian Studies), Occasional Papers No. 1.

Bernbach, Udo [1994]. *Der Wahn des Gesamtkunstwerks: Richard Wagners politisch-ästhetische Utopie* (Frankfurt: Fischer).

Bertellini, Giorgio (ed.) [2004]. *The Cinema of Italy* (London: Wallflower).

Blum, Cinzia Sartini [1996]. *The Other Modernism: F. T. Marinetti's Futurist Fiction of Power* (Berkeley, CA: University of California Press).

Blumenberg, Hans [1987]. *The Genesis of the Copernican World* (Cambridge, MA: The MIT Press [1975]), transl.

Blunt, Anthony [1937-1938]. "The Hypnerotomachia Poliphili in 17th Century France," *Journal of the Warburg Institute*, 1: 117-137.

Boedeker, Deborah Dickmann [1974]. *Aphrodite's Entry into Greek Epic* (Leiden: E. J. Brill).

Boland, Richard J., Jr. & Fred Collopy (eds.) [2004]. *Managing as Designing* (Stanford, CA: Stanford Business Books).

Bolter, J. David [1984]. *Turing's Man* (London: Penguin).

Bondanella, Peter [1987]. *The Eternal City: Roman Images in the Modern World* (Chapel Hill, NC: University of North Carollina Press).

——— [1992]. *The Cinema of Federico Fellini* (Princeton, NJ: Princeton University Press).

——— [2001]. *Italian Cinema: From Neorealism to the Present* (New York: Continuum), 3rd ed.

Borsi, Franco [1977]. *Leon Battista Alberti: The Complete Works* (New York: Electa/Rizzoli [1973]), transl.

Botting, Douglas [1977]. *Rio de Janeiro* (Amsterdam: Time-Life Books).

Bougainville, Louis Antoine de [1958]. *Voyage autour du monde* (Paris: Clubs des Librairies de France).

Bourdieu, Pierre [1991]. *The Political Ontology of Martin Heidegger* (Stanford, CA: Stanford University Press), transl.

Breker, Arno [1990]. *The Collected Writings* (New York: West-Art), transl.

Brock, Gillian & Harry Brighouse (eds.). *The Political Philosophy of Cosmopolitanism* (Cambridge: Cambridge University Press).

Bronnenmeyer, Walter [1983]. *Richard Wagner, Bürger in Bayreuth: Wechselspiel von Allianz und Mesalliance* (Bayreuth: Ellwanger).

Bruford, W. H. [1962]. *Culture and Society in Classical Weimar, 1775-1806* (Cambridge: Cambridge University Press).

Brunette, Peter [1989]. *Roberto Rossellini* (New York: Oxford University Press).

Bruni, Leonardo [1987]. *The Humanism of Leonardo Bruni: Selected Texts* (Binghampton, NY: Medieval and Renaissance Texts and Studies), G. Griffiths, J. Hankins & D. Thompson (eds. & transl.).

Buonarroti, Michelangelo [1987]. *Life, Letters, and Poetry* (Oxford: Oxford University Press), transl.

——— [1991]. *The Poetry of Michelangelo: An Annotated Translation* (New Haven, CT: Yale University Press), transl.

Burckhardt, Jacob [1869]. *Die Cultur der Renaissance in Italien* (Leipzig: Seemann), 2nd ed.

——— [1941]. *Weltgeschichtliche Betrachtungen* (Bern: Hallwag), Werner Kaegi (ed.).

——— [1990]. *The Civilization of the Renaissance in Italy* (London: Penguin), transl.

Burian, Jarka [1983]. *Svoboda: Wagner—Josef Svoboda's Scenography for Richard Wagner's Operas* (Middletown, CT: Wesleyan University Press).

Campari, Roberto [1980]. *Hollywood-Cinecittà: Il racconto che cambia* (Milan: Feltrinelli).

Cardullo, Bert [2002]. *Vittorio de Sica: Director, Actor, Screenwriter* (Jefferson, NC: McFarland & Co.).

Carrasco, David [1982]. *Quetzalcoatl and the Irony of Empire: Myths and Prophecies in the Aztec Tradition* (Chicago: University of Chicago Press).

Carroll, David [1987]. *Paraesthetics: Foucault, Lyotard, Derrida* (New York: Methuen).

Castells, Manuel [2001]. *The Internet Galaxy: Reflections on the Internet, Business, and Society* (Oxford: Oxford University Press).

Champanier, S. [1989]. "Quo vadis Cinecittà?" *La revue du Cinéma*, 451: 67.

Chandler, Alfred D., Jr. [1977]. *The Visible Hand: The Managerial Revolution in American Business* (Cambridge, MA: Harvard University Press).

——— [1990]. *Scale and Scope: The Dynamics of Industrial Capitalism* (Cambridge, MA: Harvard University Press).

Chatman, Seymour [1983]. *Antonioni, or, The Surface of the World* (Berkeley, CA: University of California Press).

Chipp, Herschel B.(ed.) [1968]. *Theories of Modern Art: A Source Book by Artists and Critics* (Berkeley, CA: University of California Press).

Chvatík, Ivan [1992-3]. "Solidarity of the Shaken," *Telos*, 94: 163-6.

——— [2003]. "The Heretical Conception of the European Legacy in the Late Essays of Jan Patočka," Center for Theoretical Study, Prague, Czech Republic, Working Paper CTS-03-14 (September).

Chytry, Gabriel [2005]. *L'état de bonheur dans la démocratie libérale contemporaine* (M.A. thesis, Faculté des sciences et économiques, Institut Catholique de Paris).

Chytry, Josef [1989]. *The Aesthetic State: A Quest in Modern German Thought* (Berkeley, CA: University of California Press).

——— [1999a]. Review of Rabinbach [1997], *German Politics and Society*, 17:2 (Summer), 94-100.

——— [1999b]. Review of Marchand [1996], *American Historical Review*, 104:3 (June), 1019-1021.

——— [2003]. "Between *Polis* and *Poiēsis*: On the 'Cytherean' Ambiguities in the Poetry of James G. March," *Industrial and Corporate Change*, 12:4, 943-960.

——— [2004]. "Fair Play," *History and Theory*, 43:1, 83-106.

——— [2005]. *Cytherica: Aesthetic-Political Essays in an Aphrodisian Key* (New York & Berne: Peter Lang).

——— [2006a]. "On the 'Terror' of Polis Freedom: From Martin Heidegger to Jan Patočka and the Czech Velvet Revolution," in Goi & Dolan [2006], 119-172.

——— [2006b]. "Bordering the Civilization of Greater California: An Inquiry into Genealogy, Treaty-Making, and Influence," *Western Humanities Review*, 60:2 (Fall), 27-50.

——— [2007]. "'Aphrodisian Bliss' for the Artful Firm: Wagner, Nietzsche, and the Idea of Bayreuth in Relation to Organization and Management Theory," *Aesthesis,* 1:2, 43-53

——— [2008a]. "California Civilization and European Speculative Thought: An Evolving Relationship," *California History*, 89:4, 50-69,73-75.

——— [2008b]. "Organizational Aesthetics: The Artful Firm and the Aesthetic Moment in Organization and Management Theory," *Aesthesis*, 2:2, 60-71.

Clark, Martin [1984]. *Modern Italy 1871-1982* (London: Longman).

Cohen, Eliot A. [1996]. "A Revolution in Warfare," *Foreign Affairs*, 75: 2 (March/April), 37-54.
Cohen Peter (director) [1989]. *The Architecture of Doom*. Documentary Film.
Colonna, Francesco [1999]. *Hypnerotomachia Poliphili: The Strife of Love in a Dream* (New York: Thames & Hudson), J. Godwin (transl.).
Conn, Robert T. [2002]. *The Politics of Philology: Alfonso Reyes and the Invention of the Latin American Literary Tradition* (Cranbury, NJ: Associated University Presses).
Connor, W. Robert [1971]. *The New Politicians of Fifth-Century Athens* (Princeton, NJ: Princeton University Press).
——— [1984]. *Thucydides* (Princeton, NJ: Princeton University Press).
Corbin. Henry [1969]. *Creative Imagination in the Sūfism of Ibn 'Arabī* (Princeton, NJ: Princeton University Press [1958]), transl.
Coulanges, Fustel de [1956]. *The Ancient City: A Study on the Religion, Laws and Institutions of Greece and Rome* (Garden City, NY: Doubleday [1873]), transl.
Cowart, Georgia [2001]. "Watteau's 'Pilgrimage to Cythera' and the Subversive Utopia of the Opera-Ballet," *The Art Bulletin*, 83:3 (September), 461-478.
Crow, Thomas [1985]. *Painters and Public Life in Eighteenth-Century Paris* (New Haven, CT: Yale University Press).
Curtis, Kimberley [1997]. "Aesthetic Foundations of Democratic Politics in the Work of Hannah Arendt," in C. Calhoun & J. McGowan (eds.), *Hannah Arendt and the Meaning of Politics* (Minneapolis, MN: University of Minnesota Press).
Cyert, Richard M. & James G. March [1992]. *A Behavioral Theory of the Firm* (Cambridge, MA: Black Business), 2nd ed.
Daraki, Maria [1986]. "Michel Foucault's Journey to Greece," *Telos*, 67 (Spring), 87-110, transl.
Day, Barbara [1999]. *The Velvet Philosophers* (London: The Claridge Press).
Derrida, Jacques [1995]. *The Gift of Death* (Chicago: University of Chicago Press), transl.
——— [2002]. *Acts of Religion* (New York: Routledge), transl.
Dickinson, Paul (author) & Neil Svensen (designer) [2000]. *Beautiful Corporations: Corporate Style in Action* (New York: Prentice Hall).
Dobson, John [1999]. *The Art of Management and the Aesthetic Manager: The Coming Way of Business* (Westport, CT: Quorum)
——— [2006]. "Aesthetics as a Foundation for Business Activity," *Journal of Business Ethics* (online).
Dolan, Frederick M. [1994]. *Allegories of America: Narratives, Metaphysics, Politics* (Ithaca, NY: Cornell University Press).
Dosi, Giovanni; David J. Teece & Josef Chytry (eds.). [1998]. *Technology, Organization, and Competitiveness: Perspectives on Industrial and Corporate Change* (Oxford: Oxford University Press).
——— [2005]. *Understanding Industrial and Corporate Change* (Oxford: Oxford University Press).
Doumos, Christos [1992]. *The Wall-Paintings of Thera* (Athens: The Thera Foundation).
Eagleton, Terry [1990]. *The Ideology of the Aesthetic* (Cambridge, MA: Basil Blackwell).
Else, Gerald F. [1965]. *The Origin and Early Form of Greek Tragedy* (Cambridge, MA: Harvard University Press).
Elson, Charles [1913]. *Wieland and Shaftesbury* (New York: Columbia University Press).
Englund, Steven [1984]. *Grace of Monaco: An Interpretive Biography* (Garden City, NY: Doubleday).
Erim, Kenan T. [1986]. *Aphrodisias: City of Venus Aphrodite* (New York: File on File Publications).

Etlin, Richard A. [ed.] [2002]. *Art, Culture and Media under the Third Reich* (Chicago, IL: University of Chicago Press).

Evenson, Norma [1973]. *Two Brazilian Capitals: Architecture and Urbanism in Rio de Janeiro and Brasilia* (New Haven, CT: Yale University Press).

Fay, Brian [1975]. *Social Theory and Political Practice* (London: Allen & Unwin).

Fellini, Federico [1972]. *"Roma" di Federico Fellini* (Bologna: Capelli), B. Zapponi (ed.).

——— [1989]. *Cinecittà* (London: Studio Vista [1988]), transl.

Ferry, Luc [1993] *Homo Aestheticus: The Invention of Taste in the Democratic Age* (Chicago, IL: University of Chicago Press [1990]), transl.

Fierz-David, Linda [1987]. *The Dream of Poliphilo: The Soul in Love* (Dallas, TX: Spring Publications [1950]), transl.

Findlay, Edward F. [2002]. *Caring for the Soul in a Postmodern Age: Politics and Phenomenology in the Thought of Jan Patočka* (Albany, NY: State University of New York Press).

Fink, Eugen [1960]. *Spiel als Weltsymbol* (Stuttgart: W. Kohlhammer).

——— [2003]. *Nietzsche's Philosophy* (London: Continuum [1960]), transl.

——— & Jan Patočka [1999]. *Briefe und Dokumente: 1933-1977* (Freiburg: Alber).

Finley, John H. [1963]. *Thucydides* (Ann Arbor, MI: University of Michigan Press [1942]).

Finney, Ben R. & Eric M. Jones {eds.) [1985]. *Interstellar Migration and the Human Experience* (Berkeley, CA: University of California Press).

Fitton, J. Lesley [2002]. *Minoans* (London: British Museum Press).

Fletcher, Richard [1992]. *Moorish Spain* (New York: Henry Holt).

Foreman, Walter C. [1980]. "Fellini's Cinematic City: *Roma* and Myths of Foundation," *Forum Italicum*, 14: 78-98.

Forrest, W. G. [1968]. *A History of Sparta 950-192 BC* (New York: W. W. Norton).

——— [1970]. *The Emergence of Greek Democracy 800-400 BC* (New York: McGraw-Hill [1966]).

Foster, Hal (ed.) [1983]. *The Anti-Aesthetic: Essays on Postmodern Culture* (Port Townsend, WA: Bay Press).

Foucault, Michel [2003]. *The Essential Foucault: Selections from Essential Works of Foucault, 1954-1984* (New York: New Press [1994]), transl. P. Rabinow & N. Rose (eds.).

Frederiksen, Rune [2002]. "The Greek Theatre: A Typical Building in the Urban Center of the *Polis*?," in Thomas Heine Nielsen (ed.), *Even More Studies in the Ancient Greek* ***Polis***: *Papers from the Copenhagen Polis Centre 6* (Stuttgart: Franz Steiner), 65-124.

Freeman, Chris & Francisco Louçã [2001]. *As Time Goes By: From the Industrial Revolutions to the Information Revolution* (Oxford: Oxford University Press).

Friedrich, Carl [1978]. *The Meaning of Aphrodite* (Chicago, IL: University of Chicago Press).

Fry, Roger [1924]. *Vision and Design* (New York: Brentano's).

Gadamer, Hans-Georg [1972]. *Wahrheit und Methode: Grundzüge einer philosophischen Hermeneutik* (Tübingen: J. C. B. Mohr), 3rd ed.

Gadol, Joan [1969]. *Leon Battista Alberti: Universal Man of the Early Renaissance* (Chicago, IL: University of Chicago Press).

Gaines, Thomas A. [1991]. *The Campus as a Work of Art* (New York: Praeger).

Geertz, Clifford [1980]. *Negara: The Theatre State in Nineteenth-Century Bali* (Princeton, NJ: Princeton University Press).

Gelernter, David [1998]. *Machine Beauty: Elegance and the Heart of Technology* (New York: Basic Books).

Gerber, Jane S. [1992]. *The Jews of Spain: A History of the Sephardic Experience* (New York: The Free Press).

Gethmann-Siefert, Annemarie & Otto Pöggeler (eds.) [1988]. *Heidegger und die praktische Philosophie* (Frankfurt: Suhrkamp).

Giesler, Hermann [1978]. *Ein anderer Hitler: Bericht seines Architekten Hermann Giesler: Erlebnisse Gespräche Reflexionen* (Leoni am Starnberger See: Druffel-Verlag).

Gilbert, Felix [1965]. *Machiavelli and Guicciardini: Politics and History in Sixteenth-Century Florence* (Princeton, NJ: Princeton University Press).

Gimbutas, Marija [1999]. *The Living Goddesses* (Berkeley, CA: University of California Press).

Ginsborg, Paul [1990]. *A History of Contemporary Italy: Society and Politics 1943-1988* (London: Penguin).

Glick, Thomas F. [1979]. *Islamic and Christian Spain in the Early Middle Ages* (Princeton, NJ: Princeton University Press).

Goebbels, Joseph [1937]. *Michael: Ein deutsches Schicksal in Tagebuchblättern* (Munich: Zentralverlag der NSDAP [1929]).

——— [1987]. *Michael: A Novel* (New York: Amok Press [1929]), transl.

——— [1993]. *Die Tagebücher von Joseph Goebbels* (Munich: K. G. Saur). Vol. II (Diktate 1941-1945), No. 9 (July-September 1943). Elke Fröhlich (ed.).

Goehr, Lydia [1998] *The Quest for Voice: On Music, Politics, and the Limits of Philosophy* (Berkeley, CA: University of California Press).

Goffman, Ken & Dan Joy [2005]. *Counterculture through the Ages: From Abraham to Acid Rock* (New York: Villard Books).

Goi, Simona & Frederick M. Dolan (eds.) [2006]. *Between Terror and Freedom: Philosophy, Politics, and Fiction Speak of Modernity* (Lanham, MA: Lexington Books).

Goléa, Antoine [1967]. *Entretiens avec Wieland Wagner* (Paris: Éditions Pierre Belfond).

Gossman, Lionel [2000]. *Basel in the Age of Burckhardt: A Study in Unseasonable Ideas* (Chicago, IL: University of Chicago Press).

Govinda, Anagarika [1991]. *Buddhist Reflections* (York Beach, ME: Samuel Weiser).

Grabar, Oleg [1978]. *The Alhambra* (Cambridge, MA: Harvard University Press).

Grafton, Anthony [2000]. *Leon Battista Alberti: Master Builder of the Italian Renaissance* (Cambridge, MA: Harvard University Press).

Green, Martin [1976]. *Children of the Sun: A Narrative of 'Decadence' in England after 1918* (New York: Basic Books).

Grigson, Geoffrey [1976]. *The Goddess of Love: The Birth, Triumph, Death and Return of Aphrodite* (New York: Stein and Day).

Guillet de Monthoux, Pierre [2004]. *The Art Firm: Aesthetic Management and Metaphysical Marketing from Wagner to Wilson* (Stanford, CA: Stanford Business Books).

——— [2006}. *Liedership: Franz Schubert's Schwungsongs for Aesthetic Management*, CD.

———; Claes Gustafsson & Sven-Erik Sjostrand (eds.) [2007]. *Aesthetic Leadership: Managing Fields of Flow in Art and Business* (London: Palgrave Macmillan).

Habermas, Jürgen [1996] *Between Facts and Norms: Contributions to a Discourse Theory of Law and Democracy* (Cambridge, MA: The MIT Press [1992]), transl.

Habicht, Christian [1997]. *Athens from Alexander to Antony* (Cambridge, MA: Harvard University Press [1995]), transl.

Hägg, R. & N. Marinatos (eds.). [1984]. *The Minoan Thalassocracy: Myth and Reality* (Stockholm: Skrifter utgivna av Svenska institutet i Athen).

Hall, Peter Geoffrey [1998]. *Cities in Civilization* (New York: Pantheon).

Hallward, Peter [2006]. "Staging Equality: On Rancière's Theatrocracy," *New Left Review*, 37 (January-February), 109-129.

Hamann, Brigitte [2002]. *Winifred Wagner oder Hitlers Bayreuth* (Munich: Piper).

Hancock, Philip & Melissa Tyler [2001]. *Work, Postmodernism and Organization: A Critical Introduction* (London: Sage).

Hansen, Mogens Herman [1987]. *The Athenian Assembly in the Age of Demosthenes* (Oxford: Basil Blackwell).

Harrison, R. B. [1974]. *Hölderlin and Greek Literature* (Oxford: Clarendon).

Havel, Václav [1978]. "The Power of the Powerless [1978]," in Havel [1991], 129-214.

——— [1990a]. *Disturbing the Peace: A Conversation with Karl Hvížďala* (New York: Alfred A. Knopf), transl.

——— [1990b]. *Moc bezmocných* (Prague: Lidové noviny).

——— [1991]. *Open Letters: Selected Writings 1965-1990* (New York: Alfred A. Knopf), transl.

——— [1992]. *Summer Meditations* (New York: Alfred A. Knopf), transl.

——— [2007]. *To the Castle and Back* (New York: Alfred A. Knopf), transl.

Hawkes, Jacquetta [1972]. *Dawn of the Gods* (London: Sphere Books [1968]).

Heckscher, W. S. [1956]. "The *Anadyomene* in the Medieval tradition (Pelagia-Cleopatra-Aphrodite): A Prelude to Botticelli's 'Birth of Venus'," *Nederlands Kunsthistorisch Jaarboek*, 7: 1-38.

Hedin, Astrid [2004]. "Stalinism as a Civilization: New Perspectives on Communist Regimes," *Political Studies Review*, 2: 166-184.

Heidegger, Martin [1966]. *Einführung in die Metaphysik* (Tübingen: Max Niemeyer), 3rd ed.

——— [1967]. *Wegmarken* (Frankfurt: Vittorio Klostermann).

——— [1969]. *Zur Sache des Denkens* (Tübingen: Niemeyer).

——— [1975]. *Die Grundprobleme der Phänomenologie* (Frankfurt: Vittorio Klostermann).

——— [1975 -]. *Gesamtausgabe* (Frankfurt: Vittorio Klostermann), in process.

——— [1977]. *The Question Concerning Technology and Other Essays* (New York: Harper & Row), transl.

——— [1978]. *Metaphysische Anfangsgründe der Logik in Ausgang von Leibniz* (Frankfurt: Vittorio Klostermann).

——— [1984a]. *Hölderlins Hymne 'Die Ister'* (Frankfurt: Klostermann [1942]).

——— [1984b]. *The Metaphysical Foundations of Logic* (Bloomington, IN: Indiana University Press [1978]), transl.

——— [1991]. *Nietzsche, Volumes I and II* (San Francisco, CA: HarperSan Francisco [1961]), transl.

——— & Eugen Fink [1993]. *Heraclitus Seminar* (Evanston, IL: Northwestern University Press [1970]), transl.

Heine-Geldern, Robert [1956]. *Conceptions of State and Kingship in Southeast Asia* (Cornell University Southeast Asia Program Data Paper No. 18 [April]).

Heller, Agnes [1985]. "The Great Republic," *Praxis International*, 5:1 (April), 23-34.

——— [1997]. "Parmenides and the Battle of Stalingrad," *Graduate Faculty Philosophy Journal*, 20:1 (1997), 247-262.

Hermassi, Karen [1977]. *Theatre and Polity in Historical Perspective* (Berkeley, CA: University of California Press).

Herodotus [1960]. *Historiae* (Oxford: Clarendon [1927]), 3rd ed., 2 vols.

Hesiod & Homer [1914]. *Hesiod, the Homeric Hymns and Homerica* (Cambridge, MA: Harvard University Press), W. G. Evelyn-White (transl.), Greek text & transl.

Hillach, Angar [1979]. "The Aesthetics of Politics: Walter Benjamin's 'Theories of German Fascism,'" *New German Critique*, 17 (Spring), 99-119.

Hipple, Jr., Walter John [1957]. *The Beautiful, The Sublime & The Picturesque in Eighteenth-Century British Aesthetic Theory* (Carbondale, IL: The Southern Illinois University Press).

Hitler, Adolf [1925]. *Mein Kampf: Eine Abrechnung* (Vol. 1) (Munich: Franz Eher).

——— [1927]. *Mein Kampf: Die nationalsozialistische Bewegung* (Vol. 2) (Munich: Franz Eher).

——— [1943]. *Mein Kampf* (Boston: Houghton Mifflin [1925-1927]), transl.

——— [2000]. *Hitler's Table Talk 1941-1944: His Private Conversations* (New York: Enigma [1953]), transl.

Holmes, George [1969]. *The Florentine Enlightenment, 1400-50* (London: Weidenfeld & Nicolson).

Homer [1970]. *Homerus Ilias Odyssee* (Haarlem: Willink & Zoon N.V.).

——— [1990]. *The Iliad* (New York: Viking Penguin), Robert Fagles (transl.).

Honohan, Iseult [2002]. *Civic Republicanism* (London: Routledge).

Horowitz, Jason [2003]. "An American Sequel to Cinecittà's Dolce Vita," *The New York Times* (25 June 2003).

Hoyt, Edwin Palmer [1993]. *199 Days: The Battle for Stalingrad* (New York: Tor).

Huener, Jonathan & Frank H. Nicosia (eds.) [2006]. *The Arts in Nazi Germany: Continuity, Conformity, Change* (New York: Berghahn Books).

Husserl, Edmund [1970]. *The Crisis of European Sciences and Transcendental Phenomenology: An Introduction to Phenomenological Philosophy* (Evanston, IL: Northwestern University Press, [1954]), transl.

——— [1962]. *Die Krisis der Europäischen Wissenschaften und die Transzendentale Phänomenologie* (The Hague: Martinus Nijhoff), Walter Biemel (ed.), 2nd ed.

Jameson, Fredric; Ernst Bloch et al. [1977]. *Aesthetics and Politics* (London: NLB), transl.

Janik, Allan & Stephen Toulmin [1973]. *Wittgenstein's Vienna* (New York: Simon & Schuster).

Jay, Martin [1992]. "'The Aesthetic Ideology' as Ideology: Or What Does It Mean to Aestheticize Politics?," in *Cultural Critique*, 21 (Spring), 41-61.

——— [1993]. *Force Fields: Between Intellectual History and Cultural Critique* (New York: Routledge).

——— [2005]. *Songs of Experience: Modern American and European Variations on a Univesal Theme* (Berkeley, CA: University of California Press).

Jayyusi, Salma Khadra (ed.) [1992]. *The Legacy of Muslim Spain* (Leiden: Brill), 2 vols.

Jones, A. H. M. [1969]. *Athenian Democracy* (Oxford: Basil Blackwell [1957]).

Jones, Michael Owen; Michael Dane Moore & Richard Christopher Snyder (eds.) [1988]. *Inside Organizations: Understanding the Human Dimension* (London: Sage).

Jukes, Geoffrey [1985]. *Hitler's Stalingrad Decisions* (Berkeley, CA: University of California Press).

Kagan, Donald [1991]. *Pericles of Athens and the Birth of Democracy* (New York: The Free Press).

Kaiser, David Aram [1999]. *Romanticism, Aesthetics and Nationalism* (Cambridge: Cambridge University Press).

Kātz, Barry [1998]. *The Invisible City* (Palo Alto, CA: unpublished manuscript).

Kaufman, Hank & Gene Lerner [1982]. *Hollywood and Tevere* (Milan: Sperling & Kupfer).

Keane, John [1999]. *Václav Havel: A Political Tragedy in Six Acts* (London: Bloomsbury).

Kemal, Salim & Ivan Gaskell (eds.) [2000]. *Politics and Aesthetics in the Arts* (Cambridge: Cambridge University Press).

Kerr, Clark [1963]. *The Uses of the University* (Cambridge, MA: Harvard University Press).
Kershaw, Ian [1998]. *Hitler: Hubris, 1889-1936* (New York: W. W. Norton).
——— [2000]. *Hitler: Nemesis, 1936-1945* (New York: W. W. Norton).
Kezich, Tullio [1999]. *Primavera a Cinecittà: Il cinema italiano alla svolta della 'Dolce Vita"* (Rome: Bulzoni Editore).
Kirk, G. S. & J. E., Raven [1969]. *The Presocratic Philosophers: A Critical History with a Selection of Texts* (Cambridge: At the University Press).
Kirkeby, Ole Fogh [2000]. *Management Philosophy: A Radical-Normative Perspective* (Berlin: Springer [1998])
Kittler, Friedrich [1995]. "Eros und Aphrodite," in Elfi Bettinger and Julika Funk (eds.), *Maskeraden: Geschlechterdifferenz in der literarischen Inszenierung* (Berlin: Erich Schmidt), 33-40.
——— [2004]. "Universities: Wet, Hard, Soft, and Harder," *Critical Inquiry*, 31: 244-255.
——— [2006]. *Musik und Mathematik. Band 1: Hellas, Teil 1: Aphrodite* (Munich: Wilhelm Fink).
——— & Cornelia Vismann [2001]. *Vom Griechenland* (Berlin: Merve).
Kohák, Erazim [1989]. "Jan Patočka: A Philosophical Biography," in Patočka [1989],1-135.
Köhler, Joachim [2000]. *Wagner's Hitler: The Prophet and his Disciple* (Cambridge: The Polity Press [1997], transl.
Kolb, Frank [1981]. *Agora und Theater, Volks- und Festversammlung* (Berlin: Gebr. Mann Verlag).
Kotkin, Stephen [1997]. *Magnetic Mountain: Stalinism as a Civilization* (Berkeley, CA: University of California Press).
Kubizek, August [1955]. *The Young Hitler I Knew* (Boston: MA: Houghton Mifflin [1954]), transl.
Kukral, Michael Andrews [1997]. *Prague 1989: Theater of Revolution: A Study in Humanistic Political Geography* (New York: Columbia University Press [East European Monographs, Boulder]).
Kulke, Hermann [1978]. *The Devarāja Cult* (Cornell University Southeast Asia Program Data Paper no. 108 [January]).
Küng, Hans [2002]. *My Struggle for Freedom: Memoirs* (Grand Rapids, MI: Eerdmans [2000], transl.
Lacoue-Labarthe, Philippe [1987]. *La fiction du politique: Heidegger, l'art et la politique* (Paris: Christian Bourgois).
Laignel-Lavastine, Alexandra [1998]. *Jan Patočka: L'Esprit de la dissidence* (Paris: Éditions Michalon).
Landino, Cristoforo [1980]. *Disputationes Camaldulenses* (Florence: Sansoni).
Landy, Marcia [1987]. *Fascism in Film: The Italian Commercial Cinema, 1931-1943* (Princeton, NJ: Princeton University Press).
——— [2000]. *Italian Film* (Cambridge: Cambridge University Press).
Lane Fox, Robin [1987]. *Pagans and Christians* (New York: HarperCollins).
Lawler, Lillian B. [1964]. *The Dance in Ancient Greece* (London: Adam & Charles Black).
Lee, Haiyan [2006]. "Governmentality and the Aesthetic State," *East Asia Cultures Critique*, 14:1, 99-129.
Legras, Horacio [2003]. "El Ateneo y Los Origenes del Estado ético en México," *Latin American Research Review*, 38:2, 34-60.
Lévêque, P. & P. Vidal-Naquet [1996]. *Cleisthenes the Athenian* (Atlantic Highlands, NJ: Humanities Press), transl.

Lévi-Strauss, Claude [1964]. *Le cru et le cuit* (Paris: Plon).
Liehm, Mira [1984]. *Passion and Defiance: Film in Italy from 1942 to the Present* (Berkeley, CA: University of California Press).
Lind, Michael [1994]. "In Defense of Liberal Nationalism," *Foreign Affairs*, 73:3 (May/June), 87-99.
Linforth, Ivan M. [1919]. *Solon the Athenian* (Berkeley, CA: University of California Press).
Linstead, Stephen and Heath Höpfl (eds.) [2000]. *The Aesthetics of Organization* (London: Sage).
Löwith, Karl [1949]. *Meaning in History: The Theological Implications of the Philosophy of History* (Chicago: University of Chicago Press).
Lust, Claude [1966]. *Wieland Wagner et la survie du théâtre lyrique* (Lausanne: Editions l'Age d'Homme).
McAdams, Robert [1966]. *The Evolution of Urban Society: Early Mesopotamia and Prehispanic Mexico* (Chicago, IL: Aldine).
McGlew, James F. [2002]. *Citizens on Stage: Comedy and Political Culture in the Athenian Democracy* (Ann Arbor, MI: University of Michigan Press).
MacIntyre, Alasdair [1984]. *After Virtue* (Notre Dame, IN: University of Notre Dame Press), 2nd ed.
——— [1998]. *Whose Justice? Which Rationality?* (Notre Dame, IN: University of Notre Dame Press).
Machiavelli, Niccolò [1950]. *The Prince and The Discourses* (New York: Modern Library), transl.
Mack Smith, Denis [1981]. *Mussolini* (London: Weidenfeld & Nicolson).
Magee, Bryan [2000]. *The Tristan Chord: Wagner and Philosophy* (New York: Henry Holt).
Man, Paul de [1996]. *Aesthetic Ideology* (Minneapolis, MN: University of Minnesota Press).
Mann, Thomas [1948]. *Doktor Faustus: Das Leben des deutschen Tonsetzers Adrian Leverkühn, Erzählt von einem Freunde* (Stockholm: Bermann-Fischer).
Manuel, Frank E. & Fritzie E. Manuel [1979]. *Utopian Thought in the Western World* (Cambridge, MA: Harvard University Press).
Manville, Brook & Josiah Ober [2003]. *A Company of Citizens: What the World's First Democracy Teaches Leaders about Creating Great Organizations* (Boston, MA: Harvard Business School Press).
March, James G. [1974]. *Academic Notes* (London: Poets' and Painters' Press).
——— [1977]. *Aged Wisconsin* (London: Poets' and Painters' Press).
——— [1980a]. *Autonomy as a Factor in Group Organization: A Study in Politics* (New York: Arno).
——— [1980b]. *Pleasures of the Process* (London: Poets' and Painters' Press).
——— [1985]. *Slow Learner* (London: Poets' and Painters' Press).
——— [1990]. *Minor Memos* (London: Poets' and Painters' Press).
——— [1994]. *A Primer on Decision Making: How Decisions Happen* (New York: The Free Press).
——— [1999]. *The Pursuit of Organizational Intelligence* (Oxford: Blackwell, 1999).
——— [2000]. *Late Harvest* (Palo Alto, CA: Bonde Press).
——— [2005]. *Footprints* (Palo Alto, CA: Bonde Press).
——— [2006]. "Poetry and the Rhetoric of Management: Easter 1916," *Journal of Management Inquiry*, 15:1 (March), 70-72.
——— [2008]. *Quiet Corners* (Palo Alto, CA: Bonde Press).
——— & Johan P. Olsen [1995]. *Democratic Governance* (New York: The Free Press).

——— & Herbert Simon [1958]. *Organizations* (New York: John Wiley).
——— & Herbert Simon [1993]. *Organizations* (Cambridge, MA: Blackwell), 2nd ed.
——— & Thierry Weil [2003]. *Le leadership dans les organisations: Un cours de James March* (Paris: Les Presses de l'École des Mines).
——— & Thierry Weil [2005]. *On Leadership* (Oxford: Blackwell), transl.
Marchand, Suzanne L. [1996]. *Down from Olympus: Archaeology and Philhellenism in Germany, 1750-1970* (Princeton, NJ: Princeton University Press).
Marcus, Millicent [2002]. *After Fellini: National Cinema in the Postmodern Age* (Baltimore, MD: The Johns Hopkins Press).
Marcus Aurelius Antoninus [1916]. *The Communion with Himself of Marcus Aurelius Antoninus Emperor of Rome* (London: William Heineman), Greek text & transl.
Marcuse, Herbert [2005]. *The New Left and the 1960s: Collected Papers of Herbert Marcuse, Volume Three* (New York: Routledge), Douglas Kellner (ed.)
——— [2007]. *Art and Liberation: Collected Papers of Herbert Marcuse, Volume Four* (New York: Routledge), Douglas Kellner (ed.)
Marinatos, Nanno [1993]. *Minoan Religion: Ritual, Image, and Symbol* (Columbia, SC: University of South Carolina Press).
Marinatos, Spiridon [1972]. *Life and Art in Prehistoric Thera* (London: Oxford University Press).
Marinetti, F. T. [1983]. *Teoria e invenzione futurista* (Milan: Arnoldo Mondadori), Luciano De Maria (ed.).
——— [2002]. *Selected Poems and Related Prose* (New Haven, CT: Yale University Press), transl.
Martin, F. David [1981]. *Sculpture and Enlivened Space: Aesthetics and History* (Kexington, KY: The University Press of Kentucky).
Matuštik, Martin J. [1993]. *Postnational Identity: Critical Theory and Existential Philosophy in Habermas, Kierkegaard, and Havel* (NY: Guilford Press).
Megill, Allan [1985]. *Prophets of Extremity: Nietzsche, Heidegger, Foucault, Derrida* (Berkeley, CA: University of California Press).
Meiggs, Russell [1972]. *The Athenian Empire* (Oxford: Clarendon).
Mendelsohn-Martone, Leatrice [1978]. *Benedetto Varchi's 'Due Lezzioni':* Paragoni *and Cinquecento Art Theory* (Ph.D. dissertation, New York University).
Menocal, María Rosa [2002]. *The Ornament of the World: How Muslims, Jews, and Christians Created a Culture of Tolerance in Medieval Spain* (Boston: Little, Brown).
——— ; Raymond P. Scheindlin & Michael Sells (eds.) [2000]. *The Literature of Al-Andalus* (Cambridge: Cambridge University Press).
Miller, Molly [1971]. *The Thalassocracies* (Albany, NY: State University of New York Press).
Moon, Beverly [2000]. "Aphrodite, Ancestor of Kings," in Elisabeth Benard & Beverly Moon (eds.), *Goddesses Who Rule* (Oxford: Oxford University Press), 17-31.
Moore, Henry [1967]. *Henry Moore on Sculpture* (New York: Viking), Philip James (ed.).
Morgan, Lyvia [1988]. *The Miniature Wall Paintings of Thera: A Study in Aegean Culture and Iconography* (Cambridge: Cambridge University Press).
Morrow, Glenn R. [1960]. *Plato's Cretan City: A Historical Interpretation of the* ***Laws*** (Princeton, NJ: Princeton University Press).
Mostra Internazionale del Nuovo Cinema [1985]. *Cinecittà I: Industria e mercato nel cinema Italiano tra le due guerre* (Venice: Marsilio Editori).
Mumford, Lewis [1938]. *The Culture of Cities* (New York: Harcourt, Brace & Co.)

——— [1961]. *The City in History: Its Origins, Its Transformations, and Its Prospects* (New York: Harcourt, Brace Jovanovich).

Murphy, Peter [1993]. "Romantic Modernism and the Greek Polis," *Thesis Eleven*, 34: 42-66.

——— [1998]. "The Triadic Moment: The Anti-Genealogy of Hellenist Marxism," *Thesis Eleven* 53 (May): 102-113.

——— [2001]. *Civic Justice: From Greek Antiquity to the Modern World* (Amherst, NY: Humanity Books).

Muschamp, Herbert [2007]. "Rome, the Sequel," *The New York Times Magazine* (7 January 2007), 52-58.

Mussolini, Benito [1932]. *Mussolinis Gespräche mit Emil Ludwig* (Berlin: Paul Zsolnay Verlag).

Nelson, Richard R. [2005]. *Technology, Institutions, and Economic Growth* (Cambridge, MA: Harvard University Press).

Newman, Ernest [1976]. *The Life of Richard Wagner* (Cambridge: Cambridge University Press [1937-1946]), 4 vols.

Nietzsche, Friedrich [1930]. *Der Wille zur Macht: Versuch einer Umwertung aller Werte* (Leipzig: Alfred Kröner).

——— [1966]. *Werke in Drei Bänden* (Munich: Carl Hanser), 3 vols. Karl Schlechta (ed.).

——— [1975-2004]. *Kritische Gesamtausgabe: Briefe* (Berlin: Walter de Gruyter), Giorgio Colli & Mazzino Montinari (eds.)

Nonaka, Ikujiro & Noburu Konno [1998]. "The Concept of 'Ba': Building a Foundation for Knowledge Creation," *California Management Review*, 40:3 (Spring), 40-54.

——— & Toshihiro Nishiguchi (eds.). [2001] *Knowledge Emergence: The Social, Technical and Evolutionary Dimensions of Knowledge Creation* (Oxford: Oxford University Press).

North, Michael [1991]. *The Political Aesthetic of Yeats, Eliot and Pound* (Cambridge: Cambridge University Press).

Nowell-Smith, Geoffrey (with James Hay & Gianni Volpa) [1996]. *The Companion to Italian Cinema* (London: Cassell).

Olsen, Erik J. [2006]. *Civic Republicanism and the Properties of Democracy: A Case Study of Post-Socialist Political Theory* (Lanham, MA: Lexington).

O'Neill, James L. [1995]. *The Origins and Development of Ancient Greek Democracy* (Lanham, MD: Rowman & Littlefield).

Onians, Richard Broxton [1988]. *The Origins of European Thought: About the Body, the Mind, the Soul, the World, Time, and Fate* (Cambridge: Cambridge University Press [1951]).

Ott, Hugo [1985]. "Martin Heidegger und die Universität Freiburg nach 1945: Ein Beispiel für die Auseinandersetzung mit der politischen Vergangenheit," *Historisches Jahrbuch*, 105: 95-128.

——— [1988]. *Martin Heidegger: Unterwegs zu einer Biographie* (Frankfurt: Campus Verlag).

Overbey, D. (ed.) [1979]. *Springtime in Italy: A Reader in Neo-Realism* (Hamden, CT: Archon Books), transl.

Panofsky, Erwin [1972]. *Renaissance and Renascences in Western Art* (New York: Harper & Row [1960]).

Parker, Geoffrey [2004]. *Sovereign City: The City-State Through History* (London: Reaktion Books).

Pasolini, Pier Paolo [1969]. *Pasolini on Pasolini: Interviews with Oswald Stack* (Bloomington, IN: Indiana University Press), transl.

——— [1988]. *Heretical Empiricism* (Bloomington, IN: Indiana University Press [1972]), transl.

——— [2003]. *Le ceneri di Gramsci* (Milan: Garzanti).

Patočka, Jan [1976a]. "Erinnerungen an Husserl," in Walter Biemel (ed.), *Die Welt des Menschen—Die Welt der Philosophie: Festschrift für Jan Patočka* (The Hague: Martinue Nijhoff), vii-xix.

——— [1976b]. *Le monde naturel comme problème philosophique* (The Hague: Martinus Nijhoff), transl.

——— [1977]. "Charter 77 Manifesto," *Telos*, 31: 148-50, transl.

——— [1989]. *Philosophy and Selected Writings* (Chicago, IL: University of Chicago Press), transl.

——— [1990a]. *Kacířské eseye o filosofii dějin* (Prague: Academia).

——— [1990b]. *Sókratés: Přednášky z antické filosofie* (Prague: Státní pedagogické nakladtelství [1947]).

——— [1992]. *Co jsou Češi? Malý přehled fakt a pokus o vysvětlení* (Prague: Panorama).

——— [1995]. *Tělo, společenství, jazyk, svět* (Prague: Oikoumene).

——— [1996a]. *An Introduction to Husserl's Phenomenology* (Chicago, IL: Open Court), transl.

——— [1996b]. *Heretical Essays in the Philosophy of History* (Chicago, IL: Open Court), transl.

——— [1997]. *Body, Community, Language, World* (Chicago, IL: Open Court), transl.

——— [1997-]. *Sebrané Spisy Jana Patočky* (Prague: Oikoumene), iii: Péče o Duši, third part: Kacířské eseje o filosofii dějin, and related work, 2002, Ivan Chvatík & Pavel Kouba (eds.); ix: Komeniologické studie, first part [1941-1958]), Ivan Chvatík & Pavel Kouba (eds.).

——— [2002]. *Plato and Europe* (Stanford, CA: Stanford University Press), transl.

Perry, W. J. [1968]. *The Children of the Sun: A Study in the Early History of Civilization* (London: Methuen & Co. [1923]).

Petropoulos, Jonathan [1996]. *Art as Politics in the Third Reich* (Chapel Hill, NC: University of North Carolina Press).

——— [2002]. "From Seduction to Denial: Arno Breker's Engagement with National Socialism," in Etlin [2002], 205-229.

Pine, B. Joseph II and James H. Gilmore [1999]. *The Experience Economy: Work is Theatre and Every Business a Stage* (Boston, MA: Harvard Business School Press).

Pirro, Robert [1994]. Review of Steinweis [1993], *German Politics and Society*, 31 (Spring 1994), 140-148.

——— [2001]. *Hannah Arendt and the Politics of Tragedy* (DeKalb, IL: Northern Illinois University Press).

——— [2002]. "Václav Havel and the Political Uses of Tragedy," *Political Theory*, 30:2 (April), 228-258.

Plato [1902]. *Res Publica* (Oxford: Clarendon).

——— [1962]. *Platonis Opera* (Oxford: Clarendon [1902]), vol. 5.

Plax, Julie-Anne [2000]. *Watteau and the Cultural Politics of Eighteenth-Century France* (Cambridge: Cambridge University Press).

Plutarch [1914]. "Pericles," in *Plutarch's Lives* (Cambridge, MA: Harvard University Press), vol. 3, transl.

Pocock, J. G. A. [2003]. *The Machiavellian Moment: Florentine Political Thought and the Atlantic Republican Tradition* (Princeton, NJ: Princeton University Press [1975]), with new afterword.

Podlecki, Anthony J. [1998]. *Perikles and his Circle* (London: Routledge).

Poggioli, Renato [1968]. *The Theory of the Avant-Garde* (Cambridge, MA: Harvard University Press [1962]), transl.

Postrel, Virginia [2003]. *The Substance of Style: How the Rise of Aesthetic Value is Remaking Commerce, Culture, and Consciousness* (New York: HarperCollins).

Pothen, Philip [2002]. *Nietzsche and the Fate of Art* (Aldershot, Hampshire: Ashgate).

Potter, Pamela M. [2006]. "The Arts in Nazi Germany: A Silent Debate," *Contemporary European History*, 15:4, 585-599.

Pound, Ezra [1996]. *The Cantos of Ezra Pound* (New York: New Directions Books [1993]).

Proust, Marcel [1954]. *A la recherche du temps perdu* (Paris: Bibliothèque de la Pléiade), vol. 3.

Rabinbach, Anson [1997]. *In the Shadow of Catastrophe: German Intellectuals between Apocalypse and Enlightenment* (Berkeley, CA: University of California Press).

Rabinowitz, Nancy Sorkin [2006]. *Greek Tragedy* (Oxford: Clarendon).

Ramirez, Rafael [1991]. *The Beauty of Social Organization* (Munich: Accedo).

Rancière, Jacque [2004].. *The Politics of Aesthetics: The Distribution of the Sensible* (London & NY: Continuum [2001]), transl.

Rawls, John [1971]. *A Theory of Justice* (Cambridge, MA: Harvard University Press).

——— [2001]. *Justice as Fairness: A Restatement* (Cambridge, MA: Harvard University Press).

Rawson, Philip [1997]. *Sculpture* (Philadelphia, PA: University of Pennsylvania Press).

Read, Herbert [1961]. *The Art of Sculpture* (Princeton, NJ: Princeton University Press [1956]).

——— [1965]. *Henry Moore: A Study of his Life and Work* (London: Thames and Hudson).

Redfield, Marc [1996]. *Phantom Formations: Aesthetic Ideology and the Bildungsroman* (Ithaca, NY: Cornell University Press).

——— [2003]. *The Politics of Aesthetics: Nationalism, Gender, Romanticism* (Stanford, CA: Stanford University Press).

Reichel, Peter [1991]. *Der schöne Schein des Dritten Reiches: Faszination und Gewalt des Faschismus* (Munich: Carl Hanser).

Reignier, Philippe [1991]. *Singapore: City-State in Southeast Asia* (Honolulu, HI: University of Hawaii Press [1987], transl.

Reuth, Ralf Georg [1993]. *Goebbels* (New York: Harcourt Brace [1990]), transl.

Rhodes, Anthony [1959]. *The Poet as Superman: A Life of Gabriele D'Annunzio* (London: Weidenfeld & Nicolson).

Rhodes, P. J. (ed.). *Athenian Democracy* (Edinburgh: Edinburgh University Press).

Rockmore, Tom [1992]. *On Heidegger's Nazism and Philosophy* (Berkeley, CA: University of California Press).

Roebuck, Carl [1959]. *Ionian Trade and Colonization* (New York: Archaeological Institute of America).

Rogers, L. R. [1983]. "Sculpture, Space and Being within Things," *British Journal of Aesthetics*, 23:2 (Spring), 164-168.

Rombach, Ursula [1991]. *Vita Activa und Vita Contemplativa bei Cristoforo Landino* (Stuttgart: Teubner).

Romilly, Jacqueline de [2006]. *Actualité de la democratie athénienne: Entretiens avec Fabrice Amedeo* (Paris: Bourin Éditeur).

Ronell, Avital [2008]. *The ÜberReader: Selected Works of Avital Ronell* (Urbana, IL: University of Illinois Press).

Rorty, Richard [1991]. "The Seer of Prague," *The New Republic* (1 July 1991), 35-40.

Rosenthal, Franz [1992]. *The Classical Heritage in Islam* (London: Routledge [1965]), transl.

Rousseau, Jean-Jacques [1968]. *The Social Contract* (Harmondsworth: Penguin), transl.

——— [1990]. *Essai sur l'origine des langues: Où il est parlé de la mélodie et de l'imitation musicale* (Paris: Éditions Gallimard).

Ruberto, Laura E. & Kristi M. Wilson (eds.) [2007]. *Italian Neorealism and Global Cinema* (Detroit, MI: Wayne State University Press).

Ruggles, D. Fairchild [2000]. *Gardens, Landscape, and Vision in the Palaces of Islamic Spain* (University Park, PA: The Pennsylvania State University Press),
Sabine, George H. [1973]. *A History of Political Theory* (Hinsdale, IL: Dryden Press), 4th ed. T. L. Thorson rev.
Savio, Francesco [1979]. *Cinecittà Anni Trenti* (Rome: Buzoni Editore), 3 vols.
Saxonhouse, Arlene W. [1996]. *Athenian Democracy: Modern Mythmakers and Ancient Theorists* (Notre Dame, IN: University of Notre Dame Press).
Scarry, Elaine [1999]. *On Beauty and Being Just* (Princeton, NJ: Princeton University Press).
Schiller, Friedrich [1966]. *Werke* (Frankfurt: Insel), 3 vols.
——— [1967]. *On the Aesthetic Education of Man in a Series of Letters* (Oxford: Clarendon), E. M. Wilkinson & L. A. Willoughby (eds. & transl.)
Schilling, Robert [1954]. *La religion romaine de Vénus, depuis les origines jusqu'au temps d'Auguste* (Paris: E. de Boccard).
Schmitt, Bernd & Alex Simonson [1997]. *Marketing Aesthetics: The Strategic Management of Brands, Identity, and Image* (New York: The Free Press).
——— ; David L. Rogers & Karen Vrotsos [2004]. *There's No Business That's Not Show Business: Marketing in an Experience Culture* (Upper Saddle River, NJ: Prentice Hall).
Schopenhauer, Arthur [n.d.]. *Die Welt als Wille und Vorstellung* (Cologne: Atlas).
Schumpeter, Joseph [1976]. *Capitalism, Socialism and Democracy* (New York: Harper [1950]), 3d ed.
——— [1997]. *Theorie der wirtschaftlichen Entwicklung: Eine Untersuchung über Unternehmergewinn, Kapital, Kredit, Zins und den Konjunkturzyklus* (Berlin: Duncker & Humblot [1934], 9th printing of 4th ed.
Scobie, Alex [1990]. *Hitler's State Architecture: The Impact of Classical Antiquity* (University Park, PA: Pennsylvania State University Press).
Scully, Stephen [1990]. *Homer and the Sacred City* (Ithaca, NY: Cornell University Press).
Seigel, Jerrold [1986]. *Bohemian Paris: Culture, Politics and the Boundaries of Bourgeois Life, 1830-1930* (New York: Viking Penguin).
Seligsohn, Andrew J. [2006]. "'The Stirring Up of Passion': Must We Fear an Aesthetic Politics?," in Goi & Dolan [2006], 87-117.
Serke, Jürgen [1987]. *Böhmische Dörfer: Wanderungen durch eine verlassene literarische Landschaft* (Vienna: Paul Zsolnay).
Servadio, Gaia [1983]. *Luchino Visconti: A Biography* (New York: Franklin Watts [1981]).
Shlegel, Dorothy B. [1956]. *Shaftesbury and the French Deists* (Chapel Hill, NC: University of North Carolina Press).
Singer, Alan [2003]. *Aesthetic Reason: Artworks and the Deliberative Ethos* (University Park, PA: The Pennsylvania University Press).
Sitney, P. Adams [1995]. *Vital Crises in Italian Cinema: Iconography, Stylistics, Politics* (Austin, TX: University of Texas Press).
Skilling, Gordon H. [1981]. *Charter 77 and Human Rights in Czechoslovakia* (London: Allen and Unwin).
——— & Paul Wilson (eds.) [1991]. *Civic Freedom in Central Europe: Voices from Czechoslovakia* (London: Macmillan).
Sluga, Hans D. [1993]. *Heidegger's Crisis: Philosophy and Politics in Nazi Germany* (Cambridge, MA: Harvard University Press).
Sombart, Werner [1967]. *The Quintessence of Capitalism* (New York: Howard Fertig [1915]), transl.
Sontag, Susan [1981]. *Under the Sign of Saturn* (New York: Vintage [1980]).

Speer, Albert [1970]. *Inside the Third Reich* (New York: Avon [1969]), transl.
——— [1975]. *Spandauer Tagebücher* (Frankfurt: Propyläen).
Spengler, Oswald [1969]. *Der Untergang des Abendlandes: Umrisse einer Morphologie der Weltgeschichte* (Munich: Beck [1923].
Spinosa, Charles; Fernando Flores & Hubert L. Dreyfus [1997]. *Disclosing New Worlds: Entrepreneurship, Democratic Action, and the Cultivation of Solidarity* (Cambridge, MA: The MIT Press).
Spotts, Frederic [1994]. *Bayreuth: A History of the Wagner Festival* (New Haven, CT: Yale University Press).
——— [2002]. *Hitler and the Power of Aesthetics* (Woodstock, NY: The Overlook Press).
Stadter, Philip A. [1989]. *A Commentary on Plutarch's Pericles* (Chapel Hill, NC: University of North Carolina Press).
Ste. Croix, G. E. M. de [1972]. *The Origins of the Peloponnesian War* (Ithaca, NY: Cornell University Press).
Steinweis, Alan E. [1993]. *Art, Ideology, & Economics in Nazi Germany: The Reich Chambers of Music, Theater, and the Visual Arts* (Chapel Hill, NC: The University of North Carolina Press).
Stirling, Monica [1979]. *A Screen of Time: A Study of Luchino Visconti* (New York: Harcourt Brace Jovanovich).
Stockton, David [1990]. *The Classical Athenian Democracy* (Oxford: Oxford University Press).
Stoppard, Tom [2006]. *Rock'n'Roll* (New York: Grove).
Strati, Antonio [1999]. *Organization and Aesthetics* (London: Sage).
——— [2000]. "The Aesthetic Approach in Organization Studies," in Linstead & Höpfl [2000], 13-34.
Strong, Tracy [1988]. "Nietzsche's Political Aesthetics," in M. Gillespie & T. Strong (eds.), *Nietzsche's New Seas* (Chicago: University of Chicago Press).
Swain, Simon [1996]. *Hellenism and Empire: Language, Classicism, and Power in the Greek World AD 50-250* (Oxford: Clarendon).
Tambiah, S. J. [1976]. *World Conqueror and World Renouncer: A Study of Buddhism and Polity in Thailand against a Historical Background* (Cambridge: Cambridge University Press).
Taylor, A. J. P. [1964]. *The Origins of the Second World War* (Harmondsworth: Penguin [1961]).
Thomas, Hugh [1995]. *Conquest: Montezuma, Cortés, and the Fall of Old Mexico* (New York: Touchstone [1993].
Thorley, John [1996]. *Athenian Democracy* (London: Routledge).
Thucydides [1992]. *Historiae* (Oxford: Clarendon [1902], 2nd ed., 2 vols.
Tibi, Amin T. [1986]. *The Tibyān: Memoirs of 'Abd Allāh Buluggīn, Last Zīrid Amīr of Granada* (Leiden: Brill), transl.
Time Magazine [1954]. "Hollywood on the Tiber," *Time* (10 August 1954), 54-61.
Tsafrir, Yoram [1999]. "The Holy City of Jerusalem in the Madaba Map," in Michele Piccirillo & Eugenio Alliata (eds.), *The Madaba Map Centenary 1897-1997: Travelling through the Byzantine Umayyad Period* (Jerusalem: Studium Biblicum Franciscanum), 155-163.
Tucker, Aviezer [2000]. *The Philosophy and Politics of Czech Dissidence from Patočka to Havel* (Pittsburgh, PA: University of Pittsburgh Press).
Turner, Paul Venable [1984]. *Campus: An American Planning Tradition* (Cambridge, MA: The MIT Press).
Turner, Victor [1982]. *From Ritual to Theatre: The Human Seriousness of Play* (New York: Performing Arts Journal Publications).

Varchi, Benedetto [1550]. "Lezione delle quale si disputa della maggioranza delle arti e qual sia più nobile, la scultura o la pittura," in Barocchi [1960], 1-82.
Veszelits, Thomas [2006]. *Die Monaco AG: Wie sich die Grimaldis ihr Fürstentum vergolden* (Frankfurt: Campus).
Virgil [1966]. *P. Vergili Maronis Opera* (Oxford: Clarendon [1900]).
Voegelin, Eric [1957. *Order and History* (Baton Rouge, LA: Lousiana State University Press, 1957), 3 vols.
Wackernagel, Martin [1981]. *The World of the Florentine Renaissance Artists: Projects and Patrons, Workshop and Art Market* (Princeton, NJ: Princeton University Press [1938]), transl.
Wagner, Richard [1914]. *Richard Wagners Gesammelte Schriften* (Leipzig: Hesse & Becker). Julius Kapp (ed.). Multiple volumes.
——— [1963]. *Mein Leben: Erste authentische Veröffentlichung* (Munich: List).
——— [1967]. *Richard Wagner Sämtliche Briefe* (Leizpig: Deutscher Verlag für Musik). Gertrud Strobel & Werner Wolf (eds.), multiple volumes.
Wagner, Wieland (ed.) [1962]. *Richard Wagner und das neue Bayreuth* (Munich: Paul List).
Wagner, Wolfgang [1994]. *Lebens-Akte: Autobiographie* (Munich: Albrecht Knaus), 2nd ed.
Waley, Daniel [1969]. *The Italian City-Republics* (London: Weidenfeld & Nicolson).
Walker, Henry J. [1995]. *Theseus and Athens* (New York: Oxford University Press).
Wasserstein, D. [1985]. *The Rise and Fall of the Party-Kings: Politics and Society in Islamic Spain 1002-1086* (Princeton, NJ: Princeton University Press).
Weber, Samuel [2004]. *Theatricality as Medium* (New York: Fordham University Press).
Weil, Thierry [2000]. *Invitation à la lecture de James March: Réflexions sur les processus de décision, d'apprentissage et de changement dans les organisations* (Paris: Les Presses de l'École des Mines).
Weiner, Amir (ed.) [2003]. *Landscaping the Human Garden: Twentieth-Century Population Management in a Comparative Framework* (Stanford, CA: Stanford University Press).
Weiser, Christian Friedrich [1916]. *Shaftesbury und das deutsche Geistesleben* (Leipzig: Teubner).
Westernhagen, Curt von [1978]. *Wagner: A Biography* (Cambridge: Cambridge University Press), 2nd ed., transl., 2 vols.
Wheatley, Paul [1971]. *The Pivot of the Four Quarters: A Preliminary Enquiry into the Origins and Character of the Ancient Chinese City* (Chicago, IL: Aldine).
Wheeler, Brett R. [2001]. "Modernist Reenchantments I: From Liberalism to Aestheticized Politics," *The German Quarterly*, 74:3, 223-236.
——— [2002]. "Modernist Reenchantments II: Aestheticized Politics to the Artwork," *The German Quarterly*, 75:2, 113-126.
Wiedemann, Fritz [1964]. *Der Mann, der Feldherr werden wollte: Erlebnisse und Erfahrungen des Vorgesetzten Hitlers im I. Weltkrieg und seines späteren Persönlichen Adjutanten* (Ullstein: blick + blick Verlag für politische Bildung).
Wiggershaus, Rolf [1986]. *Die Frankfurter Schule: Geschichte, Theoretische Entwicklung, Politische Bedeutung* (Munich: Carl Hanser).
Willetts, R. F. [1962]. *Cretan Cults and Festivals* (New York: Barnes & Noble).
——— [1991]. *The Civilization of Ancient Crete* (Amsterdam: Adolf M. Hakkert), 2nd ed.
Winkler, John J. & Froma I. Zeitlin (eds.) [1990]. *Nothing to Do with Dionysos? Athenian Drama in its Social Context* (Princeton, NJ: Princeton University Press).

Winthrop-Young, Geoffrey [2002]. "Drill and Distraction in the Yellow Submarine: On the Dominance of War in Friedrich Kittler's Media Theory," *Critical Inquiry*, 28:4 (Summer), 825-854.

Witte, William [1949]. *Schiller* (Oxford: Blackwell).

Wohl, Victoria [2002]. *Love among the Ruins: The Erotics of Democracy in Classical Athens* (Princeton, NJ: Princeton University Press).

Wolin, Richard (ed.) [1991]. *The Heidegger Controversy: A Critical Reading* (New York: Columbia University Press).

——— [2001]. *Heidegger's Children: Hannah Arendt, Karl Löwith, Hans Jonas, and Herbert Marcuse* (Princeton, NJ: Princeton University Press).

Wolin, Sheldon [2004]. *Politics and Vision: Continuity and Innovation in Western Political Thought* (Princeton, NJ: Princeton University Press), expanded ed.

Wood, Mary P. [2000]. "Representations of Rome in Italian Cinema: Space and Power," *Journal of the Institute of Romance Studies*, 8 (2000), 211-221.

——— [2005]. *Italian Cinema* (Oxford: Berg).

Wycherley, R. E. [1976]. *How the Greeks Built Cities* (New York: W. W. Norton [1962]), 2nd ed.

Wyke, Maria [1997]. *Projecting the Past: Ancient Rome, Cinema and History* (New York: Routledge).

Xenophon [1966]. "Athenaion Politeia," in *Opera Omnia* (Oxford: Clarendon [1920]), vol. 5.

Yarshatar, Elisan (ed.) [1988]. *Persian Literature* (Albany, NY: Bibliotheca Persica).

Zavattini, Cesare [1970]. *Zavattini: Sequences from a Cinematic Life* (Englewood Cliffs, NJ: Prentice-Hall), transl.

FSC
www.fsc.org
MIX
Papier | Fördert gute Waldnutzung
FSC® C083411

Kolibri 360 GmbH
Ferdinand-Jühlke-Straße 7
99095 Erfurt, Deutschland
produktsicherheit@kolibri360.de